The Arab Spring

THE ARAB SPRING

*The Hope and Reality
of the Uprisings*

2ND EDITION

Edited by

MARK L. HAAS

Duquesne University

and

DAVID W. LESCH

Trinity University

WESTVIEW
PRESS

Westview Press was founded in 1975 in Boulder, Colorado, by notable publisher and intellectual Fred Praeger. Westview Press continues to publish scholarly titles and high-quality undergraduate- and graduate-level textbooks in core social science disciplines. With books developed, written, and edited with the needs of serious nonfiction readers, professors, and students in mind, Westview Press honors its long history of publishing books that matter.

Westview Press books are available at special discounts for bulk purchases in the United States by corporations, institutions, and other organizations. For more information, please contact the Special Markets Department at 2300 Chestnut Street, Suite 200, Philadelphia, PA 19103, or call (800) 810-4145, ext. 5000, or e-mail special.markets@perseusbooks.com.

Text set in 11.5 Adobe Jenson Pro

Library of Congress Cataloging-in-Publication Data
Names: Haas, Mark L., editor. | Lesch, David W., editor.
Title: The Arab Spring : change and resistance in the Middle East / edited by Mark L. Haas, David W. Lesch.
Description: Second edition. | Boulder, CO: Westview Press, 2017. | Includes bibliographical references and index. | Description based on print version record and CIP data provided by publisher; resource not viewed.
Identifiers: LCCN 2016021908 (print) | LCCN 2016015319 (ebook) | ISBN 9780813350332 (ebook) | ISBN 9780813349749 | ISBN 9780813349749q (hardcover : alk. paper) | ISBN 9780813350332q (ebook)
Subjects: LCSH: Arab Spring, 2010– | Arab countries—Politics and Government—21st century. | Revolutions—Arab countries—History—21st century. | Arab countries—History—21st century.
Classification: LCC JQ1850.A91 (print) | LCC JQ1850.A91 A77 2017 (ebook) | DDC 909/.097492708312—dc23
LC record available at https://lccn.loc.gov/2016021908

10 9 8 7 6 5 4 3 2 1

Mark dedicates the book to his aunt Trudy and uncle John,
for a lifetime of love, support, and interest in his work and well-being.
He cannot thank them enough for all they have done.

David dedicates this book to his wife, Judy Dunlap,
for her unswerving support, energy, and love,
without which tasks such as this would be impossible.

Contents

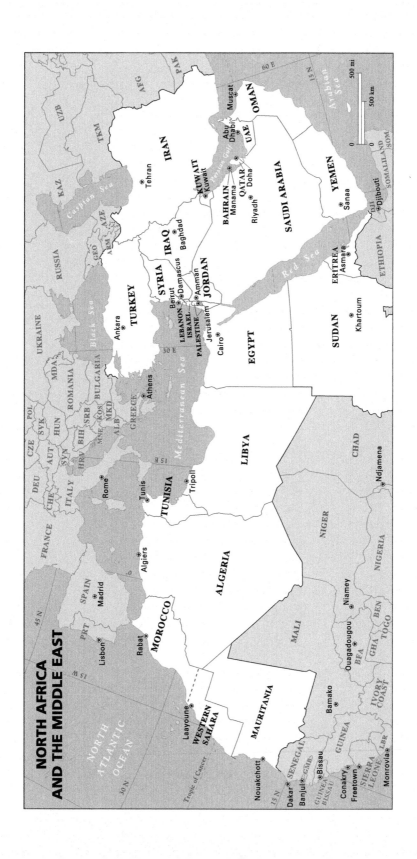

Preface

Writing or commenting on current or recent events in the Middle East is a hazardous business. The fluidity of the moment and the different possible outcomes of a particular course of events, frequently resting on the whim of individuals, often make predicting anything an exercise in futility—or a book risking being partially outdated before it is even published. Who would have guessed that a twenty-something fruit vendor in Tunisia, by setting himself on fire in late 2010 in abject frustration and anger at his lot in life, would unleash a torrent of protest that has rewritten the landscape of the Middle East? Sometimes, however, such is the importance of a series of events that they demand coverage and examination in the short term. This is the case with the so-called Arab Spring, which engulfed the region—and riveted the world—beginning in late 2010. Although the ultimate impact of the uprisings of the Arab Spring may not become truly apparent for a generation, attempting to understand the origins of the uprisings, the actual course of events in particular countries directly and indirectly hit by the Arab Spring, and the regional and international responses is necessary in order to acquire a level of comprehension that will allow us to track and give meaning to all this history and politics in the making.

Of course, as more time goes by, our ability to update events and our understanding of them grows. Hence the value of the second edition of this volume, which resulted in major revisions of all the chapters (often from scratch) as well as a brand-new chapter on Iraq. Even the volume's subtitle has been altered to reflect the fluidity of events, from "Change and Resistance in the

Middle East" to "The Hope and Reality of the Uprisings." This change reflects the continued, and often increased, instability and conflict in the region, which have dashed the initial hopes of many for greater freedom and prosperity. The reality of what lies ahead for the region is now better understood, even if this reality is far from what was anticipated in 2011 and even though much uncertainty remains.

We selected the countries and topics to be examined. We are, as always, mindful of page count—and thus of the price of a book—in order to make this volume affordable. We are very happy with the final tally of authors, topics, and pages. We believe that it was necessary to paint a broad picture of the Middle East in order to account for the interplay between actors and states at the domestic, regional, and international levels. As such, we have chapters on Arab countries that gave rise to the term "Arab Spring" as well as chapters examining regional and international players that have become deeply involved in the Arab uprisings and/or have been deeply affected by it. This volume is intended to introduce and explain events for the interested general public as well as students and scholars of the Middle East in a way that will help them understand how all of this came about and what might happen in the near- and long-term future of the region and beyond. This book should act as an in-depth introduction to the Arab uprisings and/or a supplementary reader for courses on modern Middle East history, politics, and international relations.

The Organization and Content of the Book

The book is divided into two main sections. Julia Clancy-Smith (Tunisia), Jeannie L. Sowers and Bruce K. Rutherford (Egypt), Karim Mezran and Laurentina Cizza (Libya), and David W. Lesch (Syria) begin Part I by examining the Arab countries hit most dramatically by the Arab Spring. These chapters appear in the order in which the protests occurred. Although the political upheavals in these states shared some important characteristics, the causes and courses of the uprisings as well as regime responses and actions by external actors were different, with some ending fairly cleanly (at least at first) with the removal of the authoritarian leader and others continuing with the dictatorial regime tenaciously fighting back to remain in power.

These four case studies are followed by chapters by Steve A. Yetiv, Curtis R. Ryan, and Ibrahim Al-Marashi, who analyze developments in Saudi Arabia, Jordan, and Iraq, respectively. The central focus of these chapters is to explore why these countries, at least for the present time, have been able to escape large-scale revolutionary pressures. Comprehending variations in outcomes in those states that witnessed massive uprisings, as well as why some countries have not experienced such protests, is critical to both prediction and prescription. Almost all analysts and policymakers were caught off guard by the Arab Spring. Correctly understanding the sources, successes, and failures of these protests will not only reduce the likelihood of similar surprises in the future but also, perhaps, help to shape outcomes toward desired ends.

Part II explores the policies of non-Arab states that have major interests at stake in the uprisings. Narges Bajoghli and Arang Keshavarzian (Iran), Mark L. Haas (Turkey), Ilan Peleg (Israel), Robert O. Freedman (Russia), and Jeremy Pressman (United States) examine the threats and opportunities that the Arab Spring protests created for these outside powers as well as these states' responses to the revolts. All five of these countries sometimes supported and sometimes opposed particular uprisings, though the dominant tendency in favor of revolution or reaction varied considerably among them. The chapters in this section highlight how the Arab demonstrations affected the material and ideological interests of the non-Arab powers and how the latter tried to protect and even advance both sets of interests in the wake of the protests. Like the first half of the book, the second is preceded by an introductory chapter that summarizes key issues and patterns. James L. Gelvin concludes the volume with an analysis of some of the common themes of the Arab Spring as well as an examination of some of the myths about and common misinterpretations of these uprisings.

ACKNOWLEDGMENTS

The editors first and foremost want to thank the contributors, whose expertise and dedication to their work are recognized and much appreciated. They had a small window of time in which to write their chapters. This collection represents quite the compilation of well-known specialists in their respective fields, and we feel particularly fortunate to have gathered such an esteemed group.

We are grateful to the reviewers who provided us with insightful feedback on the first edition, including Andrea Grove (California State University, Channel Islands), Curtis Richardson (Northwest Missouri State University), Beverly Tsacoyianis (University of Memphis), and others who wish to remain anonymous. We also want to thank the people at Westview Press for their professional and efficient handling of the process, particularly Ada Fung, Grace Fujimoto, Krista Anderson, and Connie Oehring. When we approached editors at Westview Press with the idea for the first edition, they instantly saw the value of it and acted accordingly in an expeditious fashion in order to get the book out in a timely manner.

Most importantly, we want to profusely thank our families, without whose support none of this would be possible.

—Mark L. Haas
—David W. Lesch

A Note on the Text

ONE OF THE CHALLENGES of compiling an edited volume is ensuring stylistic and spelling consistency among chapters written by different contributors. In particular, many authors have used their own systems of transliteration. We generally retained each author's style except for names, places, and terms that appear throughout the text. In these cases, we selected one variation of spelling, which is often the more recognizable version rather than a strict transliteration: for example, Assad rather than Asad; Hussein rather than Husayn; and Gadafi rather than Qadhdhafi, Kaddafi, Qaddafi, or numerous other transliterations of the name of the former Libyan leader.

Also, as is the case with every other region on earth, Middle East history, politics, and even geography are subject to many different interpretations depending upon who is doing the talking or writing. As such, wars, events, and places are often referred to in sometimes drastically different ways. Even the term "Arab Spring," as pointed out in the Part I introduction and in several other chapters, is not at all universally accepted and is something of a misnomer. As a historical example, the 1973 Arab-Israeli War (the most neutral and objective of all appellations for the event) has been called the October War, the Ramadan War, the War of Liberation, and the Yom Kippur War. In the few cases such as this one, authors sometimes employ one particular term; however, the reader should be aware that oftentimes there are other references as well that have meaning to different populations, and for the most part these variations have been pointed out by the authors and/or editors.

PART I

Uprisings in the Arab World: Tyranny, Anarchy, and (Perhaps) Democracy

MARK L. HAAS AND DAVID W. LESCH

THE SO-CALLED ARAB SPRING unexpectedly erupted in late 2010 and early 2011. It was characterized in the beginning by huge and largely peaceful popular protests in a number of Arab countries against long-standing entrenched regimes. It began in Tunisia, where a young man trying to eke out a living as a street vendor set himself on fire as an act of defiance against the government. His action was borne of frustration and disillusionment over the socioeconomic malaise and political repression in his country. Little did he know that he would light a fire across the region. Shortly thereafter, mass protests pushed the Tunisian president, Zine El Abidine Ben Ali, out of office.

In neighboring Egypt, suffering from many of the same systemic maladies, throngs of protesters gathered at Tahrir Square in the center of Cairo, eventually forcing President Husni Mubarak from power. Similar events transpired in Yemen, where President Ali Abdullah Saleh fled the country in June 2011 in response to popular pressure, leaving Vice President Abdrabbuh Mansour Hadi as acting president. Protests sprang up elsewhere in the Arab world from the Persian Gulf to North Africa, most spectacularly leading to the death of

1

Libyan President Muammar al-Gadafi following a campaign of armed popular resistance supported militarily by NATO and the Arab League. Then the regime in Syria, which many had thought would weather the storm of the Arab Spring, began to encounter mass protests. The regime, however, unleashed a brutal crackdown against the opposition, displaying a resiliency that confounded the prognostications that it, too, would soon fall. As a result of these contending forces, Syria has been plunged into a savage five-year civil war that continues at the time of this writing.

All the while, certain countries in and outside the Middle East, such as Iran, Israel, Turkey, the United States, and Russia, have a significant stake in what the Arab Spring means in terms of their own interests and objectives. They continue to look on in fascination and confusion as to how to respond to the tremendous changes occurring before their eyes. These countries have frequently responded to events by military intervention, either directly using force or actively supporting groups that are engaged in armed combat.

Debates in both academic and policymaking circles about the meaning, consequences, and likely outcomes of the mass protests abound. Indeed, the very name "Arab Spring" is controversial. As a number of the contributors to this volume point out, this term is something of a misnomer. Ask the Syrian protesters in Syria fighting against a brutal crackdown ordered by a repressive regime in the spring of 2011 or 2012 if they feel that they are in an "Arab Spring." You will likely get laughed at or punched in the mouth. However, we employ the term in the title of this volume primarily for recognition purposes because, rightly or wrongly, most of what this volume addresses—the protests, their origins, and the repercussions—is frequently known by that name.

Beyond the matter of labeling, the events beginning in 2010 have created a host of questions that have major implications for regional and global politics. Were the uprisings a spontaneous combustion caused by the unique confluence of factors that produced a "perfect storm" of dissatisfaction and dissent? Or were there important historical antecedents, of which the Arab Spring is only the latest, albeit most dramatic, manifestation? Or both? Will the Arab Spring eventually usher in a period of democratic development and prosperity? Or will authoritarian leaders, many of whom have successfully fought back against protesters, continue to remain in power? Has the Arab Spring cleared the road for Islamist parties, long suppressed across the region, to take and maintain power, at least in some places? If so, what will this mean for domestic and international politics?

The mass demonstrations throughout the Arab world that began in 2010 took most analysts by surprise. The Middle East and North Africa were an important exception to what prominent political scientist Samuel Huntington labeled the "third wave" of democratization that swept across much of Eastern Europe, Latin America, and Asia after the end of the cold war.[1] Analysts consistently ranked the Arab states as the least free in the world, and few in 2010 were predicting that popular pressures for democratization would be sufficiently powerful to change this situation.

Soviet leader Leon Trotsky reportedly asserted that revolution is impossible until it is inevitable.[2] The logic underlying this statement applies to the Arab Spring protests. In retrospect, it is clear that there were very powerful forces pushing people across the Arab world to revolt and that some authoritarian governments had feet of clay: They were not nearly as invulnerable to popular pressures for change as widely believed.[3] A particularly important source of protest is the fact that states in the Middle East and North Africa have more "youth bulges"—a disproportionate number of young people in a particular state—than any other region in the world. Throughout the entire Middle East and North Africa, roughly one of every three people is between the ages of ten and twenty-four.[4] Youth bulges were particularly pronounced in those countries that experienced the most widespread and powerful demonstrations during the Arab Spring. In Tunisia in 2010, more than 42 percent of the population was under twenty-five. This number was 48 percent in Libya, 51 percent in Egypt, and 57 percent in Syria.[5]

Youth bulges, as numerous studies have documented, frequently create highly combustible social and political environments. Large numbers of young people are much more likely than other demographic cohorts to act on their grievances in an attempt to rectify them, even if such action requires large-scale protests and even violence.[6] Arab youth before the Arab Spring began certainly had pressing grievances against their governments, including the systematic denial of basic rights, massive governmental corruption, extreme levels of unemployment, widespread poverty, and steady increases in the cost of living (including food prices). There was also a general hopelessness that none of these conditions would improve without major pressure for political and economic change. Youth bulges and widespread dissatisfaction with the status quo, combined with the socioeconomic challenges created by the 2008 global financial crisis, were critical to the origins of the protests and their spread throughout the Arab world. Many of the authors in the first part of this volume, who concentrate on the Arab countries that were most dramatically affected by the protests, examine these shared grievances as key conditions that led to the demonstrations.

These commonalities help explain why the protests spread throughout much of the Arab world. They do not account, though, for major variations in both the intensity of the demonstrations and the success in achieving their objectives. Explaining these variations based on analyses of key national differences among Arab countries is another core goal of the chapters in Part I. Some protests, such as those in Jordan, Iraq, and Saudi Arabia (the last of which were minor), sought to push the government to adopt various political and economic reforms, whereas demonstrations in other countries—including those in Tunisia, Egypt, Libya, and Syria—sought to overthrow existing authoritarian governments. Perceived legitimacy of existing rulers was obviously a central factor that led to popular preferences for reform over revolution. As Steve Yetiv points out in Chapter 5, Saudi Arabia's King Abdullah was one of the most popular leaders in the Arab world. Support for King Abdullah of Jordan has also remained strong, as Curtis Ryan argues in Chapter 6. Although many Iraqis perceive their government to be highly ineffective, the fact that Grand Ayatollah Ali al-Sistani, who is one of the most revered figures in Iraq, continues to support reform and changes in leadership within the existing political system and not revolution helps explain the lack of support for the latter, at least among the Shia population (see Ibrahim Al-Marashi's analysis in Chapter 7). By contrast, in states where rulers' legitimacy was low due to widespread views of corruption and profligacy—including Tunisia, Egypt, and Libya (see Chapters 1, 2, and 3 by Julia Clancy-Smith, Jeannie L. Sowers and Bruce K. Rutherford, and Karim Mezran and Laurentina Cizza, respectively)—protesters were much more likely to push for revolutionary over reformist objectives.

The timing and temperament of the protests have also played major roles in shaping preferences for reform over revolution. The entire world has witnessed the turmoil, the floods of refugees, and the mass killings that have plagued both Libya after Gadafi's ouster in September 2011 and Syria as various groups pushed for the overthrow of the Bashar al-Assad regime in the spring of that same year (on the latter, see the analysis by David Lesch in Chapter 4). The overthrow or attempted overthrow of existing governments has also allowed for the empowerment of radical, brutal Islamist groups, particularly the Islamic State of Iraq and Syria (ISIS). The more revolutionary forces and outcomes in the Middle East are associated with chaos and violence, the more likely it is that the legitimacy of existing governments will be enhanced.

Authoritarian leaders are well aware of this relationship. Dictators in the Arab world have long used the fear of the rise of radical groups to power as a tactic designed to increase their popular support. The intense violence that has accompanied the weakening of autocrats in Syria and Libya has reduced the pressure for revolution in those countries that remained quiet in the early months of the Arab Spring, as the chapters on Saudi Arabia, Jordan, Iraq, and Iran all document. While the early successes of the Arab uprisings originally inspired people in other countries—hence the spread of the demonstrations throughout the region—the highly negative outcomes, especially in Libya and Syria, that resulted from the protests have since created powerful disincentives against revolution in other states. If the metaphor of a wave captures part of the early dynamics of the Arab Spring (see James Gelvin's concluding chapter), time has revealed that descriptions of a "double" or "reverse" wave are actually more apt. This alternative image captures the tension between revolution and reaction, referring to both the spread of the protests due to the initial successes of the demonstrations and the increasing disincentives against revolution that followed due to revulsion created by large-scale violence in some of the revolutionized states.

In addition to variation in the political objectives of the protesters (reform versus revolution), there have also been major differences in outcomes. Some protesters have been much more successful in achieving their goals than others. Tunisian, Egyptian, and Yemeni protesters were able to topple their governments, or at least force out current leaders; Libyan rebels did so only with significant foreign military aid; demonstrators in Bahrain and Syria have thus far been unsuccessful in their efforts; and protests in Saudi Arabia barely got off the ground. A number of factors account for these differences, and the chapters in this volume highlight the most important. When a state's military largely comprises ethnic, religious, and/or kinship minorities (Assad's government and military, for example, are dominated by the minority Alawite sect, and many in the Saudi military are members of the royal family), there is an increased likelihood that military personnel will remain loyal to the regime, even if this loyalty requires firing on fellow citizens engaged in political protests. Minority groups will fear that the creation of a more democratic regime will result in their ouster from power or even their persecution. These fears create powerful incentives to do whatever it takes to remain in positions of influence.

Large revenue streams that are controlled by the government, such as that created by Saudi Arabia's massive oil wealth, further tip the balance in favor of the political status quo. Oil wealth in fact provides multiple barriers to change (see Chapter 5). These resources not only allow a government to maintain patronage systems (including for the military) to help ensure loyalty and assuage some popular grievances but also increase its ability to adopt activist foreign policies against revolutionary groups outside the state, while reducing the likelihood that oil-dependent countries will push hard for the oil exporter to adopt major domestic changes. As long as repressive governments are able to continue vast financial support systems, and especially when their militaries remain willing to brutally crush dissent, it will be very difficult for revolutionary forces to achieve their objectives.

Conversely, when governments do not control large resource-based wealth that can be used to maintain patronage systems and buy off protesters (as in Syria, Egypt, and Yemen), or when states possess professional militaries whose leaders and personnel are drawn from the dominant ethnic and religious groups in a society (as in Tunisia and Egypt), revolutionary forces are advantaged. In the latter scenario, militaries can reasonably anticipate that they will remain in power even after a regime change. The incentives for militaries to support current governments to the bitter end against popular protests are, as a result, much lower in these instances.[7]

Even in those cases in which protesters are able to topple dictatorial governments, however, the creation of stable democratic regimes in their place is far from guaranteed. The same factors that spur protests in the first place are likely to work against such political transitions. Youth bulges and high levels of youth unemployment will continue to create highly unstable and violence-prone environments. Moreover, the pernicious effects of authoritarianism, even after the dictator has been overthrown, are likely to continue to plague new governments. Authoritarian regimes that crushed independent sources of power, thereby preventing the creation of a thriving civil society; inhibited widespread respect for democratic principles and political pluralism; and prevented the creation of democratic institutions and leaders often greatly handicap future efforts at state building, sometimes for generations. One 2005 study found that of sixty-seven countries trying to transition from authoritarian regimes, roughly only half were judged to be "free" a generation after the transition began.[8]

The evolution of events in the Middle East and North Africa indicates that skepticism about the political future of the region is unfortunately warranted. Indeed, the course of the Arab Spring has demonstrated the accuracy of what political scientists sometimes refer to as a "tyranny-anarchy loop."[9] This term refers to the tendency for many societies to fluctuate between the opposing political outcomes of tyranny and anarchy while finding it very difficult to exit the cycle and establish stable democracies.

The origins of this loop are rooted in the fact that the overthrow of dictatorial regimes, while obviously beneficial in key respects, also has potential major costs if overwhelming governmental power is necessary to maintain order among opposing societal groups. The more divided a society, the more governmental power must be exerted to prevent these divisions from devolving into violence. Many countries in the Middle East and North Africa are riven by fierce ethnic (e.g., Kurds versus Arabs), religious (e.g., Sunni versus Shia Muslims), and ideological (e.g., various types of Islamists, liberals, and secular authoritarians) divisions. As authoritarian regimes weaken or are overthrown, these disputes are much more free to turn violent. Overthrowing tyrannies in these conditions is more likely to result in anarchy and widespread civil conflict than in democracy. At the time of this writing, this tendency is most powerfully on display in Syria. The weakening of Assad's regime has allowed sectarian and ideological animosities to explode. Thus, the civil war in Syria is much more than a product of the Syrian people struggling to liberate themselves from a dictator. It is also a struggle both between Syria's Sunni Muslim majority and the minority Alawite Muslim sect (to which Assad belongs), who fear repression and reprisals if they lose their position of political dominance, and among extremist Islamists, moderate Islamists, and secular groups, all of which are part of the opposition.

In further support of the analytic value of the tyranny-anarchy loop is the fact that all four of the countries that ousted a dictator in 2011 (Tunisia, Egypt, Libya, and Yemen) either suffered or are currently suffering from the effects of anarchy created by weak governments and powerful societal divisions. Yemen at the time of this writing is in civil war, divided between forces loyal to the government, separatists in the southern part of the country, rival radical Islamist groups (including al-Qaeda affiliates and factions loyal to ISIS), and Houthi militias (a Shia sect).[10] Libya, too, is racked by armed hostilities involving multiple enemies, including conflict between two competing governments (one democratically elected, the other controlled by the Muslim Brotherhood) as well as militants loyal to ISIS who have carried out a series of executions, beheadings, and amputations.[11] Frequent mass political protests both for and against the Muslim Brotherhood–led government in Egypt (which began governing in June 2012) helped pave the way for a military coup in July 2013. Egypt under the subsequent government led by Abdel Fattah el-Sisi (a former general) has in some ways become even more repressive than it was during Mubarak's reign.[12] As is often the case, the tyranny-anarchy loop has come full circle in Egypt.

Only in Tunisia has the tyranny-anarchy cycle appeared to have stopped on democracy, though the situation remains fragile. In 2015, Tunisia was listed as a free country by Freedom House, a nonpartisan democracy-advocacy group. This was the first such designation of an Arab country by the organization in over forty years. Freedom House justified the classification based on Tunisia's "adoption of a progressive constitution, governance improvements under a consensus-based caretaker administration, and the holding of free and fair parliamentary and presidential elections, all with a high degree of transparency."[13]

Only time will tell whether Tunisia will maintain its democracy or, if it does, whether it will serve as a model or an exception to the region. Understanding the forces that have led to the remarkable era of the Arab Spring—at once full of hope and despair—and how Arab and non-Arab states have responded to it is, however, the first step in accurately predicting the region's likely political trajectory. It is to precisely these fundamental objectives that this volume is dedicated.

NOTES

1. Samuel Huntington, *The Third Wave: Democratization in the Late Twentieth Century* (Norman: University of Oklahoma Press, 1991).

2. Bruce Crumley, "Tunisia Pushes Out Its Strongman: Could Other Arab Countries Follow?," *Time* online, January 14, 2011, www.time.com/time/world/article/0,8599 ,2042541,00.html.

3. On this last point, see Jack A. Goldstone, "Understanding the Revolutions of 2011," *Foreign Affairs* 90, 3 (May-June 2011): 8–16.

4. Antonello Cabras, "The Implications of the Youth Bulge in Middle East and North African Populations," NATO Parliamentary Assembly, November 20, 2010, www.nato -pa.int/Default.asp?SHORTCUT=2342.

5. United Nations, *World Population Prospects: The 2010 Revision* (New York: United Nations Population Division, 2011), http://esa.un.org/unpd/wpp/unpp/panel_indicators .htm.

6. See, for example, Henrik Urdal, "A Clash of Generations? Youth Bulges and Political Violence," *International Studies Quarterly* 50, 3 (September 2006): 607–629.

7. For similar analysis, see F. Gregory Gause III, "Why Middle East Studies Missed the Arab Spring," *Foreign Affairs* 90, 4 (July-August 2011): 81–90.

8. Cited in "People's Revolutions Don't Guarantee Democracy," Reuters, February 13, 2011, http://in.reuters.com/article/idINIndia-54856920110213.

9. As the theologian and international relations theorist Reinhold Niebuhr put it, "The political life of man must constantly steer between the Scylla of *anarchy* and the Charybdis of *tyranny*." Reinhold Niebuhr, *Christianity and Power Politics* (New York: Scribner, 1940), p. 14.

10. Jeremy M. Sharp, "Yemen: Civil War and Regional Intervention," Congressional Research Service, October 2, 2015.

11. Missy Ryan and Hassan Morajea, "In Libya, Trying to Make One Government Out of Two," *Washington Post*, September 18, 2015; Stephanie Nebehay, "Islamic State Tightens Grip in Central Libya with Executions," Reuters, November 16, 2015, www .reuters.com/article/2015/11/16/us-libya-security-warcrimes-idUSKCN0T51CM2015 1116#IjQIU800M6YAtubS.97.

12. "Worse Than Mubarak: Abdel-Fattah al-Sisi Has Restored Order in Egypt, but at Great Cost," *Economist*, May 2, 2015, www.economist.com/news/middle-east-and-africa /21650160-abdel-fattah-al-sisi-has-restored-order-egypt-great-cost-worse.

13. Freedom House, "Tunisia," https://freedomhouse.org/report/freedom-world/2015 /tunisia, accessed November 16, 2015.

Lessons from a Small Place: The Dignity Revolutions in Tunisia, North Africa, and the Globe

JULIA CLANCY-SMITH

The Norwegian Nobel Committee has decided that the Nobel Peace Prize for 2015 is to be awarded to the Tunisian National Dialogue Quartet for its decisive contribution to the building of a pluralistic democracy in Tunisia in the wake of the Jasmine Revolution of 2011. The Quartet was formed in the summer of 2013 when the democratization process was in danger of collapsing as a result of political assassinations and widespread social unrest. It established an alternative, peaceful political process at a time when the country was on the brink of civil war. It was thus instrumental in enabling Tunisia, in the space of a few years, to establish a constitutional system of government guaranteeing fundamental rights for the entire population, irrespective of gender, political conviction or religious belief.[1]

PRELUDES

ON DECEMBER 17, 2010, a young man, Mohamed Bouazizi, who scrambled to earn a living as a street vendor in the town of Sidi Bou Zid, set himself on fire. While his exact motivations remain contested, this desperate gesture focused instantaneous national and international attention on the miserable plight of youth as well as the relentless oppression of the citizenry.

Severely burned, he eventually died on January 4, 2011. The spatial coordinates of what transpired in Bouazizi's hometown are key to the geography and ethnography of the revolutions in gestation.[2] Local teachers in Sidi Bou Zid transported him to the capital for treatment in the country's only burn center. Zine El Abidine Ben Ali's decision a few days later to ostentatiously visit the terminally injured young man at his hospital bedside, with hyped fanfare on state-muzzled TV and in newspapers, proved fatal to the president-for-life. This calculated act laid bare the deplorable political tone-deafness of autocracy in its terminal stages. The despot was himself absurdly on display, although he failed to realize it because he had long been seduced by his own power. Images of this cruel attempt at self-promotion flooded cell phones, Facebook pages, and other digital communication across the nation and the Tunisian diaspora. The national army, a conscript citizen military that differs greatly from that of Egypt, allowed massive, largely nonviolent street protests to unfold and continue.[3]

On January 14, 2011, Ben Ali and his entourage fled the country, at first seeking refuge in France and Italy, then finding welcome in Saudi Arabia, an irony given the ex-president's flagrantly licentious lifestyle and repression of various expressions of Islam. Thus came the fall of Tunisia's second dictator.[4]

Mohamed Bouazizi's sacrificial self-immolation in December 2010 and the regime's cynical response provided one of many triggers for heightened and expanded collective nationwide action. But his was not the first case of suicide; nor were the interior town and province of Sidi Bou Zid, from which Bouazizi hailed, unique.[5] For years, citizens in villages and towns in that area had protested land and water seizures, environmental degradation, lack of a genuine voice in local or national policies, and corruption. A number of young people had killed themselves before 2010 due to a pervasive sense of hopelessness generated by unemployment, poverty, and grim life prospects. Indeed, the fact that a "culture of suicide" had developed utterly shocked Tunisian society.[6] In a cruel irony, the United Nations declared 2010–2011 the "Year of Youth," and in October 2010, the World Bank report on Tunisia "gushed with enthusiasm for the country's economic performance."[7] But by early 2011, Tunisia, Arab nations, their youth, and the world had a hero as well as a martyr to global authoritarianism: Mohamed Bouazizi.[8]

This chapter proposes a *longue durée* approach to the Tunisian Dignity Revolutions.[9] It employs the plural because evidence suggests that complex short- and long-term social movements converged to produce uprisings, resulting in radical transformation. Insistence on the deep past stems from my historical training. But history also offers an antidote to the "presentism" of policy literature and media coverage—the tendency to seek causation and meaning in very recent time.[10] Moreover, many political analysts were caught off guard by the revolutions, which raises questions about their theoretical frames and assumptions. In searching for causation or etiology, the flagrant injustices, state lawlessness, and moral outrages of Ben Ali's presidency undoubtedly incubated individual and collective grievances that coagulated over time from protests into mass civic action. For the historian, however, the story is more complicated. Many of the processes nurturing discontent and breeding revolution boasted longer historical pedigrees, predating the rule of Habib Bourguiba (1956–1987) and Ben Ali (1987–2011).

In addition, this chapter adopts a trans-Maghrib perspective. Algeria and Morocco are frequently relegated to the status of sidebars in scholarly, and especially popular, studies of the Arab Spring movements. Ceaseless, indeed daily, protests in these two countries have not been deemed sufficiently combustive to stoke the kinds of collective resistance leading to genuine change. But there is much to question here, and, moreover, the political purchase of older transregional connections remains significant. Not only have conventional borders between and among North African states recently become ever more porous and ungovernable, but recognized frontiers—territorial, legal, and other—have ominously collapsed in places.

A critical issue is the historical relationship between the fall of empire, decolonization, and the six decades from 1956 until 2011 of single-party rule under Bourguiba and Ben Ali. One fundamental argument advanced here is that decolonization did not unfold according to the neat, linear political and geostrategic paradigms conventionally proposed—or imagined—by theorists. Indeed, decolonization has yet to become a reality in much of the formerly colonized world. In a directly related topic, I argue that "small" places allow glimpses of imperceptible tectonic shifts transpiring on scales far beyond the "national" level. Methodologically, I posit that scholarly fields of vision need to capture transnational, weblike forces that convey both continuities and ruptures from the past and that "national" histories have always been constructed in transnational contexts.[11]

Three interrelated clusters of problems are examined: first, institutions and traditions of collective action or protest; second, Islam, women, and education; and finally, food security, the agrarian sector and interior, and the environment.

The conclusion appraises the global repercussions of the Tunisian revolutions as well as new and alarming targets for violence. Not discussed in detail here is the critical role of social media and digital communications, which has been treated at length by many scholars.[12]

The next section investigates the recent democratic movements in relationship to traditions of militant action directed against different kinds of states, stretching back not only to the collapse of France's North African Empire, 1956–1962, but also to the colonial and precolonial periods. How did older movements shape the terrain of collective action today? Let's start in the contemporary era.

Traditions, Targets, and Symbols

"Get lost," "Get out" (*irhal*), "Game over," chanted tens of thousands of people in Tunis and across the country as they waved signs in Arabic and a number of other languages.[13] Images of the jubilant crowds demonstrated social diversity—old, young, men, women, people from the countryside or bidonvilles, tony urbanites, and women in Islamic apparel. The photos of protesters brandishing baguettes in early January 2011 could easily have been misinterpreted by uninformed foreign media at the time to signal that economic grievances and household security were principally at stake. However, Tunisians quickly dispelled that myth-in-the-making. The baguettes meant quite the opposite—that they could not be "bought off," as the Ben Ali government had hoped (along with international financial institutions, such as the World Bank and International Monetary Fund), by empty promises of a middle-class existence, sorely undermined by years of stupendous venality that filled foreign bank coffers. Tunisians were prepared to "subsist on bread and water alone," but they could no longer live under the regime.[14] Did the fact that Bouazizi was a food vendor resonate with rallying protesters—thus, the baguettes? Or had demonstrators accessed leaked US Embassy cables dispatched from Tunis to Washington, D.C., in 2009 that were published in early December 2010 by the British *Daily Mail* and instantly circulated widely in digital formats across the world? These came to be known as TunisLeaks.

In one cable entitled "Mafia family," dated June 2009, the US ambassador to Tunisia, Robert F. Godec, characterized the Tunisian president and his in-laws, the Trabelsis, as "The Family," comparing them to the Mafia due to their stranglehold on the economy and monopoly of the means of violence.[15] Godec also described the lavish dinner parties hosted by Ben Ali family members at their sumptuous Mediterranean palaces. What kinds of culinary delights were served to their guests? "The menu included perhaps a dozen dishes, including fish, steak, turkey, octopus, and fish couscous. The quantity was sufficient for a very large number of guests." The main meal over, the guests were "served ice cream and frozen yoghurt ... brought in by plane from Saint Tropez," probably in one of Ben Ali's private jets.[16] In conclusion, the US ambassador observed, "As for the dinner itself, it was similar to what one might experience in a Gulf country, and out of the ordinary for Tunisians." The cable concluded prophetically: "The opulence with which El Materi and Nesrine [the president's in-laws] live and their behavior make clear why they and other members of Ben Ali's family are disliked and even hated by some Tunisians. The excesses of the Ben Ali family are growing."[17]

The cables only confirmed what Tunisians already knew through raging rumor and informal news exchanges. But another message broke through—that the US ambassador, and perhaps Washington, D.C., no longer regarded Ben Ali as a close ally but rather as a liability. The extent to which the leaked cables triggered more and larger protests will surely be subject to scholarly debate for years to come. Godec's diplomatic missives bring us to the all-important matter of Mediterranean palaces as symbols, targets, and evidence of corruption.

As soon as Ben Ali, formerly minister of the interior, claimed the presidency in 1987 under murky and contested circumstances, he ordered the construction of a super-Walmart-sized palace on the Mediterranean adjacent to the chic village of Sidi Bou Said, a main tourist attraction. It soon assumed the guise of a luxurious, if garish, citadel and stronghold. Then the Trabelsi clan set about seizing through illegal mechanisms prime real estate in the capital city region and along the coast; these properties had previously either held the status of *mulk al-dawla* (state lands) or were privately owned by Tunisian families. More luxury palaces with infinity pools, splendid views, and rare antiques went up. In 2007, Leila Trabelsi (the president's wife) purchased a palace on the marina in Hammamet measuring more than 3,000 square meters for the absurdly small sum of €50. In effect these structures represented highly visible, concrete expressions of the elaboration of a murderous police state and its architecture of subjugation, humiliation, and expropriation. The critical transnational link between Ben Ali's seaside land grabs and real estate trends worldwide during the boom years from the 1990s to 2008 was that high-end property around the Mediterranean rim, for example in Spain and Sardinia, was also subject to escalating illegal corporate seizures.[18]

After Ben Ali and his entourage took flight in January 2011, throngs surged to the presidential villas, which were sacked, burned, and photographed with cell phones. The looted palaces were transformed into political shrines, or pilgrimage sites, where crowds, indeed families with their children, assembled to meditate on and celebrate the fall of the dictator. Numerous other buildings, monuments, and symbols have been desacralized, desecrated, or recommemorated as the revolutionaries have invested spaces with novel meanings and uses. At the far end of the Avenue Bourguiba in downtown Tunis, the clock tower hailing Ben Ali's 1987 coup was partially dismantled; it now bears the name of the martyr-hero Bouazizi.[19]

After the fall of Ben Ali, a functioning interim government, in a series of such bodies, was successfully formed in late January 2011. The Tunisian minister of justice at that time, Lazhar Karoui Chebbi, a lawyer, initiated criminal investigations into the financial holdings of the Ben Ali clan. Foreign banks were served notice of legal action. Switzerland agreed to freeze toxic assets, and international arrest warrants were issued. Between June and July 2011, civilian courts convicted Ben Ali and Leila Trabelsi, in absentia, of money laundering; embezzlement of public funds; and smuggling of arms, narcotics, and archaeological objects; they were sentenced to many years in prison. In two military trials, Ben Ali received life sentences, once again in absentia, for the premeditated deaths of protesters from across the country during 2010. Saudi Arabia, the "land of fallen tyrants," where Ben Ali languishes today in perpetual exile, refused Tunisia's request to extradite the former president. According to the rumor mill in Tunisia, the ex-president arrived in Jeddah, not bearing gifts but transporting one and a half tons of gold.[20]

In contrast to the second president, Tunisia's first postcolonial leader, Habib Bourguiba (ca. 1903–2000), died in rather modest social circumstances, owning only a few meager possessions. A visit to a monument erected in his memory in Bourguiba's hometown of Munastir demonstrates that, unlike Ben Ali, he did not regard Tunisia's wealth and resources as his personal property or fief. And after his government was bloodlessly overthrown in November 1987, the dethroned president lived out the rest of his life in a villa donated by a supporter. From 2000 until the 2010–2011 uprisings, Bourguiba's mausoleum functioned as both a national museum and a discreet shrine for discontented citizens. The structures built during the Ben Ali years tell a rather different story. They yielded proof of astonishing depravity, stoked collective fury, and ultimately furnished potent targets and symbols for prodemocratic mobilization. Nevertheless, by the time of his ouster in 1987, Bourguiba, father of the nation, had assumed the mantle of the autocrat, which sparked organized resistance to the "Supreme Combatant" himself during the 1970s and 1980s.[21] In order to understand how this transpired, we must examine the power of two organizations that possessed sufficient legitimacy and appeal to challenge the power of the state: unions and political Islamists.

In contrast to the other three Maghribi countries, Tunisia's labor activism has deep roots. Organized urban workers had opposed unpopular Protectorate policies in mass strikes even before World War I, notably on the Tunis tramways, which employed both Italian and Tunisian workers.[22] By 1919, the main French labor union in Tunisia admitted "natives," but only at an inferior rank. In a breakaway move, the Confédération Générale des Travailleurs Tunisiens was formed in 1924, making it the second-oldest labor union in all of Africa. Its formation and mass base fueled the nationalist movement, or Neo-Dustur Party, whose leader by the interwar period was Habib Bourguiba. By the 1930s, an indigenous industrial labor force had matured in the interior's mining zones, notably in the phosphate-rich Gafsa region. There a local theater of protest crystallized in which militant workers communicated anti-French messages to the populace through staged plays and satirical productions—the Facebooks of the day.[23]

World War II exerted a tremendous, and as yet largely unacknowledged, impact upon Tunisia. In 1946, Farhat Hached established the new Union Générale Tunisienne du Travail (UGTT), which played a key role in breaking free from France; he served as its first secretary general. The threat that Hached and the UGTT posed to France's rule in the Maghrib is underscored by his untimely death. In December 1952, French intelligence operatives assassinated Hached at his home in a Tunis suburb in retaliation for his strategy of internationalizing Tunisia's cause through cooperation with international trade unions, such as the International Confederation of Free Trade Unions and the Word Federation of Trade Unions.[24] Indeed, in 1952, he had participated in meetings held in San Francisco of the AFL and CIO, which backed the Tunisian nationalist movement. As the Algerian uprisings of 1954 turned into full-scale revolution, Tunisian nationalists capitalized upon mounting disorders across the borders and in France to push for full independence.

Some scholars argue that the 1864 revolt and largely tribal opposition to France's invasion between 1881 and 1883 represented the last time in modern Tunisian history that the south and border areas engaged in concerted political action—until the twenty-first century. But this argument is historically inaccurate. Between 1955 and 1956, guerrilla fighters (*fallaqa*) from the interior fought hard against France in order to represent the interests of the people there. In a revealing countermove undercutting these same anticolonial forces, Bourguiba, who was negotiating the terms of Tunisia's liberation from France, enlisted the colonial army and police, then preparing to repatriate to France, to quash the rebellion.[25]

Thus, at independence, trade unionism already constituted an esteemed and institutionalized mode of sociopolitical action. Moreover, various strands of unionism combined with feminism, both Islamic and secular, figure in the history of collective protest and resistance. By World War II, several women's organizations existed. Bachira Ben M'Rad, whose father was a leading nationalist, established the Muslim Union of Tunisian Women. Nabiha ben Milad and Gladys Adda cofounded the Union of Women of Tunisia (UFT), which recruited female members from families adhering to the Tunisian branches of the Communist and Socialist Parties. The Muslim Union's objectives were to provide educated women access to teaching posts and to organize girls' clubs, including a girls' section of the Scouts. The UFT campaigned to ameliorate conditions for North African workers and soldiers in Europe and to address wartime shortages of foodstuffs in Tunisia, which was utterly ravaged by Allied-Axis bombardments and military campaigns. After 1945, the UFT pressed for clinics to redress the colonial regime's neglect of women's health and for education. France's civilizing mission meant that nearly nine-tenths of Tunisian women were unlettered at independence.[26]

From 1956 until now, relations between Tunisia's unions and the state have generally mirrored not only the national economy's boom-and-bust cycles but also trans-Maghribi and international political and economic trends. During the global crises of the mid-1970s, sparked by oil embargoes after the 1973 Arab-Israeli War, unionized workers' grievances mounted in Tunisia. UGTT members chafed under the growing autocracy of Bourguiba's single party—the Parti Socialiste Dusturien (Dustur Socialist Party, or PSD).[27] In January 1978, the UGTT and its leadership openly broke with the self-appointed president-for-life and his inner circle after the regime sought to handpick union leaders. Countrywide strikers voiced unequivocal demands for pluralism, democracy, and social equality. On "Black Thursday" (January 26, 1978), demonstrations across Tunisia turned into fierce clashes; once again, worker militancy in the phosphate mining zones of Gafsa was pivotal. Violent state measures snuffed out those movements. Habib Achour, the respected head of the UGTT, was imprisoned, along with countless other activists.[28] The unions, particularly their top-level leadership, have also suffered intimidation and manipulation. Like Bourguiba, Ben Ali sought to co-opt the unions' executive officers.

It should be noted that the UGTT has grown into a federation, or super-umbrella organization, that represents unions of engineers, physicians, women, health care professionals, postal employees, university teachers and professors, and workers in the commercial and artisanal sectors. Its nationwide federated structure and grassroots socioeconomic sinews meant that the UGTT, long under the thumb of a single-party system, represented one of only two organizations with sufficient mass-populist legitimacy to oppose, or at least manage, the damage inflicted upon civil society by the state. The other was the Islamic party, known today as al-Nahda.

WOMEN, ISLAM, AND EDUCATION

From a comparative historical perspective, women's status fundamentally distinguishes Tunisia from other Maghribi nations. With the recent revolutions, women and religion—different understandings of the family, gender norms, secularization, Islam, and what it means to be Muslim in Tunisia—came to the foreground during intense, and at times tense, debates among citizens over the new constitution and the organization of the first truly democratic elections. But these crucial questions, which go to the very heart of society, belief, faith, ethics, morals, and identities, were not new by any means.[29]

Under Bourguiba, several programs directly affecting women's status—education and family planning—had made strides, although these had much older histories. The first North African woman to earn a medical degree was Tawhida ben Shaykh (1909–2010), who graduated from the Paris School of Medicine in 1936 with a specialty in pediatrics. Upon her return to Tunis, she was denied a physician's position in European colonial hospitals but opened one of the country's first private women's clinics during the interwar period.[30] Despite insistent calls from Tunisian Jews and Muslims for expanded schooling from the late nineteenth century on, the French Protectorate for political reasons was parsimonious in funding native children's education, especially for girls. After 1956, the nationalist elite (Bourguiba held a French law degree) stressed modern schooling for girls and boys and adult literacy. In 1991, universal education for all children became compulsory by law. Spectacular results had already been achieved relative to other Arab or African nations: 85 percent of school-age boys were enrolled and 70 percent of girls. By the 1990s, the World Bank estimated that a majority of Tunisians regarded themselves as middle class, largely due to free public education. But modern schooling ironically created inevitable discontents. For university graduates, employment consonant with degrees proved elusive, and institutions in the capital city and on the coast were almost always better endowed than those in the interior. Thus began the *fuite de cerveau*, or brain drain, that scattered highly educated and skilled Tunisians across the world.

As collective hopes for true democracy were dashed, society concluded an implicit Faustian pact with Bourguiba, a bargain seen elsewhere in the world. In exchange for middle-class existence and consumer culture achieved mainly through education, open dissent was generally muted on a daily basis. In return, the Bourguiba regime refrained from interference in the national baccalaureate examinations scheduled annually in early summer. These exams, indispensable for university admission, were the Tunisian version of an educational Ramadan. For weeks, all eyes were glued to this "bac" process, which was fair and honest for the most part, although social class played a considerable role, as it does everywhere. Results were published with great fanfare in Arabic and French newspapers, often with photos of the winning students, and jubilant families threw parties. The losers got another crack at university exams the next year. But the Ben Ali regime gradually, if furtively, began corrupting the selection process, creating an enormous sense of grievance and moral outrage. In effect, families were blackmailed, obliged to collaborate, in order to assure their children's future. This factor is rarely, if at all, mentioned in analyses of the Dignity Revolutions.[31]

Among Bourguiba's principal boasts was that he had liberated women through not only education but also radical legal reforms.[32] With France's departure came a second watershed—the August 1956 promulgation of the Code of Personal Status (CPS), the most progressive family law code in the Middle East and North Africa, with the exception of Turkey. According to Mounira Charrad, the CPS "placed the country at the forefront of the Arab world in regard to women's rights."[33] It abolished polygamy and repudiation, instituted judicial divorce, and declared legal equality of the sexes; it was continuously amended and became more comprehensive in following decades. Nevertheless, the initial motivations for, and social responses to, the CPS were extremely complicated. Significantly, after this new legislation, Bourguiba immediately established the National Union of Tunisian Women (l'Union Nationale de la Femme Tunisienne), "merging" other existing women's associations with it; the union was paired with the single party, the Neo-Dustur. State feminism was launched, enduring for much of Bourguiba's presidency. Only during the 1980s did a new generation of women's rights advocates, including Muslim feminists, dare critique the Women's Union as a stark manifestation of state patriarchalism.

Bourguiba and Ben Ali managed women's emancipation as a political hedge fund against national and above all international accusations of human rights abuses.[34] Both presidents were masters of disseminating messages about modernity as evidenced by the relatively (and undeniably) better status of the country's women: "Every foreign guest, each diplomatic delegation or international meeting in Tunisia was provided with ample documentation regarding female rights and progress."[35] (It should be noted that the French Protectorate, as it sought to promote a positive image of colonialism, had manipulated the condition of women and girls through public support for the newly created School for Muslim Girls in Tunis after 1900.[36])

Bourguiba declared August 13 a national holiday to mark the passage of the reformed family law code, proclaiming that the CPS enshrined the "Tunisian personality." But not all citizens agreed—then and now—above all, the Islamist movements. Scholars generally sort political Islam, that is, religious organizations militating for states grounded in their interpretation of Islam, into three ideological categories: (1) so-called hard-liners, whose conservatism is most glaring in the related realms of law, religion, and women; (2) pragmatic conservatives, who also insist upon Islamic law as the basis for legitimacy but who nevertheless favor modern economic systems and citizen engagement; and (3) liberal Islamists, who interpret sacred law as permitting democracy, pluralism, and women and minority rights, but within limits.[37] Proponents of all three of these socioreligious and political positions have been present in Tunisia, but the third type, liberal Islamists, has been in the majority—for historical reasons.[38]

As with women's status, Bourguiba and Ben Ali manipulated international opinion about Islamists, cultivating alarm about the specter of radical Islam to justify denying citizens a voice and a vote. Throughout the 1990s, the second president warned repeatedly of the dangers looming across the western border. These were Algeria's "dark years" of near civil war that pitted members and sympathizers of the Islamic Salvation Front (Front Islamique du Salut, or FIS) against the postcolonial government and security forces. Sparked by contested, and tainted, elections in Algeria, that conflict was constantly evoked by Tunisian ruling elites to quell legitimate opposition. Finally, Bourguiba and Ben Ali staged Tunisia's allegedly "unique Mediterranean identity" for European consumers as a way of not talking about Islam and Muslims on Europe's southern frontiers.

Strong religiously based opposition to the CPS existed from 1956 on. Indeed, one could argue that the solidification of Islamic or Islamist opposition in Tunisia and elsewhere was the fruit of the fundamentally contentious "woman question." In 1981, Rachid al-Ghannouchi (1941–) and Abdelfattah Mourou cofounded the Islamic Tendency Movement (Harakat al-Ittijah al-Islami), which demanded, among other things, an equitable allocation of resources; a multiparty system; and institutionalized support for Islam in public, the law, education, and daily life. They pledged nonviolent action to achieve these goals but were equivocal from the start about the nature and degree of women's emancipation. Due to repression by the Bourguiba regime after 1984, the party was reorganized to operate clandestinely as well as publicly. Seeking legal recognition, it assumed its current name, Hizb al-Nahdah ("Renaissance Party," also known as Ennahda or al-Nahda) in 1989. By then Ghannouchi, who had been imprisoned and tortured by the Bourguiba regime, was in exile in Europe (from 1988 until 2011). The party remained illegal throughout the Ben Ali administration.[39] Significantly, in 1985, the Islamist Tendency Movement called for a national referendum on the PSC, equating it with state-enforced secularization. Moreover, Muslim groups have persistently argued that the PSC not only violated Islamic principles, notably the religious-sanctioned existence of different, though complementary, spheres for man and woman, but also promoted female equality in the job force, thereby depriving men of employment.[40]

After Ben Ali was forced out, the al-Nahdah Party gained legal recognition and the right to enter candidates in forthcoming elections. Over one hundred parties presented candidate lists for the October 23, 2011, elections for the 217-member National Constituent Assembly (NCA), authorized to appoint an interim cabinet and draft a new constitution. An array of international bodies provided expertise on democratic process. The American Bar Association's Rule of Law Initiative held in-country training sessions for hundreds of Tunisian lawyers during the summer of 2011, addressing issues such as best practices for election law, procedures, monitoring, and resolving disputed votes.[41]

In May 2011, Tunisia passed a "parity law" emulating French legislation that required political parties to ensure that at least 50 percent of their candidates were female. Some 5,000 women stood for the NCA. Al-Nahda marshaled superior organizational and mobilizing skills and endorsed the parity law as a tactical move; it ran the largest number of female candidates.[42] The party won 90 seats, a clear majority, and sent the largest bloc of female lawmakers to the assembly. Figures for voter turnout remain disputed; some sources claim nearly 70 percent while others advance lower numbers, such as 53 percent of the eligible electorate. Complicating democratic process was that tens of thousands of Tunisians in the diaspora had been given the right to vote, but hastily organizing eligible voter rolls and stations in distant places, such as North America, posed daunting logistical problems.

Once again, the disparity between major cities and interior towns became patent on election day, Sunday, October 23, 2011. In Kasserine, the international media captured an image of, and message from, a group of women, most of whom wore head scarves. "We are from the south, and we want to vote," they declared. But no one had informed them that they had to first register to cast a ballot; they were turned away from the polling station housed in a local school. Debates raged until 2014 about the place of women's rights and religion in the new constitution. These frequently disrupted institutions of learning. Confrontations between secular and Islamist students and faculty plagued public education; incidents at the University of Tunis's Manouba campus, the largest in the system, bear witness to this.[43] As enshrined in the 1956 PSC, Tunisian feminism has been largely urban, middle-class, and secular, but democracy requires listening to dissenting voices, desires, and worldviews.

Following the largely nonviolent October 2012 elections, a severe crisis marked 2013 after the murders of two leading members of the Popular Front Coalition, allegedly by Islamists. Chokri Belaïd was assassinated in Tunis on February 6, 2013; daily protests were held at the Ministry of the Interior to demand justice. On July 25, 2013 (Tunisian Independence Day), Mohamed Brahmi, an opposition member of the NCA, was gunned down in the streets of the capital. Brahmi's slaying was absurdly incongruous; a leftist, he represented

Sidi Bou Zid, where it had all begun. In that town, a furious crowd torched al-Nahda's local headquarters, and the UGTT called a nationwide strike.[44] In response, coalition opposition parties demanded the resignation of the Islamist-led government and dissolution of the NCA, but al-Nahda clung to its electoral legitimacy, refusing to relinquish power. At this momentous juncture, the UGTT put forth an initiative to resolve the tense stalemate, which was greatly influenced by events across the Middle East and above all in Egypt.

There, President Husni Mubarak had been toppled in 2011 by mass demonstrations that had been directly sparked by Tunisia's ease in ousting its own dictator. Elections in 2012 had brought the Muslim Brotherhood under Muhammed Morsi to power. But by June 2013, millions of Egyptians in Cairo's streets called for Morsi's resignation on the first anniversary of his election due to mounting violence, social chaos, and economic disarray. If the Tunisian example inspired Egyptians to overthrow a long-ensconced, US-backed military regime, if only temporarily, then Egypt helped break the impasse in Tunis.

A national coalition known as the "Quartet," composed of al-Nahda and other party leaders and representatives of the UGTT; the Tunisian Union of Industry, Commerce, and Handicrafts (which represents employers); the Bar Association; and the Human Rights League, convened to hammer out a "consensual road map." This three-pronged document advocated preserving the NCA, forming a nonpolitical government, and setting dates for general elections. On January 26, 2014, the first democratic constitution was adopted, despite almost insurmountable obstacles and near failures.[45] At the same time, in June 2014, Moncef Marzouki, president of the NCA, and Mustapha Ben Jaafar, prime minister, announced the newly established Truth and Dignity Commission (TDC), again setting a precedent. The declaration came during the international conference organized by the Tunisian Ministry of Justice, Human Rights, and Transitional Justice in collaboration with the United Nations Development Programme (UNDP), the Office of the High Commissioner for Human Rights (OHCHR), and the International Centre for Transitional Justice (ICTJ). Tellingly, this commission, whose armature includes both judicial and nonjudicial mechanisms, has been gathering evidence on human rights violations committed by the Tunisian state since 1956. Victims would be afforded compensation and rehabilitation.[46]

One of the most awful truths to emerge from the TDC hearings regards women's brutalization under Ben Ali. At least 12,000 individuals came forward with documentation on torture and extrajudicial incarceration, the vast majority of them men. "But what has surprised even long-time human rights activists is the number of women starting to tell stories of extreme cruelty, sexual violence, and rape."[47] Women as truth-bearers about sexual-political crimes are particularly fraught for societies that place the highest moral value on female virtue but shame and shun women (and their families) who are victimized by such crimes. As the journalist and rights activist Sihem Bensedrine stated in May 2015, "We had this paradox. . . . Ben Ali did a lot of feminization but there were massive violations against women, especially rape, more than we thought."[48] This newfound audacity by some women to discuss sexual assault and humiliation in public might be compared to the deafening silence among Algerians for decades after the war for independence (1954–1962); rape had been systematically employed as a "weapon of mass destruction." Only recently has the heavy silence about Algerian women's afflictions at the hands of French military, police, and civilian authorities been broken. It is appalling to realize that torture methods employed systematically by Ben Ali's secret police were identical to those used by the United States at Bagram air base, the notorious Abu Ghraib prison in Iraq, and Guantanamo Bay—waterboarding, electric shocks to the genitals, crippling psychological abuse, rape, and other horrors. In fact, these practices were being deployed at the very same time.

Tunisia has a long, if precarious—and nonlinear—history of constitution-making. In 1861, the first Dustur (constitution) in the Arab world was proclaimed just prior to the 1864 rebellion. A century and a half ago, that constitution proved stillborn in the midst of a rebellion where intersecting national and transnational forces converged. But the 1861 constitution was again invoked during the Dignity Revolutions. Most significantly, the Nobel Committee awarded the 2015 Peace Prize to Tunisia for the consensual processes resulting in the 2014 constitution. For the first time, this document contained explicit provisions guaranteeing state protection for the environment, which is the subject to which I turn next.

FOOD SECURITY, WATER, AND THE ENVIRONMENT

Why, if the colonial tree produced bitter fruit, has the tree of national independence provided us only with stunted and shriveled crops?[49]

The current malaise of the agricultural sector and the North African interior has deep historical roots. Moreover, precedents for collective action symbolized and concretized by the notion of food security go far back to the precolonial and colonial eras. Since the nineteenth century, North Africa's economies have been progressively integrated into world market forces, frequently at a disadvantage. Due to the growing clout of transnational finance, imperialism, and modern communications, the Mediterranean rim became firmly enmeshed in European-controlled trans-sea and transatlantic/global circuits.[50] A pattern can be detected—autocratic regimes, whether colonial or postcolonial, almost always neglect rural peoples and the subsistence agrarian sectors.[51] As Habib Ayeb and Roy Bush bluntly state, "Here lies a paradox. Small farmers in Egypt and Tunisia are among the most productive and clever in the world. . . . In Tunisia's arid southeast, particularly in the Gabes region, farmers demonstrate immense skill and knowledge."[52]

From 1964 until 1973, small-farmer agriculture in Tunisia was badly bruised by ill-conceived collectivization programs imposed by the minister of planning, Ahmad Ben Salah. By then, farm exports largely to European markets did not cover even 50 percent of the cost of imported food. After 1974, state planners abandoned socialized agriculture for free-market strategies. By the early 1980s, food insecurity had increased to intolerable levels in the interior. Windfall oil revenues dropped off, and Tunisia, an agrarian-based economy, was beset by poor harvests due to unfavorable climatic conditions. In the same period, fortress Europe began shutting its doors more tightly against North Africans of any educational background or social class searching for a secure livelihood through expatriation. Government and public debt ballooned. The International Monetary Fund (IMF) and World Bank dictated austerity measures in 1983, pressing for termination of state subsidies on basic foodstuffs in exchange for loans. And a hitherto unthinkable event occurred: Bourguiba's car was stoned in a symbolic act "indicative of the depth of frustration and rage among the poorest and most afflicted Tunisians."[53]

When late in December of 1983 the government doubled the price of bread and other staples, it came as no surprise that a series of disturbances erupted throughout the country. The peoples of the south and interior were the first to rebel; unrest rapidly spread to northern provinces and coastal cities. Peasants, youths, seasonal agricultural laborers, and the unemployed were joined by students who declared a national solidarity strike. The police were overwhelmed; a state of emergency was declared, and the army mobilized to put down the revolt. The resulting repression was nothing short of draconian. It revealed that the social pact among Bourguiba, the state-controlled single party (the PSD), and citizens that had been concluded long before independence in 1956 was unraveling. The food subsidies were restored, but the agribusinesses and large landowners thrived. During the 1980s, the Islamist party became politically active, campaigning for the underprivileged. In the aftermath of the 1983–1984 rebellion, Ben Ali was reappointed director-general of national security.[54] Characterizing the events of 1984 as "bread riots" is not only a misleading label but also an intellectually bankrupt notion. It downgrades the socioideological and moral content of civic mass action to a story only about food.

Today, 80 percent of national production is concentrated in cities from Bizerte to Sfax. The provinces of the southwest and center-west, home to 40 percent of the total population of more than 10 million, claim only 20 percent of GDP. Nonetheless, Tunisians have enjoyed relatively secure access to food in comparison with much of Africa or the Middle East. Meat, poultry, eggs, and milk products have been available, at least in coastal cities, towns, and villages. Indeed, in fossil-fuel-rich Algeria, families crossed the borders regularly to shop for food in Tunisia due to shortages at home. But even before the recent crash, a small can of tuna, fished from the waters off the Cap Bon, had become pricey, even by American standards, because the country's high-quality tuna was exported to Japan. Food subsidies remained in place for bread, oil, and couscous so critical to urban populations living beyond the margins of rising middle-class prosperity and, above all, to rural households. Then came 2008, the twenty-first century's version of the Great Depression.[55] Under- and unemployment grievously affected specific regions, notably the interior, and specific social demographics. Impoverished young men between the ages of eighteen and twenty-five were deprived of income adequate for them to marry and establish households—in other words, masculinity was a critical issue. By the eve of the revolutions, the visibility and audibility of the economic and cultural rift between the disadvantaged interior and the urban, cosmopolitan coast could no longer be concealed, much less denied.

Water is an increasingly scarce resource worldwide but especially in the Maghrib, where the Great Sahara is expanding steadily and rapidly northward. After 1987, the regime embarked on a pillage-cum-privatization campaign with substantial backing from foreign corporations. Targeted for expropriation were aquifers in the Sidi Bou Zid governorate, where farmers depended upon food processing and citrus export to Europe. "Irrigation is 100 percent dependent upon groundwater, coming from springs in oases and wells in the steppe. Small farmers in this region eked out an existence until the early 1990s, when investors undermined them by drilling more wells for their large-scale irrigation schemes."[56] The Ben Ali clan organized the Hayet Water Company and constructed a pipeline extracting the governorate's "blue gold" for distribution to the large industrial city of Sfax. This fanned social anger because local growers had to buy their own water back from Hayet.[57] This scheme lined the already well-lined pockets of the regime and its cronies and threatened the agrarian economy on which social relations depend. The ultimate irony—and a cruel one at that—was the company name, Hayet, which in Arabic means "life"; its slick branding smacks of Madison Avenue–type marketing devices. Moreover, "the main centers of water consumption are situated within the coastal region, while water resources are mainly located in the North and in the interior of the country."[58] But there was nothing Tunisian about the water grab—global companies such as Eaux Canada, Vivendi, Suez, and Bechtel have been privatizing water for decades.

Two of the greatest ecological threats to the sustainability of the entire Mediterranean Sea—fossil fuels and/or industrial waste, and tourism—have converged upon Tunisia with great force. The Gulf of Gabes, a dumping ground for toxic phosphate-processing chemicals, has become an ecological disaster zone. Local people there refer to the Gulf as "the shore of death" because of its unprecedented outbreaks of environmentally induced illnesses, disappearance of species, and habitat destruction.[59] One alarming consequence of the recent upheavals is that industrial pollution has soared. "'In our country, there's no control at all,' says Mohammed, an environmental activist with Kulna Tunis, tossing the empty blue and red shell casings to the ochre sand. 'The el-hbara birds and el-ghzel are being hunted wildly; it is a catastrophe.' [Tourist] Companies are taking advantage of Tunisia's weak central authority and deteriorating economy by bringing in hunters to illegally poach gazelles and birds for profit."[60]

The centrality of environmental issues distinguishes current activism from past mobilization. In the same way that the practices and grammar of international human rights carved out a limited space for dissent under Tunisia's two dictators, so the discourse of the environment offers a language for claiming rights. Now the degradation of habitats can be publicly debated—it is enshrined in the 2014 constitution. Algeria's ruling party has been profoundly shaken by events in Tunisia, particularly in view of the persistence of decades-old Berber autonomy movements.[61] But local Algerians have taken heart from their neighbor to the east, particularly in the realm of environmental political action and the current "shale rush." At Ain Salah in the Sahara, peaceful protests against a pilot project in fracking shale for gas have been ongoing and spread to northern Algeria. The methods involved in this pilot program are prohibited today in France for environmental reasons.[62] Yet the postcolonial corporate collaboration between SONATRACH (the state-owned gas and oil company) and France Total not only endures but also brings us back in time—to when European and US empires employed overseas territories and peoples as experimental testing grounds. Perhaps in Algeria, "the country of perpetual protest," the fossil-fuel party will come to an end. One of the major grievances among demonstrators is that fracking, as we know from the United States, wastes huge amounts of water and pollutes drinking sources.

Tunisia's enormous tourist industry infrastructure has deeply distinguished it from Libya and Algeria for decades. By the 1980s, high-end as well as mass international tourism, mainly from Europe, had taken off, furnishing much-needed hard currency and employment but fueling socioreligious and cultural discontents.[63] The extraordinary expansion of Tunisia's middle class—among the largest in the Arab world—was intimately tied to international tourism as well as to worker remittances, the country's phosphate industry, and relocation of light manufacturing from Europe to Tunisia to exploit local laborers. But global investment capitalism cum tour industry has sinister dimensions—it siphons off large quantities of water and responds instantaneously to political or economic crises. The 2008 bust and the revolutions have severely depressed the tourist industry, which suffered a calamitous drop after 2011. But tourism is not just about "a room with a view," and a direct connection can be established between the tourist industry revenues and the apparatus of the Ben Ali police state.

The Bardo Museum in Tunis, once a palace for the precolonial dynasty, boasts some of the most splendid artifacts from North Africa and the Mediterranean area in the world. It has been a prime international attraction since the colonial period. On March 18, 2015, gunmen stormed the museum in Tunis; British, Japanese, French, Italian, and Colombian tourists and a Tunisian were among the twenty-four dead. Two Tunisians and one Algerian, members of the Okba Ibn Nafa Brigade, a jihadist group that had previously attacked security forces, were held responsible. It is thought that the gunmen had been trained in Libya.[64] On March 29, thousands of Tunisians and foreign visitors demonstrated in the streets in solidarity against violence.

This was not the first nor the last time that tourists were targeted. In October 2013, a suicide bomber detonated explosives on a beach in the resort

of Sousse, killing himself. Tragically, on June 27, 2015, Islamic State operatives murdered some thirty-nine tourists, mainly vacationers from the United
Kingdom. The police killed one of the perpetrators, Seifeddine Rezgui, a student at Kairouan University. In 2014, tourism provided employment to about
400,000 people and constituted at least 7 percent of GDP. Currently, hotel
rooms are empty and hotel managers wonder whether to shut their doors.[65]
Tourism as a political target mimics a series of extremist attacks on luxury
hotels in Cairo and elsewhere in Egypt. In January 2013, the Semiramis Intercontinental near Tahrir Square suffered six assaults. This is not new to Egypt
but goes back to the early 1990s.[66]

Conclusion: Transborder Repercussions and Global Aftershocks

A recent assessment of Tunisia as "small, peripheral, and docile" and "an island
of comparative tranquility because it barely casts a shadow beyond its borders"
seems not only historically specious but also simply wrongheaded.[67] People,
groups, and organizations across the globe have tracked the fortunes of the
Dignity Revolutions. In 2011, Chinese prodemocracy organizers embraced
the notion of a "Jasmine Revolution," the name some used for the uprisings
in Tunisia. Labor's newly energized leadership role explains why the World
Social Forum (WSF) convened in Tunis in March 2013, the first time in an
Arab country. Some 50,000 visitors from 128 countries gathered for seminars,
workshops, concerts, and marches. Organized in Porto Alegre, Brazil, in 2001,
the WSF initially focused on Latin American struggles against authoritarian
regimes allied with the IMF and other transnational entities. A decade later,
the Tunisian revolutions resonated with the WSF's expanded objectives.

Climate change was the principal theme for 2013, but austerity economics,
public and social indebtedness, and human dignity were on the table as well.
Predictably, women's legal rights, religion, and freedom of expression proved
especially controversial. Local civil society activists hoped that the WSF would
boost social demand for democracy as the Tunisian secular left wing under-
stands it. In March 2015, the biannual WSF met again in Tunis—the second
time in a row. During the five-day event, 70,000 delegates from more than
4,000 organizations representing 120 countries debated climate justice, immigration, media freedom, women's rights, refugees, energy, and divestment. That
two WSF meetings took place there drew world attention to the country's part

in gestating the Occupy Wall Street movements.[68] Kalle Lasn, "leader" of the leaderless Occupy Wall Street movement, stated during an interview, "Back in the summer of 2011 we were all talking about what we were going to do . . . and we were all inspired by what happened in Tunisia and thought that America was ripe for this type of rage."[69]

By the new millennium, the EU regarded North Africa as "Europe's dangerous southern Mediterranean frontier" due to massive clandestine immigration. The magnitude of the fallout from the first Arab uprisings was front-page news in 2016 as hundreds of thousands of refugees from Syria and elsewhere beat at the doors of Western Europe. But the first mass transborder movements were thousands of Libyans who fled to Tunisia (and Egypt) after the virtual destruction of Muammar Gaddafi's state by October 20, 2011. During that period, the Tunisia–Lampedusa crossing for refugees seeking a haven in Europe has become not only a global human trafficking highway but also a passageway to a watery grave.[70] The future for Tunisia and its new constitution is perilous because of the very mass uprisings that they inspired elsewhere. In Libya, the absence of a state has not only triggered refugee flows and human smuggling but also accelerated the circulation of weaponry and fighters across fungible North African borders. Older patterns in the geography of armed resistance have reasserted themselves. The *bled al-siba*, historically situated in the inaccessible terrain of the Chaambi Mountains on the Algerian-Tunisian borderlands, currently shelter Islamist rebels in ways similar to the past.[71] Thus, the issues of borders, radical or violent militant action, and targets are critical.

This leads to a question: What is specifically Arab about the Arab Spring? The phenomenon of transnational North Africans residing permanently outside the Maghrib is historically quite old and predates independence from France. Indeed, many in the diaspora across the world are French (or Canadian or American, etc.) citizens. These communities have maintained close ties with family and fellow citizens "back home" who suffered under repressive regimes; they furnish forbidden news, information, and new ideas. Functioning as "political offshore" communities, the expatriates as makers of revolution have not yet drawn the scholarly attention they deserve.

This chapter's intent has been less to search for definitive triggers and causalities of mass protest and radical social change than to troll the past for long-term, tectonic transformations as well as manifest or semiconcealed continuities and ruptures. Some of the causes for the ongoing upheavals are not necessarily new to our already deeply troubled century. The youth bulge, globalization, and the novel social media, so critical for ideological conscious-ness, communication, and mobilization, provoked and facilitated collective protest in earlier periods. Globalization, the unequal incorporation of econ-omies and state structures into transnational, transregional structures, was well under way by the twentieth century. Finally, I argue here that in contrast to Morocco, Algeria, and Egypt, Tunisia does not have a "minority problem," whether defined as ethnic or religious. However, before the Dignity Revolu-tions, the "interior" functioned as an internal or domestic "other," although the newly seated National Assembly in Tunis seeks to change this.[72]

Two final questions arise. First, why did women, the environment, and youth as clusters of interrelated issues—about what the future holds—fail to attract serious scholarly attention in Middle East and North African studies until very recently?[73] Indeed, the current Moroccan sultan, Muhammad VI, is playing the "woman game," as did Bourguiba and Ben Ali in years past, to quell permanent unrest and persuade international audiences of his democratic in-tentions.[74] Second, did decolonization really happen?

Small places and states can prove as intellectually provocative as the big players such as Egypt, and now Syria. Tunisia provides critical lessons on multiple scales—from the intertidal to the intergalactic—for thinking about and formulating theories of collective action and more. As noted by the Nobel Committee, the challenges that lie ahead are enormous.

NOTES

1. Norwegian Nobel Committee, "The Nobel Peace Prize for 2015," www.nobelprize.org/nobel_prizes/peace/laureates/2015/press.html.

2. Julia Clancy-Smith, *Tunisian Revolutions: Reflections on Seas, Coasts, and Interiors* (Washington, DC: Center for Contemporary Arab Studies and Georgetown University Press, 2014), 26–28; and Eric Goldstein, "Before the Arab Spring, the Unseen Thaw," 2012, www.hrw.org/world-report-2012/arab-spring-unseen-thaw. The explosion of publications in print and electronic format as well as international conferences, meetings, and other forums on the Arab Spring makes comprehensive citations impossible. See, for example, David McMurray and Amanda Ufheil-Somers, *The Arab Revolts: Dispatches on Militant Democracy in the Middle East* (Bloomington and Indianapolis: Indiana University Press, 2013), a compilation of articles from the *Middle East Report*. The *Journal of North African Studies* has closely chronicled the revolutions, for example, the special issue "Women, Gen-der and the Arab Spring," 19, 2 (2014), as have the *Journal of Middle East Women's Studies* and the *International Journal of Middle East Studies*. The most sophisticated analysis of the

Ben Ali regime is Béatrice Hibou, *The Force of Obedience: The Political Economy of Repression in Tunisia* (Cambridge: Cambridge University Press, 2011), an expanded and updated version of the French edition, *La force d'obéissance: Economie politique de la répréssion en Tunisie* (Paris: La Découverte, 2006).

3. As Shir Hever astutely observed in "The People Want: A Radical Exploration of the Arab Spring," *Review of Middle East Studies* 48, 1 & 2 (2014): 54, "The country in which the uprising was the most successful and met with least amount of violence was Tunisia, a country defined by its small military."

4. Natasha Ezrow and Erica Frantz's *Dictators and Dictatorships: Understanding Authoritarian Regimes and Their Leaders* (New York: Continuum, 2011) undervalues the potential of mass civic action in the unmaking of dictatorial systems of rule, which this chapter disputes.

5. For an analysis of Bouazizi's death as one among many triggers for collective action, see Nouri Gana, ed., *The Making of the Tunisian Revolution: Contexts, Architects, Prospects* (Edinburgh: Edinburgh University Press, 2013), 1–31.

6. Mehdi Mabrouk, "A Revolution for Dignity and Freedom: Preliminary Observations on the Social and Cultural Background to the Tunisian Revolution," *Journal of North African Studies* 16, 4 (2011): 625–635; on the "culture of suicide," 629. See also Amy Aisen Kallander, "Tunisia's Post–Ben Ali Challenge: A Primer," *MERIP Middle East Report Online*, January 26, 2011, www.merip.org/mero/mero012611; and the articles in Ahmed Jdey, ed., special issue of *EurOrient*, "La Tunisie du XXIe siècle: Quels pouvoirs pour quelle modèle de société?," No. 38 (Paris: L'Harmattan, June 2012).

7. Quoted in Francis Ghilès, "North African Diversities: A Tunisian Odyssey," *open Democracy*, May 22, 2012, www.opendemocracy.net/print/65987.

8. Isabelle Mandraud, "Un portfolio sonore sur Sidi Bouzid," *Le Monde*, December 17, 2011.

9. A heated debate exists regarding the moniker "Jasmine Revolution," which first emerged when Ben Ali seized power in 1987; some scholars maintain that the CIA coined the term as a marketing device. Since 2010, Tunisians have generally employed Thawra al-Karamah (The Dignity Revolution), Thawra Sidi Bou Zid (The Revolution of Sidi Bou Zid), or al-Thawra al-Tunisiyya (The Tunisian Revolution).

10. The distressing deficit of historical knowledge about the Maghrib among journalists has committed astonishing errors to print. One pervasive fiction was that 2010–2011 witnessed the Arab world's *first modern* revolutions. See, for example, Angelique Chrisafis's "The Arab World's First Modern Popular Revolution," *Guardian*, February 9, 2011, a historically inaccurate assertion. Other commentators opined that Tunisia experienced less violence than Egypt because it had been so thoroughly colonized by Rome and that the French or, as improbably, the British had "liberated" North Africa from Ottoman imperial rule.

11. Julia Clancy-Smith, "Ruptures? Governance in Colonial-Husaynid Tunisia, 1870–1914," in *Colonial and Post-Colonial Governance of Islam: Continuities and Ruptures*, ed. Veit

Bader, Annelies Moors, and Marcel Maussen (Amsterdam: University of Amsterdam Press, 2011), 65–87; and Farina Mir, "Introduction" to the American Historical Association's Roundtable, "The Archives of Decolonization," *American Historical Review* 120, 3 (June 2015): 844–851.

12. Sonia Shiri, "Co-constructing Dissent in the Transient Linguistic Landscape: Multilingual Protest Signs of the Tunisian Revolution," in *Conflict, Exclusion and Dissent in the Linguistic Landscape,* ed. Rani Rubdy and Selim Ben Said (New York: Palgrave McMillan, 2015); Silvia Marsans-Sakly, "The Tunisian Revolution: Making and Meaning of an Event," *EurOrient,* No. 38 (Paris: L'Harmattan, June 2012); and Mohamed Kerrou, "New Actors of the Revolution and the Political Transition in Tunisia," in *The Arab Spring: Will It Lead to Democratic Transitions?,* ed. Clement Henry and Jang Ji-Hyang (Seoul: Asian Institute for Policy Studies, 2012), 80–99.

13. See Denis Bocquet's "Reflections on Public Spaces in Revolutionary and Post-Revolutionary Tunis," a review of Chiara Sebastiani's study *Una città, una rivoluzione. Tunisi e la riconquista dello spazio pubblico* (Cosenza, Italy: Luigi Pellegrini Editore, 2014) in *Jadaliyya,* April 17, 2015.

14. An arresting photo of the baguettes in Tunis on January 18, 2011, appears in Nadia Marzouki, "From People to Citizens in Tunisia," *Middle East Report* 259 (Summer 2011): 16–19. See also Hibou, *The Force of Obedience;* Mabrouk, "A Revolution"; and "Food and the Arab Spring," *Economist,* March 17, 2012, 59.

15. Juan Cole, "US Ignored Tunisian Corruption: Diplomatic Cables Suggest US Was Aware of Deep-Rooted Corruption Among Tunisia's Elite," Al Jazeera, January 18, 2011, www.aljazeera.com/indepth/opinion/2011/01/20111171299907176.html.

16. On November 28, 2010, WikiLeaks and five international newspapers including the *Guardian* agreed to simultaneously publish a number of leaked diplomatic cables from US embassies around the world, covering the period from 1966 to early 2010. The report on Ben Ali's son-in-law, "US Embassy Cables: The 'OTT' Lifestyle of Tunisian President's Son-in-Law, Including Pet Tiger," was published in the *Guardian,* December 7, 2010, www.guardian.co.uk/world/us-embassy-cables-documents/218324.

17. Ibid.

18. Nathan E. Richardson, *Constructing Spain: The Re-imagination of Space and Place in Fiction and Film, 1953–2003* (Lewisburg, PA: Bucknell University Press, 2012), documents the expropriation of Mediterranean vacation properties by international investors. In some places, as in Spain during the summer of 2009, villages were deliberately torched to drive their aging owners out; their land was subsequently "purchased" by transnational corporations and developed.

19. Clancy-Smith, *Tunisian Revolutions.* Ukrainians' reactions in February 2014 to the overthrow of Viktor F. Yanukovych were identical. In Noi Petrivtsi, home to the former president's pleasure palace, crowds assembled in anger and astonishment inside the 350-acre estate; Steven Erlanger, "An Abandoned Ukrainian Palace, an Anxious Look Toward the Future," *New York Times,* February 28, 2014.

20. The editors of *Encyclopedia Britannica*, "Zine al-Abidine Ben Ali," *Encyclopedia Britannica*, accessed September 22, 2015, www.britannica.com/biography/Zine-al-Abidine -Ben-Ali; and Ellen Knickmeyer, "A Five-Star Retirement Home for Dictators: Welcome to Sunny Saudi Arabia, Land of Fallen Tyrants," *Foreign Policy*, June 23, 2011, http://foreign policy.com/2011/06/23/a-five-star-retirement-home-for-dictators-2.

21. See Sophie Bessis and Souhayr Belhassen, *Bourguiba* (Tunis: Elyzad, 2012); and Pierre-Albin Martel, *Habib Bourguiba: Un homme, un siècle* (Paris: Jaguar, 1999).

22. Omar Carlier makes a critical link between North Africans employed by French urban tramways and the gestation of organized anticolonial labor movements in "Les tra-minots algériens des années 30: Un groupe social médiateur et novateur," *Le Mouvement Social* 146 (1989): 61–89. Women, however, are often absent from histories of trade unionism. A good example is Gladys 'Adda (1921–2012), a labor and women's rights activist and journalist originally from Gabes who joined the Tunisian Communist Party during World War II to fight against Fascism and for workers.

23. Today, Tunisia is the world's fifth-largest exporter of phosphoric acid, whose processing has extensively damaged the environment. See Christopher Alexander, *Tunisia: Stability and Reform in the Modern Maghreb* (Oxon, UK: Routledge, 2010); Nouradin Dougi, *Histoire d'une grande entreprise coloniale: La Compagnie des Phosphates et du chemin de fer de Gafsa, 1897–1930* (Tunis: Faculté de la Manouba, 1995); Silvia Finzi, ed., *Mestieri e professioni degli Italiani di Tunisia* (Tunis: Éditions Finzi, 2003); and Samya El Mechat, *Tunisie: Les chemins vers l'indépendance (1945–1956)* (Paris: L'Harmattan, 1995).

24. Kenneth J. Perkins, *A History of Modern Tunisia* (Cambridge: Cambridge University Press, 2004), 157–176; and Afef Abrougui, "Foundation Formed to Honor Farhat Hached," Tunisialive, December 5, 2013, www.tunisia-live.net/2013/12/05/farhat-hached /#sthash.CPwfweOa.dpuf.

25. Perkins, *A History of Modern Tunisia*, and Abdesslem Ben Hamida, "Marginalité et nouvelles solidarités urbaine en Tunisie à l'époque coloniale," *Cahiers de la Méditerranée* 69 (2004): 51–61.

26. Habib Kazdaghli, ed., *Nisa' wa dhakira/Mémoire de femmes: Tunisiennes dans la vie publique, 1920–1960* (Tunis: Éditions Média Com, 1993).

27. Formerly known as the New Constitution (Neo-Dustour) Party, which led the country to independence from France, the party was renamed in 1964 as the Socialist Dustour Party (Parti Socialiste Dusturien, or PSD). The party's names harken back to the 1861 Tunisian constitution.

28. Perkins, *A History of Modern Tunisia*.

29. Mounira M. Charrad, *States and Women's Rights: The Making of Postcolonial Tunisia, Algeria, and Morocco* (Berkeley and Los Angeles: University of California Press, 2001); Jane Tchaïcha and Khedija Arfaoui, "Tunisian Women in the Twenty-First Century: Past Achievements and Present Uncertainties in the Wake of the Jasmine Revolution," *Journal of North African Studies* 17, 2 (March 2012): 215–238; and the special issue devoted to the

uprisings, *International Journal of Middle East Studies* 43, 3 (August 2011). See also Lilia La-bidi's important research on women and oral history: *Joudhour al-harakat al-nisa'iyya: Ri-wayat li-shakhsiyyat tarikhiyya* (Origins of feminist movements in Tunisia: Personal history narratives) (Tunis: Imprimerie Tunis-Carthage, 2009) and *Qamus as-siyar li-lmunadhilat at-tunisiyyat, 1881–1956* (Biographical dictionary of Tunisian women militants) (Tunis: Imprimerie Tunis-Carthage, 2009).

30. Julia Clancy-Smith, "From Household to School Room: Women, Trans-Mediterranean Networks, and Education in North Africa," in *French Mediterraneans: Transnational and Imperial Histories*, ed. Patricia M. E. Lorcin and Todd Shepard (Lincoln: University of Nebraska Press, 2015), 200–231.

31. I gathered evidence for this during years of interviews and conversations in Tunis with high school teachers who drew up, oversaw, and corrected the annual examination as well as with the families of students presenting themselves for the bac. An arresting photo appeared in 2011 of an unemployed teacher in Kasserine sitting dejectedly by abandoned rail lines on a flat, dusty plain. He did have a university degree, but he was one of an estimated 3,000 certified teachers without schools and classrooms. Yet there is nothing inherently Tunisian, North African, Arab, or Muslim about this image. The jobless teacher might well be from West Texas, southern Arizona, or rural Mississippi, anywhere in the United States—or the globe—beset by growing structural-social inequities.

32. Julia Clancy-Smith, "Changing Perspectives on Colonialism and Imperialism: Women, Gender, Empire," in *Historians and Historiography of the Modern Middle East*, ed. Israel Gershoni and Amy Singer (Seattle: University of Washington Press, 2006), 70–100.

33. Mounira M. Charrad has published the most comprehensive work on the CPS as well as on women in North Africa comparatively and historically in *States and Women's Rights*; see also Mounira M. Charrad, "Tunisia at the Forefront of the Arab World: Two Waves of Gender Legislation," *Washington and Lee Law Review* 64 (2007): 1513–1527; and Mounira M. Charrad and Amina Zarrugh, "The Arab Spring and Women's Rights in Tunisia," e-International Relations, www.e-ir.info/2013/09/04/the-arab-spring-and-womens-rights-in-tunisia. The quotation is from Charrad and Zarrugh, "The Arab Spring," 6.

34. On human rights organizations, see Hibou, *The Force of Obedience*, 95–105.

35. Lilia Labidi, "Islamic Law, Feminism, and Family: The Reformulation of *Hudud* in Egypt and Tunisia," in *From Patriarchy to Empowerment: Women's Participation, Movements, and Rights in the Middle East, North Africa, and South Asia*, ed. Valentine M. Moghadam (Syracuse, NY: Syracuse University Press, 2007); and Sophie Bessis, "Le féminisme institutionnel en Tunisie," *CLIO: Histoire, femmes et sociétiés* 9 (1999), accessed May 10, 2012, http://clio.revues.org/286, doi: 10.4000/clio.286.

36. Julia Clancy-Smith, "Envisioning Knowledge: Educating the Muslim Woman in Colonial North Africa, 1850–1918," in *Iran and Beyond: Essays in Middle Eastern History in Honor of Nikki R. Keddie*, ed. Beth Baron and Rudi Matthee (Los Angeles: Mazda Press, 2000), 99–118.

37. On these three categories, which can overlap, see the introductory chapter by Mark L. Haas and David W. Lesch, *The Arab Spring: Change and Resistance in the Middle East* (Boulder, CO: Westview Press, 2013), 5–6.

38. Charrad, *States and Women's Rights*; Tchaïcha and Arfaoui, "Tunisian Women in the Twenty-First Century."

39. Azzam Tamimi, *Rachid Ghannouchi: A Democrat Within Islamism* (New York: Oxford University Press, 2001).

40. Perkins, *A History of Modern Tunisia*, 135–139; Charrad, *States and Women's Rights*, 219–231.

41. On the ABA's role in the elections, see American Bar Association, "ABA ROLI, Tunisian Bar Association Work for Fair and Transparent Elections," October 2011, www .americanbar.org/advocacy/rule_of_law/where_we_work/middle_east/tunisia/news/ news_tunisia_aba_roli_tunisian_bar_association_support_transparent_elections_1011 .html.

42. Feminist historian Joan W. Scott has raised serious questions about the ideology and practice of parity (*parité*) in *The Politics of the Veil* (Princeton, NJ: Princeton University Press, 2007). For another perspective advanced by the daughter of the Nahda Party leader, see Soumaya Ghannoushi, "Perceptions of Arab Women Have Been Revolutionised," *Guardian*, March 11, 2011.

43. The dean of the Faculty of Letters at the University of Tunis, Manouba, Professor Habib Kazdaghli, was only recently acquitted in a court trial of false accusations of assaulting female students wearing the *niqab* who had forcefully broken into his office, trashing it, in March 2012.

44. Juan Cole, "Tunisia Plunged into Crisis by Second Political Assassination," *Informed Comment*, July 27, 2013, www.juancole.com/2013/07/tunisia-political-assassination .html. See also Carlotta Gall, "Tunisia Says Assassination Had Links to Al Qaeda," *New York Times*, July 27, 2013.

45. A solid source for current human rights in Tunisia is the Carter Center for Peace; see "Tunisia: Election Monitoring Reports," www.cartercenter.org/news/publications/peace /democracy_publications/tunisia-peace-reports.html.

46. See Heather McRobie, "Will Tunisia's Truth and Dignity Commission Heal the Wounds of the Authoritarian Past?," Oxford Human Rights Hub, February 20, 2015, http://ohrh.law.ox.ac.uk/will-tunisias-truth-and-dignity-commission-heal-the-wounds -of-the-authoritarian-past.

47. Carlotta Gall, "Tortured and Violated in Tunisia, Then Shamed," *New York Times*, May 29, 2015, A1, A8 (quotation A1).

48. Ibid., A8.

49. Albert Memmi, *Decolonization and the Decolonized*, trans. Robert Bononno (Minneapolis: University of Minnesota Press, 2006), 21. Memmi was born in Tunis in 1920.

50. Julia Clancy-Smith, *Mediterraneans: North Africa and Europe in an Age of Migration, c. 1800–1900* (Berkeley and Los Angeles: University of California Press, 2011); John R.

McNeill, *Mountains of the Mediterranean: An Environmental History* (Cambridge: Cambridge University Press, 1992); and Faruk Tabak, *The Waning of the Mediterranean, 1550–1870: A Geohistorical Approach* (Baltimore, MD: Johns Hopkins University Press, 2008).

51. Clancy-Smith, *Tunisian Revolutions.*

52. Habib Ayeb and Ray Bush, "Small Farmer Uprisings and Rural Neglect in Egypt and Tunisia," *Middle East Report* 272 (Fall 2014): 2–11 (quotation 4).

53. Perkins, *A History of Modern Tunisia,* 157–165 (quotation 170); and Stephen J. King, "Economic Reform and Tunisia's Hegemonic Party," in *Beyond Colonialism and Nationalism in the Maghrib: History, Culture, and Politics,* ed. Ali Abdullatif Ahmida (New York: Palgrave, 2000), 165–193.

54. Ayeb and Bush, "Small Farmer Uprisings"; and Rikke Hostrup Haugbølle and Francesco Cavatorta, "Beyond Ghannouchi: Islamism and Social Change in Tunisia," *Middle East Report* 260 (Spring 2012): 20–25.

55. Sarah Chayes, *Thieves of State: Why Corruption Threatens Global Security* (New York: W. W. Norton, 2015). See also the interview with Sarah Chayes of the Carnegie Endowment by Amy Goodman, "Nobel Peace Prize to Tunisian Civil Society Groups for Democratization Efforts After Arab Spring," Democracy Now!, Friday, October 9, 2015, www.democracynow.org/2015/10/9/nobel_peace_prize_to_tunisian_civil.

56. Ayeb and Bush, "Small Farmer Uprisings," 4.

57. Maude Barlow and Tony Clarke, *Blue Gold: The Fight to Stop the Corporate Theft of the World's Water* (New York: New Press, 2005); and Stewart M. Patrick, "Not a Drop to Drink: The Global Water Crisis," Council on Foreign Relations, May 8, 2012, http://blogs .cfr.org/patrick/2012/05/08/not-a-drop-to-drink-the-global-water-crisis.

58. Maamar Sebri, "Residential Water Industry in Tunisia: A Descriptive Analysis," *Journal of North African Studies* 18, 2 (2013): 305–306. See also Philp McMichael, ed., *Food, Energy, and Environment: Crisis of the Modern World System—Special Issue of the Review* (Fernand Braudel Center) 33, 2–3 (2010): introduction, 95–102.

59. Justin Hyatt, "In Southern Tunisia, Pollution No Longer Swept Under the Rug," Inter Press Service News Agency, June 7, 2013, www.ipsnews.net/2013/06/in-southern -Tunisia-pollution-no-longer; Samuel T. McNeil and Radhouane Addala, "Pollution in Gabes, Tunisia's Shore of Death," Al Jazeera, June 14, 2013, www.aljazeera.com/indepth/ features/2013/06.

60. Samuel T. McNeil and Radhouane Addala, "Environmental Crimes Run Rampant in Tunisia: Climate Change, Illicit Dumping, and a Two-Year Drought Are Gravely Affecting Tunisia's Landscape," Al Jazeera, November 27, 2013, www.aljazeera.com/indepth/ features/2013/11/environmental-crimes-run-rampant-tunisia-201311251180934679.html.

61. The "Berber Spring" of 1980 needs to be directly tied through attentive scholarship to the "Arab Spring." In 1980, bloody protests exploded in the Kabylia and elsewhere in Algeria, demanding official recognition of Berber as a national language and its use in media and educational curricula. Rapidly suppressed by the state, the Berber Spring nurtures transregional and transnational identities and politics that now include Libyans and

Moroccans. See Judith Scheele, *Village Matters: Knowledge, Politics, and Community in Kabylia, Algeria* (Suffolk, UK: James Currey, 2009).

62. Carolotta Gall, "Shale Gas Project Encounters Persistent Foes Deep in Algerian Sahara," *New York Times*, February 26, 2015, A4, A10.

63. Bill Bramwell, *Coastal Mass Tourism: Diversification and Sustainable Development in Southern Europe* (Clevedon: Channel View Press, 2004); and Hibou, *The Force of Obedience*, 31, on the Ben Ali regime's abuses of the internationally financed tourist industry. As for mass tourism to the Mediterranean rim during the summer, when demand skyrockets, the average Spaniard uses an estimated 250 liters per week; tourists consume between 440 and 880 liters per week diverted to pools and golf courses (these data are from the World Wildlife Fund and World Trade Organization).

64. It was the deadliest terrorist attack in Tunisian history, surpassing the 2002 Ghriba synagogue bombing in Djerba, which killed twenty-one people, most of whom were European tourists. However, the 2002 attacks differed because they were directly related to Palestine and Israel.

65. Simon Calder, "Tunisia Tourism: Will Holidaymakers Ever Return?" *Independent*, July 17, 2015, www.independent.co.uk/travel/news-and-advice/tunisia-tourism-will -holidaymakers-ever-return-10395859.html.

66. See "25 Arrested After InterContinental Hotel Attacked for 6th Time," Ahram Online, January 30, 2013, http://english.ahram.org.eg/News/63649.aspx, for tourist attacks in Egypt.

67. Mustafa Marrouchi, "Willed from the Bottom Up: The Postcolonial Turned Revolutionary," *Journal of North African Studies* 18, 3 (2013): 389.

68. Jon Queally, "As Neoliberal Order Wreaks Havoc, World Social Forum Gathers in Tunisia," Common Dreams, March 26, 2013, http://commondreams.org/headline /2013/03/26-0. See also Medea Benjamin, "A Participant's Account of the World Social Forum in Tunisia," April 3, 2013, http://rabble.ca/news/2013/04/participants-account-world -social-forum-tunisia; and Hoda Baraka, "World Social Forum 2015: Another World Is Possible," March 28, 2015, http://350.org/world-social-forum-2015-another-world-is-possible.

69. Quoted in Kenneth Rapoza, "The Brains Behind 'Occupy Wall Street': Kalle Lasn Talks to Kenneth Rapoza," *Forbes*, October 14, 2011, www.forbes.com/sites/kenrapoza /2011/10/14/the-brains-behind-occupy-wall-street-and-where-its-heading. Lasn conceived of the Occupy Movement in Vancouver; born in Estonia, he resided in Australia and is now a Canadian citizen. After the initial launch, spin-off Occupy movements burst out across North America and the globe.

70. Julia Clancy-Smith, "Mediterranean Historical Migrations: An Overview," in *Encyclopedia of Global Human Migration*, ed. Dirk Hoerder and Donna Gabaccia (London: Wiley Blackwell, 2012). In 2011, *Time* reported that "as many as 250 people were missing after a fishing boat overloaded with refugees and migrants from North Africa sank near the Italian island of Lampedusa, located about 70 miles off the Tunisian coast. The island has been overwhelmed by more than 20,000 people fleeing turmoil in Tunisia and Libya."

"Caught in the Storm," *Time*, April 18, 2011, 15. Compare this with the reports by the Office of the UN High Commissioner for Refugees, "Mediterranean Crisis 2015 at Six Months: Refugee and Migrant Numbers Highest on Record," press releases, July 1, 2015, www .unhcr.org/5592b9b36.html.

71. The Associated Press, Algiers, reported that on March 14, 2014, Algerian security forces apprehended seven militants as they attempted to cross over the border into Tunisia near the city of Tebessa. According to Algeria's Interior Ministry, a large cache of weapons and ammunition was also discovered. "Algerian Forces Kill 7 Militants Near Tunisia," March 14, 2014, www.yahoo.com/news/algerian-forces-kill-7-militants-near-tunisia -173345181.html.

72. Isabelle Mandraud, "Un portfolio sonore sur Sidi Bouzid," *Le Monde*, December 17, 2011.

73. Edmund Burke III and Kenneth Pomeranz, eds., *The Environment and World History, 1500–2000* (Berkeley: University of California Press, 2009).

74. Dörthe Engelcke, "The Ongoing, Steady Gains of Morocco's Islamist Party," *Jadaliyya*, September 29, 2015, www.jadaliyya.com/pages/contributors/232388. See also Aida Alamioct, "Moroccan Government Cracks Down on Journalists and Activists," *New York Times*, October 11, 2015, 2015, www.nytimes.com/2015/10/12/world/africa/moroccan -government-cracks-down-on-journalists-and-activistshtml?ribbon-ad-idx=12&rref =world/middleeast&_r=0.

2

Revolution and Counterrevolution in Egypt

JEANNIE L. SOWERS AND BRUCE K. RUTHERFORD

OVER EIGHTEEN DAYS in January 2011, Tahrir Square in Cairo was featured in broadcasts around the world as the epicenter of Egypt's *thawra*, or revolution. Festooned with flags and signs and posters, pulsing with the beat of music and speakers and protest chants from loudspeakers and stages, and filled with the sense of changing history, the square was temporarily transformed by thousands of protesters from a large traffic circle into an iconic protest forum.[1] The Tahrir protests inspired the takeover and makeover of other squares in Arab capitals, including the Pearl roundabout in Manama, Bahrain, and the "change square" in Sana'a, Yemen. In only eighteen days, the scale and intensity of the protests across Egyptian cities induced Egypt's army high command to announce that Husni Mubarak, a former air force commander who had been in power since 1981, would step down. In his place, the army would rule temporarily until a new president and parliament were elected.

By the autumn of 2015, there was little evidence of the heady days of popular protest in Tahrir Square. The square was once again as it had long been under thirty years of Husni Mubarak's rule: a traffic circle surrounded by the Egyptian National Museum, an imposing governmental building known as the Mugama'a, an array of tourist shops and fast-food restaurants, and the old campus of the American University in Cairo. Revolutionary graffiti had been whitewashed in the surrounding neighborhood, and couples sat placidly on the few benches on a small green lawn at the entrance to the underground Metro. A new large four-story underground parking garage had opened in front of the museum, built by the Osman family's Arab Contractors, the largest state-owned construction company in Egypt.

Re-creating an appearance of normality and predictability, for both international and domestic audiences, has been central to the appeal and the strategy of Egypt's current president, the former head of military intelligence and former secretary of defense Abdel Fattah al-Sisi. If one leaves Tahrir for nearby side streets, however, the state security apparatus that enforces this "stability" through the threat and exercise of coercion is plainly visible, as it was under the long-standing previous president, Mubarak. The roads that run from Tahrir a few blocks down to the Ministry of Interior and the Parliament building remain blocked off with large concrete barriers.[2] Behind the Omar Makram mosque, the distinctive blue transport vans of Egypt's Central Security Forces again wait lined up, and white-uniformed traffic police have returned to the corners of many intersections.

Between January 2011 and the winter of 2015, Egyptians voted in five national elections and three constitutional referenda, that is, yes or no votes on constitutional changes proposed largely by Egypt's military high command. Yet these elections did not mark a transformation to a more democratic or accountable polity. Instead, each cycle of elections was marked by deepened political and social polarization, increasingly low voter turnout, and grave economic concerns.[3] Economic crisis, political uncertainty, and a steep rise in personal and collective insecurity after 2011 disillusioned many Egyptians with the revolutionary process.

The most famous slogan of the uprising in 2011 was *Al sha'ab yureed iskat al-nizam* (The people want the fall of the regime). However, by 2015, the new regime, with Sisi at the helm, looked very much like the old in its central institutions and political practices. The much-amended constitution still enshrined both extensive executive power and military privilege, while the coercive apparatus of the state was as powerful and shielded from scrutiny as ever. Draconian measures against protest and labor strikes were again codified in law, while a coordinated media campaign across state and privately owned outlets whipped up nationalist feelings and portrayed dissenters as terrorists.

This chapter examines why one of the most promising of the Arab uprisings, in which expectations for revolutionary change ran high, resulted instead in what many would consider a series of counterrevolutions. We analyze long-term developments in the political economy that underpinned revolutionary upheaval, considering the widespread social, political, and economic grievances that precipitated sustained cycles of popular street protests. We then explore the tumultuous period of uncertainty, economic crisis, and political polarization that emerged in Egypt after 2011, resulting in a new regime that very much resembled the old.

Economic Restructuring and Marginalization Under Mubarak

When Husni Mubarak became president after Anwar Sadat's assassination by Islamic militants in 1981, Egypt faced a number of enduring and major economic problems. The state-owned sector produced 50 percent of GDP and consumed 75 percent of gross domestic fixed investment.[4] Egypt resorted to sustaining public investment and subsidies by external borrowing on international credit markets and increasingly relied on worker remittances sent back from Egyptians working in the newly flush oil economies of the Persian Gulf. By the late 1980s, Egypt had one of the largest debt burdens in the world—184 percent of GDP, if calculated at the free-market exchange rate.[5]

By the early 1990s, the United States and Europe had forgiven some of the external debt after Egypt agreed to join the US-led coalition against Iraq in the 1991 Gulf War. Advised by the International Monetary Fund, the US Agency for International Development, and European aid lenders, Egypt then embarked on a neoliberal reform plan in 1991. The public sector would be largely sold off, the subsidy system cut, and the state's role in the economy reduced. The architects of this reform plan were sensitive to the political repercussions of dismantling this safety net and attempted to design their plan to minimize its pain. Public sector firms would be privatized, but at a market price and only to buyers who agreed not to dismiss workers for several years. Workers made redundant by downsizing were supposed to receive training to help them find new jobs. The implementation of the plan, though, fell far short of these goals. Public sector firms were sold at bargain-basement prices, often to businessmen with close political connections to Mubarak and his family. Promises to keep workers on the payroll were evaded or ignored, leading to widespread dismissals. Assurances of additional training and benefits went unfulfilled. At the same time, state subsidies were cut and state investment in the public sector was sharply curtailed.

The regime and its advisers hoped that the private sector would pick up the slack and establish new, dynamic enterprises that would create thousands of new jobs. Indeed, a new private sector emerged. Some parts of the Egyptian economy grew, but growth was primarily in real estate; construction; fossil fuels; financial services; and, to a lesser extent, technology services and agricultural exports.

As medical care, agricultural productivity, and nutrition improved with state intervention, Egypt's population grew rapidly. Egypt's population in 1952 was 22.2 million; in 1981, it had doubled to 44.2 million.[6] The population more than doubled again by 2015, when Egypt's Central Agency for Public Mobilization and Statistics reported 87.9 million Egyptians in the country and 8 million living outside it.[7]

Unemployment, Urbanization, and Rising Poverty

Egypt's population exhibits a youth bulge, as does much of the Middle East, sub-Saharan Africa, and South Asia, with roughly 30 percent of its population between the ages of fifteen and twenty-nine.[8] Young people can often be a source of economic dynamism if they are employed. Yet most youths cannot find jobs; labor force participation among fifteen- to twenty-nine-year-olds for the Middle East was only 30.3 percent and for North Africa only 33.3 percent in 2010, significantly lower than for other developing regions.[9] The unemployment picture has two additional important dimensions: the unemployment of women and of graduates with a college education. In 2006, 87 percent of young female Egyptians were out of the labor force, compared to 39 percent for men.[10] In 2008, unemployment among Egyptian university graduates was estimated at 25 percent, a figure that did not include those who had given up seeking work.[11] Thus, as the number of job seekers has increased with population growth, neither the Egyptian nor the broader Middle East regional economy has provided sufficient jobs, resulting in exceptionally high unemployment rates for women, youths, and college graduates by global standards.[12] For those who do manage to find work, the jobs rarely meet expectations or provide adequate wages. The International Labour Organisation (ILO) found that only 19 percent of Egyptian men between the ages of eighteen and forty-nine had ever obtained what the ILO defined as a "good job."[13]

Without an independent means of earning a living, many Egyptians into their twenties and often thirties are stranded in what Diane Singerman terms "waithood"—an inability to establish autonomous lives and move into adulthood.[14] Relying on extended-family support for survival, they are unable to afford marriage or the cost of having children, to obtain decent housing, or to accrue the kind of social status that is associated with becoming an adult and contributing to the broader community. The economic exclusion of many youths, particularly those with educational degrees, has undermined confidence in incumbent governments and institutions.

Furthermore, Egyptians generally feel that their quality of life has been declining over the past several decades. Through a combination of rural-to-urban migration, land speculation, and natural increase, Egypt's main cities of Cairo and Alexandria have grown rapidly, and in Cairo, the population density is among the highest in the world. Urban air pollution is a significant problem, as are traffic; poor water quality; lack of green and communal spaces; and unsafe, poor-quality construction that frequently results in collapsed buildings and deaths. Cairo remains by far the largest city in Africa: Over 20 million people, out of approximately 87 million Egyptians, live in the urban provinces that make up Greater Cairo. There is a housing shortage as well. Given a paucity of reliable investment outlets, many Egyptians buy apartments as an investment, leaving millions of vacant-but-owned units in both old and new cities.

Public water and sanitation networks have not been able to keep pace with urban expansion, and the high cost of land and housing means that many Egyptians live in informal areas without adequate public services. Even in areas with water connections, service interruptions are frequently reported in the Egyptian media, especially but not exclusively in the summer months. Water shortages are experienced both in the irrigation system and in the urban drinking-water networks.

Official GDP growth rates of 6–7 percent in the mid-2000s thus masked the fact that most Egyptians were excluded from economic growth. Public sector workers, civil servants, and pensioners saw their incomes remain largely stagnant while inflation rose at double-digit rates for much of the 2000s. Families who thought of themselves as solidly middle class saw their standard of living steadily decline until they were poor. Many of those on the edge of poverty slipped into it.

As in other countries, poverty has long been unequally distributed across Egypt, with metropolitan areas generally exhibiting both greater income inequality and generally higher levels of income than rural areas. Crucially, however, between 2005 and 2009, real income declined across Egypt; the decline in income was most severe in the largest cities, Cairo (14 percent) and Alexandria (16 percent).[15]

One of the reasons for this decline was the global spike in food prices, driven by drought and supply shortages in Russia and other grain-producing regions as well as volatility produced by the spectacular growth of speculative financial instruments in commodity markets. Egypt is the largest importer of wheat globally, and the government must generate enough foreign currency to purchase grain and other food imports. When food prices rise sharply, ordinary Egyptians find it difficult to purchase adequate food and government budget deficits worsen significantly. Food prices rose 37 percent in the two years prior to the uprising.[16]

As many Egyptians watched the purchasing power of their salaries fall, food prices rise, new job seekers fail to obtain employment, and corruption become endemic, popular support for the Mubarak regime waned. The state was widely viewed as unable to meet even the smallest expectations of the public for the services that had been promised by the glowing rhetoric of the Nasser era. Popular perception saw instead a corrupt and ineffective state that served the interests of a small elite consisting of the regime, businessmen with close ties to the regime, and Mubarak's family and close confidants, backed by the military and security services.

THE SPREAD OF ACTIVIST NETWORKS AND MOVEMENTS

As the legitimacy of the regime steadily declined and the economic situation for many citizens deteriorated, Egyptians had few peaceful ways to express their anger. Opposition parties had been permitted since the mid-1970s, but they had long been rendered mute and politically irrelevant. Mubarak's men sometimes allowed them to win a few seats in Parliament, but they did not play a role in the formulation of policy and were prevented from building a national organization that might lead to real political power.

The Muslim Brotherhood proved a tenacious and durable opponent that the regime managed with a variety of tactics, including brutal repression under Nasser; a brief opening under Sadat, followed by another round of repression; and limited freedom in the early years of Mubarak's rule, followed by waves of repression in the 1990s and 2000s as Mubarak came to believe that the Brotherhood was an irredeemable threat to him and his regime. A wide array of civil society groups also existed—from professional associations to charitable groups to human rights organizations.

To deal with the state monopolization of formal civil and political spaces, activists increasingly turned to horizontal and informal forms of organizing. These included wildcat strikes and unauthorized labor actions that culminated in the growth of a movement for independent unions autonomous from the state. Between 2004 and 2008, more than 1,900 labor actions of various sizes took place to protest poor wages, inadequate benefits, and declining working conditions.[17] On a few occasions, these labor actions managed to achieve some significant concessions from employers and from the state. In doing so, they showed that the regime would accommodate rather than simply repress sufficiently large-scale collective protests.

Horizontal networks often led by educated young people coalesced around specific issues. Youth activists thus gained experience in conducting protest campaigns that combined street protests, demonstrations, and online organizing. These campaigns tackled a number of issues, ranging from foreign policy—such as opposing Israeli attacks on Gaza and the US-led Iraq War in 2003—to domestic concerns. For instance, campaigns against polluting factories in the port city of Damietta from 2008 on helped forge activist networks that linked the provincial periphery to the media and political scene in Cairo.[18] The Kefaya (Enough) movement organized demonstrations in 2005 that called for Mubarak to leave office. In 2008, the April 6 movement was formed. The network was initially established to support striking workers in Egypt's Delta region but soon expanded to call for broad political and economic reform. The April 6 website had 70,000 members on the eve of the uprising.[19] Facebook, blogs, and other social media thus played an important role in building a shared identity and facilitating coordination among critics of the regime.

As Maha Abdelrahman argued, by 2011 these various networks had engaged in significant cross-ideological cooperation (particularly among reformist youth) and developed new forms of organization and activism. "The central defining feature of the pro-democracy movement and its constituent groups," she notes, "was the ability to take the struggle onto the streets and to liberate activism from the confines of underground meetings and the closed offices of formal political groups. During this decade, demonstrations, rallies, sit-ins, and street blockades progressively became a daily occurrence in Egypt's main squares, workplaces, university campuses, major roads, and residential neighborhoods."[20]

Abdelrahman termed this the "normalization" of protest; whereas protest had long been an exceptionally risky action, the increased tempo of street protest across classes and regions made it more likely for others to do the same. In public opinion surveys conducted by the Arab Barometer a few years before the uprisings, the increase in protest experience was evident: 30 percent of Egyptian youths aged eighteen to twenty-four reported that they had participated in protest activity.[21] Egypt's changing media landscape was also crucial, as new independent and private newspapers, online and citizen journalists, blogs, and regional satellite stations covered protest campaigns extensively. Publicizing protest made it seem routine, even as many more Egyptians were initiated into repeated confrontations with the security services.

The security services had an extensive established system of surveillance in place. When the Mubarak regime sought to destroy radical Islamist movements in the early 1990s, particularly in southern Egypt, it granted the security services even greater autonomy. There were few legal constraints on arresting, detaining, and torturing citizens. It became routine for anyone suspected of a crime to face beatings at the local police station and for persons suspected of political subversion to face long detention without trial. From targeting leftists and Islamists, the security services increasingly responded to workers, farmers, street vendors, and anyone in the wrong place at the wrong time.[22] Along with the normalization of protest came the normalization of abuse and detention and the ability to document and publicize these experiences.

Long documented by a handful of Egyptian and international human rights organizations, the advent of social media in the 2000s publicized the expanding abusive practices by internal police and security forces to an unprecedented extent. Cell-phone videos of torture in police stations uploaded to YouTube and other sites went viral. When a young man was pulled from an Internet café in Alexandria and beaten to death in broad daylight in the street in 2010, his family uploaded photographs taken at the morgue to the Web. Wael Ghoneim's Facebook page to commemorate him, "Kullina Khaled Said" (We are all Khaled Said) attracted 400,000 members in the months preceding the uprising.[23]

As many citizens' economic situation deteriorated, the political institutions that ostensibly represented them became even less responsive. This was particularly true during the parliamentary election in November 2010. In the previous election in 2005, opposition parties had managed to win 22 percent of the seats, with most of these held by the Muslim Brotherhood (88 seats)—not enough to pose a meaningful challenge to the ruling party's control of the chamber but enough to provide a forum for venting public anger at the status quo. In November 2010, Mubarak and his advisers lost all sense of proportion and managed the elections to produce a lopsided victory for the ruling party. The National Democratic Party (NDP) won 93 percent of the seats, and the Brotherhood won only 1 seat. The regime also embarked on a new round of steps to rein in the opposition press and limit the capacity of private satellite stations to criticize the government. In addition, it took steps to silence the reformist wing of the judiciary, which had been an important voice for electoral honesty in the 2005 elections.

On top of these deteriorating economic and political conditions, there were growing rumors about Mubarak's health and uncertainty about who would succeed him. He was eighty-three years old in 2011 and had spent several months abroad for medical treatment in 2010. It was widely believed that Mubarak was steering the succession toward his son Gamal Mubarak, a Western-trained banker with long-standing connections to big businessmen who had benefited from the privatization process.

Egypt's generals in particular were concerned about who would succeed Mubarak as president; his son was part of the elite business community rather than the military hierarchy. The military high command felt increasingly marginalized during the last years of Mubarak's rule, as police forces claimed an ever larger share of state resources and big business representatives moved upward in the NDP and into Parliament.[24] There was particular criticism of the privatization process, which many believed provided sweetheart deals to well-connected business families. The secretive military rarely expressed these criticisms publicly, but they occasionally leaked out through statements and letters by retired officers and indicated increasing dissatisfaction with Mubarak's leadership.[25]

THE OUSTING OF MUBARAK: EIGHTEEN DAYS IN JANUARY–FEBRUARY 2011

The key to the success of Egypt's uprising in January and February 2011 was the unprecedented mass mobilizations in the streets and the refusal of the military to deploy in Egypt's cities to counteract them. By some estimates, the protests between January 25 and February 11 exceeded 1 million people on several occasions.[26] The sheer number of demonstrators led the key supporters of Mubarak in the military and in the United States to conclude that it was time for a new leader.

No one was more surprised by the size and diversity of the crowds than the relatively small youth activist networks that called Egyptians to protest on Police Day, January 25.[27] Although many more Egyptians had engaged in street protest in the preceding decades, most demonstrations remained small and were easily dispersed by the security services. Yet many more people than expected came down to Tahrir on January 25. This may well have been due to the euphoria experienced across the Arab world when the Tunisian uprising forced Tunisia's long-standing president, Zine al-Abidine Ben Ali, to flee the country for Saudi Arabia. Egyptians found inspiration in the departure of Tunisia's dictator after thirty days of mass protests in a country widely considered more repressive than Mubarak's Egypt.

Egypt's activist networks had also adapted their strategies for demonstrations, seeking novel ways to outmaneuver the vast security apparatus. They tricked the security police into sending troops to the wrong sites, mobilized unexpected groups (particularly from the poor neighborhoods near Tahrir Square) for the first big march on the square on January 25, and made skillful use of the international media.[28] The brutal tactics employed on February 2 and 3 to disperse the demonstrators were broadcast for all to see by the Qatari-owned al-Jazeera network, adding moral urgency to the cause of confronting the regime. The TV images led more people to conclude that the regime was vulnerable and that demonstrations were worth the risk. As more people turned out, the demonstrations became ever larger, and the vulnerability of the regime became even more apparent.

All of these efforts would have been for naught if the military had intervened to disperse the demonstrators. The military leadership's decision not to fire on the protesters was pivotal; once it became clear that the military would not step in, this fact emboldened ever more Egyptians to take to the streets. For his part, Mubarak underestimated the popular appeal of the demonstrators and missed several opportunities to offer concessions that might have slowed their momentum.[29] Instead, he remained dismissive of the "children" in the square and sent in thugs from the security forces to subdue them.

The Generals in Power (2011–2012)

The military thus decided to jettison its patron of thirty years and take the reins of power itself as the Supreme Council of the Armed Forces (SCAF). This committee of twenty senior generals assumed all executive and legislative power on February 11, 2011, when Mubarak stepped down, suspending the constitution and disbanding Parliament. It announced plans to supervise elections for a new Parliament and president and to preside over the drafting of a new constitution. In November, the SCAF-appointed cabinet released a "proposal of basic principles for the new constitution" that rejected civilian scrutiny of the military and identified the armed forces as the "protector of constitutional legitimacy."[30] Presaging the military coup in 2013, this language showed that the SCAF sought to construct a legal basis for the military to remove a popularly elected government.

The military's actions during its period of direct rule also presaged the crackdown on dissent that came in July 2013 with the military coup. More than 12,000 civilian demonstrators were tried in military courts without any compelling legal reason beyond the assertion of the need to obtain quick convictions. This number was greater than the total number of civilians tried before military courts during the entire thirty years of Mubarak's rule.[31] When the much-despised Emergency Law expired on May 31, 2012, the SCAF effectively continued its key provisions by asserting that military personnel still had the authority to arrest civilians and try them before military courts.[32] When soldiers were accused of human rights abuses, the military took little action to investigate the claims or to discipline those responsible. Civil society groups remained tightly monitored and, in some cases, faced a degree of repression that exceeded that under Mubarak's rule.[33] Reports surfaced of the military interfering with the media, enforcing de facto censorship over coverage of numerous issues.[34]

Egypt's 2011–2012 Parliamentary Elections: Brothers, Salafis, and Liberals Compete

The SCAF's decision to hold early parliamentary elections in late 2011 and early 2012 was a similarly divisive and controversial political decision that in retrospect helped polarize the Egyptian public sphere. Many of the young activists who had helped lead the January 25 uprising opposed holding early elections without the process of constitution-writing first, in order to guarantee civil liberties and basic political rights. They also rightly feared that elections would privilege Islamist organizations with long-standing organizational outreach as well as the business and political elites of the old regime with the wealth and connections to run campaigns. These activist networks launched a number of initiatives and protests to contest the SCAF's decision, but these efforts gained little traction with the generals. Faced with the reality of approaching elections, forty new parties organized by the "revolutionary" youth registered, and twenty-three parties eventually put forward candidates.[35]

The platforms put forward by various competing parties provide a glimpse into the commonalities and differences of Egypt's various political currents in the first open and free parliamentary elections. Old and new liberal parties competed in the elections, including the Wafd Party, the Justice Party, the Free Egyptians, the Democratic Front Party, the Social Democratic Party, and the Free Egypt Party. Supporters of these parties joined a long tradition of liberal thought that extends back to the late nineteenth century and reached its heyday in the early years of Egypt's independence in the 1920s. These networks advocated for a civil state in which military and religious institutions played no role in politics, with laws originating in an elected Parliament rather than in the executive branch, checks and balances among branches of government, an independent and well-trained judiciary, equality of all citizens, and protection of basic civil and political rights. However, the liberal parties and new youth-led parties were unable to translate street protest into effective campaigning. The oldest liberal party, the Wafd, won only 7.5 percent of the seats in the lower house (the People's Assembly) and 8 percent in the upper house (the Shura Council). An alliance of other liberal parties, the Egyptian Bloc, won 6.7 percent of the seats in the lower house and 4.5 percent in the upper house.

The Muslim Brotherhood was the only competitor with a strong national organization, which paid off in getting supportive voters to the polls. Running under the aegis of their newly created Freedom and Justice Party (FJP), Brotherhood-affiliated candidates won 45 percent of the seats in the lower house and 58 percent of the contested seats in the upper house.

The Muslim Brotherhood had been vague about its political goals for much of its eighty-four-year history. The organization's famous slogan, "Islam is the solution," offered few concrete policy proposals until the mid-1990s, when the Brotherhood issued documents drawing upon the ideas of several reformist Islamic thinkers, including Yusuf al-Qaradawi, Tariq al-Bishri, Kamal Abu

al-Magd, and Muhammad Salim al-Awwa. The reformist trend became especially pronounced during the 2005 parliamentary elections. Held under
Mubarak-era emergency laws, these managed elections informally allowed
Brotherhood candidates to run as "independents." Their campaign materials
adapted Islamic tradition and doctrine to advocate legal and institutional constraints on state power, protection of many civil and political rights, and the
rule of law.

After 2011, FJP politicians continued to develop this political outlook,
which can be termed Islamic constitutionalism. However, they also articulated
illiberal, controversial positions, stating that women and Coptic Christians
should not hold the office of president and arguing that religious scholars
should be allowed to review legislation. The party also called for repealing laws
from the Mubarak era that broadened women's rights (particularly their right
to divorce) on the grounds that these laws had been imposed under foreign
pressure. The Brotherhood ran very few women on the FJP's parliamentary
list, and as a consequence, there were only 7 women in the FJP's parliamentary
delegation of 213. No women held significant leadership positions within the
Brotherhood.

The other major party to emerge in the 2012 parliamentary elections was
the al-Nur Party, affiliated with the Islamist Salafi movement, which won 25
percent in the lower house and 25 percent in the upper house. This came as
a surprise to many observers. The Salafis were a highly conservative set of Islamic networks that had been uninvolved in formal politics prior to 2011. The
Salafi movement, like the Brotherhood, had long-standing networks of influence based on preaching, charities, and social outreach, particularly in the city
of Alexandria. However, because state security forces frequently targeted its
leaders and members, the movement kept a particularly low profile. Its leaders
castigated formal politics as a corruption of faith-based outreach and activity
and initially opposed the 2011 uprising on the grounds that it was better to
accept Mubarak's authority than to risk disorder from a change of regime.

With the political opening that followed the 2011 uprising, however, some
Salafi thinkers and leaders began to engage the media and take public positions. Some prominent Salafists—particularly Emad al-Din Abd al-Ghafur,
Nadir al-Bakaar, and Yusri Hamaad—soon coalesced into the al-Nur Party.
Al-Nur called for an Islamic state, largely adopting the language of Islamic
constitutionalism publicized by the Brotherhood's FJP. Al-Nur's party plat-
form called for "democracy within the framework of *shari'a*" and a wide range

of civil and political rights. Al-Nur political figures, however, generally emphasized a conservative social agenda that included banning alcohol, limiting the mixing of genders outside the home, and regulating media and books to ensure that they uphold Islamic moral standards. In general, they were more critical of Western culture and ties to the West than were the Brotherhood's FJP politicians.

Despite these significant differences, liberal parties, the Muslim Brotherhood, and the Salafi movement generally converged in their views on Egypt's long-standing relationship with and dependency on the United States. For most of Egypt's political currents, Egypt's decline in regional power and status stemmed in large part from its close ties to the United States. In this view, Mubarak's regime became an appendage of US policy in the region and failed to defend the country's distinct national interests. Many Egyptians had long felt that Anwar Sadat had negotiated the Camp David Accords from a position of weakness, giving up Egypt's regional role as the only viable Arab military force and abandoning the Palestinian cause by signing a separate peace agreement between Egypt and Israel. Thus, while Egypt's new politicians stated that they would abide by Egypt's existing international treaties, they also emphasized the need to assist the Palestinians. In addition, political parties generally agreed on the need to broaden Egypt's foreign alliances away from the United States and strengthen linkages to other Arab countries, Africa, Turkey, the Islamic world, and Asia.

THE MUSLIM BROTHERHOOD AND THE 2012 PRESIDENTIAL ELECTION

In March 2012, the Brotherhood decided to enter the race for the presidency, despite having promised liberal parties initially that it would not do so.[36] This decision marked the beginning of a series of strategic miscalculations that alienated the activist youth movements, more-liberal parties, and ordinary Egyptians. Widespread discontent culminated in the July 2013 military coup, which saw President Mohamed Mursi imprisoned and tried for treason on trumped-up political charges and the Muslim Brotherhood declared a "terrorist" organization by the new regime.

Thirteen candidates received the necessary approvals to compete in the first round of presidential elections held in May 2012.[37] As in the parliamentary elections, however, the revolutionary and liberal vote was split among competing candidates. For instance, Abd al-Monam Abu al-Fatuh, a prominent former leader of the Brotherhood who had led efforts in the 1990s and 2000s to revise Brotherhood doctrine to support a more open and democratic political system, was supported by a range of moderate parties as well as the Salafi al-Nur.[38] Hamdeen al-Sabahi also appealed to revolutionary currents as a Nasserist and a poet who emphasized workers' rights and expanding social services. The Brotherhood ran Mohamed Mursi, the head of its political party, after its first choice was disqualified. Mursi's presidential campaign in spring 2012 emphasized several conservative themes, in contrast to the more moderate positions staked out by the FJP in the parliamentary elections. For example, he called for implementation of *shari'a* rather than simply drafting legislation within the framework of *shari'a*, asserted that the Quran should serve as the foundation for the new constitution, and expressed his personal opposition to women and Coptic Christians running for the presidency.

With the Brotherhood supporters voting as a bloc, Mursi received the largest share of the vote, with 24.8 percent, while Ahmed Shafiq, former head of Egypt's air force from 1996 to 2002, was runner-up with 23.7 percent, setting the stage for a runoff election. Many supporters of Egypt's revolution were disappointed with this limited choice. Mursi was widely viewed as lacking experience, charisma, and the political skills needed to run the country. Shafiq's commitment to the goals of the revolution was in serious doubt, as he was closely associated with Mubarak's regime. Indeed, he described Mubarak as his role model and criticized the January 25 demonstrators as disrespectful children who had slapped their father.[39]

Two days before the runoff election began on June 16, the Supreme Constitutional Court issued a dramatic ruling that declared the law governing the election of Parliament or the Majlis al-Sha'ab (the People's Assembly) unconstitutional.[40] Based on this ruling, the SCAF dissolved the People's Assembly with its large numbers of Islamist delegates. The Brotherhood and some observers asserted that the court ruling and the SCAF decision to dissolve the People's Assembly were politically motivated efforts to deny the Brotherhood the political power that it had earned at the ballot box, undermining the democratic aspirations of the 2011 uprising.

Mursi thus campaigned as the "candidate of the revolution" and won by a small margin (52 percent to Shafiq's 48 percent). However, as Ellis Goldberg and others have noted, Mursi did not carry the principal urban governorates of Cairo, Alexandria, or Suez, the locus of revolutionary activism and protest.[41]

The Muslim Brotherhood mistook its electoral victories for widespread support, ignoring the fact that other parties and currents were organizing and were fearful that the Brotherhood would monopolize political life and state institutions.

THE MURSI PRESIDENCY (2012–2013): POWER IN NAME ONLY?

Mursi took office in a climate dominated by increasing security challenges, political polarization, and economic crisis. Some of the challenges he faced were not of his making; others were. Egypt was still in a revolutionary moment— the rules of the political game were uncertain; expectations for rapid and substantive change were high; and large numbers of people remained ready to take to the streets.

While the Brotherhood had won the presidency, the SCAF was determined to maintain a large role within the emerging Egyptian regime. Within hours of the presidential election, the SCAF had amended the constitution to significantly expand its authority vis-à-vis other political institutions. With Parliament already disbanded by court order, the amendments granted the SCAF legislative authority previously held by Parliament, complete control over all matters related to the military, immunity from civilian oversight, and the capacity to block virtually any policy initiative that the new president might pursue. The amendments also gave the SCAF the authority to appoint a new constitutional assembly if the existing assembly failed to complete its work and a formal mechanism for the SCAF to object to specific clauses in any proposed constitution.

The generals justified their intervention in political life on the grounds that the SCAF was stabilizing Egyptian politics at a critical moment and preventing the Muslim Brotherhood from dominating the formation of Egypt's new political order. The SCAF's stance appeared to enjoy some popular support, particularly among Coptic Christians and some mainstream Muslims who feared that the Brotherhood would infringe on their civic and personal rights. In this view, the military was the only institution capable of balancing the power of Islamists, the defender of a civil state at a time when some populist figures in the Brotherhood and the Salafi movement were calling for a state with a strong Islamic character. Many activist youths, however, viewed these constitutional amendments as a de facto coup aimed at frustrating the will of the people.

Over the summer of 2012, Mursi seemingly pushed back against the expansion of military power. He released over 500 prisoners detained by the SCAF. After Egyptian security forces were attacked in the Sinai Peninsula by gunmen who then commandeered an Egyptian military vehicle and crashed it into an Israeli border checkpoint, he dismissed the Mubarak-era chief of intelligence and several other internal security officials. A few days later, he went further, suspending the military's constitutional amendments and appointing a judge as his civilian vice-president. He also announced that he was replacing the Mubarak-era minister of defense, Mohamed Hussein Tantawi, with a younger member of the SCAF, General Abdel Fattah al-Sisi, who would later lead the military's coup against Mursi. The commanders of the different armed services branches were also shuffled. While this move was initially seen as a sidelining of the power of the generals, senior Muslim Brotherhood leaders told the press that the rotation of personnel came after extended discussions between the SCAF and Mursi.[42] More likely, then, a significant number of military leaders felt that the deteriorating security situation required a younger and more capable leadership.

Two basic challenges, however, quickly illustrated the limits of Mursi's control over Egypt's sprawling state apparatus: fuel and security. Egypt's extensive state bureaucracy represents a variety of institutionalized and often conflicting interests. As Nathan Brown notes, the Egyptian state's reach into society and economy is not only wide and deep but also balkanized, fragmented into a number of state agencies and authorities that see themselves as above and separate from the vicissitudes of politics and politicians.[43] In other words, though Mursi won elections, there was no guarantee that Egyptian state authorities would cooperate with the new presidential regime.

Electricity cuts had been relatively rare under the Mubarak regime; after 2011, however, electricity cuts and fuel shortages were increasingly experienced across the country. These shortages quickly intensified after Mursi took office. Gasoline and other fuels became in scarce supply, creating long lines at gas stations and affecting transportation and industrial activity across the country. When the power went out, water treatment plants, sewage treatment plants, and water and sanitation networks also shut down. Shortages of energy thus made water scarce as well.

As importantly, the continued lack of any police presence generated widespread insecurity. Police disappeared from the streets after pitched battles with demonstrators in January–February 2011, while the government reportedly released thousands of criminals from prison to deepen insecurity. Volunteer watch committees formed in many neighborhoods to fill the void. None of the governments after 2011, however, made headway in creating a civilian police force separate from the Ministry of Interior. Increasingly, the lack of enforcement of traffic rules and criminal activity undermined citizens' confidence. In Cairo, traffic became much worse, lengthening commutes for rich and poor alike. But it was on the peripheries, in southern Egypt and in the Sinai, that the lack of security was most acutely felt.

Because the FJP had been a banned and suppressed organization for most of its history, its leaders did not trust the upper echelons of Egypt's sprawling state apparatus, nor did they know how to make it work. Neither the Brotherhood nor the FJP developed lines of communication to many important state ministries. Midlevel officials reported stasis and confusion, as lines of authority were unclear.[44] For its part, the Mursi administration increasingly argued that elements of Egypt's "deep state" were working against it in its efforts to provide basic security and goods.

Within days of the military's ouster of Mursi the following summer, energy shortages disappeared and the internal security forces were rapidly redeployed across the country. It thus seems likely that the Brotherhood was in part correct: Elements of the old regime had worked hard to make ordinary life unbearable for Egyptians during Mursi's tenure. This loose coalition likely included much of the military and security establishments, large-business tycoons threatened by the new business interests that accompanied the change of presidential regime, and personnel in key state ministries such as oil and gas. As one retired police officer told *New York Times* reporters, "You had officers and individuals who were working under a specific policy that was against Islamic extremists and Islamists in general. . . . Then all of a sudden the regime flips and there is an Islamic regime ruling. They could never psychologically accept that."[45]

Egyptians were also acutely feeling the contraction of Egypt's economy. Hit by capital flight (both domestic and foreign), declines in tourism, inflation, continuing high food prices, and a declining value to its currency, Egypt's debt increased further, while its foreign exchange reserves, essential for importing grain and food, shrank. While Mursi engaged in protracted negotiations with the International Monetary Fund for a $4.8 billion loan that would have required cutbacks in spending on food and fuel subsidies, Qatar provided the Mursi government with a reported $8 billion in cash and loans. Qatari support for the Muslim Brotherhood–led government, however, was controversial in Egypt, providing fodder for critics in the media and elsewhere that Egypt was being "sold" to external powers.[46]

Faced with escalating criticism, a deteriorating economy, and large swaths of Egypt's state-owned sector that he could not control, Mursi attempted to further consolidate power in the presidency. Mursi viewed the judiciary, which had been largely appointed by Mubarak but was also viewed as one of the more autonomous state institutions in Egypt, as undermining and delaying the creation of a new political order. As previously noted, the judiciary had dissolved the lower house of Parliament in 2012 on constitutional grounds. Moreover, liberal parties had filed suit in the courts to have the constitution-writing assembly chosen by the Islamist-dominated Parliament disbanded. An agreement among the Brotherhood and various political parties and prominent figures to create a more balanced constitutional assembly in the summer of 2012 soon broke down, prompting most liberal and Coptic representatives to boycott the assembly.

In November 2012, Mursi issued a constitutional decree that sought to bypass the authority of the judiciary.[47] The first article called for reopening the court cases against Mubarak and regime cronies, responding to ongoing protests calling for greater justice for protesters killed and wounded in the 2011 uprising. The decree also called for a more expansive investigation of "crimes of terror committed against the revolutionaries by anyone who held a political or executive position under the former regime." The second article asserted that presidential decrees could not be appealed by any entity nor countered through judicial proceedings of any kind; similarly, the fourth article announced that the judiciary could not dissolve either the constitutional assembly or the upper house of Parliament, where the Muslim Brotherhood dominated representation.

The decree had the immediate effect of uniting opposition to Mursi, bringing political groups together that had little in common other than their sense that the Muslim Brotherhood was consolidating power. Much as Mubarak's inability to adequately respond to the street protests had helped crystallize his removal as the basic goal of the 2011 uprising, Mursi's attempt to place the president beyond the judiciary galvanized widespread opposition. Mursi's move also discomfited those very elements of the deep state that opposed the Brotherhood (described by activists as the *fulul*, the debris of the old regime). The *fulul*, state officials and big businessmen alike, had no interest in revolutionary prosecutions of its past actions. The Brotherhood, long suppressed by the state apparatus, had thus tried to reassure the generals and security forces of their position in Egypt's politics yet had also taken up the rhetorical mantle of revolutionary change, calling for accountability for the excesses of these same actors.

In early December, the Islamist-dominated constitutional assembly finished its work in an all-night session to meet its deadline. Mursi formally rescinded the controversial November decree but insisted on calling for a referendum on the newly written constitution. By this point, Mursi and the opposition groups had staked out irreconcilable positions. Mursi and the Brotherhood were focused on enshrining a constitution whose drafting had been boycotted by most other political forces; the opposition was focused on stopping it. The military was increasingly concerned and called on Mursi to engage in serious dialogue with the opposition, something the opposition would undertake only if Mursi agreed to rebalance the constitutional assembly and start afresh. Neither side was willing to make these compromises.

In the spring, Mursi announced parliamentary elections in April; the judiciary promptly declared the electoral law unconstitutional and annulled the elections, a ruling that Mursi appealed. Mursi raised further fears of the Brotherhood controlling the state and its provincial offices through several decisions. He reshuffled the cabinet, appointing eleven Brotherhood-affiliated ministers out of thirty-five total, and he appointed seven Brotherhood-affiliated governors to Egypt's provinces. This included appointing a governor of Luxor from the Al-Gama'a Al-Islamiyya, an Islamist group that had claimed responsibility for massacring tourists and Egyptians in the same city in 1997.

As a result, protesters returned to Tahrir and elsewhere, demanding that Mursi cancel the decree and disband the constitutional assembly. Supporters of Mursi also began their own protests in support of the constitutional assembly. Violent clashes between supporters and opponents of Mursi broke out around Egypt, including around the Presidential Palace, forcing Mursi to abandon the palace at one point and resulting in hundreds of injuries. Arson attacks on FJP offices across Egypt were successful, showing that the security forces were unwilling to protect the party or its officials.

Meanwhile, Mursi's foreign policy stances also raised concerns among the military's senior command.[48] When Mursi helped broker a cease-fire between Israel and Hamas, a move heralded in the United States and European Union as a sign of the Brotherhood's moderation, reports surfaced that senior generals were worried that Egypt would be held responsible for future Hamas actions. More publicly, Egyptian TV aired live footage of a meeting between Mursi and various political party leaders in which Egypt's politicians openly talked about options to stop Ethiopia from building a new large-scale dam (the "Grand Renaissance Dam") upstream from Egypt on the Blue Nile River. The casual, somewhat reckless discussion of one of Egypt's deepest security concerns—its access to Nile River water—further deepened perceptions among the political and military elite that Mursi lacked competence. Mursi also cut ties with Syria in mid-June and supported the Syrian opposition, saying a *jihad*, or holy struggle, against Syria's Bashar al-Assad was legitimate and that Egyptians could join. For the security apparatus, which had waged a brutal war on Egyptian Islamists during the 1990s, particularly in Upper Egypt, this statement was unacceptable.[49]

In late spring 2013, several young activists capitalized on this discontent and launched a petition calling on Mursi to resign. Calling itself Tamarrud (rebellion), the movement soon received significant financial and logistical support from the various currents in the opposition and wealthy businessmen as well as the security services and the military. The Tamarrud movement thus quickly became a vehicle for the otherwise disparate elements that had come to oppose Mursi, from the old regime actors to the activist youth networks. Although the numbers have not been verified, the campaign claimed that millions of Egyptians signed the petition within a few weeks. Based on subsequent reports, it seems that coordination between senior military and security officials and Tamarrud activists was substantial.[50]

Grassroots support was amplified by an orchestrated media campaign against Mursi and the Muslim Brotherhood, which sought to systematically portray them as a fanatic minority working for and with foreign interests. Mursi's minister of defense, Sisi, had been the head of military intelligence. Like Vladimir Putin in Russia, both men were familiar with the powerful role that propaganda and mass media can play in shaping public opinion and mobilization and had access to an extensive surveillance network, state-owned media outlets, and big private businessmen opposed to the Brotherhood who owned much of the private media. Thus, the media steadily heightened fears about the "disintegration" of Egypt's state, the "Brotherhoodization" of state institutions, and threats to Egypt's security. Media outlets and commentators also attacked the United States and other countries for acknowledging Mursi's electoral legitimacy and thereby "supporting" the Brotherhood. As one military source told Reuters, "What we have now is an information war with the Muslim Brotherhood."[51]

THE 2013 POPULAR COUP

The Tamarrud campaign and other anti-Brotherhood currents called for a massive street protest on June 30, 2013, for a second "revolution" to overthrow Mursi. In the run-up, escalating protests and clashes intensified. Sisi reportedly met with Mursi, asking him to share power with the opposition or the military would impose a solution. Mursi and the FJP leaders refused, noting that Egyptians could simply elect a new president in a few months and that using street protests to bring down a democratically elected government was illegitimate.

The FJP was also counting on a show of support from its own constituents, who had established sizable sit-ins at Raba'a al-Adawiya mosque in the Nasr City district of Cairo and elsewhere. Ten Islamist parties sided with the Brotherhood and joined the protests, chanting that the "legitimacy [of the elected president] is the red line." At the same time, however, leaders from various Salafi parties also tried to convince Mursi to compromise with opposition demands.

In line with the ultimatum, the June 30 mass protest was openly supported by the military. While the January 25 protest was planned by loose, horizontal networks of activists who had no idea whether the military or police would turn out against them, on June 30, military helicopters dropped Egyptian flags on the crowds and the Egyptian army deployed men and vehicles sporting stickers in support of Tamarrud. Some activists later told journalists that security arrangements had been coordinated in advance with intelligence and military officials. Egyptian state media carried nonstop coverage of the anti-Mursi protests, in stark contrast to January 2011, when state media had refused to cover the Tahrir protests. As in 2011, however, antigovernment protests were not confined to Cairo but also emerged in Egypt's other major cities and industrial zones, including Suez, Mahalla al-Kubra, Alexandria, and Port Said.[52]

Sisi used the escalating situation to issue a public ultimatum on July 1, read on state television, that Mursi had to compromise with public demands (these were left vague) within forty-eight hours or the military command would impose its own "road map." The military statement came shortly after ten ministers, including the remaining technocratic, non-Islamist members of the cabinet, submitted their resignations. The following day, the rest of the cabinet resigned, while large-scale public celebrations in the streets supported the military declaration. On July 3, Sisi announced that Mursi had been ousted and that Adly Mansour had been appointed interim president. The SCAF promised presidential and parliamentary elections once a new elections law had been approved by Egypt's highest court.

Sisi and the military and intelligence agencies moved quickly to consolidate control. Their first target was Mursi and the larger organizational hierarchy of the Muslim Brotherhood. Mursi was arrested, charged with a variety of crimes, and sentenced in different trials to life in prison and to death over the next few years. Returning to Mubarak-era laws, Sisi declared the Muslim Brotherhood a banned terrorist organization and rounded up thousands of Brotherhood members or suspected members. The charges against Mursi and other Brotherhood leaders reflected the strategy of demonizing the Brotherhood by accusing its leaders of working with foreigners against Egypt's national security. Mursi was accused of working with Hamas, Hizballah, and Iran's Republic Guards; of espionage; and of ordering the deaths of anti-Mursi protesters outside the Presidential Palace. Mursi remained incarcerated as this chapter went to press. The judicial proceedings were equally suspect in other mass trials of Brotherhood and Islamists, with 1,200 people sentenced to death in two trials in 2014, prompting criticism from the United Nations and human rights organizations. Such death sentences in Egypt are rarely carried out; those convicted typically languish in prison instead.

The most significant indication that the new political regime would unleash systematic violence against its opponents was the bloodbath that occurred in early August during the two large pro-Mursi sit-ins as well as smaller protests across the country. Regarding the dispersal of the largest sit-in at Raba'a al-Adawiya Square in August 2013, Human Rights Watch concluded that, "using armored personnel carriers (APCs), bulldozers, ground forces, and snipers, police and army personnel attacked the makeshift protest encampment, where demonstrators, including women and children, had been camped out for over 45 days, and opened fire on the protesters, killing at least 817 and likely more than 1,000."[53] Protesters were besieged by internal security forces and attacked from five main entrances from dawn until dusk, while security forces detained an additional 800 or more persons. Using similar indiscriminate tactics, the security forces also attacked a sit-in at al-Nahda Square near Cairo University.

But repression and detention soon spread beyond the Brotherhood. The new regime rapidly passed a draconian antiprotest law that criminalized protest and free expression and required prior consent for protests from the Ministry of Interior, exactly as previous laws under Mubarak had done. Soon some of the most well-known youth activists of the 2011 uprising who dared challenge these prohibitions found themselves detained, tried, and convicted for organizing or participating in protests, sit-ins, or other forms of expression.[54] Journalists and photographers were detained and tried for reporting on such events or simply for trying to report on or photograph unstable areas, such as Egypt's Sinai Peninsula. Since July 2013, human rights organizations estimate that more than 22,000 people have been detained in Egypt. Some of these have simply "disappeared" into military intelligence and security prisons, with no access to their families or legal representation.[55] The practice of referring civilians to military tribunals, which emerged during the first period of SCAF rule, was resumed, but for many more individuals; between October 2014 and November 2014, more than 3,700 civilians were tried in military courts.[56]

Taken together, these measures meant not simply a return to the Mubarak regime but the creation of a more repressive regime. Under Sisi, noted Joshua Stacher, "state elites are using organized violence to formalize a new narrower ruling coalition and to break their opponents, to proactively restructure Egypt's political arena, and reregulate state-societal relationships."[57]

Violence was supplemented with media campaigns to ensure some public support and overwhelm dissident voices. In the weeks before the massacres, Egyptian officials and the media explicitly called for forcibly dispersing the sit-ins, portraying pro-Mursi demonstrators as violent extremists who intimidated residents, detained and abused suspected infiltrators, and negatively impacted nearby neighborhoods. The facts that the vast majority of the protesters were peaceful and that regular policing tactics could have been used to clear the squares were conspicuously missing from state-sponsored discourse. In this climate, pro-Mursi protests on university campuses and areas around Egypt were quickly quelled as security forces redeployed with a vengeance. The media and intelligence apparatus also sought to create a cult of personality around Sisi, portraying him as a new Nasser, the savior of Egypt from external and internal enemies.

The reaction from the United States, European countries, and most of the monarchies in the Persian Gulf was quiet support for the coup. Most refused to call the SCAF's assumption of power a military coup; in the United States, such an acknowledgment would have triggered a suspension of US arms sales under US law. The United States temporarily froze the transfer of some military equipment, but within a few months, the United Kingdom, France, and the United States had not only resumed arms and aid transfers but were actively soliciting future arms sales. The Egyptian stock market, representing large domestic capital, also rallied in the wake of the coup against Mursi. On the foreign policy front, Sisi emphasized restoring the "prestige" and "integrity" of the state and the Egyptian nation in the face of internal and external threats and sought a rapprochement with Ethiopia over the building of the Grand Renaissance Dam.

Repression combined with propaganda campaigns has had several important political effects. The first is to create a self-fulfilling prophecy about terrorism. Criminalizing the Muslim Brotherhood; designating members, organizations, and charities allegedly or actually affiliated with the Brotherhood as "terrorists"; and subjecting them to arbitrary detention and torture have again driven Islamists underground. In response, armed groups have again emerged, particularly but not exclusively in the Sinai, such as Ansar Beit al-Maqdis, which later renamed itself Province of Sinai and pledged itself to the so-called Islamic State of Iraq and Syria (ISIS). These armed groups have launched a number of attacks, specifically targeting police and army personnel and installations. In the summer of 2015, the violence moved to Cairo, where the general public prosecutor was assassinated and the Italian consulate was bombed.

Second, this political climate has served to manufacture the appearance of almost universal support for Sisi, despite the evident diversity of political expression that flourished after 2011. This support was aptly demonstrated in both the referendum on the constitution, held in January 2014, and the subsequent presidential election later that year. The constitutional amendments continued to allow the most influential state institutions—the military, security services, and judiciary—to operate with little accountability to an elected parliament or other state oversight institutions. The amendments also allowed the president to issue decrees with the force of legislation in the absence of a sitting Parliament (recall that the 2012 Parliament had been dissolved by judicial ruling). The media ran an overt "Yes" campaign, and the amendments passed with 98 percent of those who participated voting yes.

With the passage of the constitutional amendments, Sisi declared that he would run for the presidency, an outcome called for by a petition campaign and media outlets since the coup. Only one candidate dared to run against him—Hamdeen al-Sabahi, who had run for president against Mursi in 2012. With state institutions and media endorsing Sisi, most leading Egyptian politicians and personalities simply declared that they would not run. Potential candidates may have remembered how Ayman Nour had been imprisoned after running against Mubarak in the only presidential election of his regime. Many revolutionary parties, youth movements, and activists chose to boycott the presidential election, while others chose to support Sisi. In a tally reminiscent of the Mubarak era, Sisi was declared the winner with 96.6 percent of the vote and a voter turnout of 47.5 percent. Parliamentary elections held in the fall of 2015 were also stacked to result in a staunchly backed Sisi regime.

On the economic side, Sisi's first priority was to secure short-term relief for the cash-strapped government. Significant infusions of funds from Saudi Arabia and the United Arab Emirates were the first solution. These conservative monarchies were eager to see the Muslim Brotherhood crushed in Egypt, as they saw the prospect of broadly based Islamic parties winning popular elections as one of the greatest threats to their own political systems.

For longer-term sources of rent, Sisi quickly returned to the development model of the Mubarak years: grandiose national projects, typically portrayed as encouraging domestic and foreign private investment; tourism; the development of new industrial and export zones; and an attempt to reduce government spending through better targeting of subsidies on fuel and food.

As under Mubarak, large-scale infrastructure projects were intended to project an image of regime stability and competency. Yet, as under the old regime, such projects reinforced the favored position of small circles of business elites with symbiotic relationships to the state. Under Mursi, the Brotherhood had brought with it a new crop of much smaller business groups, but these were not large enough nor well enough integrated with state institutions to enable them to dominate the economy as the "fat cats" of the Mubarak era had done. Thus, there had been space for smaller private entrepreneurs, as there had been for smaller political parties.[58] With a return to the style of the old regime, the government reverted to issuing major contracts for the military, large private and public construction firms, and international conglomerates.

The most publicized national project was the expansion of shipping lanes in the Suez Canal, which was completed in a year but cost $8.2 billion. With global shipping trade slowing—the number of ships transiting through the canal down 20 percent compared with 2008—the government's projected revenues may or may not materialize.[59] Another announced project, a new administrative capital on the outskirts of Cairo, was a joint venture between the government's Ministry of Housing and the United Arab Emirates–based real estate investment fund Capital City Partners. Critics argue that the planned city for public servants and government ministries does little to help with overcrowding and deteriorating public services in Cairo proper.[60] Moving administrative offices outside Cairo also reflects the interests of those who can afford to flee the congestion and pollution of central Cairo for outlying suburbs and satellite cities.

CONCLUSION

As Hesham Sallem has observed, "the Arab revolutions should be viewed as living, contested phenomena rather than a set of well-defined, discrete outcomes."[61] Any narrative of the political tumult and conflict in Egypt of the past few years is thus inevitably embroiled in a set of ongoing political contestations about what has actually transpired and what were the possibilities for change. To supporters, Sisi "saved" Egypt from the breakdown of security, economic crisis, and the incompetency of the Muslim Brotherhood leadership. To critics, he has reentrenched the old regime in a more brutal fashion, riding a wave of public support manufactured in part by reviving the central role of internal security and police forces. Now, as in the past, internal security forces, state ministries, the military, and well-connected business elites compete with each other and dominate the political scene and economic activity. The new regime has further polarized society by driving dissenting and Islamist currents from the public sphere.

The same economic problems of poverty, unemployment, unaffordable food and housing, urban sprawl, traffic, and pollution that underpinned widespread discontent and mass protest in 2011 remain. Many Egyptians can barely earn enough to feed their families as global food prices remain high and Egypt continues to overlook investment in its own agricultural sector.[62] For a dismal comparison, "60 percent of Egyptians live at income levels inferior to that of the poorest 1 percent of Americans."[63] Widespread poverty and economic challenges are compounded by limited natural resources—little arable land, rainfall, and dependence on the Nile, with many upstream countries interested in expanding Nile River consumption. Rural areas and informal urban settlements, as well as regions of the country in the south and in the Sinai, remain marginalized politically and economically.

At sixty-one, Sisi is of a younger generation of military commanders than Mubarak, now eighty-seven and in a military hospital in Cairo. But Sisi and his generation remain far older than more populous, younger cohorts of Egyptians in their twenties, thirties, and forties who are stuck with stagnant economic opportunities, many unable to achieve the markers of a stable middle-class existence attained by some of their parents. For several generations mired in waithood, the primary concern is attaining decent livelihoods through jobs and public services.

In the face of these challenges, the Sisi regime's initial formula for legitimacy—aptly summarized by Joseph Massad as one of "love of the army and fear of the Muslim Brotherhood"[64]—will not long sustain itself without improvement in the economic situation of many Egyptians. Both the Egyptian regime and its Gulf allies know this well and have endeavored to prop up the economy through significant external infusions of cash. As seen with the new Suez Canal and capital city projects, however, the new-old political elite has again focused on large-scale projects in which the trickle-down effect on jobs and income is likely to be insufficient. The solution of migrating out of the country and sending money home has become difficult in recent years as Europe further seeks to limit migration from Middle Eastern countries.

Repression, as the Sisi regime knows well, has its limits. Structural changes in the public sphere and economy—access to information, educational attainment, and the spread of horizontally linked social movements—will continue to enable new forms of networked activism whatever the legal and coercive mechanisms adopted by the government. The "old" bastions of protest, such as the professional syndicates, university campuses, and human rights organizations, also remain active despite the crackdown on their members and activities by the reempowered internal security services. Thus, while the history of Egypt's 2011 revolution remains a contested and unfinished project, future prospects for a more just and accountable politics cannot yet be foreclosed.

NOTES

1. For a good firsthand account in English, see Ahmed Shukr, "The Eighteen Days of Tahrir," in *The Journey to Tahrir: Revolution, Protest, and Social Change in Egypt*, ed. J. Sowers and C. Toensing (London: Verso Press, 2012), 41–46.

2. Closing off streets predated the 2011 uprising; after the 9/11 attacks, Egyptian authorities blocked the streets near the US and Canadian Embassies in the adjacent neighborhood of Garden City.

3. Nathan Brown, "Egypt's Failed Transition," *Journal of Democracy* 24, 4 (October 2013): 45–58.

4. Khalid Ikram, *The Egyptian Economy, 1952–2000: Performance, Policies, and Issues* (New York: Routledge, 2006), 92.

5. Ibid., 56.

6. Population figures taken from the US Census Bureau and compiled at www.data360 .org/dataset.aspx?Data_Set_Id=317, accessed November 15, 2015.

7. "Egypt's Population Grows by over 3.5 Million Since 2014," Ahram Online, September 3, 2015, http://english.ahram.org.eg/NewsContent/1/64/139602/Egypt/Politics-/Egypts -population-grows-by-over--million-since--CA.aspx.

8. Michael Hoffman and Amaney Jamal, "The Youth and the Arab Spring: Cohort Differences and Similarities," *Middle East Law and Governance* 4 (2012): 169.

9. Gilbert Achcar, *The People Want: A Radical Exploration of the Arab Uprising* (Berkeley: University of California Press 2013), 27.

10. Diane Singerman, "Youth, Gender, and Dignity in the Egyptian Uprising," *Journal of Middle East Women's Studies* 9, 3 (Fall 2013): 11.

11. *Egypt Human Development Report, 2008* (New York: United Nations Development Programme, 2008), 296.

12. Achcar, *The People Want*, 26–35.

13. Cited in Singerman, "Youth, Gender, and Dignity in the Egyptian Uprising," 10.

14. Ibid, 9–15. See also M. Chloe Mulderig, "An Uncertain Future: Youth Frustration and the Arab Spring," Pardee Papers Series, No. 16, Boston University, April 2013.

15. Ibid., p. 49.

16. "Food and the Arab Spring: Let Them Eat Baklava," *Economist*, March 17, 2012, 59. The world price for wheat more than doubled between July 2010 and January 2011 due to drought and brush fires in Russia, Ukraine, and Kazakhstan. Egypt is the world's largest importer of wheat. Sarah Johnstone and Jeffrey Mazo, "Global Warming and the Arab Spring," *Survival* 53, 2 (April-May 2011): 12.

17. Joel Beinin, *The Struggle for Worker Rights in Egypt* (Washington, DC: Solidarity Center, 2010), 14.

18. For detailed accounts of these and other environmental campaigns, see J. Sowers, *Environmental Politics in Egypt: Activists, Experts, and the State* (New York: Routledge, 2012).

19. April 6 Youth Movement website, http://6april.org.

20. Maha Abdelrahman, *Egypt's Long Revolution: Protest Movements and Uprisings* (New York: Routledge, 2015), p. 31.

21. Hoffman and Jamal, "The Youth and the Arab Spring," 177.

22. Abdelrahman, *Egypt's Long Revolution*, 16–20.

23. "Kullina Khaled Said," www.facebook.com/ElShaheeed.

24. Hazem Kandil. *Soldiers, Spies, and Statesmen: Egypt's Road to Revolt* (New York: Verso Books, 2012).

25. See Bruce K. Rutherford, "Egypt: Citizens and Soldiers," *Montréal Review*, March 2011, www.themontrealreview.com/2009/Egypt-Citizens-and-Soldiers.php.

26. Adel Iskandar, "Egypt Defies All," *Huffington Post*, February 14, 2011, www.huffington post.com/adel-iskandar/egypt-defies-all_b_822336.html.

27. Other youth movements included We Are All Khalid Said and the youth organizations of the Muslim Brotherhood, Kefaya, and the Democratic Front Party.

28. See Wael Ghonim, *Revolution 2.0: The Power of the People Is Greater Than the People in Power: A Memoir* (New York: Houghton Mifflin Harcourt, 2012); and Ashraf Khalil, *Liberation Square: Inside the Egyptian Revolution and the Rebirth of a Nation* (New York: St. Martin's Press, 2012). See also Charles Levinson and Margaret Coker, "The Secret Rally That Sparked an Uprising," *Wall Street Journal*, February 10, 2011.

29. See Emad Shahin, "Mubarak's 5 Fatal Mistakes," *Atlantic*, February 24, 2011, www .theatlantic.com/international/archive/2011/02/mubaraks-5-fatal-mistakes/71661.

30. The text of the supraconstitutional principles is available at www.masrawy.com/ news/Egypt/Politics/2011/November/2/4559080.aspx%2f4559080.aspx#. A translation is available at http://fjponline.com/article.php?id=84.

31. Amnesty International, *Year of Rebellion: The State of Human Rights in the Middle East and North Africa* (London: Amnesty International, 2012), 9–15.

32. This authority was granted by the SCAF-appointed minister of justice. At the time of this writing, an administrative court had suspended implementation of this order.

33. Human Rights Watch, "Egypt: National and International Human Rights Organisations Are Under Attack," December 29, 2011, www.hrw.org.

34. Human Rights Watch, "Egypt: A Year of Attacks on Free Expression," February 11, 2012, www.hrw.org.

35. Abdelrahman, *Egypt's Long Revolution*, 86.

36. The Brotherhood initially nominated its most prominent financier and strategist, Khairat al-Shater. However, he was disqualified by the Presidential Election Commission and replaced by Mohamed Mursi, the president of the FJP.

37. Several prominent candidates were disqualified by the commission for failing to meet the legal requirements for entering the race. Omar Suleiman, a former head of Egyptian intelligence and a close adviser to Husni Mubarak, was disqualified for not having enough signatures on his petitions for candidacy. Khairat al-Shater, the Muslim Brotherhood's leading strategist and financier, was prevented from running because of a conviction for fraud during the Mubarak era.

38. Abu al-Fatuh was expelled from the Brotherhood in June 2011. At the time, the Brotherhood leadership decided that the organization would not run a candidate for president and that no member of the organization should run for the post. Abu al-Fatuh disregarded this order and announced his candidacy. He was promptly expelled for defying the organization's leadership.

39. David D. Kirkpatrick and Kareen Fahim, "In Egypt's Likely Runoff, Islam Vies with the Past," *New York Times*, May 25, 2012.

40. The law stated that two-thirds of the seats in the People's Assembly would be chosen through competition among party lists and one-third would be selected by competition among individual candidates. The law allowed members of parties to run both as members of a party list and as individual candidates. The Supreme Constitutional Court ruled that this structure gave candidates with party affiliations an unfair advantage over independent candidates, as they effectively had two opportunities to win a seat in the chamber.

41. Ellis Goldberg, "The Urban Roots of the Arab Spring," April 20, 2014, http://ssrn.com/abstract=2426960.

42. See, for example, Ernesto Londoño, "Egypt's Morsi Replaces Military Chiefs in Bid to Consolidate Power," *Washington Post*, August 12, 2012, https://www.washingtonpost.com/world/middle_east/egypts-morsi-orders-retirement-of-defense-minister-chief-of-staff-names-vp/2012/08/12/a5b26402-e497-11e1-8f62-58260e3940a0_story.html.

43. Nathan Brown, "Egypt's Wide State Reassembles Itself," *Foreign Policy Online*, June 17, 2013, http://foreignpolicy.com/2013/07/17/egypts-wide-state-reassembles-itself.

44. Interviews by Jeannie L. Sowers, Cairo, May 2012 and January 2013.

45. Ben Hubbard and David D. Kirkpatrick, "Sudden Improvements in Egypt Suggest Campaign to Undermine Morsi," *New York Times*, July 10, 2013, www.nytimes.com/2013/07/11/world/middleeast/improvements-in-egypt-suggest-a-campaign-that-undermined-morsi.html?_r=0.

46. Maria Abi-Habib and Reem Abdellatif, "Qatar's Aid to Egypt Raises Fears on Motives," *Wall Street Journal*, May 17, 2013, www.wsj.com/articles/SB10001424127887324031404578480771040838046.

47. The full text of the decree in English is available at "English Text of Morsi's Constitutional Declaration," Ahram Online, November 22, 2012, http://english.ahram.org.eg/News/58947.aspx.

48. See, for example, Yasmin Salah and Paul Taylor, "Special Report: Mursi's Downfall," Reuters, July 5, 2013, www.reuters.com/article/2013/07/05/us-egypt-protests-downfall-specialreport-idUSBRE9640SP20130705#AwySpRQxvrbYBIdw.97.

49. "Egypt's Army Says Morsi Role at Syria Rally Seen as Turning Point," Voice of America, July 2, 2013, www.voanews.com/content/egypt-army-says-morsi-role-at-syria-rally-seen-as-turning-point/1693911.html.

50. Jennifer Baker, "A Founder of the Tamarod Movement Admits Taking Orders from Army," Revolution News, April 17, 2014, http://revolution-news.com/founders-tamarod-movement-admits-movement-taking-orders-army.

51. Quoted in Salah and Taylor, "Special Report on Mursi's Downfall."

52. Matt Bradley and Reem Abdellatif, "Widespread Opposition Protests Grip Egypt," *Wall Street Journal*, June 30, 2013.

53. Human Rights Watch, "All According to Plan: The Raba'a Massacre and Mass Killings of Protesters in Egypt," August 12, 2014, https://www.hrw.org/report/2014/08/12/all-according-plan-raba-massacre-and-mass-killings-protesters-egypt.

54. Alastair Beach, "The Return of Egypt's Police State," *Independent*, November 29, 2013, www.independent.co.uk/news/world/africa/the-return-of-egypt-s-police-state-8973 863.html.

55. Amnesty International, "Blood, Death, and Flames: Memories of Egypt's Rabaa Massacre," August 14, 2015, www.amnesty.org/en/latest/news/2015/08/egypt-blood-death -and-flames-memories-of-the-rabaa-massacre.

56. For additional details, see the open letter sent to Sisi by US-based scholars of Egypt, "Egypt Scholars Protest Crackdown on Freedom of Expression," November 18, 2015, www.merip.org/scholars-egypt-protest-crackdown-freedom-expression?ip_login_no _cache=2a0c45f0372e0486db911f5f15062963.

57. Joshua Stacher, "Fragmenting States, New Regimes: Militarized State Violence and Transition in the Middle East," *Democratization* 22, 2 (2015): 269, doi: 10.108/13519347 .2015.1010810.

58. Interviews by Jeannie L. Sowers with private agricultural investors, Cairo and 6th of October City, September 2015.

59. Ahmed Feteha, "Egypt Shows Off 8 Billion Suez Canal Expansion That the World May Not Need," Bloomberg News, August 4, 2015, www.bloomberg.com/news/articles /2015-08-04/egypt-shows-off-8-billion-suez-canal-gift-world-may-not-need.

60. The US-based design firm hired for the project, SOM, like the United Arab Emirate's Capital City Partners, has been involved in a number of high-profile real estate and urban developments in the Persian/Arabian Gulf.

61. Hesham Sallem, "The Egyptian Revolution and the Politics of Histories," *PS: Political Science and Politics* 46, 2 (April 2013): 248.

62. Ray Bush, "Food Security in Egypt," in *Food Security in the Middle East*, ed. Zahra Barbar and Suzi Mirgani (London: C. Hurst Publishers, 2014), 89–114.

63. Paolo Verme, Branko Milanovic, Sherine Al-Shawarby, Sahar El Tawila, May Gadallah, and Enas Ali A. El-Majeed, *Inside Inequality in the Arab Republic of Egypt: Facts and Perceptions Across People, Time, and Space* (Washington, DC: World Bank, 2014), www.worldbank.org/content/dam/Worldbank/egypt-inequality-book.pdf.

64. Joseph Massad, "Love, Fear, and the Arab Spring," *Public Culture* 26, 1 (2013): 127–152.

3

The Libyan Spring:
From Dream to Disillusionment

KARIM MEZRAN AND LAURENTINA CIZZA

T HE LIBYAN REVOLT was perhaps the most improbable of the uprisings of the so-called Arab Spring. On the eve of the 2011 revolution, the
three pillars that propped up the Muammar al-Gadafi regime showed little
sign of buckling. On the surface, his system of coercion, divide and rule mostly
through tribal manipulation, and resource distribution appeared as sturdy as
ever.[1]

The fact that the regime lasted so long and withstood so many challenges
and threats is a clear demonstration of the effectiveness of its coercive apparatus. While the army was intentionally kept powerless, paramilitary forces such
as the security brigades, personally headed by Gadafi's family members, grew
in strength. The real power, nevertheless, rested in the security service, buttressed by the revolutionary committees (RCs).[2] The RCs, established in 1977,
were central to the coercion of Gadafi's Jamahiriya system, which consisted of
popular committees and congresses founded on the tribal model of consultation and representation.[3] By 1980, the RCs, initially created to incite popular
participation, had infiltrated all of Libya's security institutions, universities,
and professional and media organizations[4] and reported directly to Gadafi.
They monitored their fellow citizens and hunted down opposition figures inside and outside Libya.[5] Although the RCs were forced to scale back their role
in the late 1980s, their influence remained pervasive in Libya until the time of
the 2011 revolution. The manipulation of clans and tribes according to a precise
divide-and-rule strategy was also in place and actively pursued. No crack in

the realm of tribal obedience to the regime could be detected. Economically, the country was doing well, and the standard of living of the population at large was improving considerably. The distributive capacity of the regime was at its highest. A few weeks before the revolution, Gadafi announced a set of initiatives to curry the favor of the population, such as financing the purchase of houses by newly married couples, allowing free access to a new car to recent university graduates to travel to their jobs, and the complete subsidization of household electricity.

So why did Libyans rebel? In his work *The Anatomy of Revolution*, Crane Brinton explains that "revolutions . . . clearly were not born in societies economically retrograde; on the contrary, they took place in societies economically progressive. . . . Thus we see that certain economic grievances—usually not in the form of economic distress, but rather [in] a feeling on the part of some of the chief enterprising groups that their opportunities for getting on in this world are unduly limited by political arrangements—would seem to be one of the symptoms of revolution."[6]

This "symptom" was at work in Libya in 2011. The perception by Libyans of the regime's elites changed dramatically in the first decade of the new millennium. The facade of the frugality and purity of Gadafi's lifestyle was uncovered by the many reports in the foreign media, by then accessible to a large part of the population, that revealed the extravagances of the leader and his family. The wealth accumulated by figures close to the regime, through blatant corruption and other illegitimate means, had also become more visible. It became clear to all Libyans that the elites were squandering the country's wealth and preventing a large part of the population from the possibility of benefiting from it. The revolt that took place against all odds was a call for dignity, respect, and greater participation in the political and economic development of the country.

Another important question to answer is whether the uprising was a revolution or a simple revolt that turned violent. Samuel Huntington defines a revolution as a "rapid, fundamental, and violent domestic change in the dominant values and myths of a society, in its political institutions, social structure, leadership, and government activities and policies."[7] The ouster of Gadafi apparently presents all the conditions listed by Huntington to define a revolution. The whole Jamahiriya project and its "socialist and somewhat esoteric values . . . were swept away, and the political institutions such as the popular committees and the security apparatus, including the military and paramilitary state organizations, were dismantled or foundered."[8] All government and central state activities ceased.

Unfortunately, as has become more evident, the Libyan case was not only a revolution, or not simply a revolution. The regime had a relatively widespread base of consensus among some tribal and social sectors of society. The support of these groups for the regime was downplayed by the propaganda machine of the revolutionaries, who preferred to assert the narrative that the revolution was a revolt by an entire cohesive population against a brutal dictator and his mercenaries. That it was more of a civil war than a revolution became clearer with the passing of time.[9] The cleavages and fractures historically present in Libyan society, which were exploited by the regime for the sake of maintenance of power, came to the fore immediately after the liberation of Tripoli when militias from different cities started positioning themselves against each other in order to advance their respective bids for power. With time, these cleavages became rapidly militarized and entrenched. The political and military crisis of today is nothing less and nothing more than the prosecution of the civil war that brought about the fall of the Gadafi regime.

How Did Libya Get to Its Current Crisis?

The wave of enthusiasm that engulfed Libya in the postrevolutionary period lasted only a few months, from the death of Colonel Gadafi on October 20, 2011, to the General National Congress (GNC) elections on July 7, 2012.[10] The GNC elections were held with little delay and with a 60 percent turnout rate. Mahmoud Jibril and his National Front Alliance (NFA) emerged as the forerunners, with 48 percent of the vote and 39 parliamentary seats. The Islamist bloc, represented by the Justice and Construction Party (JCP), the political arm of the Muslim Brotherhood movement, came in second with a mere 10 percent of the national vote and 17 parliamentary seats.

The collective euphoria that had erupted following the fall of the Gadafi regime faded quickly as the GNC proved incapable of disbanding the revolutionary militias, of bringing order to the country, and of initiating a process of nation-building. Revolutionaries refused to disarm, adducing as a pretext that they could not trust the new state's representatives, many of whom had not actively participated in the fighting. Several members of the National Transitional Council (NTC), the organ that ruled Libya from the beginning of the revolution until the GNC elections, as well as many members of the GNC, had held high-level positions in the Gadafi regime.[11] This fact generated resentment among political and revolutionary factions such as the Islamists and the Misratans, who had suffered total marginalization under the former regime and great losses during the revolution.

Both the NTC and the GNC lacked the capacity to implement a demobilization, disarmament, and reconciliation (DDR) campaign because of the progressive entrenchment of the militias in their respective localities. Moreover, since they could not appeal to a strong prior national identity for legitimacy, Libya's budding national institutions could not prevent groups with decentralized appeal, such as the federalists in Cyrenaica, the Amazigh in the western mountains, or some of the tribes in the south, from pursuing their own agendas at the expense of the nation's. In September 2012, armed groups killed US ambassador Christopher Stevens in the Benghazi consulate, while in October 2013, armed groups briefly abducted Prime Minister Ali Zeidan from a Tripoli hotel. By November 2013, the government was struggling to expel Ansar al-Shariah—the group that had spearheaded the attack on the US consulate—from Benghazi. In the meantime, the GNC's internal dynamics had shifted such that the Islamist bloc and its allies gained the upper hand in passing conservative and very often unpopular legislation. As a result, when the GNC refused to dissolve at the end of its mandate on February 7, 2014, protests erupted across the country. In the face of such public outrage, the GNC resolved to hold presidential and parliamentary elections by July 2014. Due to Islamist opposition, however, in the new road map drafted on March 11, 2014, the GNC agreed that the legislature elected in July would determine how the president should be chosen.[12]

The rivalry between the two political factions and their militant affiliates has led to the country's progressive polarization and the erosion of political security. Tensions reached a tipping point in May 2014, when Khalifa Haftar, a former general under Gadafi, launched Operation Dignity—an assault intended to expel all Islamist groups from the country. An agglomeration of secular groups, tribal militias, and soldiers of the former regime responded to General Haftar's call to arms. But the general's lumping together of all Islamists caused the militias of Benghazi to unite with each other and link arms with groups in Tripoli and Misrata to launch Libya Dawn, a coordinated counterattack in Benghazi and throughout most of Western Libya.

Haftar's wide definition of terrorism pushed moderate Islamists and militants into a tactical alliance with more extremist groups such as Ansar al Shariah.[13] The launching of Operation Dignity had the adverse effect of strengthening Islamist appeal where it had previously been lacking. With the support of the powerful Misratan militias, the Islamist brigades forced the newly elected, largely secularist parliament, the House of Representatives (HoR), to seek refuge in the eastern city of Tobruk under the protection of General Haftar's troops. Since the summer of 2014, Libya has been paralyzed in a civil war between two rival factions—each one supporting a separate parliament, the HoR in Tobruk and the GNC in Tripoli, and government.

Among the Libyan fighting units that returned from the conflict in Syria and Iraq to fight Haftar was the pro–Islamic State (IS) Bitar Battalion. This fact likely facilitated the arrival of IS emissaries from Saudi Arabia and Yemen to Derna.[14] By mid-October, one of the main Islamist groups in Derna, the Majlis Shura Shabab al-Islam (MSSI), had pledged allegiance to the Islamic State and established an Islamic court under the guidance of the IS emissaries who had arrived with the express purpose of establishing the Libya province of the Islamic State, which in the east of the country took the name Wilayat al-Barqa.[15] Since then, the IS in Libya has been replicating its model of expansion used in Syria and Iraq, albeit on a smaller scale.

REASONS FOR THE LIBYAN CRISIS

The reasons for the failure of Libya's new political class to build new state institutions and to ensure a smooth transition to an open and pluralistic system are many. Some of the causes rest in the history of Libya itself, a country that never experienced true unity and never constructed a national identity. While King Idris saw himself more as the spiritual leader of a Sufi lodge than the leader of a modern nation, Gadafi emphasized transnational values such as pan-Arabism, Islamism, and Africanism. Other causes for postrevolutionary Libya's struggles are more recent. Gadafi's divide-and-conquer tactics forged fresh cleavages in Libyan society, while his support for terrorist movements led to Libya being ostracized by the international community, thus preventing the country from developing a class of internationally exposed, well-educated elites. There are also more proximate causes—original sins of the revolution and major mistakes made by the post-Gadafi governments—that are discussed in the following sections.[16]

Libya as a Divided Nation

Regionalism has been a defining feature of Libya's development as a nation. Historically, the natural boundaries of the Sahara Desert and the Gulf of Sirte allowed the eastern region of Cyrenaica and the southern region of Fezzan to maintain political and economic autonomy from the weak state in Tripoli. From the Phoenicians in the twelfth century to the Ottomans in the eighteenth century, Libya's numerous invaders failed to penetrate the nomadic interior of the country, their authority withering past the coastal towns. Since its establishment in the 1550s, Ottoman Tripoli has often competed with tribal confederations and regional states such as Awlad Muhammad's Fezzan (1550–1812) and the Sanusi state in Cyrenaica (1870–1911). In addition to physical distance from Tripoli, the regional governments and tribal confederations enjoyed socioeconomic ties to neighboring markets and tribes, which allowed them to challenge central authority. The tribes of western Tripolitania formed confederations with tribes in southern Tunisia and the larger Muslim communities of the Sahara and the Maghreb. Tribes in Fezzan traded with and recruited soldiers from populations in the Lake Chad region, while Cyrenaican tribes looked to western Egypt for sanctuary in times of war and for trade in times of peace.[17] The three regions of Tripolitania, Cyrenaica, and Fezzan were not united into a single administrative unit until 1934 under the Italian governor-general Italo Balbo.

When independence came in 1951, the Libyan regions reluctantly bowed to the pressure of the great powers and unified as the United Kingdom of Libya. At the outset of the cold war, Britain, France, and the United States regarded Libya's independence and unity as essential to preventing the Soviet Union from gaining a foothold in the Mediterranean. However, Libya's main regions had diverging interests and ambitions.[18] Eventually, the requests of Cyrenaica prevailed, and Libya was unified with a federal system of government under Sanusi leadership. Therefore, unlike its newly emancipated neighbors, the modern Libyan nation was not born out of a crucial struggle for unification, independence, and self-determination but rather came out of a combination of regional interests and international pressures. When independence came, most Libyans still identified in terms of familial, tribal, ethnic, or religious ties. A national identity was fundamentally absent.[19]

King Idris I struggled to spearhead the state-building process. He took limited direct interest in the administration of the country and instead relied heavily on his inner circle, the *diwan*, whose excesses and corruption would later cost him the throne.[20] He favored his frugal residence in Bayda over the extravagant royal palace in Tripoli, which had served as the Italian governor's residence. Besides creating logistical issues, the king's remoteness from Tripoli led Libyans to suspect that he preferred to reside by the British air base or near the Egyptian border, where, if need be, loyal tribes could help him escape. Less generous critics accused him of avoiding his royal duties.[21]

The king did little to extend his support base beyond his tribal stronghold in Cyrenaica, which also discouraged the development of institutions capable of projecting state authority across the country. He made sure that the Royal Libyan Army never grew large enough to constitute a threat to the monarchy by balancing it against the Cyrenaican Defense Force—an elite tribal militia— and the Tripolitanian Defense Force. He also banned political parties in 1952. The king feared that parties based in Tripolitania, whose population exceeded that of Cyrenaica and Fezzan combined, could gain the upper hand in elections and amend the constitution to the detriment of the other regions.[22] As a result, despite its meticulous representation of all major tribes, the national parliament did little more than provide a stamp of approval for the policies of the king's *diwan*.

Libya's dismal economic prospects prior to the discovery of oil in 1959 added to the national apathy that inhibited the development of national institutions.[23] At the time of discovery, Libya had no strong political class that could oppose the king and his *diwan* and lacked a state apparatus that could regulate the oil industry or design an effective development plan. By prompting Libya to develop a unified state apparatus for the first time in its history, the discovery of oil in 1959 represented the most momentous event since the creation of the country. A 1963 constitutional amendment did away with the federal system and enhanced the authority of the national government by dissolving the provincial assemblies, bureaucracies, and courts. The government created the National Oil Company and the Central Bank, which reported directly to the *diwan*.[24] Unfortunately, government intervention was implemented through the monarchy's patronage system and strengthened the regime's distributive capabilities to the detriment of state institutionalization.[25]

Subnational divisions—rather than national unity—have been the defining features of Libya's political development. Under both the federal and unitary systems, the monarchy's patronage system favored the development of subnational affiliations at the expense of a Libyan identity. These divisions were further compounded by the new revolutionary regime of Colonel Gadafi, who in 1969 launched his coup in the name of pan-Arabism rather than Libyan nationalism. He preferred to lean on the rhetoric of pan-Arab, Islamic, and African identities rather than construct a Libyan identity.[26] Much like the king before him, Gadafi kept himself afloat with generous oil revenues and an extensive patronage network based on personal, familial, and tribal loyalties.[27] The February 17, 2011, revolution unshackled age-old resentments, rivalries, and identities that Gadafi's authoritarian bondage had utilized and restrained. Today, Libya's subnational identities and interests have found expression in the pattern of alliances that has emerged in the current political conflict between the two contending governments based in Tobruk and Tripoli.[28]

The Gadafi Legacy: Divide and Conquer

Gadafi's policies amplified the preceding divisions. A main pillar of his regime was the policy of divide-and-rule tactics, which he successfully applied until almost the end of his rule. Upon staging his bloodless coup in 1969, Gadafi struggled to mobilize the Libyan people with the pan-Arab single-party system that he admired in Nasser's Egypt. Having failed to solicit the nationalist fervor of the Libyan people, Gadafi embarked on his Jamahiriya political experiment (the system of popular committees and congresses founded on the tribal model of consultation and representation), believing that it would lead to the self-governance of the Libyan masses.[29] He dismantled the hierarchy of representative and state institutions, which he argued interfered with democratic representation, and set up a system of bottom-up participation that gave the appearance of direct democracy while neutralizing any potential for rivalry from other government institutions.[30] This system corresponded perfectly with Gadafi's divide-and-rule purposes.

In the early years of his reign, Gadafi attempted to downplay Libya's tribal and regional identities to foster the development of a united pan-Arab identity. However, as his popularity dwindled in the 1980s, Gadafi resorted to manipulating regional divisions and tribal loyalties for the sake of maintaining his grip on power. In particular, following the 1986 American bombing campaign against Tripoli and Benghazi, he decided to shore up the support of Libya's traditional power brokers. He began to leverage tribalism as a weapon against his critics in the intelligentsia and the middle class, who called for modernization, by promoting rural customs and traditions at the expense of urban culture.[31] Gadafi's political and economic policies tended to favor the southern and central parts of Libya, where he enjoyed support among the clans. The

Qadhafa tribe and its allies, the Maqarha and the Warfalla, formed the back-bone of the regime and occupied high-ranking positions in the security appa-ratus and the revolutionary committees.[32] Manipulating the tribes was thus part and parcel of Gadafi's divide-and-rule policy. In 1993, Gadafi institution-alized the role of the tribes with the creation of the Popular Social Leadership, which brought the tribal leaderships under state coordination in a nationwide municipality-based system. In this way, the regime developed an alliance sys-tem that boosted, perhaps artificially, the role of the tribe.[33]

Gadafi intentionally marginalized and neglected the eastern province of Cyrenaica, which was the traditional seat of the Sanusi monarchy, stamping out all the fledgling institutions that had flourished under King Idris I. His-torically, moderate Islamism and apolitical Salafism tended to find greater ex-pression in Cyrenaica than in the rest of Libya; therefore, it appeared natural that the east became the operational safe haven of an armed Islamist resistance movement from the late 1970s to the early 1990s. By 2011, Gadafi had not re-lented in his marginalization of the east. The fact that the February 2011 revo-lution originated in Benghazi therefore did not surprise most analysts.

Original Sins of the Revolution

Although Libya's historical social structures, weak national institutions, and Gadafi-era policies may lie at the root of the current conflict, Libya's post-revolutionary elites committed some crucial mistakes that exacerbated pre-existing fractures and weaknesses. Two "original sins" of the NTC in particular soured the development of the revolution. The first was its failure to recognize that the 2011 uprisings were not a simple revolt of an entire population against a dictatorship but a conflict between various components of a society, some against and some in favor of the Gadafi regime. In this light, the revolution resembled a civil war more than an insurrection. This shortsightedness kept officials from embarking on a national reconciliation process that would give Libyans the opportunity to overcome their grievances. By this omission, the authorities alienated almost a quarter of the population—the supporters of the former regime—which has reacted by actively destabilizing the new state and undermining its newly acquired legitimacy.

The second original sin of the new Libyan elites was to minimize the impor-tance of foreign support in the fall of the regime.[34] Eager to reinforce the public perception that Libya had freed itself of the Gadafi regime on its own, the au-thorities too readily dismissed Western assistance in managing the transition.

Similarly, Western powers were all too eager to avoid involvement in capacity-building efforts like those being attempted in Iraq. Nevertheless, no sooner had the initial euphoria of the first few months after liberation passed than political infighting over power positions began to dampen the transition to constitutional democracy. The rising political tensions and the stalling DDR efforts exacerbated insecurity as the central government failed to exercise control over the militant factions swamping the country.[35] Thus, failure on the part of Libya's authorities to initiate a national reconciliation process and to solicit foreign support for DDR efforts could be considered among the main causes of the consequent political crisis.

Mistakes of Successive Governments

The original sins and the naïveté in which they were founded led the NTC and the GNC to adopt too soft an approach to the militias that refused to turn in their weapons. In particular, the NTC and the GNC's policy of appeasement toward Libya's armed groups created an environment hostile to national institution-building, which led instead to political polarization and a fractured security sector.[36]

When the first postrevolutionary NTC government began forming a cabinet of ministers, the cities with the heaviest number of militias in Tripoli—mainly Misrata and Zintan—agreed to participate in the new government only in exchange for large concessions. Having inherited the remnants of Gadafi's toothless army and police forces, and with ethnic and tribal clashes becoming increasingly common throughout the country, the NTC leadership felt it had little choice but to appease the armed groups. As a result, the NTC awarded the Ministry of Defense to Misrata and the Ministry of Interior to Zintan.[37] The Ministry of Defense began to subsidize most of the armed groups that had fought against Gadafi during the revolution, organizing them into the Libya Shield Force, which served as the country's army, and the Preventative Security Apparatus, which served as a counterintelligence force, while the Ministry of Interior organized the Supreme Security Committee, which resembled a police force. The result was a sort of hybrid security sector in which these armed groups worked alongside the weaker and smaller national army and police forces.[38]

Despite the NTC's intentions, the policy devolved into a sort of Faustian bargain[39] whereby the militias agreed not to rebel in exchange for government subsidies and status. As the militias' sense of entitlement grew, so did the government subsidies as both the NTC and the GNC strove to placate the militias, which had begun intervening in the political process. The Libyan government's appeasement of the militias created an incentive for the armed groups to obstruct the national DDR efforts, which would have deprived them of their privileged position. Ultimately, this policy of appeasement encouraged the proliferation of "revolutionary" armed groups, emboldened the militias to pursue their own agendas, and thwarted the development of a national army.[40]

The Libya Shield project in particular suffered from several damning design flaws that entrenched provincialism and the influence of the militias. First, despite the hybrid nature of the security policy, regular forces and the armed groups rarely served in integrated units. Distrust, hostility, and poor coordination characterized relations between the two sides. While regular Libyan security forces viewed the militias as Islamist and highly politicized, the armed groups viewed the regular forces as corrupt vestiges of the ancien régime. Second, Libya Shield's high salaries attracted recruits away from the regular army and police forces, giving young men an incentive to falsely claim "revolutionary" credentials.[41] Following the 2011 Libya Shield policy announcement, the number of militants seeking "deputization" skyrocketed to 250,000—a number that far exceeded the 30,000 revolutionaries who had genuinely fought against Gadafi.[42] As a result, Libya's various governments have continued to pay nonexistent militias and to pay recruits for services in two, or sometimes three, security bodies.[43] The policy of garrisoning Libya Shield division recruits in their towns and regions of origin rather than across the country reinforced parochialism and regionalism at the expense of Libyan national identity.[44]

Most alarmingly, however, the Libya Shield project emboldened the militias to take rogue action and pursue their own ideological, political, and criminal agendas rather than serve the interests of the state. The security policy allowed whole armed groups to join the army as units. In many cases, the militants remained more loyal to their unit commanders than to the government-appointed Libyan army officer of the Shield unit. Government-sanctioned militias, much like their nonsanctioned counterparts, engaged in the smuggling and feuding they were employed to prevent.[45] For example, in April 2012, rather than quell the ethnic clashes in Kufra and Sabha, the eastern Libya Shield force sided with the Arabs against the Tebu.[46] Likewise, authorized brigades—in particular those with Islamist sympathies—disobeyed government orders, refusing to seriously oppose their unauthorized peers, such as Ansar al Shariah.

As the armed representatives of their communities, the militias became emboldened to disrupt political proceedings to advocate their short-term populist causes. GNC appeasement encouraged their behavior. When armed militants from Zawiyya interrupted cabinet appointment discussions in October 2012, the GNC added Zawiyyan concerns as items to vote on during the debate instead of calling in other units to disperse the protesters. When in March 2013 armed protesters stormed the GNC to ensure the passage of the political isolation law, the GNC amended the Temporary Constitutional Declaration to state that the law could not be declared unconstitutional in the future.[47] Appeasement was rooted in a desire to not appear despotic. However, this approach allowed the stronger militias to become substate actors capable of delivering welfare, administering justice, creating jobs, and keeping their political and military patronage networks under control.[48]

The deleterious effects of this last trend on political unity were greatly magnified by the increasing polarization of the militias. In the immediate aftermath of Gadafi's fall, revolutionary Libyans united in a loose and unusual coalition over the desire to consolidate the revolution. The anti-Gadafi brigades, the politicians of the NTC, the Islamist groups writ large, anti-Gadafi tribes and their militias, and the Eastern Federalists all pitted themselves against loyalists such as the Warfalla and the Magarha. It was only a matter of time before the interests and backgrounds of the broad anti-Gadafi coalition began to splinter. Two groups emerged: the "hard-line" revolutionaries who insisted on the exclusion of Gadafi-era officials from the new Libya and "moderate" revolutionaries who limited political isolation to Gadafi loyalists. The Muslim Brotherhood, the Salafists, Misrata, the Islamists, and Eastern Federalists fell in the hard-line camp, while parties that had vested political and economic interests dating back to the Gadafi era fell in the moderate camp. These included the politicians and bureaucrats of the NTC and the tribal brigades, such as the Zintanis, that defected from the Gadafi regime early in the revolution.[49]

With the increasing polarization of the GNC, appeasement of the militias turned to politicization as Libya's key political blocs began to utilize the militias to ensure the implementation of their agendas. The bonds between political actors and the armed groups go beyond ties of kinship, town, and tribe. Rather, patronage and exclusion under the old regime, a desire to settle old grievances, and competition for legitimacy have emerged as the most polarizing elements in Libyan society. Few instances are more indicative of the militias' politicization along these lines than the Political Isolation Law, a bill stipulating the exclusion of former regime officials from politics.

Libya's first parliamentary elections in July 2012 demonstrated that the Islamist coalition enjoyed little popular appeal. Aware of their unpopularity, the Islamists saw in the Political Isolation Law an opportunity to undermine powerful political opponents such as Mahmoud Jibril, leader of the most popular party, the NFA, and gain the upper hand in the GNC. Similarly, by endorsing the Political Isolation Law, the Misratan militias, which aspired to dominate the new Libyan army, could exclude former members of Gadafi's army—their only skilled competitors—from positions of power in the new military institution.[50] Through internal politicking and with armed pressure, the JCP, the Islamist Loyalty to Martyrs' Blood, and their armed affiliates obligated the GNC to put the Political Isolation Law into effect in May 2013. The NFA's numerical dominance did not stop the Islamist bloc from forming a coalition and supporting the exclusionist legislation. The JCP's skillful alliance-building with independents, the Salafists, and the hard-line urban revolutionaries made resisting the passage of the bill almost impossible for the NFA and its allies.

Mohammad Magarief, the GNC chairman, and other high-ranking politicians resigned in protest, and on July 4, 2013, the whole NFA temporarily withdrew from the GNC. The JCP-dominated GNC replaced Magarief with Nuri Abu Sahmein, an independent representative of the Amazigh minority from Zuara and a hard-line revolutionary affiliated with the Loyalty to Martyrs' Blood bloc. The rivalry between the two political factions and their militant affiliates has led to the country's progressive polarization—a process aggravated by the intervention, coercion, and manipulation of the political process by militias loyal to the rival factions. This erosion of political security and numerous assassinations plaguing the country, particularly in Benghazi, have greatly contributed to the grave crisis we witness today.

International Mediation

Soon after Bernardino Leon assumed the role of UN special envoy to Libya in September 2014, he began plans for political dialogue between warring factions. Though a small group of HoR parliamentarians met in September, this dialogue began occurring regularly only after several intervening months. Ongoing fighting in Benghazi, regular bombings across the country, air strikes on Misrata, attacks on oil installations, and increasing violence in both the east and the west delayed negotiations repeatedly. On January 16, 2015, the United Nations succeeded in bringing together various Libyan stakeholders, including local councils and rival parliamentarians, in Geneva and Ghadames. However, despite repeated UN calls for a cease-fire and recognition by Libyan parties that the violence is unsustainable and counterproductive to political stability, fighting and bombings continued across the country, leaving the dialogue to attempt to make political arrangements in the midst of what was already becoming an all-out civil war, albeit one between fragmented and still diverging poles.

In March 2015, Leon gathered HoR and GNC representatives for indirect talks in Skhirat, Morocco. The result was discouraging: The Islamist-dominated GNC as well as General Haftar refused to endorse an agreement. As a result, continued fighting on the ground and a failure to meet crucial demands has slowed the negotiations several times. Though the political track captures the spotlight, Leon planned for additional, parallel tracks bringing together women's leadership, civil society, and security forces. Of these, the security track may be the most crucial. Militias empowered and entrenched by the warring governments are the loci of power in Libya, and no peace agreement can hold without considerable buy-in on the part of some of these forces.

In late July 2015, finally, representatives of most Libyan parties, except the GNC, signed a fifth draft of an agreement in Skhirat. The Libyan Political Agreement (LPA) foresees, among other details, the establishment of a Government of National Accord (GNA), led by an executive council formed by the prime minister and two deputies. The HoR remains the main legislative body, and a new assembly with advisory powers will be appointed to accommodate demands from GNC members. Leon and foreign diplomats were able to bring GNC representatives back to the table with the aim of producing a definitive agreement and forming a unified government by the end of August 2015.[51]

Unfortunately, this did not happen, and Bernardino Leon, having exhausted his term, left and was replaced by the German Martin Kobler. Under the latter's guidance, the Libyan political dialogue continued until December 2015, when the majority of the delegates signed the LPA, and a prime minister was nominated in the person of Fayez Serraj. Along with him, a Presidential Council (PC) of nine members was appointed as the main institutional governing body. While the international community has declared the GNA the legitimate government of Libya and the HoR has approved the LPA "in principle," the HoR has still not approved the unity government that the PC nominated in February. At the end of March, members of the PC, including Serraj, arrived in Tripoli, and less than a week later, the Tripoli government announced that it would step down. As of April 2016, the situation was still uncertain.

There are many challenges to be overcome before the agreement can be successfully implemented. The prolonged mediation efforts have unfortunately created fractures within the ranks of the rivaling factions. When the majority of Misratan commanders voted in favor of signing the agreement in June 2015, antinegotiation hard-liners split from the Islamist-affiliated Libya Dawn coalition and formed the Steadfastness (Samoud) Front. Led by Misratan GNC member and militia commander Salah Badi, the Front views the militias of Zintan and General Khalifa Haftar as existential enemies of Misrata and rejects the idea of compromise. The pronegotiation moderates include groups of Misratan businessmen and staunch Islamists such as the mayor of Tripoli, Mehdi al-Harati, and the political leader of the Libyan Muslim Brotherhood, Mohammad Sawan, both of whom signed the UN draft agreement in Skhirat. The Tobruk-based HoR also suffers from internal divisions. The assembly itself is divided between supporters of federalism and secession and those who want to maintain a united Libya as well as between those who favor an agreement with the Tripoli government and those who are absolutely against it. Among the HoR supporters are also many spoilers. Primary among them is General Haftar, who by launching spoiler attacks in the periods preceding the talks has established himself as the head antinegotiation hard-liner. However, reports suggest that disagreements between Haftar and his subordinates are becoming increasingly frequent.

Fragmentation between the rival camps, however, represents only one of the various challenges facing the formation of a GNA. To these rivals, who see their future only in achieving military success, there also should be added criminal organizations and terrorist groups such as the IS, which will continue working for the failure of the political process and for a permanent state of anarchy in the country. Moreover, even if all participants were to sign the UN agreement, Libya lacks a security network capable of defending GNA members from these spoilers. Although Libyan politicians on both sides have publicly disqualified the possibility of foreign intervention for fear of appearing unpatriotic, many recognize the country's inability to solve its own security problems and thus the need for an international peacekeeping or stabilization force to guarantee security.

CONCLUSION

With oil exports almost at a standstill and foreign exchange reserves rapidly declining, Libya is nearing an economic—not to mention human—breaking point. In this light, even the partial signing of the draft agreement in Skhirat represents a positive step toward solving the crisis, although there are many critics of this deal. Opponents and supporters alike recognize the lack of capacity of a nascent GNA to protect its members and vital infrastructure from the attacks of criminal organizations, extremists, and militia groups not represented in a new government. Some critics of the deal prefer a peace process that works on a local and regional level, addressing the myriad territorial grievances in which they identify the root of Libya's insecurity. They fear that an agreement on the national level is a short-term fix that will fail to address the causes of the civil war, dooming future peace.[52] Others point out that, even if working on a national level is feasible, the militias, who wield real power and are increasingly independent of the political actors, are not included in this deal.

However, skeptics of the UN mediation process overlook the fact that while the roots of the Libyan conflict are local, the aspirations of both the warring factions and the spoilers are national. Both the HoR-sponsored government in Tobruk and the GNC-sponsored government in Tripoli aspire to national rule and national control. Likewise, General Haftar's ambition is to control Libya much as his fellow military strongman Abdel Fatah al-Sisi controls Egypt. Salah Badi and his Steadfastness Front aim to defeat the Zintanis and impose their interests at the national level as well. The UN agreement will not be perfect, but it is better than nothing. A UN peace deal represents an initial framework through which Libyans can begin addressing the local grievances that have destabilized the country. This also means including local stakeholders to negotiate cease-fires and develop local security strategies. Therefore, the pursuit of an international strategy to address Libya's national conflict does not preclude the pursuit of negotiations at the ground level. With continuous attacks on key cities, infrastructure, and political institutions, Libya cannot afford to eschew a national solution in favor of a purely ground-up approach focused on local-level conflict. If the Libyan problem is not addressed as a national conflict immediately, there will be no Libya left to speak of.

NOTES

1. Luis Martinez, *The Libyan Paradox* (London: Hurst, 2007), 91–100.

2. Ibid., 92.

3. Alison Pargeter, "Jamahiriyah in Practice: A Revolutionary Decade," in *Libya: The Rise and Fall of Gadafi* (New Haven, CT: Yale University Press, 2012), 97.

4. Ibid., 99

5. Dirk Vandewalle, "After Gadafi," *Foreign Affairs* (November-December 2012): https://www.foreignaffairs.com/articles/libya/2012-09-16/after-Gadafi.

6. Crane Brinton, *The Anatomy of Revolution* (New York: Prentice Hall, 1952), 36.

7. Samuel P. Huntington, *Political Order in Changing Societies* (New Haven, CT: Yale University Press, 1968), 264.

8. Mary-Jane Deeb, "The Arab Spring: Libya's Second Revolution," in *The Arab Spring: Change and Resistance in the Middle East*, ed. Mark Haas and David Lesch (Boulder, CO: Westview Press, 2013), 69–75.

9. Florence Gaub, "Civil Wars: A Very Short Introduction," European Union Institute for Security Studies, Paris, October 18, 2013, www.iss.europa.eu/publications/detail/article/civil-wars-a-very-short-introduction.

10. Dirk Vandewalle, "Libya's Uncertain Revolution," in *The Libyan Revolution and Its Aftermath*, ed. Peter Cole and Brian McQuinn (London: Hurst, 2015), 18.

11. Ibid., 21.

12. Jason Pack, Karim Mezran, and Mohamed Eljarh, *Libya's Faustian Bargains: Breaking the Appeasement Cycle*, Atlantic Council Rafik Hariri Center for the Middle East, May 2014, 57–58, www.atlanticcouncil.org/publications/reports/libya-s-faustian -bargains-breaking-the-appeasement-cycle.

13. Frederic Wehrey, "Ending Libya's Civil War: Reconciling Politics, Rebuilding Security," Carnegie Endowment for International Peace, September 24, 2014, http://carnegie endowment.org/2014/09/24/ending-libya-s-civil-war-reconciling-politics-rebuilding -security.

14. Frederic Wehrey, "Mosul on the Mediterranean? The Islamic State in Libya and U.S. Counterterrorism Dilemmas." Carnegie Endowment for International Peace, December 17, 2014, http://carnegieendowment.org/2014/12/17/islamic-state-in-libya-and-u.s. -counterterrorism-dilemmas.

15. Kalam Institute for Network Science, Report, *Islamic State Activity in Libya*. February 3, 2015. Web. February 10, 2015.

16. See Karim Mezran, "Libya in Transition: From *Jamahiriya* to *Jumhuriyyah*?," in *The New Middle East: Protest and Revolution in the Arab World*, ed. Fawaz Gerges (New York: Cambridge University Press, 2014), 309–331.

17. Ali Abdullatif Ahmida, "The Myth of the Hilali Conquest," in *The Making of Modern Libya*, ed. Ali Abdullatif Ahmida (New York: State University of New York Press, 2009), 11–19.

18. See Majid Khadduri, *Modern Libya* (Baltimore, MD: Johns Hopkins University Press, 1963).

19. Dirk J. Vandewalle, *A History of Modern Libya* (Cambridge: Cambridge University Press, 2006), 43–76. See also Karim Mezran, *Negotiation and Construction of National Identities* (Leiden, The Netherlands, and Boston: Martinus Nijhoff Publishers, 2007).

20. John Oakes, "The Kingdom of Libya: The Shepherd King and the Oil Barons," in *Libya: The History of Gaddafi's Pariah State* (Stroud, Gloucestershire: History Press, 2011), 93–94.

21. Ibid., 94.

22. Ibid., 97.

23. Ibid., 102.

24. Ibid., 103.

25. Dirk Vandewalle, "Shadow of the Past: The Sanusi Kingdom," in *Libya Since Independence: Oil and State-Building* (Ithaca, NY: Cornell University Press, 1998), 55.

26. Ruth First, *Libya: The Elusive Revolution* (London: Penguin Books, 1974).

27. See Mansour O. El-Kikhia, *Libya's Gadafi: The Politics of Contradiction* (Gainesville: University Press of Florida, 1997).

28. Wolfram Lacher, "Faultlines of the Revolution: Political Actors, Camps and Conflicts in the New Libya," Report 4, Stiftung Wissenschaft und Politik German Institute for International and Security Affairs, Berlin, May 2013.

29. "Jamahiriya" does not have a precise translation but could be roughly translated as the "state of the masses."

30. Vandewalle, "After Gadafi."

31. Ali Abdullatif Ahmida, "Why Gadafi Has Already Lost," *New York Times*, March 16, 2011.

32. Ronald Bruce St. John, "The February 17th Revolution in Libya," Middle East Institute, August 1, 2011, www.mei.edu/content/february-17th-revolution-libya.

33. George Joffé, "Civil Activism and the Roots of the 2011 Uprisings," in *The 2011 Libyan Uprisings and the Struggle for the Post-Qadhafi Future*, ed. Jason Pack (London: Palgrave Macmillan, 2013), 28–30.

34. On foreign intervention in the 2011 revolution, see Christopher Chivvis, *Toppling Gadafi: Libya and the Limits of Liberal Intervention* (New York: Cambridge University Press, 2014).

35. Pack, Mezran, and Eljarh, *Libya's Faustian Bargains*, 13–14.

36. Ibid., 1. See also Karim Mezran and Eric Knecht, "Actors and Factors in Libya's Revolution," in *Political and Constitutional Transitions in North Africa*, ed. Justin Frosini and Francesco Biagi (New York: Routledge, 2015).

37. Ibid., 12.

38. Wehrey, *Ending Libya's Civil War*, 6.

39. Pack, Mezran, and Eljarh, *Libya's Faustian Bargains*, 2.

40. Ibid., 3.

41. Wehrey, *Ending Libya's Civil War*, 7.

42. Pack, Mezran, and Eljarh, *Libya's Faustian Bargains*, 2.

43. Wehrey, *Ending Libya's Civil War*, 8.

44. Ibid., 9.

45. Ibid., 3.

46. Pack, Mezran, and Eljarh, *Libya's Faustian Bargains*, 46.

47. Ibid., 20.

48. Ibid., 12.

49. Rosan Smits, "Revolution and Its Discontents: State, Factions, and Violence in the New Libya," Clingendael: Netherlands Institute of International Relations, September 2013, 23, www.clingendael.nl/publication/revolution-and-its-discontents-state-factions-and-violence-new-libya.

50. Pack, Mezran, and Eljarh, *Libya's Faustian Bargains*, 42.

51. See Karim Mezran, "Libya: Half an Agreement Is Better Than No Agreement," MENASource, August 12, 2015, www.atlanticcouncil.org/blogs/menasource/libya-half-an-agreement-is-better-than-no-agreement.

52. Fadil Aliriza, "Libya's Bad Peace Deal Is Worse Than No Peace Deal," *Foreign Policy*, August 7, 2015, http://foreignpolicy.com/2015/08/07/libyas-bad-peace-deal-is-worse-than-no-peace-deal.

4

Anatomy of an Uprising:
Bashar al-Assad's Fateful Choices
That Launched a Civil War

DAVID W. LESCH

SYRIAN PRESIDENT BASHAR AL-ASSAD'S speech to the nation on March 30, 2011, his first to address the protests in Syria that had intensified following the debacle in Deraa in mid-March, was, in my opinion, a seminal moment in modern Syrian history. It seemed that the whole country, supporters and opposition, waited with bated breath to hear what he had to say. The country had barely heard a peep from him in the two weeks since the incidents at Deraa, where, reportedly, in response to a number of teenaged children having been arrested and tortured by Syrian security for having written antiregime graffiti on a wall, relatives, friends, and other residents marched out against local authorities demanding redress. The situation soon devolved into bloodshed as the protesters and government forces clashed, news of which spread like wildfire amid the heady days of the Arab Spring, and protests and clashes began to pop up in other Syrian towns.

Assad's speech, given in front of a crowd of adulatory supporters in the National Assembly, is now famous for having offered very few concessions to meet the protesters' demands. On the contrary, it was a defiant speech, blaming the uprising on the insidious actions of terrorists and armed groups supported by Syria's external enemies in the region and internationally. Assad was taken to task in the international media for what was viewed as a blatant misdirection from the real socioeconomic and political factors that had laid the foundation for the unrest—either this or he and his inner circle were blind to the real causes of the protests. Certainly, the protesters were immensely disappointed, but so were many of Assad's supporters in and outside the Syrian government.[1]

From interviews I conducted with a number of former Syrian officials who were close to or in the decisionmaking apparatus behind Assad's policies, it seems that the Syrian president definitely had a choice of what direction to take in his March 30 speech.[2] Different factions within the regime apparently advocated a variety of responses, from one group wanting to make what it felt were necessary concessions to dampen the rising tide of protests to another group that obviously influenced the president to make the speech he did in fact give, one that laid the groundwork for the regime's crackdown on protesters in the days and weeks to come. Some of these officials went to the National Assembly or watched the speech on television expecting the more lenient draft they had figured (or been told) Assad would give, only to be surprised by what actually happened. It is clear that there was a tussle back and forth within the opaque Syrian decisionmaking apparatus surrounding Assad, with the decision by the Syrian president on what course to take, in effect which version of the speech to give, having taken place only a short time before he delivered it.[3]

Why did Assad choose to deliver the more defiant and harsh version rather than the more conciliatory one? In essence, the answer to this question begins to answer the question of why the Syrian regime chose to brutally put down the uprising, setting in motion a chain of events that has led to over four years of devastating conflict. Was it an individual decision on the part of Bashar al-Assad and perhaps a few of his closest advisers, or was it the result of something more systemic, that is, the way in which the Syrian regime, or at least enough of the officials therein, uniquely viewed the nature of threat based upon its own conceptual paradigm?

Ultimately, we may never know for sure, but I think there is enough circumstantial evidence and knowledge of recent Syrian history to suggest how it all might have come down. Whatever the case, that March 30 speech may be the single most important decision in modern Syrian history, one that sent Syria in a trajectory toward a catastrophic war that has forever changed the country; indeed, it has changed the heartland of the Middle East itself, and the repercussions of these changes are still being felt.

BASHAR AL-ASSAD CAUGHT UNAWARES?

In late 2010 and early 2011, Syria seemed to be a fairly stable place, especially when compared to Tunisia, Egypt, and Yemen, where events of the so-called Arab Spring were beginning to percolate. Bashar al-Assad had improved his own and his country's image; earlier in the decade, and particularly in the aftermath of the 2005 assassination of former Lebanese prime minister Rafiq Hariri, which was widely blamed on Damascus, that image had been severely tarnished. However, in Paris in December 2010, the Syrian president and his wife, Asma al-Assad, were widely photographed in their haute couture clothes, visiting museums and being hosted (if not feted) by the French elite.

In retrospect, Assad's apparent complacency, denial of the facts, and/or ignorance amid the turmoil of the Arab Spring were vividly on display in an interview he gave to journalists from the *Wall Street Journal* in late January 2011.[4] Assad stated in the interview that the protests in Tunisia, Egypt, and Yemen signaled a "new era" in the Middle East, where rulers would need to meet the rising political and economic demands of the people. He noted, "If you didn't see the need of reform before what happened in Egypt and Tunisia, it's too late to do any reform." He went on to say, "Syria is stable. Why? Because you have to be very closely linked to the beliefs of the people. This is the core issue. When there is divergence . . . you will have this vacuum that creates disturbances."

This was actually a reference to Syria's position on the Israeli-Palestinian issue as well as to Assad's perceived triumphal resistance to the "American project" in the region. The Syrian president also seemed confident in the level of reform he had implemented in Syria over the years. He admitted that he wished there had been more but commented that his country needed more time to build up institutions and improve education in order to absorb such levels of reform. In this vein, he asked, "Is it going to be a new era toward more chaos or more institutionalization? That is the question."

Two essays in the February 2011 issue of *Forward Magazine*, a progovernment English-language monthly published in Damascus, dovetailed with Assad's *Wall Street Journal* interview.[5] One essay was by the periodical's editor in chief and a leading Syrian commentator, Sami Moubayed, who was well connected to the upper echelons of the Syrian regime; the other was by Bouthaina Shaaban, one of the president's closest and most influential advisers. Political essays in this periodical are heavily vetted and at this important juncture were no doubt purposely placed in the publication, thus reflecting regime sentiments.

In his essay, Moubayed repeatedly hammers home the point that the dictators in the Arab world who had either fallen by then (President Ben Ali in Tunisia) or were on their way out (President Husni Mubarak in Egypt and President Abdullah Saleh in Yemen) were being run out of office by widespread popular protest primarily because over the years they had been lackeys of the West, and particularly the United States. Like Moubayed, Shaaban castigates the West for being at the root of the unrest in the Arab world. Interestingly, she seems to recognize the pervasive socioeconomic problems in the region, and by implication also in Syria, that in part gave rise to the unrest. However, she also identifies what in her (and Assad's?) mind were the real reasons for the upheavals: Arab neglect of, and complicity, in the Palestinian problem; Israeli brutality; and related US policies. In other words, if an Arab leader, such as Bashar al-Assad, has been on the correct side of history by opposing such policies and supporting the Palestinians and other Arabs suffering under stagnant, obsequious autocracies and foreign imperialism, he should be safe because he is on the side of the people. She ends her article by saying, "If anger is directed today against governments and aims are to change rulers and their methods, there is no doubt that the position of these rulers over the question of the liberation of Palestine from Israeli occupation will be a major factor in what happens over the coming weeks and months." It was the correct identification of symptoms, but it was also the wrong diagnosis.

In addition, there were comments by Syrian officials that painted Assad as someone who was relatively young, technologically savvy, and thus in tune with the people, especially the younger generations at the epicenter of protests elsewhere. He was not the septuagenarian or octogenarian entrenched autocrat who was totally out of touch with the people, such as Mubarak in Egypt. He was popular because he had opposed the West, Israel, and their lackeys in the region. Surely Assad was immune to the popular unrest he was witnessing around him in neighboring Arab states.

It is almost certain that Bashar al-Assad was shocked when the so-called Arab Spring uprisings seeped into his country in force in March 2011. I believe he truly thought he was safe, secure, and popular beyond condemnation. He probably believed so much in his own popularity in Syria that he thought any protests must have been foreign-inspired. But this was not the case in the Middle East of 2011, where the stream of information via social media could not be controlled as it once had been. The perfect storm in the Arab world of higher commodity prices, which made basic items more expensive, and a youth bulge that created an irreparable gap between mobilization and assimilation threw into sharp relief the widespread socioeconomic problems (especially gross unequal income distribution and growing poverty), corruption, and restricted political space marked by *mukhabarat*-enforced (security/intelligence) political repression. In these respects, Syria was no different. And after the popular uprisings in Tunisia and Egypt led to the removal of the ancien régimes in each country, the barrier of fear of the repressive apparatus was broken.

Assad thought Syria would be different. He was obviously wrong. As mentioned before, Assad portrayed his country as almost immune to such domestic unrest. The mouthpieces of the Syrian regime consistently echoed this view, even to the point of expressing support for the protesters in other Arab states. Indeed, calls by anti-Assad elements inside and outside the country for similar protests to be held in Syrian cities in January and February 2011 failed to elicit much response, as only a few dozen showed up, rather than the hoped-for thousands that had demonstrated in Tunisian and Egyptian cities. These protests usually fizzled out rapidly or were easily dispersed by security. There just did not seem to be the same energy for opposition in Syria as in other countries, and this only made the regime feel that much more secure.

Assad's supporters, as noted before, emphasized that the septuagenarian and octogenarian leaders of those other Arab states had been out of touch with their people and had been corrupt lackeys of the United States and Israel. The implication, of course, was that Assad—forty-five years old at the time—was young by comparison and therefore in sync with Arab youth. He had also consistently confronted the United States and Israel in the region and had supported the resistance forces of Hamas and Hizbullah. He could thus brandish credentials that played well in the Arab street—not only in Syria but throughout the Arab world. This may have bought him some time, but it was a misreading of the situation—or a denial of it. As it turned out, Syria had been suffering from many of the same underlying socioeconomic woes that existed in the non-oil-producing Arab countries and that created a well of disenfranchisement and disempowerment, especially among an energized and increasingly frustrated youth.

There were, indeed, several tangible factors that led Assad and his supporters to believe that they could weather the storm rising in the Arab world, or at least deflect and contain it if it did enter Syrian space. First, because of Syria's turbulent political development following independence in 1946, Syrians have generally disdained engagement in actions that could produce instability. In the decade prior to the Arab Spring, they had only to look across their borders, on either side, toward Lebanon and Iraq—two countries that, like Syria, are ethnically and religiously diverse—to see how political disorder can violently rip apart the fabric of society. Of course, this trepidation was constantly stoked by the regime to reinforce the necessity of maintaining stability at all costs. The regime frequently portrayed itself as the only thing standing between stability and chaos. As long as Assad remained the only viable alternative in the minds of many Syrians, they were not going to participate in an opposition movement that could destabilize the country over the long term. And the brutality of the Syrian government crackdown, with the memory of Hama in 1982 within the consciousness of most Syrians, the repressive apparatus of the state—military, *mukhabarat*, paramilitary groups—was daunting to anyone contemplating taking it on.[6]

Second, the fate of the Syrian military and security services is closely tied to that of the regime. In contrast to Egypt, these institutions have not been separate from the political leadership. They have aggressively led the violent crackdown on the protesters since the beginning of the uprising. And after a decade in power, by 2011, Assad had successfully manipulated the ruling apparatus, both military and civilian, to have in place an extremely loyal and tight leadership at the top. There have been remarkably few high-placed defections from the Syrian government when compared to other Arab states convulsed by uprisings, and by now their fates are tied together more than ever.

Third, the minority-ruled Syrian regime, infused as it is with Alawites in important positions, had always represented itself as the protector of all minorities in a country that is about 65 percent Sunni Arab. In addition to the 10–11 percent Alawite population, there are various Christian sects comprising about 10 percent of the population, plus Druze (3 percent) and a smattering of smaller Shiite sects. The Sunni Kurdish population in Syria (another 10 percent) has often been a restless and repressed minority in Syria under the Assads; however, the Syrian government made a number of concessions to the Kurds, mostly in the area of political autonomy, in the early part of the uprising in order to at the very least keep most of them neutral in the conflict. The Assads have skillfully played the minority card over the years, practically guaranteeing themselves at least a 20–30 percent support base in the country by playing on fears of the potential for repressive, even fanatical, Sunni

Muslim rule and/or instability, in which minorities typically pay a high price. Then there are loyal Sunnis from the business class who have long been co-opted into supporting the Assads as well as numerous Sufi Muslim orders in Syria that were actively cultivated and supported by the Assads, especially by Bashar al-Assad. All of these elements added together probably account for about half of the Syrian population. For an authoritarian regime, this is not a bad percentage. By employing coercion, a pervasive spy apparatus, carefully constructed tribal and family alliances, co-optation, and the tactics of divide and rule, maintaining control over the remaining half of the population is not as difficult for a minority-ruled regime as it would, on the surface, seem to be.

Fourth, Bashar al-Assad, prior to the uprising, was generally well liked in the country—or at least not generally reviled. He tended to live modestly and had a popular wife, and they were both much better at domestic public diplomacy than his father had ever been. The image cultivated was that he and his family were normal—not distanced from the masses but rather aware of and concerned about their problems. Indeed, Assad's supporters would often talk about him in reverential terms, almost like a prophet delivered to Syria to bring the country forward. Of course, this sort of sycophancy only fed Assad's delusion that emerged over the years that the well-being of the country was synonymous with his well-being.

In a related point, Assad gained a good bit of credit in the eyes of many Syrians for giving up his passion, ophthalmology, to serve the country when it needed him following his brother's death in 1994 and his father's passing in 2000. Of course, this sacrifice was promoted as regime propaganda, and it may have bought Assad a longer learning curve and more public patience with his incremental reform efforts, simply because the image was that he had not been groomed to be president. Quite to the contrary, Assad was portrayed as having kept the country together despite the regional and international pressures applied against Syria during the previous decade and as deserving the gratitude of the Syrian people for having done so. In addition, there was some economic growth, albeit very uneven, as well as fiscal, administrative, and education reform that perhaps has been too easily dismissed in the wake of the civil war.

Finally, Syria's internal and external opposition prior to the uprising were often uncoordinated and divided, with no generally recognized leadership, and this has carried over into the civil war itself. The Syrian regime had done a good job over the years of ensuring this fragmentation. There was little if any experience with politics in a populace where there existed political repression and very restricted political space. As such, there was no real alternative to Assad, especially after the regime survived—and indeed consolidated power—following the existential threat in the wake of former Lebanese prime minister Rafiq Hariri's assassination in 2005.

TO SPEECH OR NOT TO SPEECH

In response to the growing protests, the Syrian government announced a series of reforms on March 24, 2011. This response seemed to repeat the pattern established by fallen regimes in Tunis and Cairo as well as other governments in the Arab world experiencing problems at the time. Regime insiders told me that Assad went back and forth between making concessions (and announcing them in a conciliatory speech) and cracking down hard on the protesters. The March 24 announcement included the formation of a committee to investigate and bring to justice anyone who had committed unlawful acts, including government soldiers and personnel.

Bouthaina Shaaban, the political and media adviser to the president who had now assumed the role of government spokesperson, stipulated that the wages of government workers be raised by 20 to 30 percent (thus keeping an important support base mollified) and that there would be income-tax cuts and pension increases. She then spoke in general terms about new health reforms, judicial reform, the relaxation of media restrictions, the establishment of a new mechanism to fight corruption, and allowing more political parties to compete in elections. She also announced that a committee would be formed to examine the need to lift the state-of-emergency law (Decree No. 51) that had been in place since the Ba'thist coup in 1963.

Of course, Syrians had heard these promises before with little to no implementation. The real question people were asking amid the rising protests was "Where is Bashar?" He had not been heard from since the protest movement had begun in earnest in Deraa in mid-March, and he seemingly had retreated into seclusion.

There are some possible reasons why Assad was not personally responding to the growing crisis. I firmly believe he—and the Syrian leadership as a whole—was caught off guard by the ferocity of the protests and how they spread from Deraa to other cities and towns. It is not as though the regime did not consider and take measures in the wake of what had happened elsewhere in the Arab world. Before Deraa erupted, Assad had apparently ordered three separate security studies to examine the likelihood of the Arab Spring spreading into Syria. The quality and methodology of the studies (and which branch or branches of the government carried out the studies) can, perhaps, be questioned, but all three concluded that Syria was safe and secure.[7] In addition, in Damascus, police authorities were given orders to be more lenient in terms of traffic violations and other unlawful activities in order to minimize any potential incidents that could incite the public.[8] And there was certainly a mobilization of military and security forces just in case something happened, mostly in and around Damascus. Assad likely still believed he had a target on his back dating from the days of the Hariri assassination, and the security chiefs never believed that they were entirely safe from siege. Some certainly felt that after Egypt, Syria had to be on the lookout.[9] So it was not as though the regime were totally complacent, but it obviously was focusing on Damascus (and perhaps Aleppo), as the protests in other Arab countries, particularly in Egypt, had tended to focus on and have the most significant impact in their respective capital cities, whereas the Syrian uprising began and continued for some time as a mostly rural phenomenon outside Damascus.

Regardless, the regime seemed to be rocked back on its heels by the events at Deraa. There were apparently pronounced differences in the inner circle surrounding the president over how to react.[10] Should the protests be repressed ruthlessly, as had been the Syrian way in the past? Or should Assad announce, and implement, meaningful reforms? There appeared to be a great deal of confusion within the inner circle, with varying responses to these questions, and comments and actions by the regime in these crucial two weeks made it seem as though it were talking out of both sides of its mouth, saying one thing while regime forces were doing quite the opposite on the ground. In my interviews with both regime and opposition figures, I heard a wide variety of stories and recollections about exactly what had happened in Deraa in those crucial days of March 2011. Some of these tales may be filtered through agenda-ridden or traumatized lenses, and enough ambiguity exists that an accurate history of what actually went down in Deraa remains to be written. One top regime insider told me that Assad had intended to go down to Deraa and be apologetic and conciliatory, possibly even to get rid of his cousin, the governor Atif Najib, whom many held responsible for the civilian deaths.[11] This response would have met many of the local demands and possibly would have taken the air out of the expanding protests. However, according to this official, there was a massacre (unreported in the media) of about a dozen policemen in Deraa in late March by locals bent on revenge, and after this, Assad had no choice but to give the orders to respond more forcefully. Regardless of these different narratives of the events in Deraa, Assad was publicly nowhere to be found, so it appeared that the president was not taking charge.

Bashar al-Assad does not typically act or decide on important issues in an expeditious fashion. It is difficult to discern exactly what was going on in those first few days and weeks, as the Syrian decisionmaking apparatus is fairly opaque. It is also hampered by deep bureaucratic inertia that makes quick decisions on policy exceedingly difficult. The decisionmaking at the top appears to be quite compartmentalized. Small groups of advisers close to the president advise him on different issues. Some officials serve on more than one of these ad hoc committees, and competing viewpoints are often deliberately placed in the same group so that the president can hear different opinions. Assad tends to be very deliberate, often mulling things over for quite some time before making a final decision. This system is not built for quick, efficient responses and reactions.

One high-ranking Syrian official informed me in December 2011 in a meeting in Europe that one of the driving forces behind the regime's response in the initial stages of the unrest had been to *not* do what the Tunisian and Egyptian presidents had done. The logic was inescapable: Ben Ali and Mubarak had been removed from office in short order after making some concessions and not ordering widespread crackdowns; thus, Assad should do the opposite. These other leaders had given in too easily and appeared weak. I asked this Syrian official why Assad did not go in front of the cameras on live television instead of giving televised, orchestrated speeches. The official told me that a number of people had tried to get him to do this while he still had some credibility in order to connect with a people with whom he had forged a bond over the years. But other, obviously more influential members of the inner circle strongly cautioned against doing this because it was what other—by then former—Arab leaders had done.

Maybe some of the more hard-line elements in the regime thought it would be a sign of weakness for the president to admit any mistakes. Maybe they thought Assad might be able to dissociate himself from the crackdown by connecting at a more personal level with the Syrian people, thus making their own positions more vulnerable. Indeed, several former high-level Syrian officials indicated to me that talk of internal coups was in the air. One recommended to Assad that the president himself could carry out a coup against some of these hard-line elements. The president's response, according to this official, was simply "You are naive."[12] Another well-placed former Syrian official, who had direct access to Assad and was one of the more influential officials in Damascus, blatantly accused certain Ba'th Party officials in cahoots with the security establishment of using the crisis as an opportunity to force out the more reformist elements in the regime, of which he was one. Clearly there was confusion and intrigue at the top during this crisis period, and Assad had to navigate his position—and his response—very carefully.

Perhaps, as well, Assad's decision to make a televised speech reflected his unswerving commitment to what is often the fiction of institutions; therefore, he spoke first at the People's Assembly on March 30, spoke to his newly sworn-in cabinet in April, and addressed a cast of supporters in an auditorium at Damascus University in June. It could be that Assad, who is not the greatest orator and does not have a commanding presence, felt (or his advisers did) that he needed to be surrounded by supporters as a kind of prop, to create the spectacle and theater of drama he was seeking, with almost scripted applause and adulation that are familiar to anyone who has heard speeches by him or his father in such venues.

A Speech Not Worth Waiting For

There was a great deal of anticipation regarding Assad's March 30 speech. Many were hoping that the Syrian president would be magnanimous and humble, announcing serious political reforms. This was the moment when Assad would finally come through, would finally live up to the high expectations raised when he first came to power over a decade earlier. Those listeners were to be disappointed. Many Syrians in the opposition later identified Assad's speech as a turning point; their disappointment in the speech made them realize that Bashar, in the end, wasn't any different from his father, and this realization galvanized the protests.[13] In addition, the fact that Assad did not punish his cousin, the governor of the province of Deraa, at least as a symbolic gesture in reaction to the civilian deaths in the city of Deraa, reinforced the view that any real concessions by the government would be few and far between. A number of Syrian opposition elements from inside the country, both civilians and armed activists, concede that if he had done one or both of these things, the uprising might never have occurred. As one progovernment Hizbullah figure told us,

Bashar had real popularity in Syria. It was not 90 percent, it was not total or unconditional support, but he had—I think that we had a clear majority who was hoping that Bashar was going to transform the system, little by little. Perhaps some of them were becoming less patient, but when the contestation movement began, if he had taken some measures to directly sanction the guy who tortured the kids in Deraa, if he had taken some anticorruption measures, even if it was symbolic, it would have made things better. He had to take the decision to confront some clans inside the leadership and the Syrian apparatus and administration and I think that he could have—this kind of measure would have divided the ranks of the contestation, and he would have had a larger popular base.[14]

One Syrian opposition activist frankly stated that Assad could have remained in power "if he stayed with the Syrian people."[15]

A former high-level Syrian government official who was a part of the decisionmaking apparatus at the time said that Assad made a "terrible strategic mistake that [week after the March 15 Deraa incident] by not deciding what's the nature of this conflict. And I tried to say this is not a singular crisis, this is a multidimensional crisis, economic and political. Have a package, and a package that's clear in one particular direction. Don't give signals in two hundred directions. . . . Let me put it simply: First, sack the governor. Then sack all the heads of security so his cousin doesn't stand out. That is what we used to do whenever there was trouble in any governorate."[16] He (and others) also advised Assad to rain some largesse on Deraa—new roads, schools, and so forth—and then send ministers, or even the president himself, to Deraa to meet with city elders and tribal leaders to pacify the protesters.[17]

These hypotheses are difficult to prove in hindsight, but it is clear, in my opinion, that at least some of the energy of the growing unrest would have been dampened had Assad initiated bold moves. This, in my view, is one of the great tragedies of the conflict: unlike a Mubarak, a Gadafi, or even a Ben Ali, Bashar al-Assad still enjoyed a level of genuine popularity (or even residual popularity) in his country, and he could possibly have rallied the people, if not all of the security forces or Ba'th Party leadership, behind him to compel the country in a more ameliorative direction rather than a confrontational one. It's easy for armchair historians to speculate. We are not the ones putting our lives on the line, and surely hard-line elements in Damascus would have vigorously opposed any moves by the Syrian president to enact reforms that could undercut the power base of important factions in the government. However, it is times like these that separate the great leaders, who might save a country rather than plunging it into the depths and despair of five years and counting of civil war, from the also-rans and conformists.

Despite some references to the socioeconomic causes of the unrest in Syria, Assad's speech was clearly dominated by the attempt to place the blame on external forces and on the seditious activities of their domestic co-conspirators; indeed, the word "sedition" was used repeatedly during the speech. Toward the end, in a clear—and chilling—warning to opposition elements, Assad said, "The Holy Quran says, 'sedition is worse than killing.' So all those involved intentionally or unintentionally in it contribute to destroying their country. So there is no compromise or middle way on this. What is at stake is the homeland and there is a huge conspiracy."

It seems that ultimately, Assad and a critical mass of the Syrian leadership concluded that the protests had to be eliminated. The regime had to reassert control and stability through force and by playing on the penchant of the Syrian population to believe conspiracy theories. Assad ended his speech by stating, "I shall remain the faithful brother and comrade who will walk with his people and lead them to build the Syria we love, the Syria we are proud of, the Syria which is invincible to its enemies." That he ended his speech with the word "enemies" revealed the direction the regime was taking in terms of its public evaluation of the main source of the crisis as well as the nature of its response.

It was no surprise that Assad blamed the protests largely on conspirators inside and (especially) outside the country. Anyone who has spent time in Syria can recognize the national paranoia. This conspiratorial mind-set is commonplace even among the educated elite, many of whom attended university in the West. The problem is that there have been just enough actual foreign conspiracies in Syria over the decades to lend credence to such claims. And the regimes of both Hafiz and Bashar al-Assad have nurtured this paranoia through propaganda and censorship, in part to justify the necessity of the security state. So the president probably figured he was preaching to the converted, certainly within the parliamentary chamber in which he was speaking. And a good many Syrians outside the chamber probably believed in the conspiracy as well. But in the new information age, a growing number of people could no longer be cowed or brainwashed as they had been in the past. The Arab Spring had changed the perspectives and the level of demands of ordinary citizens. By blaming unseen forces of conspiracy, the government denied responsibility for, and recognition of, the very real socioeconomic and political problems, and for the growing clamor of Syrians expressing frustration with the government for lack of accountability, corruption, political repression, and rising poverty. Assad did not adequately address these issues, which had become much more important to ordinary citizens because they had seen in other Arab countries a way to finally combat them.

No Going Back

Beyond his closest supporters, the reactions to Assad's speech were almost universally negative. In its wake, protests broke out across the country (with the exceptions of Aleppo and Damascus for the most part) and were followed by violent crackdowns by government forces. Regime officials were likely taken aback that the speech was not the panacea they had thought it would be. Assad replaced the cabinet and announced a number of other measures, such as the termination of the 1963 emergency law; however, other announcements and provisions—and above all actions—effectively made null and void any apparent concessions made by the regime. The Syrian population was used to announcements of reforms followed by very little substance, much less implementation—this was no different. If I could have spoken with Bashar al-Assad during the early weeks and months of the uprising, I am sure he would have insisted that he had made serious concessions and that they were not appreciated in the West or by duplicitous, naive elements of the growing opposition movement. And rather than lying through his teeth, he might have truly believed he was going far more than halfway to meet various demands. But what neither side understood particularly well was that the Arab Spring had raised the bar and that expectations were greater than what a *mukhabarat* regime could possibly meet.

In the end, Assad fell back into the default position, convinced by certain elements in his inner circle and security apparatus that the uprising could be taken care of in a matter of weeks. As one former high-ranking Syrian military figure who was close to the inner circle stated, "[Bashar] was tilting on both sides. At some point [the security chiefs] must have told him, move aside, relax, and we'll deal with it."[18] Perhaps this is just the typical response under the Assads: When a domestic threat appears, there is a push-button response of quick and ruthless repression. No one questions it, and the *mukhabarat* and the elite units of the military swing into action. Assad likely did not fret over it much once the initial shock of the protests wore off, as this was simply business as usual in the *mukhabarat* state. Assad had been convinced—or he had convinced himself—that he was actually saving the country from the enemies of the state.

During the first month or two of the uprising, while the regime continued to make some concessions and announce reform measures to present an image of calm and cool control,[19] the military and security forces intensified their crackdown in cities across Syria. To the outside observer, this approach may seem contradictory and indicative of fissures within the ruling elite on how to respond to the crisis. But from the perspective of Assad and his inner circle, it was two sides of the same coin. Both Assad regimes followed the axiom of power politics that one offers concessions only from a position of strength, never from a position of weakness. Therefore, while there was a practical side to the Assad approach in terms of quelling the unrest, it also clearly indicated that the regime wanted to portray itself as making concessions and offering reforms (actually just reiterating measures previously made so as not to seem as if it were caving in to pressure) only from a position of strength. The regime hoped that announced reforms could separate the wheat from the chaff of the opposition, thus enabling it to land a knockout punch in relatively short order. But, of course, that never happened.

Ultimately, Bashar al-Assad had little faith that anything other than his continuance in power could lead the way forward. Assad's strategic vision (dream, even) for an internationally respected and integrated Syria became consumed by a Syrian paradigm of political survival. He was either unwilling or unable to stop what in Syria is a reflexive response to perceived threat. He retrenched and retreated into a typically Syrian authoritarian mode of survival, an Alawite fortress to protect the sect's chokehold on power. In the end, when the pressure was greatest, Assad was not the enlightened, Western-educated ophthalmologist. He was—as he always really has been—a child of the Arab-Israeli conflict; the superpower cold war; and, most importantly, Hafiz al-Assad.

Yes, Assad had a choice in the hours before giving his speech on March 30, 2011. But considering the parameters under which he was ruling, the conceptual paradigm of his perception of the nature of threat, and a worldview that had been shaped by modern Syrian history, maybe in the end there was really only one option.

CONCLUSION: CIVIL WAR

As is well known, the following months saw an exponential increase in violence all over Syria as the regime crackdown hardened and the once peaceful protests turned more violent. In response to the regime, the Free Syrian Army (FSA) was formed in the summer of 2011, an amalgam of soldiers who had defected from Syrian armed forces and others seeking an organizational body to coordinate opposition military efforts. Outside Syria, political opposition groups comprised mostly of Syrian exiles established the Syrian National Council (SNC), a civilian body that attempted to become the internationally recognized opposition to the Syrian regime. Neither the FSA nor the SNC developed into anything close to what their supporters had envisioned, the former due to fragmentation, lack of coordination, and a dearth of military hardware and the latter due to the fact that it lacked any legitimacy inside the country for the armed opposition groups who were doing the fighting and dying. One of the primary problems of the Syrian conflict early on became evident in these two attempts to form viable opposition bodies; that is, various elements in each were supported by different outside players (such as Saudi Arabia, Qatar, and Turkey) who often had different agendas in terms of whom they wanted to support and by what means they wanted to counter the Assad regime.

In fact, by late summer and fall of 2011, when many countries, including the United States, had demanded that Bashar al-Assad step down as president, the conflict had clearly become a proxy war. On one side, in support of the Syrian government, were Russia, Iran, Hizbullah, and, increasingly, Iraq. The main players arrayed against the Syrian regime, ostensibly in support of various Syrian opposition groups, were the United States and its European allies, Turkey, Saudi Arabia, and Qatar. While the violence and death toll increased, along with more and more Syrian refugees crossing the borders into Turkey, Lebanon, and Jordan, the United Nations arduously worked for a cease-fire. There were some cease-fires on the ground negotiated by the United Nations (and its special envoy, former UN secretary-general Kofi Annan), but they were too small-scale and inevitably broke down, especially as the increasing fragmentation of the armed opposition made it almost impossible to implement a cease-fire of any breadth or duration.

The conflict developed into something of a stalemate, where neither side had the wherewithal to land a knockout punch. The regime largely held on to the main cities and immediate surrounding areas, while various opposition groups made gains in the countryside, in small cities and towns, and in the suburbs of some major cities. This picture fluctuated from time to time, with the opposition appearing to be on the uptick at certain moments and the regime at others. By the summer and fall of 2012, the fighting had intensified to the point where one could label the conflict as an all-out civil war. Aleppans reluctantly became ensnared in the war by the fall of 2012, with the city fast becoming split between regime forces on one side and opposition groups on the other, a situation that persists as of this writing.

As the conflict deepened, the Syrian opposition, while becoming more fragmented, also became more (Sunni) Islamist. The leading roles in this regard have been played by such groups as Ahrar al-Sham, the al-Qaida affiliate Jabhat al-Nusra (established in early 2012), and the Islamic State in Iraq and Syria (ISIS), particularly with the latter's seizure of Raqqa, which became the capital of the self-described Islamic State. Several factors fed into this trend. Syria increasingly became a failed state, and typically in such chaos people retreat toward subnational identities, which in Syria's case means religious sectarianism (or ethnicity, as in the case of the Kurds, who, with regime acquiescence, carved out semiautonomous zones in northern and northeastern Syria). So, as the regime came to be seen more and more (some of it due to the regime's own propaganda) as the sinecure of Alawite survival; the protector of religious minorities such as Christians, Druze, and other Shiites; and the last bastion of secular diversity (some of it also due to the regime's own propaganda), the opposition naturally gravitated toward a more conservative brand of Sunni Islam, comprising 75 percent of the population and representing more accurately the true leanings of an opposition that emerged from a more rural and traditional base. Also, since the bulk of financial support from the outside emanated from Sunni conservative countries such as Saudi Arabia, Qatar, and Kuwait, much of the so-called moderate or secular opposition adopted the discourse and style of radical Islamists in order to acquire arms and attract recruits to the cause. Finally, as Syria disintegrated, with life becoming correspondingly more intolerable for vast numbers of Syrians, some began to find in radical Sunni Islam a way to make a living as well as a purpose and palliative for their personal, family, and societal suffering.

Of course, this trend made it difficult for Western countries to more assertively back the Syrian opposition forces for fear that any arms and ammunition supplied to them might find their way into the hands of radical Islamist groups (which did in fact happen on a regular basis), who might then use them against

Western interests. In addition, it became more problematic for some countries in the West, especially the United States, to engineer the fall of the Assad regime for fear of the chaos that would ensue, the subsequent spillover effects across Syria's borders, and the question of what would replace the Syrian regime, most probably a radical Islamist group such as ISIS.

A case in point was the Obama administration's response to the chemical attacks reportedly carried out by Syrian government forces in the Ghouta area on the edge of Damascus in August 2013 that killed scores of civilians. President Obama had previously said the use of chemical weapons by the Assad regime would be a red line that, if crossed, would, many presumed, elicit a bold military response by the West. It did not happen. Instead, Moscow used the hesitation from Washington (and London) to insert itself diplomatically, which resulted in a UN-sanctioned agreement for the Syrian government to relinquish, under international supervision, its chemical stockpile and manufacturing facilities. Over the next months, with a number of stops and starts, it appeared that Damascus had met the terms of the agreement.

Bashar al-Assad had to feel at the time that he might be able to survive after all. He was receiving direct military support from Iran, Hizbullah, and Shiite militias from Iraq and as far afield as Afghanistan. Russia's political and economic support continued, and with President Vladimir Putin's diplomatic intervention on the chemical weapons deal, Putin's ability to support Syria was enhanced. Finally, from the perspective of Damascus, it appeared that the United States had made the decision that removing Assad would cause more trouble than it was worth. And the Syrian opposition, despite some gains here and there, still remained more fragmented than not.

The ebb and flow of the war continued. The regime appeared to rebound fairly nicely in late 2014 and early 2015, but it began to experience a series of losses on a variety of fronts in the spring and summer of 2015. A number of opposition groups, including Jabhat al-Nusra, Ahrar al-Sham, elements of what was left of the FSA, and other smaller militias combined and coordinated their efforts into a new organization called the Army of Conquest (Jaish al-Fateh). The fact that regional players, such as Saudi Arabia, Turkey, and Qatar, who had supported different (and often competing) Syrian opposition groups to date, began to align their support and cooperate more in their joint efforts to remove Assad certainly helped the cause. The Army of Conquest captured the provincial capital of Idlib (and most of the rest of the Idlib province) and some other strategic spots in northwestern Syria from government forces. On the other side to the east, Islamic State forces continued to expand their control of territory in several parts of eastern Syria, and most spectacularly took the city of Palmyra, home to incomparable Roman ruins, some of which have since been destroyed by ISIS.

The Syrian regime was on its heels. Evidence of this was a speech given by Bashar al-Assad in July 2015 in which he admitted for the first time that the government was running low on manpower and resources. Until then, the regime had always presented itself as the only entity in the war that could reconstitute Syria and restore stability. In the speech, however, Assad also admitted that, at least in the short term, government forces would not be able to regain lost territory. Once again, prognosticators had the regime on its last legs, losing as much from attrition as anything else.

And once again, the prognosticators were wrong. This time it wasn't the unexpected resilience of regime forces or significantly more Iranian or Hizbullah troops that came to the rescue. It was the Russians. On September 30, 2015, Russia, which for several weeks had been moving aircraft and support troops to regime-controlled territory outside Latakia, began a sustained air campaign against Syrian opposition positions. In essence, Russia became the Syrian air force. As a result, Syrian and progovernment forces were able to go on the offensive and retake some territory (including retaking Palmyra in March 2016), thus restoring the calculus for a stalemate. Indeed, such were the military successes by Russian-supported regime forces in the first quarter of 2016 that some analysts were commenting that the only side that could produce something resembling victory was the Syrian government.

With the military intervention, Putin made an emphatic statement, basically saying to those countries who have been supporting various Syrian opposition groups that Russia was not going to let the regime of Bashar al-Assad collapse, so if any of these countries wanted to continue backing opposition groups, they had better up the ante and be prepared for the long haul. If not, they should do what they should have done all along: shift their efforts toward ending the war itself by backing the Syrian government's fight against terrorists (broadly defined by Russia as anyone fighting the Syrian regime). Moscow could then preserve its strategic interests in Syria as well as secure a central role for itself in any sort of negotiated settlement that might ensue. If successful, Putin would stand tall, rehabilitate Russia's image following its military adventure in Ukraine, and perhaps bring an end to the subsequent international economic sanctions imposed by the West, resulting in a grateful Europe, itself reeling under the weight of thousands of Syrian refugees flooding into the continent as well as the threat of terrorism, so dramatically illustrated by the terrorist attacks in Paris on November 13, 2015, that killed 130 people and in Brussels on March 22, 2016, killing 36 people.

The Russian military intervention did, in fact, reactivate diplomacy. The narrative regarding Assad began to shift, as many of the anti-Assad states, including the United States, began to show more flexibility on whether or not the Syrian president had to vacate office during or immediately following a transition process (as outlined in the Geneva II communiqué of June 2012). The United States and Russia took the lead in convening a meeting in Vienna on October 30, 2015, composed of twenty stakeholder countries and groups in the Syrian civil war, including, for the first time in such a setting, Iran. A set of agreed-upon principles was drawn up along with a plan developed at a subsequent meeting on November 14 to bring Syrian opposition groups and the Syrian government together to negotiate a political transition in 2016, leading to a new constitution and elections within eighteen months. Negotiations brokered by the United Nations commenced in Geneva in early 2016 between an amalgam of acceptable Syrian opposition elements grouped together as the High Negotiations Committee (and pointedly not including the Islamic State or Jabhat al-Nusra—and, as a result of Turkish pressure, no Kurdish representation) and the Syrian government. But despite this diplomatic momentum into 2016, there were still enormous obstacles to overcome, including the ability of the Syrian opposition to present a somewhat united front; the seriousness of the Syrian government's commitment to the negotiations, especially as Assad was more securely in power following the Russian intervention; and overall the unpredictable vagaries of a war that has taken so many twists and turns to date.

Through all of this, Bashar al-Assad is still around as of this writing, and it is certainly possible that he could serve out his current term in office (to 2021) and possibly even beyond. He might therefore think that he made the right decision in March and April 2011. Whether it was right or wrong, the price to date has been 300,000 killed, half of the 22 million population either internally or externally displaced, and the utter destruction of cities and towns across the country.

Notes

1. Excerpts from this chapter first appeared in David W. Lesch, *Syria: The Fall of the House of Assad* (London: Yale University Press, 2013).

2. Unless otherwise noted, information gleaned from interviews was generated as part of the Harvard-NUPI Trinity Syria Research Project (hereafter HNT). I developed and organized this project in late 2012, sponsored by the Harvard Negotiation Project, the Norwegian Institute for International Affairs (NUPI), and Trinity University in San Antonio, Texas. The project was funded by the Swiss and Norwegian governments and was focused on meeting with top officials in most of the stakeholder countries and other entities involved in the Syrian conflict, including members of the Syrian government and elements of the Syrian opposition both in and outside Syria. A final report was produced in the fall of 2013, the full version available confidentially only to certain parties. An abridged version of the final report ("Obstacles to a Resolution of the Syrian Conflict") was more widely circulated and can be found at the Belfer Center for Science and International Affairs website, http://belfercenter.hks.harvard.edu/publication/23675/obstacles_to_a_resolution_of_the_syrian_conflict.html. Some of the notes for this chapter include the date and location of the referenced interview; others do not because that information could reveal the identity of the interviewee.

3. I have yet to find this so-called more lenient version of the speech, if it even exists anymore, and I have not found any details of exactly what concessions Assad might have offered in this version. A *New York Times* article stated that, "according to [Syrian] officials, the speech . . . will offer significant political concessions, including the lifting of laws that restrict civil and political freedoms." Michael Slackman, "Syria's Cabinet Resigns: Concessions Expected," *New York Times*, March 29, 2011, www.nytimes.com/2011/03/30/world/middleeast/30syria.html. Also, the Syrian government, probably the Ministry of Information, sent excerpts of Assad's speech to some reporters in the West. Apparently these snippets reflected the more proreform verion of the speech rather than the harsher version, lending credence to the idea that the final form of the speech was not decided upon by Assad until just prior to his delivery of it (my thanks to Andrew Tabler for this information).

4. Jay Soloman and Bill Spindle, "Syria Strongman: Time for Reform," *Wall Street Journal*, January 31, 2011.

5. Sami Moubayed, "Lesson from Egypt: West Is Not Best," *Forward Magazine* 48 (February 2011): 4; and Bouthaina Shaaban, "The Real Evils Plaguing the Region," *Forward Magazine* 48 (February 2011): 16.

6. In February 1982, Syrian government forces bombarded and launched a ferocious attack on the city of Hama, which had been the center of Muslim Brotherhood resistance against the secular, Alawite-minority, Ba'th-ruled regime led by Hafiz al-Assad, Bashar's father. The Muslim Brotherhood and the Syrian government had been engaged in what some described as a mini–civil war since 1979. Assad decided to put an end to the Muslim Brotherhood resistance once and for all with the attack on Hama, which may have

killed upward of 20,000. Although it worked from the Syrian government's perspective, the memory of Hama still lives on in the minds of many of the Sunni rebel fighters in the current civil war who are bent on revenge for what happened in 1982.

7. Interview with a former high-level Syrian government official who received the results of the studies and discussed them with Assad, HNT.

8. Interview with a European diplomat present in Damascus in the early stages of the uprising, HNT.

9. As one activist who knew Bashar al-Assad well before joining the opposition said, "Bashar and his guys prepared for this fight before and they choose this fight. Everyone repositioned after Egypt. The cards were already shuffled; everyone wants to make the game for their side. Everyone prepared for the fight before it started. They are too smart to hesitate." Interview with opposition activist, Gaziantep, Turkey, December 2012, HNT.

10. Interviews with several former high-level Syrian government officials intimately engaged in the decisionmaking at the time, HNT.

11. Interview with top regime insider in Beirut, Lebanon, January 2015.

12. Interview with former high-level Syrian official, HNT.

13. Opposition elements were not the only ones disappointed in the speech, as a number of regime officials were unhappy with it or at least surprised by it. One top former Syrian official close to Assad said, "Normally, when he [Assad] makes a speech, he calls people back to listen to the vibes, and normally after tens of people would come and tell him 'wow,' but no one called this time." Interview with former Syrian government official, February 2013, HNT.

14. Interview with Hizbullah figure, Beirut, August 2013, HNT.

15. Interview with Syrian opposition activist, Gaziantep, Turkey, December 2012, HNT.

16. Interview with former high-level Syrian government official, HNT.

17. Ibid.

18. Interview with former high-level Syrian military figure, HNT.

19. For instance, on March 25, 2011, Syrian minister of information Muhsin Bilal said, "The situation is completely calm in all parts of the country." Alarabiya.net, "Deaths Reported as Protests Erupt Across Syria," Al Arabiya News, March 25, 2011, www.alarabiya.net/articles/2011/03/25/142927.html. A month later, a Syrian official was quoted as saying, "We will have a few months of difficult times, but I don't think it will go further. . . . It will be a period of unrest and not an overthrow of the regime. That is highly improbable." Ian Black, "Six Syrians Who Helped Bashar al-Assad Keep Iron Grip After Father's Death," *Guardian*, April 28, 2011, www.theguardian.com/world/2011/apr/28/syria-bashar-assad-regime-members. And "the state-run Syrian Arab News Agency reported that normal life had returned to all Syrian provinces." Neil Macfarquhar and Liam Stack, "Syrian Protesters Clash with Security Forces," *New York Times*, April 1, 2011, www.nytimes.com/2011/04/02/world/middleeast/02syria.html.

5

How Saudi Arabia Has Dodged the Arab Spring

Steve A. Yetiv

T HE SO-CALLED ARAB SPRING has taken a complicated turn since it launched in various different incarnations across the Middle East in 2010–2011. But, while the Arab Spring has transformed into a cornucopia of struggles and conflicts that raise the specter of state disintegration and even failures, Saudi Arabia has remained largely immune. When the Arab Spring started to catch fire at the regional level, concerns existed around the world that Saudi Arabia might also face serious instability. Unlike in Tunisia, Egypt, or even Libya, trouble in the Kingdom created the specter of much higher oil prices, which could send the American and global economy into a recession. Eyes were focused on even minor events in Saudi Arabia, such as a proposed rally in the eastern al-Hasa oil province. This instability never materialized, even though the Shia had some legitimate claims[1] and even though Riyadh, insinuating that Iran was to blame, acknowledged on October 4, 2011, that it had faced violent clashes with Shia in the eastern city of Qatif in which eleven officers had been wounded.

Much scholarly attention focuses on why the Arab Spring has largely produced quite negative results,[2] but it is also interesting to ask why it did not gain ground in the first place in some countries. In particular, why has it not so far come to Saudi Arabia? After all, real pressures for reform have already mounted there over at least the past two decades,[3] and even before the September 11 terrorist attacks, many thinkers argued that the Saudi regime faced serious internal problems and could even fall eventually.

113

After 9/11, concerns about Saudi stability were raised anew and have persisted.[4] This is partly because, as is now well known, Osama bin Laden was born and raised in Saudi Arabia, as were fifteen of the nineteen hijackers and hundreds of Afghan Arabs trained in Bin Laden's terrorist camps. They were uneasy products of the Saudi cultural, political, and religious milieu, a milieu largely shaped, controlled, or tolerated by the Saudi royal family. These realities made it easy to conclude that the profound anti-Americanism of the September 11 attackers had deep roots in a state that the United States considered an ally and on which the world counted for oil stability.

The regime has also had to deal with a population that is increasingly better educated and more connected to the world, especially to the Arab world, through the Internet and television. This creates greater potential for political activism and antiregime sentiment. Most political groups have simply wanted the Saudi regime to reform itself and to become less corrupt, but others have sought its outright overthrow.[5] While some scholars tried to explain why regimes have been stable in the Gulf, it became more common among scholars and analysts to predict trouble for the House of Saud.[6]

For a variety of reasons, I argue that the Arab Spring was "springless" in Saudi Arabia. Saudi Arabia is a rentier state that uses its oil monies in various ways to bolster its regime. Saudi Arabia has also been more stable than most observers believe, and these elements of stability have helped anchor the regime through these stormy times. We should also consider that the late King Abdullah was much more popular than other Arab autocrats, that the Saudis have strong control over their institutions, and that Riyadh has become more proactive in its foreign policy in challenging would-be plotters and instigators. Not insignificantly, the House of Saud also is not under much pressure from the United States and other countries to democratize in any serious way. Quite the contrary, the West probably prefers a slow or even no evolution over any destabilizing changes. In addition, Iran and al-Qaida and the radical forces that may sympathize with them became less—not more—able to undermine the Al Saud over time and were largely neutralized in the Arab Spring.

This chapter first develops the oil argument and then proceeds to identify these elements of stability to which I refer. The thrust of this argument is not that the Kingdom has been immune to domestic and international instabilities but rather that it appears to have coping mechanisms that, heretofore at least, have worked.

OIL POWER AND DOMESTIC STABILITY

It is fair to say that oil has suppressed democratic sentiment, probably helping explain why non-oil-rich states in the Middle East faced the most serious uprisings.[7] The modern state of Saudi Arabia, founded in 1932 by Abd al-Aziz al-Saud (also referred to as Ibn Saud), has managed a major transformation, after the territory of the present-day country was carved out largely through war and conquest in the eighteenth and early nineteenth centuries. Saudi Arabia is the only state with proven oil reserves at one-quarter of the world's total, the potential to produce consistently above its market production, and the field production and pipeline capacity to add significant amounts of oil to the world market, especially in a fairly short period of time. It is therefore especially interesting in terms of the oil-nondemocracy connection.

Democratic theorists have long struggled to explain what facilitates and sustains democratization. They have identified many variables, ranging from education to political culture, levels of hierarchical government, war, regime type, and elites. Most explanations of democratic reforms in the Middle East link the process of political change to economic crises, but wealth is one of the general conditions viewed as favorable to democracy worldwide. Yet most of the monarchies of the Middle East are oil-rich. Based on the variable of wealth, we would expect them to tend toward democracy, all other things being equal. How can we explain that they are oil-rich and democracy-poor?

Many scholars have found that oil is an impediment to democratization.[8] This literature can help illuminate how oil has impeded the Arab Spring. Terry Karl has argued that oil wealth in particular, and natural resource wealth more generally, leads almost inexorably to authoritarian or autocratic government or at least is negatively correlated with democracy, democratization, or, more broadly, political participation and accountability.[9] Using pooled time-series cross-national data from 113 states between 1971 and 1997, political scientist Michael Ross has supported this general finding via the use of regression analysis.[10] Meanwhile, economist Kevin K. Tsui, using a different methodology based on actual oil resources, has found that states that discover 100 billion barrels of oil (approximately the initial endowment of Iraq) achieve a level of democracy that is almost 20 percentage points below trend after three decades. Tsui also varied the size of oil fields and the quality of the oil discovered to see if either affects democratization. He found that the estimated effect is larger for oil fields with higher-quality oil and lower exploration and extraction costs. However, he believes that the estimates are less precise when oil abundance is measured by oil discovery per capita, and he interprets this finding to mean that politicians may care about the raw level instead of the per capita value of oil wealth.[11]

The Arab world experienced a liberal phase in the nineteenth and early twentieth centuries, which may well have been reversed, in part due to increasing oil discoveries, in the 1950s and 1960s.[12] The biggest oil producers in the region have the worst records on democracy. Freedom House, a nonpartisan American human rights group, ranks only Kuwait as partially free and the United Arab Emirates, Iran, Iraq, and Saudi Arabia as not free or as absolute dictatorships.[13] Kuwait has the best record among these countries, but it ranks lower in the democratic rankings than a number of Muslim states that lack oil, including Turkey, Bosnia, Albania, and resource-poor Bangladesh.

Oil is not necessary for autocratic government in the Middle East—or elsewhere, for that matter. For instance, former Syrian president Hafiz al-Assad would have gone to great lengths to have Kuwait's oil but had no problem dominating his own people. However, several explanations exist for the oil connection to nondemocracy.

Economists have pointed to the notion of "Dutch disease," whereby major revenue in a single sector of the economy can raise the exchange rate, which reduces the competitiveness of other sectors of the economy and impedes diversification. It has also been argued that dependency on a single commodity is an unsustainable route to development because of the likelihood of declining terms of trade.

Beyond economics, a common explanation for why Gulf states such as Saudi Arabia lack parliaments is encapsulated in rentier state theory. The theory, which predicts that oil states will not democratize, appears to be borne out by some important surveys and studies. The basic assumption is that wealth generated from rents, which can come from oil or any other good, produces a negative and different impact on democracy than wealth generated by a diversified economy.[14] Nathan Jensen and Leonard Wantchekon point out that a rentier state is characterized by high dependence on external rents produced by a few economic resources, not from production (labor), investment (interest), or management of risk (profit).[15] Rentier economies obtain most of their monies from foreign sources based on one good, which they sell at a much higher price than it costs them to produce it. A minority of their people generates the rent and also controls it, while the majority is involved only in its distribution and use.[16] Some democracies also benefit from external rents from energy and other exports, but these funds are treated differently. They are often managed professionally and are not used for political means. By contrast, in authoritarian regimes, most of these rent monies are controlled by and bolster the elites.

A prominent version of the theory posits that these states lack parliaments because their enormous oil resources free them from having to tax their citizens and also allow them to provide major services to their citizens free of cost.[17] As a result, they do not have to bargain with their citizens, which is the purpose of parliaments and which is one of the main reasons that they arise in the first place. These states are not accountable to the citizenry, which cannot demand representation.[18] Without the need for accountability to the wider population, they solidify their autocratic control, with the state surviving on rents captured from the oil industry.

Oil rents can also be used by oil-rich regimes to placate dissent, thus stifling democratic impulses, as some scholars have found in earlier studies. Oil monies can help obtain allegiance from individuals and groups that otherwise would be much more unpredictable and even volatile, including Islamists who seek to impose their own form of power, as has occurred across the Middle East.[19]

These rents may even block the formation of independent social groups that can become the bedrock of democratization. For instance, facing rigid state control, organized labor groups have been destroyed in the Persian Gulf due to the oil boom, whereas once they were the backbone of nationalist movements.[20]

Beyond suppressing democratic sentiments from which an Arab Spring could spring, oil monies also allow for controlling and cracking down on dissent if it does start to develop.[21] In fact, the Saudi regime drew on oil monies to placate potential dissenters who sought to join their Arab brethren in challenging autocratic rule in Saudi Arabia. The late King Abdullah reacted to the Arab Spring by ordering the spending of $130 billion on social benefits, housing, and jobs in efforts to quell dissent, especially from the Shiite minority. Such "riyal" diplomacy has been the modus operandi for the royal family, and it has probably placated at least some of the regime's most serious detractors. For example, in 1979, the Saudi regime was threatened. It faced a massive Iranian-inspired Shiite uprising in the oil-rich eastern province and the seizure by

Islamic zealots of the Grand Mosque at Mecca. The Saudis suppressed the revolt and then appeased the Shia with riyal diplomacy, as they are doing now to preserve stability. If it is true that Arab societies have been unable to meet the expectations of their populations,[22] that has been less a problem in Saudi Arabia due to oil wealth.

Oil-rich regimes have been more effective at deterring attempts to unseat them, and that effectiveness is related to oil.[23] On the whole, the Arab Spring unseated just one oil-rich ruler—Libya's Muammar al-Gadafi—and he might well have succeeded in suppressing dissent were it not for his clumsy threats to wipe out the dissenters and NATO's decision, behind the United States and France, to intervene on behalf of the rebels.

LEADERSHIP

Another key reason that the Saudis have not faced an Arab Spring movement has to do with their leadership, which adds to structural control of the society.[24] The Saudis have faced myriad domestic problems, and the royal family is highly disliked in some quarters. However, it is clear that the late King Abdullah, who shepherded the kingdom through the first years of the Arab Spring in the region, was far more respected than was Egypt's former president Husni Mubarak, or many other leaders in the Middle East, for that matter. Indeed, a survey conducted May 18 to June 16, 2009, by the Pew Research Center's Global Attitudes Project found him to be the most popular leader in Muslim countries. About 92 percent of Jordanians and 83 percent of Egyptians said they had complete confidence that King Abdullah would do the right things in international affairs. King Abdullah received positive ratings outside the Middle East as well, especially in largely Muslim Asian nations, such as Pakistan (64 percent) and Indonesia (61 percent).[25]

Moreover, Saudi norms militate against internal dissension, the likes of which could produce openings for regime critics. Differences have usually been reconciled within the ruling elite of the royal family, divided between the Sudeiri family and the other sons of Ibn Saud. In essence, the country is governed by key senior royal family members—and not just the king—with varying levels of importance, depending much on their lineage, position, and access. Decisionmaking has rarely been unilateral but rather has been done through a custom of consensus and consultation, which play a central role in most serious matters of domestic as well as foreign policy.

In addition to such norms, the royal family has a good sense of how to survive. Although it has been split on certain issues ranging from how to deal with domestic turmoil to managing relations with the West, the longevity of the regime has remained enviable by almost any standard. The Saudis face some serious domestic problems, which have been exacerbated by the transition to new leadership and which cannot be discounted, but they have also faced real difficulties in the past.

In addition to traditional forms of oppressive state control, the regime has used a variety of strategies to quell domestic opposition and decrease potential internal conflicts. King Fahd, for instance, took effective steps to shore up his relations with the other tribal leaders from the Nejd, his historical base.[26] Abdullah was well situated to reconcile tribal and traditional pressures with the pressures of modernization and Western ties, though it remains unclear to what extent King Salman, who took over from Abdullah in January 2015, will prove equally adept.

Riyadh has adopted a number of "evolutionary" strategies designed to accommodate various critics of the regime. These efforts, modest as they are, have included since 2003 the convening of a series of "National Dialogues" designed to foster increased tolerance and rights, including for ethnic and religious minorities; widespread educational reform; enhanced rights for women in a number of areas; and an antiterrorism campaign aimed at delegitimizing violence.[27]

In addition, unlike in Iran in 1979, the Saudis also have benefited from the fact that geography makes it hard for a large opposition to unite. The Shia of the eastern al-Hasa province have been a source of anti-Western fervor, but they represent 10 percent of the population and are not only religiously but also geographically distant from other Saudi groups.

It certainly doesn't hurt that the royal family sits above the world's largest proven oil reserves. Riyadh faces short-term and possibly longer-run economic problems, but these reserves can work in its favor over time. In addition, deposits in Western banks are enough to allow Riyadh to guarantee its external financial obligations, and the government ministry could also draw on the royal family's massive, undisclosed international investment portfolio, which may exceed one-half trillion dollars. The Saudis, despite their economic problems, have amassed major financial reserves. The purposes of the fund are to allow the country to weather any period of low oil prices and to help stabilize domestic politics through such difficult times.

The regime has also been careful not to threaten the interests of substantial segments of the population. This caution has made it harder for an anti-regime coalition that crosses tribal, class, and religious boundaries to arise. Key religious, technocratic, and tribal leaders and factions have been allowed to maintain their positions of influence and to offer informal input into the decisionmaking structure. The September 11 attacks and the campaign on terrorism, however, have forced the regime to confront the trade-offs between cracking down on those suspected of supporting al-Qaida and losing political support in some circles that are sympathetic to al-Qaida, and between curbing religious extremism and maintaining good relations with some key mullahs.

The pressure for political reform will undoubtedly continue, as will the challenges of dealing with such questions. Such pressures can produce the positive outcome of forcing the regime to liberalize slowly without threatening a violent and destabilizing upheaval. But in any case, the Saudis do not have to be as concerned as in the past that such political challenges will be stoked and intensified by revolutionary Iran, for reasons discussed later.

ROYAL FAMILY CONTROL OF INSTITUTIONS

Ousting the royal family would require a revolution or coup. Yet, as suggested earlier, the military, like all institutions in the country, is penetrated and controlled by the thousands of princes who constitute the broader backbone of the royal family; more than seven hundred are direct descendants of Ibn Saud, and approximately four hundred are key. Revolutionaries must penetrate that hierarchical structure and develop serious alternatives to it for governance at the same time. It may well be that al-Qaida sympathizers exist in the military, but penetrating it enough to gain any influence is no easy feat. It is doubtful, in any case, that the foot soldiers of revolution currently even exist, despite rising socioeconomic and political dislocation and despite the fact that 50 percent of the Saudi population is under age eighteen.

A new generation of more politically active and disgruntled Saudis has emerged, but even many of them have shown limited enthusiasm for radical or violent change.[28] Even if they did fathom such scenarios, it is not clear that they could muster the numbers to make a difference. In that respect, Saudi Arabia is not Iran. While the forces of extremism are afoot, regimes are not overthrown by rhetoric, demonstrations, or even terror alone. Mass grassroots activity is needed, or military officers must coordinate if the deed is to be done by military coup. For grassroots activity to emerge, the regime usually has to be widely viewed as illegitimate at the core. And unlike the shah of Iran, who was viewed as enabled, controlled, and propped up by the United States, the Saudi royal family, as I noted at the outset, has the dubious distinction of having forged the state on the bloody anvil of brutal conquest.

Saudi Arabia is also different from Egypt and other Arab countries in that its institutions are not equally penetrated by royal families or the families of their current or former dictators. Mubarak had influence with the military, but his family did not run it, which was also true, for instance, of Gadafi.

A Cautionary Note: Learning from Chaos

The Saudis, already happier with their lot than most Arabs, have also now seen the effects of uprisings in other countries. This may be a further antidote to a revolutionary uprising in the Kingdom, even if one cannot rule out a combustible set of circumstances that might ignite it. These circumstances could include the strains of lower oil prices following Riyadh's decision not to cut oil production in November 2014, 2015, and well into 2016; disgruntled princes in the royal family; the rise of greater opposition among Salafis and members of the Ulema;[29] and more effective meddling by Iran and the Islamic State, which bombed Saudi sites in 2015.

However, insofar as those in and outside the al-Hasa province even contemplate a rebellion or coup, they would have to compare their current position, buttressed by oil-related benefits, to what might arise in a post–House of Saud Kingdom. Opponents and even lukewarm supporters of the royal family must consider that toppling the regime could leave them even less able to realize their goals. They could face internal chaos, be outmaneuvered by other forces filling the void, and lose present contacts with the regime. It is one thing to topple a regime and another to create a workable alternative. Democratic forces must fear that nondemocratic forces could hijack any movement toward greater democracy, and each segment of society, including competing factions within the religious establishment, must wonder how its interests will fare in such an upheaval.

Concerns about what type of regime would replace the royal family, and the absence of any clear and preferred alternative, create a serious logic of vested interests that works against significant shifts in the status quo.

The recent lessons of the Arab uprisings in other countries would give even the most ardent revolutionaries pause. Would they risk catastrophe, as other states in the region are experiencing, for a modest chance of changing the status quo? To gain substantial traction for a serious challenge, they would have to convince many people that they could succeed and generate a better Saudi Arabia than currently exists.

AN ACTIVE FOREIGN POLICY

Saudi Arabia played an unprecedented role as an interventionist state throughout the Arab Spring, working hard to manage events across the region.[30] In no place was this clearer than in Bahrain. Indeed, Saudi forces, under the rubric of acting on behalf of the Gulf Cooperation Council, moved into Bahrain. Why did Saudi tanks roll across the border to help put down the mass uprising that threatened the powers that be in neighboring Bahrain? It lent the Saudi-backed Sunni monarchy in Manama the muscle it needed to keep control of its Shia-majority population and, in turn, its hold on power. More importantly, Saudi intervention stifled momentum in Saudi Arabia's oil-rich eastern province among the newly restive Shia minority, who might have sought a repeat performance of what was occurring in Bahrain. This province had been the locus of several massive demonstrations against the regime, especially in 1979, when it appeared as if the regime were unstable enough to fall.

Could the Saudis have intervened with force in an unprecedented manner had Riyadh not been oil-rich? Possibly, but they likely would have faced global pressure not to do so, and the Saudis might well have faced their own internal insurrection, which they would have had a harder time suppressing without the requisite oil resources and largesse.

Since its 2011 uprisings, Bahrain has continued to face resistance, which far predated the Arab Spring in any case. But it has not been violent and has contrasted sharply with what has occurred in other Arab societies, including civil and sectarian strife and war, the rise of terrorist groups, and foreign military intervention.[31]

Beyond Bahrain, Riyadh has also been proactive in using foreign policy approaches to try to diminish forces that might ignite a domestic uprising, and its oil largesse has helped fund this expensive effort. The 1979 Iranian revolution generated fears in Riyadh and around the world that the Al Saud could be destabilized or even overthrown by Shiite fervor emanating from Iran. Those fears proved overdrawn, but legitimate concerns about an Iranian-inspired Shiite threat have continued[32] and have been stoked by the fall of Saddam's Iraq as a bulwark against Iran.

King Salman has largely continued, perhaps even more doggedly, Abdullah's foreign policy aimed in part at stemming Iranian-fueled Shiite power in the Middle East. These efforts range from trying to overthrow the Iranian-supported Syrian dictator to stabilizing Bahrain to intervening in Yemen's political struggles. Indeed, the fall of Yemeni president Abd Rabdu Mansour Hadi's government boosted the pro-Iranian, anti-American Shiite militia in Yemen. While it is very unlikely that Yemen's instability could ignite an uprising in the Kingdom, Riyadh started a campaign against the Shiite Houthis in March 2015 that included the creation of a coalition of Sunni Muslim states and involved sustained military attacks. These attacks, which were unprecedented in Saudi foreign policy, involved air and ground forces and appeared to diminish Houthi power and standing, albeit it is hard to predict to what extent the crisis can be resolved. It has certainly proved to be a greater and more costly struggle than the Saudis anticipated.

The Al Saud must also contend with radical Sunni groups that seek its demise, including the Islamic State, which openly calls for a caliphate in place of the royal family and has bombed targets inside the kingdom. After initially contributing indirectly to the rise of the Islamic State, Riyadh has sought to contain it, while not undermining the Sunni check on Iranian-backed Shiite militias in Iraq.

THE LACK OF EXTERNAL PRESSURE

We have much to learn about the United States and the Western role in the Arab Spring, and it will take years to gain a sound understanding. However, it is clear that the United States and its allies played a major role in some Arab revolts, but not in Saudi Arabia or Bahrain. Libya is the most obvious case. The NATO allies mounted a rather large military intervention, and some Western states were at the forefront in recognizing the Libyan transitional government, with France taking the lead. For many reasons, such action would never have been launched in Saudi Arabia or Bahrain. Nor would the United States have seriously criticized these governments for crackdowns on protesters unless they had become truly grotesque, in which case such verbal protests might have been launched.

To be sure, the Arab Spring generated Saudi-American tensions because the Saudis were furious when Washington failed to support Husni Mubarak of Egypt, and Washington raised issues when Saudi tanks rolled into Bahrain, despite the fact that such action helped stabilize global oil prices. Nonetheless, in December 2011, in what was hardly a show of disdain, Washington announced an agreement to sell F-15 fighter jets valued at nearly $30 billion to the Royal Saudi Air Force as part of a broader ten-year, $60 billion arms package that Congress had approved in 2010.

But can the absence of external pressures explain why the Arab Spring did not take off in Saudi Arabia? That's debatable, but it is fair to argue that local dissenters may take cues or gain ballast from outside powers. They may also receive material support and information as well as communications support. Local actors don't act in a vacuum. Conflicts do not occur in isolation in an interconnected world. Local actors see what others think of their plight, and those others can engage in the conflict, even as third-party actors or even bystanders. Even if military support or other forms of assistance are absent, third-party actors can affect the discursive environment in which local actors perceive their fight. And they can also use various levers to try to influence the government directly.

IRAN LESS ABLE TO EXPLOIT THE ARAB SPRING TO UNDERMINE SAUDI ARABIA

Within the region, the Saudis have been as concerned as Israel about Iran's nuclear aspirations and the rise of a Shiite arc of crisis—and they certainly have reason to be concerned. However, Iran arguably has become less able to stir discontent in the Kingdom than in the past. Were the opposite true, Iran could have stoked antiregime sentiment that may well have contributed to Arab Spring–like behavior in the Kingdom.

The 1979 Iranian revolution increased the internal threat to Saudi stability, partly by bedeviling Saudi-Iranian relations. Relations were complex at many levels, but at the core, Saudi Arabia's monarchical form of government, generally pro-Western tilt, and conservative outlook clashed with Iran's post-revolutionary clerical rule, anti-Western bent, and revisionist foreign policy. Indeed, the Saudis viewed Ayatollah Rouhollah Mousavi Khomeini as a heretic with a proclivity for violence.[33] Saudi legitimacy rested on the regime's role as the guardian of the two most holy sites of Islam, namely Mecca, the birthplace of Islam, and Medina, where the prophet Muhammad launched his mission in God's service. Unlike Pahlevi Iran, revolutionary Iran challenged Riyadh's claim to be the champion of Islam by offering an alternative Islamic model that rejected the monarchical, Islamic state and offered a theocratic one in its place. The clash between these two approaches to Islamic governance created frictions in Saudi-Iranian relations that were dramatized by the Iran-Iraq War and erupted in earnest in July 1987 over the annual pilgrimage to Mecca.

Several notable efforts were made to undermine Saudi authority in 1979. The first was in November 1979 when the Grand Mosque in Mecca was seized by several hundred armed zealots who launched an Islamic uprising to protest corruption in the royal family. The protests were small but important in that they represented the first open attack on the credibility and conduct of the royal family since the reign of Ibn Saud in 1927.[34] That prompted predictions of the fall of the royal family. With outside assistance, the Saudi National Guard successfully suppressed these zealots. But the Al Saud were concerned enough over the Mecca fallout to agree to a set of resolutions condemning the United States for its role at Camp David in the hope that this would bolster the Kingdom's credentials in the Muslim world.[35]

Eight days after the seizure of the Grand Mosque, while the Saudi National Guard was still battling the zealots at Mecca, the disturbances that erupted in Saudi Arabia's oil-rich eastern province were viewed as serious enough by the royal family that it dispatched 20,000 troops to the area. The Mecca incident further cast Saudi stability and the Kingdom's role as a pillar of Gulf security into doubt.[36]

Further clashes broke out in September and October 1981 in Medina and Mecca, respectively, between Iranian pilgrims and Saudi police. Iranian officials claimed that these disturbances were indeed an export of the Iranian revolution, aimed at destabilizing the Saudi regime. Shortly thereafter, in December 1981, Bahraini authorities arrested and subsequently convicted seventy-three individuals for plotting a coup against the regime. Bahrain charged that the coup was part of a broader strategy to overthrow the House of Saud as well and that the coup plotters at a minimum had direct connections to Tehran.[37] This came as no great surprise since Khomeini had repeatedly assailed the Gulf monarchies for being illegitimate and corrupt.

Riyadh faced the ongoing potential for Iranian-inspired subversion, but it was not until 1987 that this was manifested in stark relief. The annual pilgrimage to Mecca was disrupted by a riot touched off when Saudi security units moved in to stop a forbidden political demonstration by Iranian pilgrims in front of the Grand Mosque. Despite considerable evidence to the contrary, Iran's president, Hashemi Rafsanjani, a close friend of Khomeini's from his early days in exile and later a key adviser, denied that Iran had instigated the subversion. He asserted that the Saudis were to blame and called on Iranians as "the implementers of divine principles" to overthrow the Saudi royal family in revenge.[38] This caused alarm across the Gulf and in certain Western quarters. Iran, which competed with Saudi Arabia for leadership of the Islamic world, wanted once again to destabilize Saudi Arabia and challenge its rule over Islam's holy places. The Mecca crisis pushed the Saudis to sever relations with Iran.[39]

Over time, Iran lost some ability and will to foment instability in Saudi Arabia, partly due to the Iran-Iraq War. Iran's war failures gave moderate elements in Iran a chance to advance their political agenda. By arousing fear and focusing attention on Iran's revolution, the war made it more difficult for Khomeini to spread Islamic fundamentalism without provoking considerable alarm. Had Iraq not attacked Iran in 1980, Tehran could have spread Islamic fundamentalism in a nonmilitary and less provocative fashion, behind the tacit threat of its feared military hand. The war forced Iran to play this hand and to deplete its military arsenal.

By 1987, Iran was more concerned with consolidating and protecting the revolution within its own borders than with exporting Islam, and the Saudis were clear beneficiaries of that trend. By the late 1980s, Iran's political and economic agendas were dominated by talk about the importance of attracting foreign investment, enhancing foreign trade, and improving relations with the West.[40] These concerns were driven by the imperatives of postwar reconstruction and by Iran's dependence on oil revenues.

To be sure, Riyadh views Iran as a serious threat across the Middle East from Bahrain to Syria. The nuclear accord agreed to by Washington and Tehran in July 2015 has added to Riyadh's concerns, even if it has appeared to accept the agreement in public. Moreover, Tehran still calls for the overthrow of the Saudi monarchy. Yet, despite the ongoing Iranian threat in the region, Riyadh arguably has less to worry about now in terms of Iran's internal subversion than in the decade following the Iranian revolution. In those times, many analysts thought that the regime could fall altogether.

AL-QAIDA DIMINISHED

Anti-American views were prominent in Saudi Arabia well before 9/11, but those events highlighted them. The attacks threatened to reveal growing fissures in Saudi society and accentuate antiregime fervor. But much has changed since then, and al-Qaida and those who sympathize with it appear to have been weakened in the past decade, perhaps significantly.

Osama bin Laden, for his part, repeatedly asserted his diatribe against the presence of "infidel" forces in the land of Mecca and Medina. In his words, it was "not permitted for non-Muslims to stay in Arabia."[41] That the Saudi regime allowed US forces entry in 1991 and let some forces stay thereafter motivated Bin Laden and other Saudis who opposed the regime.

Throughout history, Islamic rulers have faced the potential of being challenged by those who portray themselves as better or purer Muslims. Bin Laden's austere existence, his invective against Western corruption, and his puritanical position on excluding infidels from Saudi land contrasted sharply with the profligacy of Saudi princes, the royal family's connection to Washington, and the allowance of US forces on Saudi territory. It is no doubt true that his sentiments struck a chord in the Saudi body politic, which exhibited quite negative views of the United States. Such anti-American views are not surprising given that most Saudis are nursed on a strict diet of religious education anchored in the extremist Wahhabi sect of Islam, sometimes referred to as Saudi Islam, an education that is perpetuated and enforced by the state. This extreme sect draws inspiration from the teachings of Muhhamad bin Abd al-Wahhab, who spread his message throughout the eighteenth century until his death in 1787.

Wahhabism takes different forms, but prominent among them is the notion that non-Muslims should not be present on Saudi soil and that aggressive jihad against them can be justified, even mandated. This does not mean that Wahhabism should necessarily spawn terrorism, a notion widely rejected by Saudi authorities, whose brand of Wahhabism differs from that of Salafism practiced by Bin Laden and his cohorts, but it could have done so.

Transnational terrorism and the appeal of Islamic extremists represent an ongoing risk factor, even though the al-Qaida movement has weakened. Systematic polling data from 2002 to 2008, as well as surveys in 2011 from the Pew Research Center's Global Attitudes Project,[42] showed that confidence in Bin Laden and al-Qaida had waned in the Muslim world well before his assassination by US Navy SEALs in 2011. Despite his death, these data can tell us something about transnational terrorism. The surveys strongly suggest that the message of al-Qaida and Bin Laden was increasingly ignored. The data are also important inasmuch as they may well indicate that radicals in the Muslim world, beyond just the terrorists, have lost influence relative to moderates, though the rise of the Islamic State shows that extremists can still wield power disproportionate to their numbers. Nevertheless, the support of moderate views suggests that the uprisings and revolutions in the Middle East, even if fraught with setbacks in the coming years, may have a greater chance of success than would otherwise be the case.

Al-Qaida increasingly has faced financial stress but, like its offshoots, shown some signs of adaptation. Witness the moves toward a partial diversification of income, including drug money, and toward the partial morphing of the organization into various local affiliates. While al-Qaida continued to gain monies in the oil-rich Persian Gulf, global cooperation in shutting down its funding also improved. Adding to its problems, al-Qaida also largely lost its base in Afghanistan and has been on the move, with many of its senior leaders killed by American forces and drone attacks.

What these developments suggest is that al-Qaida was not in a good position to stoke the Arab Spring in Saudi Arabia for purposes of undermining the regime. Had it been stronger, it might well have added some impetus for more serious uprisings against the Al Saud or at least contributed to the seeds of domestic discontent or indirectly encouraged other antiregime forces to take a stronger role.

CONCLUSION

The Arab Spring has shaken the Middle East at its core and raised myriad questions about its leaders, societies, and future direction. That the Arab Spring did not come to Saudi Arabia is a fascinating issue, even though we cannot predict the future and cannot tell what will happen in the coming years. It would, in fact, be surprising if Saudi Arabia escaped the buffeting winds of Middle East change and did not see some increased domestic upheaval. Yet, whatever does occur in the future, the issue of why Saudi Arabia was immune to the Arab Spring while other countries were not is notable.

I argue that oil wealth has been the most important factor in keeping the Arab Spring at bay. This is due to its own independent effects and also because it is tied to other crucial dynamics such as leadership and institutional control, the ability to act in foreign policy, and diminished global pressure on the Saudis to change their politics. This finding means something for the broader literature. Many scholars have found that oil impedes democratization, and this study fits into that genre. Insofar as oil monies helped insulate the Kingdom from the impulses of the Arab Spring, it helped the Al Saud prevent various manifestations of democratization that other Arab countries experienced, including freedom of expression and assembly, public rallies, antiregime statements and fervor, calls for greater suffrage and human rights protections, and uproar against ingrained and unjustified institutions of repression or status quo maintenance. Future work might do well to consider more methodically the relationship between oil wealth or oil trade as a percentage of GDP, on the one hand, and levels of democratization or antiregime activity during the Arab Spring, on the other. That could further test the oil-nondemocratization link and what it means for Middle East politics and security, and for America's foreign policy toward the region and that of other outside powers as well.

NOTES

1. On the Shia, see Toby Matthiessen, "A 'Saudi Spring?': The Shi'a Protest Movement in the Eastern Province 2011–2012," *Middle East Journal* 66, 4 (Autumn 2012): 628–659.

2. See, for instance, Jason Brownlee, Tarek Masoud, and Andrew Reynolds, *The Arab Spring: Pathways of Repression and Reform* (New York: Oxford University Press, 2015).

3. As one report shows, Saudi Arabia faces dissent but few major challenges. See Anthony H. Cordesman, "Saudi Stability in a Time of Change," (Washington, DC: Center for Strategic and International Studies, April 21, 2011), http://csis.org/files/publication/110421_saudi_stability_change.pdf. Also see Mai Yamani, "The Two Faces of Saudi Arabia," *Survival* 50 (February-March 2008): 143–156.

4. See John E. Peterson, *Saudi Arabia and the Illusion of Security* (London: Oxford University Press for the International Institute for Strategic Studies, 2002).

5. On such challenges, see Bernard Haykel, Thomas Hegghammer, and Stéphane Lacroix, eds., *Saudi Arabia in Transition: Insights on Social, Political, Economic and Religious Change* (Cambridge: Cambridge University Press, 2015); and Leigh Nolan, "Managing Reform," Policy Brief (Doha, Qatar: Brookings Center, May 2011).

6. For example, see Toby Matthiessen, *Sectarian Gulf: Bahrain, Saudi Arabia, and the Arab Spring That Wasn't* (Stanford, CA: Stanford University Press, 2013); Jill Crystal, *Oil and Politics in the Gulf: Rulers and Merchants in Kuwait and Qatar* (New York: Cambridge University Press, 1995), 75–78; and Robert Baer, *Sleeping with the Devil* (New York: Crown, 2003).

7. On how oil has affected the Arab Spring, see Kjetil Selvik and Bjørn Olav Utvik, eds., *Oil States in the New Middle East: Uprisings and Stability* (New York: Routledge, 2015).

8. One problem with the theory is that in some cases, such as in Malaysia, Norway, Chile, and Indonesia, natural resource wealth has not impeded democratization. The theory cannot account for these cases. On the broader costs of oil use, see Steve A. Yetiv, *Myths of the Oil Boom: American National Security in a Global Energy Market* (New York: Oxford University Press, 2015), chap. 8.

9. Terry Lynn Karl, *Paradox of Plenty: Oil Booms and Petro-States* (Berkeley and Los Angeles: University of California Press, 1997).

10. Michael L. Ross, *The Oil Curse: How Petroleum Wealth Shapes the Development of Nations* (Princeton, NJ: Princeton University Press, 2012). Using different data and methods, Michael Herb questions the extent of the oil-democracy connection. See Michael Herb, "No Representation Without Taxation? Rents, Development, and Democracy," *Comparative Politics* 37, 3 (2005): 297–316.

11. Kevin K. Tsui, "More Oil, Less Democracy: Evidence from Worldwide Crude Oil Discoveries," *Economic Journal* 121 (2010): 89–115.

12. Saad Eddin Ibrahim, "An Open Door," *Wilson Quarterly* 28 (Spring 2004): 36–46.

13. See the Freedom House website, www.freedomhouse.org.

14. Herb, "No Representation Without Taxation," 300.

15. Nathan Jensen and Leonard Wantchekon, "Resource Wealth and Political Regimes in Africa," *Comparative Political Studies* 37 (September 2004): 816–841.

16. Hazem Beblawi and Giacomo Luciani, eds., *The Rentier State* (New York: Croom Helm, 1987), esp. 11–16.

17. On rentier theory and challenges to it, see ibid., esp. 298–299.

18. On how oil made Kuwait and Qatar less accountable to the merchant class, see Crystal, *Oil and Politics in the Gulf*. For evidence on lack of accountability, see Kristopher W. Ramsay, "Revisiting the Resource Curse: Natural Disasters, the Price of Oil, and Democracy," *International Organization* (Summer 2011): 507–529.

19. See Shadi Hamid, *Temptations of Power: Islamists and Illiberal Democracy in a New Middle East* (New York: Oxford University Press, 2014).

20. F. Gregory Gause III, *Oil Monarchies: Domestic and Security Challenges in the Arab Gulf States* (New York: Council on Foreign Relations, 1994), 70–75.

21. On the sources of stability and instability in the Kingdom, see Haykel, Hegghammer, and Lacroix, eds., *Saudi Arabia in Transition*.

22. See Adeel Malik, "A Requiem for the Arab Development Model," *Journal of International Affairs* 68, 1 (Fall-Winter 2014): 93–115.

23. Michael L. Ross, "Will Oil Drown the Arab Spring?" *Foreign Affairs* 90, 5 (September-October 2011): 2–7. See also Ross, *The Oil Curse*.

24. On such structural control, see Jean-Pierre Filiu, *From Deep State to Islam* (New York: Oxford University Press, 2015).

25. The survey was conducted in six predominantly Muslim nations—Egypt, Indonesia,

Jordan, Lebanon, Pakistan, and Turkey—as well as in the Palestinian territories, among the Muslim population of Nigeria, and among Israel's Arab population. See Pew Global Attitudes Project, "Little Enthusiasm for Many Muslim Leaders," February 4, 2010, www .pewglobal.org/files/pdf/268.pdf.

26. Ibid.

27. On these strategies, see Mark L. Haas, *The Clash of Ideologies: Middle Eastern Politics and American Security* (New York: Oxford University Press, 2012), 260–264.

28. See Mai Yamani, *Changed Identities: The Challenge of the New Generation in Saudi Arabia* (Washington, DC: Brookings Institution Press, 2000).

29. On such challenges and responses, see Richard H. K. Vietor, "Saudi Arabia: Finding Stability After the Arab Spring," Harvard Business School Teaching Note 715-033, January 2015.

30. See John R. Bradley, "Saudi Arabia's Invisible Hand in the Arab Spring," *Foreign Affairs*, October 13, 2011, www.foreignaffairs.com/articles/136473/john-r-bradley/saudi -arabias-invisible-hand-in-the-arab-spring.

31. See Marc Lynch, *The Arab Uprising: The Unfinished Revolutions of the New Middle East* (New York: Public Affairs, 2013).

32. See Matthiessen, *Sectarian Gulf*.

33. Ayman Al-Yassini, *Religion and State in the Kingdom of Saudi Arabia* (Boulder, CO: Westview Press, 1985), 123.

34. Madawi Al-Rasheed, *A History of Saudi Arabia* (Cambridge: Cambridge University Press, 2002), 144.

35. Nadav Safran, *Saudi Arabia: The Ceaseless Quest for Security* (Cambridge, MA: Harvard University Press, 1985), 358–359.

36. For details on Saudi instability during this period, see *Middle East Contemporary Survey* 3 (1978–1979), 358–359, 736–755.

37. See Manama WAKH, Foreign Broadcast Information Service: MEA, February 25, 1982, C-3.

38. Quoted in John Kifner, "Iranian Officials Urge 'Uprooting' of Saudi Royalty," *New York Times*, August 3, 1987.

39. Ibid.

40. Anoushiravan Ehteshami, "The Foreign Policy of Iran," in *The Foreign Policies of Middle East States*, ed. Raymond Hinnebusch and Anoushiravan Ehteshami (Boulder, CO: Lynne Rienner, 2002), 288–292.

41. This section is based on several Osama bin Laden videos shown on CNN in the period September 15–October 15, 2001.

42. Pew Global Attitudes Project, "Osama bin Laden Largely Discredited Among Muslim Publics in Recent Years," May 2, 2011, http://www.pewglobal.org/2011/05/02/osama -bin-laden-largely-discredited-among-muslim-publics-in-recent-years/.

6

Jordan and the Arab Spring

Curtis R. Ryan

A S THE WINDS OF CHANGE of the "Arab Spring" swept the Middle East and North Africa in 2011 and 2012, many wondered which country would be next. Popular revolutions ousted dictators in Tunisia and Egypt. Turmoil in Yemen led to a carefully negotiated departure for the incumbent president. Civil war and foreign military intervention toppled the Gadafi regime in Libya, and Syria descended into a vicious civil war. Yet Jordan at least appeared untouched. But was Jordan an exception to the volatility of the Arab Spring? Might Jordan in fact carve out a more unique niche, navigating the Arab Spring through its own reform program and hence avoiding the revolutionary—or worse—turmoil that had engulfed so much of the region? Or is it merely a matter of time before Jordan too experiences revolutionary change?

Despite the lack of Jordanian revolution thus far, politics within the kingdom has been anything but docile or silent. Jordanians, in fact, participated in political demonstrations and rallies every Friday of the first two years of the Arab Spring. These demonstrations actually predated—by a few weeks— the larger mass movements that emerged in both Tunisia and Egypt. In the Jordanian case, however, demonstrations drew crowds numbered in the hundreds and sometimes in the thousands (in a country of approximately 6 million people) and thus did not really echo the massive gatherings of millions across Egypt. In addition to the smaller numbers, most demonstrations were also different in terms of their aims. Unlike their counterparts in Tunisia and Egypt, most Jordanian protesters called for reform, not revolution. They called for the ouster of the prime minister and his government but not for the ouster of the king.

Yet the demonstrations were nonetheless intense in tone and called for a return to reform. The implications seemed clear: If the kingdom did not return to genuine reform on its own, then the demonstrations could easily change in both size and focus, taking Jordan in a more volatile direction than the regime—and indeed most Jordanians—wanted it to go. In 2011–2012, the demands were therefore not yet revolutionary, but they were certainly real, and it would be a mistake for government or opposition to assume that the winds of change had swept by Jordan. They had not. They had simply taken a more reformist turn. But the future of the Hashemite Kingdom hinged on the decisions taken in response to these reform pressures. Could the country reform itself, or would the process fail, leaving the country open to far more revolutionary pressures?

Proregime Jordanians are often quick to acknowledge that reform remains the central point of discussion within Jordanian politics, and that this is not actually new. Nor did it begin with the Arab Spring. Jordanians have been debating these issues for decades. This very fact, however, can be taken in at least two very different ways. For more conservative Jordanians, it indicates that the kingdom is far ahead of the rest of the region and that revolutionary fervor has not reached Jordan itself precisely because the country has been slowly but steadily following a path of reform since at least 1989. For more progressive or reform-oriented Jordanians, the point of departure is the same: 1989. They too point to the inauguration of the much-heralded reform process from that era, but often with nostalgia for a more reform-oriented moment in Jordan's history. Reformers therefore almost lament the comparison of 1989 to the present, noting that the kingdom has advanced little since that promising beginning or that it has perhaps regressed in the reform process over the years. Before returning to the present, then, we must explore a key part of the past. Why exactly is 1989 so often invoked in these debates by both pro- and antireform constituencies in Jordanian politics?

1989 AND AFTER: STRUGGLES FOR REFORM

Jordan had certainly come to a crossroads by 1989. The Jordanian economy was in very poor shape, leading the government to turn to the International Monetary Fund (IMF) for help. But IMF loans always come with conditions. In Jordan, as in most cases, the conditions included a financial austerity program of the type that rocked countries such as Greece as recently as 2012. In April 1989, the government cut subsidies for basic foods, leading to massive price increases just as most Jordanians were having an especially difficult time making ends meet. The result was volatile. In the more impoverished south of Jordan, Jordanians protested the austerity measures and also launched demonstrations against political and financial corruption in government. The demonstrations soon turned into riots.

Protesters called for the ouster of Prime Minister Zayd al-Rifai and for a greater role for citizens in political life and in public policy. Their demands, in short, sounded very similar to those that would rock much of the Arab world in 2011 and 2012. In Jordan in 1989, what was especially disturbing to the regime was the fact that most demonstrators were of East Jordanian background. That is, their family origins were east of the Jordan River, unlike those of Jordan's many Palestinian citizens. The unrest, in other words, came not from Palestinian camps or urban neighborhoods but from the bedrock communities on which the regime itself was based. These were East Jordanians, many with tribal, and some with Bedouin, backgrounds.

The ethnic dimension of the riots certainly caught the attention of King Hussein. The king quickly sacked the prime minister and his government and announced that Jordan would embark on a major program of reform. This reform would include both political and economic liberalization, shifting Jordan toward a more privatized market economy while also opening the political system to greater public participation, competitive elections, a loosening of government restrictions on the media, and a lifting of martial law (which had been in place since the 1967 war with Israel).[1]

Parliamentary elections were held in November 1989, as promised, and yielded a parliament that included not only conservatives and royalists but also large numbers of Islamists (mainly affiliated with the Muslim Brotherhood) and leftist activists. By 1991, the process took another step by creating the National Charter, calling for greater pluralism and participation in governance in Jordan but in return for loyalty to the Hashemite monarchy. Following the establishment of the National Charter, political parties were legalized for the first time since the 1950s, and soon more than a dozen were officially registered, including the Islamic Action Front (IAF), the political party associated with the Muslim Brotherhood, Jordan's largest Islamist movement, and one that has historically been socially and religiously conservative but also democratic and reformist.

By the mid-1990s, the reform process seemed to have stalled or perhaps even regressed. The key factor was King Hussein's signing of the 1994 peace treaty with the state of Israel. While the treaty secured peace between the two countries, it left the future of Palestinians very much in doubt. Economic liberalization continued, but the political reform process effectively stalled in an effort to thwart domestic opposition to the unpopular peace treaty.[2] By 1999, however, Jordan had reached a turning point of another kind, as King Hussein died after many years of battling cancer. In the weeks before his death, the king shifted the line of succession from his long-serving brother, Hasan, to his eldest son, Abdullah. Educated largely in British and American schools, and with a strong military background, the new king ascended the throne with little personal political experience.[3]

Nevertheless, King Abdullah II reiterated his father's commitment to the liberalization process and pursued the economic dimensions of the program even more aggressively than his father had. The new king was determined to modernize Jordan's infrastructure, from roads and utilities to communications, Internet access, and cell-phone networks. In both domestic and foreign relations, the king emphasized the importance of trade and foreign investment in the kingdom and made sure to solidify relations with the United States, the European Union, and global financial institutions.

In terms of political reform, the king had ruled by decree for two years, having dismissed the previous parliament. By 2003, the political part of the reform process appeared to return, with new elections to parliament. Other elections followed in 2007 and 2010. But the latter two episodes were marked by widespread allegations of election rigging (especially the 2007 polls).[4] Each election, going back to 1989, has been conducted under a new temporary election law. In 1989, Islamists and other opposition forces had done so well that together they controlled more than half the parliament. In many ways, the opposition has been trying to reachieve that level of success ever since, while the regime has experimented with numerous different electoral systems, each designed to ensure that the 1989 outcome is not reproduced.

In general, it is fair to say that political reform has long lagged behind the greater priority of economic reform. This neoliberal economic model, however, was criticized within Jordan for creating greater wealth for some but also greater levels of impoverishment for others. The privatization process, while lauded by external economic and political actors, left many former employees of the public sector unemployed or underemployed, and many of these were from the East Jordanian communities that had always acted as the main pillars of support for the regime, and indeed as the main sources of recruiting for its police, armed forces, and intelligence services. The economic changes, in other words, have been disorienting for many Jordanians and have led to widespread charges that the process is not only uneven but also corrupt. Indeed, charges of corruption echo across Jordanian political debates and only escalate as Jordanians see the vast levels of wealth on display and the massive construction projects (new malls, five-star hotels, villas, high-rise luxury apartments, and so on) that they themselves cannot patronize.

The real gap, then, is between rich and poor, with a dwindling middle class. Yet these complaints too often take a more ethnically oriented tone, as many reactionary social forces attempt to sharpen the divisions in society between Jordanians of Palestinian and of Transjordanian origin; that is, between those "West Bankers" whose origins are historically in Palestine and those "East Bankers" whose families, clans, and tribes hail originally from east of the Jordan River. Yet the recurrent ethnic politics card played so often by conservative and even chauvinistic elements in Jordan (and not, therefore, by most Jordanians regardless of background) is especially effective and even dangerous in harsh economic times. Times like today.

RISING DOMESTIC AND REGIONAL TENSIONS

There is no question that ethnic-identity tensions within Jordan have dramatically increased over the past ten years. This increase is due, in part, to the severe economic hardships but also to the kingdom's extreme vulnerability to regional tensions. These include Israeli discussions of Jordan as an "alternative homeland" for Palestinians; war in Iraq and massive Iraqi refugee flows into Jordan (after 2003); and now the civil war in Syria and even fears of the state's collapse. By 2012, Jordanian officials argued that more than 120,000 Syrian refugees had crossed the northern border of the already small and economically poor kingdom.

Each of these external strains has had a harmful impact on Jordan's own internal identity politics. These identity dynamics have been most clear in the strong nativist trend that has emerged to "protect" Jordan for "real Jordanians." This has even included unprecedented levels of criticism of the regime and of the monarchy (including of the king's Palestinian wife, Queen Rania) for allegedly selling Jordan to a Palestinian economic and now increasingly governmental elite. Tensions have abounded in the largely East Jordanian southern cities and towns and between and among Jordanian tribes. High-profile criticism of the monarchy has emerged from tribal leaders and from retired military officers.[5]

Public questioning now crosses red lines that would have been unthinkable under King Hussein, including even open criticism of the king himself. For King Abdullah, as one Jordanian analyst noted, "all his choices are contested; his choice of prime minister, his choice of crown prince, his choice of wife. All are contested."[6]

Media accounts of Jordanian politics tend to pick up on these tensions, but they too often mistake the more polarized views of particular extreme Palestinian and East Jordanian political figures for the views of most Jordanians. Jordan is actually a diverse country and should not be confused with the ethnic caricatures that both Palestinian and East Jordanian chauvinists use for each other. Jordan is not the country that these more chauvinistic elements suggest. It is not, for example, a nation of tribal bigots or of disloyal rich Palestinians. Rather, it is predominantly an Arab state with a significant Circassian minority. It is a predominantly Muslim country with a large Christian minority. Some Jordanians have tribal backgrounds, but many do not. And regardless of the exclusivist and nativist trend supported by some in Jordanian politics today, all Jordanians actually have ties across one or more of the kingdom's borders. Not least among these is the Hashemite royal family itself (a point often made by former crown prince Hasan), since it hails originally from Mecca and the Hijaz region of Arabia. While political tensions in Jordan frequently manifest themselves in ethnic, tribal, or identity terms, they are more often than not more deeply about class divisions between rich and poor and between haves and have-nots. And these cut across ethnic lines.[7]

Still, violence across Jordan's borders has greatly exacerbated internal tensions. The collapse of Syria into civil war, for example, is of great concern to the Jordanian regime, but it has also caused the kingdom's own broad-based reform movement to splinter in its responses. The large Islamist movement, based in the Muslim Brotherhood and Islamic Action Front, has called for the ouster of the Assad regime and broken from many secular left opposition parties that have stood by Damascus. Some of the latter parties, originally allied with the Islamists as part of a broad reform coalition in Jordan, now fear that the Arab uprisings have led only to Islamist empowerment and a weakening of the political left across the Arab world.

As one democracy activist suggested, even within Jordan "there is also a certain sense of waiting for what will happen in Syria. It divided the opposition. Some of the Jordanian opposition backed Bashar al-Assad, because he and they take an anti-US, anti-Israel, and anticapitalist stance. This includes the old socialist Baath Party or Arab left. Their main focus isn't necessarily prodemocracy, but antiprivatization and Jordanian foreign policy." The same activist noted the contradictions in both leftist and Islamist positions regarding each other. "The secularists are sometimes so terrified that they end up supporting an authoritarian regime, while the Islamist discourse links secularism and liberalism, as though Ben Ali and Mubarak were liberal."[8]

Yet despite the various ethnic and ideological fault lines that exist in Jordanian politics, proreform and prodemocracy demonstrators (including leftist, nationalist, and Islamist parties and also nonpartisan youth movements across the country) marched and protested against corruption and for reform almost every Friday throughout 2011 and 2012.

THE 2011 AND 2012 PROTESTS

In January 2011, as protests rocked both Tunisia and Egypt, Jordanians too formed mass demonstrations calling for the ouster of the executive and his government. The executive in question was the prime minister, not the king. Prime Minister Samir al-Rifai had just been sworn in for his second term, but regional and domestic politics had taken a decidedly populist turn. Rifai was seen by many Jordanians as a neoliberal technocrat, and he became the focal point of antigovernment demonstrations. Clearly influenced by rapidly changing regional events, the regime dismissed Rifai and his government in February 2011, appointing instead Marouf al-Bakhit, a former prime minister, former general, and former head of the intelligence services—the General Intelligence Directorate (GID), or *mukhabarat*.

For conservative East Jordanian nationalists who had railed against the allegedly Palestinian Rifai government, Bakhit was a conservative East Jordanian from a major tribe, and in many ways the opposite of Rifai—save that they were both loyalist regime insiders. But for the many reform activists who had marched in the streets calling for change, they had hoped for reform and instead got a conservative member of the old guard. Youth activists were at once flush with the success of triggering a change in government and disappointed with its replacement.[9]

Still, King Abdullah argued that the Arab Spring was not a challenge to the Hashemite monarchy but rather a necessary wake-up call to Jordan and the whole region. The king suggested that the waves of change be welcomed as an opportunity for Jordan to forge a more unique path—one very different from the revolutions, civil wars, and international interventions that had changed regimes elsewhere. Jordan, he argued, would forge a path—perhaps similar to that of Morocco—in which a monarchy reformed itself.[10]

The king called for a new national dialogue committee, comprising elements from both government and some parts of the opposition, to forge a new set of reforms to the kingdom's laws on elections and political parties and even to the constitution itself. But the regime also lobbied hard for international support from its Western allies and from Gulf oil monarchies, noting the geostrategic importance of the kingdom and the severe economic hardship it was undergoing in 2011 and 2012. The regime recognized that, although many grievances were social and political, the danger of a real spark toward a more volatile situation probably lay in economic grievances and hardship. Jordan therefore lobbied urgently for increased aid to weather the storms of the Arab Spring.

Jordan even explored a tentative offer by Saudi Arabia and the Gulf Cooperation Council (GCC) to join the GCC. For critics of the kingdom, this amounted to a counterrevolutionary alliance of well-to-do monarchies, effectively shoring up the Hashemite monarchy and perhaps stifling domestic hopes for reform. For Jordanian government officials, however, being more explicitly tied to the region's wealthiest alliance was potentially an economic lifeline that could transform the kingdom's future and had no necessary bearing on the domestic reform process.

In a June 12, 2011, speech to the nation about the kingdom's reform efforts, King Abdullah ended his remarks by thanking Saudi Arabia for its invitation to Jordan to join the distinctly non-reform-oriented GCC. But the Jordanian king also called for strengthening the party system and shifting from governments that were royally appointed to those drawn from the majority bloc in a democratically elected parliament. This was a surprise. If implemented, it would meet a major opposition demand and suggest at least tentative moves toward a more constitutional monarchy.[11] Most opposition activists, however, met the speech with skepticism. As one activist put it, summarizing the general view, "It's a good idea . . . if it happens."[12]

The tepid response to the royal reform initiative is indicative of a more pervasive pessimism across the reform movement—a pessimism that has been well earned. Jordan's broad-based proreform constituency has clearly gotten tired of promises, slogans, government reshuffles, and new national committees for reform. They are suspicious, in short, of cosmetic reform and seek instead clear and irreversible steps on the ground. In the words of another opposition activist, "The whole region is moving at high speed like a BMW while we are riding donkeys . . . *donkeys*, not even horses."[13]

But regardless of the regime's ultimate intentions or level of commitment to reform, the spirit of 2011 and 2012 across the Arab world remains a major point of departure in Jordanian public life. Jordan saw the rise of extensive levels of youth activism, both in the streets and in cyberspace, from blogs to Twitter to Facebook groups. The Arab Spring also led to the revitalization of old political movements, from leftist parties to the better-organized Muslim Brotherhood and its party, the IAF (but, interestingly, none of these seem to be of interest to Jordan's energized youth). Jordan also saw a rise in public sphere discussions on virtually all topics, in cyberspace, in print, and in person. Young Jordanians, for example, hosted various discussion sessions and public debates, live-streaming the events and taking questions and comments from Twitter as well as from the local audience. The constituency for real reform in Jordan therefore stretches across Jordan's generational, class, ethnic, and gender divides. In many ways it represents the exact "modern Jordan" that the regime itself helped to create since 1999. Yet proreform Jordanians continue to feel thwarted by entrenched antireform elites.

In some respects, these various forces ran headlong into one another at a critical moment within Jordan's version of the Arab Spring—specifically on March 24 and 25, 2011. The reform movement had continued its weekly demonstrations and had been boosted by its own success in achieving the ouster of the Rifai government. The demonstrations thereafter continued every Friday, calling for an end to perceived endemic corruption, for greater inclusion in public life, and for a return to political liberalization and democratization. Specifically, demonstrators called for major changes in the electoral and political party laws, leading ultimately to a governing system characterized by checks and balances between a more constitutional monarchy and a more powerful, effective, and representative parliament.

Organized online as the March 24 Movement, Jordanian democracy and reform activists gathered at the Ministry of Interior Circle in the capital, Amman, for perhaps their most important demonstration yet. Despite the presence of myriad East Jordanian nationalist symbols, including red-checked East

Jordanian *kufiyyat* (sing. *kefiyya* or *kufiyya*) (head scarves), Hashemite and Jordanian nationalist songs, and a clearly peaceful protest, the demonstrators were attacked on March 25 by *bultajiyya* (thugs). Calling themselves the Dawa al-Watan (Call of the Nation) and believing they were saving the monarchy from "Palestinian" revolutionaries who were "occupying" their capital, they stormed the peaceful demonstration, leading to the death of one participant.[14] In many respects, March 24 represented a high point of democracy activism, while March 25 marked a low point, as peaceful democracy activists were dispersed by reactionary antireform zealots.

Despite such incidents, most Jordanians remained strongly in favor of reform rather than regime change. Meanwhile, outside Jordan, the extreme violence of the latter round of Arab uprisings—in Libya, Yemen, and, especially, Syria—may actually have helped the Hashemite monarchy, at least temporarily, since no Jordanian wants to see the country take those routes. It bought the monarchy at least some more time, and most Jordanians seemed willing to give the king a chance to join and even lead the reform effort.

For many, another decisive moment for reform occurred in October 2011, when King Abdullah dismissed the government of Prime Minister Marouf al-Bakhit. Given the pattern of previous government reshuffles, most Jordanians expected another neoliberal technocrat or a member of the East Jordanian tribal old guard, and presumably someone with a background in the army or intelligence services. The new appointee, however, was not really a politician at all. Awn Khasawneh was instead a judge on the International Court of Justice. As an internationally respected jurist, Khasawneh returned to Jordan to accept the position of prime minister, signaling perhaps a new era in Jordanian politics.

The new prime minister completed the process of presenting parliament with new laws on elections, on parties, and on the establishment of a constitutional court and an independent electoral commission. But he sparred with the monarchy over the nature of governance itself, arguing that Jordan had a parliamentary—not presidential—political system and that therefore the prime minister was the head of government and should not take directives from another executive once in office. But the *diwan* (the royal palace) did indeed make clear its views and wishes, while the Khasawneh government attempted to forge ahead on its own. The king argued that the new government was moving too slowly, dragging out the reform process.

While Khasawneh accepted the end of parliament's term in office, hoping for a newer and more effective one after national elections were held, the monarchy called for an extension of parliament in order to complete the reform process by passing the remaining reform laws. That, it turned out, was the final straw. Parliament's session was extended by royal decree while the prime minister was abroad, on a state visit to Turkey. In an unprecedented move, and after a mere six months in office, Prime Minister Khasawneh resigned while still abroad. Both prime minister and king issued letters that politely but clearly implied that the palace or the government was (respectively) to blame. But however blame is apportioned for the sudden end to the Khasawneh government, Jordanians were suddenly confronted with a fourth government in the sixteen months since the start of the regional Arab Spring.

The new government looked far more familiar, as Fayez Tarawneh, a conservative former prime minister from a powerful East Jordanian family, took office. If the reform process were to continue, it would now be led, once again, by a conservative not known for his reformist sympathies. But Tarawneh was also an economist by training and came to office at a time of severe economic hardship. Even before returning to the prime ministry, Tarawneh had noted that economic pressures were perhaps even greater than political or social strains and that the government's options were severely limited. "The demands on government are unbelievable," he noted. "People have legitimate demands for a better quality of life, but the budget deficit makes this very difficult."[15] Still, the Tarawneh government, like its predecessors in the Arab Spring era, was short-lived, lasting only from April to October 2012. Tarawneh was replaced by Abdullah an-Nsour, a moderate, reform-oriented politician who was charged with shepherding the kingdom through new reforms and new elections. The January 2013 national parliamentary elections were a far cleaner affair than those of 2007 and 2010, and Nsour was named prime minister shortly thereafter to start a second term. Unlike the various short-term governments of the Arab Spring period, Nsour's proved durable and lasted the next several years.

Beyond the Arab Spring? 2013 and After

By 2013, the politics of protest had begun to wane in Jordan. This was not necessarily a permanent condition, but regional politics had dampened the enthusiasm of many activists. Some activists argued that moderate levels of reform had been achieved; others were disillusioned with the entire process. But still others simply held back, not wanting to push matters too far, at least not for the moment, as regional conflicts across Jordan's borders grew steadily worse.

As the Syrian war dragged on, hundreds of thousands of Syrians crossed the border into Jordan. Even as the kingdom staggered under the weight of the massive refugee influx, a new threat emerged from both Syria and Iraq: the rise of the Islamic State of Iraq and Syria (ISIS), or Da'esh, as it is known in Jordan. This militant Salafi and jihadi movement at first appeared to be yet another in a long list of terrorist threats, but when it took control of entire cities in both Syria and Iraq and declared itself a "caliphate," ISIS became a territorial threat as well. It certainly had aspirations to some form of statehood, and it had designs on Jordan too.

Jordan reinforced its borders and joined a US-led coalition conducting air strikes on ISIS targets. This was a controversial move within the kingdom. Some Jordanians agreed with the king that this was a potentially existential fight against the worst form of terrorism. But other Jordanians felt that it was not their fight. When a Jordanian pilot was captured and brutally murdered by ISIS, the controversy within the kingdom only increased. Yet even as Jordan attempted to hold the line against ISIS, the kingdom was dragged into still another conflict, this time in Yemen. As Saudi Arabia led an Arab coalition in a military intervention to restore the Yemeni regime and counter Iranian-backed Houthi rebels, Jordan played a minimal role, but it made sure to back up its key regional economic allies—Saudi Arabia and the GCC.

Within Jordan, the stakes remain high for real reform. As debates over the nature and parameters of reform, political participation, and governance in Jordan proceed, the Arab uprisings continue to transform the region.[16] Jordan is not in any way immune to these pressures. As a small state, in terms of both geography and population, and with a weak economy, Jordan is especially vulnerable to regional pressures and violence. Unlike its monarchical neighbors to the south, Jordan does not have a massive oil income to co-opt opponents and buy off its own population.

For proregime conservatives, these dangerous domestic and regional currents signal a need to be slow and methodical, or perhaps to stop the talk of reform and change entirely. But for reform activists, they signal a desperate need to move faster, and more thoroughly, to transform Jordan via reform before it is too late. The question, as always in Jordanian politics, is where the king himself is in this polarized atmosphere.

Jordan's opposition, meanwhile, continues to split over both domestic and regional issues. Leftist and pan-Arab nationalist parties urged the regime to back Assad in Syria against Islamist rebels, while the Muslim Brotherhood called for Jordan to stand by rebels against the Assad dictatorship. Salafi movements grew within Jordan, and more militant elements left the kingdom for what they viewed as jihad against the Assad regime. Even Jordan's Muslim Brotherhood, a movement as old as the Hashemite monarchy itself, split into two factions—a reformist wing legally recognized by the state and a larger but more hawkish wing that felt the state was shunting it aside.

Whether united or divided, many in Jordan's various opposition movements remain frustrated with the pace of reform and frequently cite 1989 as a benchmark of hopes that remain unfulfilled, even so many years later. Others cite the 1999 monarchical transition yet make a similar argument that reform should have been achieved by now.[17] But proregime officials and supporters argue that the problem is not the monarchy or the king but a resistant old guard, an antiquated antireform elite, and an interventionist GID that thwarts not only the will of the people but also the will of the Hashemite monarchy itself.

Even reform measures are still often met with reserve rather than applause and with suspicion about motivations rather than praise. A profound lack of trust pervades Jordanian politics, and this includes a lack of faith in the regime. This does not mean looming revolution or civil war. Jordan is likely to muddle through, as it has through past challenges dating back to the birth of the state itself. And, indeed, most Jordanians still support the monarchy and want it to lead the country to genuine reform. Yet even reform moves are met with suspicion. Does reform really mean reform, or is it merely more cosmetic political change? And when the regime moves against corruption, a key opposition demand, the inconsistency of who is arrested and whether or not they come to trial leads to still more questions. For Jordanian royalists, these types of questions are infuriating. The regime, they argue, can't seem to get any credit no matter what it does. Regime critics, in contrast, argue that the cynicism comes from experience and a litany of disappointments.[18]

Conclusion

So far, Jordan has managed to avoid the regime change of Tunisia and Egypt, the violent civil wars of Libya and Syria, and the counterrevolutionary violence of Bahrain. Instead, the regime argues that it is embarking on an alternative path toward methodical homegrown reform and toward a greater pluralism and liberalization aimed at preserving the monarchy and the state, rather than replacing either. This process has a chance of succeeding, and indeed the monarchy would actually be stronger if it took a few steps back, curbed the power of the GID, and allowed parliamentary governments to emerge.

Yet the GID itself sees the kingdom's large Islamist movement as the real threat to Jordan's future and fears that greater democratization would empower Palestinians at the expense of East Jordanians and Islamists at the expense of conservative secularists. The security services fear an Islamist takeover of Jordan, with democracy as a onetime ticket to an Islamic republic and an end of the Hashemite regime. The Muslim Brotherhood and the Islamic Action Front, of course, make precisely the opposite argument: that the largely East Jordanian security forces are controlling the state, that the tribes have too much power, and that they therefore thwart democracy to preserve their own privileges.[19]

To be clear, neither a coup d'état nor a revolt is likely in Jordan, but neither are they impossible. The outcome of the Arab Spring for Jordan will depend on the influence of regional events and on the kingdom's own domestic reform efforts. Lost in much of this, as usual, is Jordan's large and well-educated youth population, which seems to have little faith in the political motivations of the regime, the GID, the Islamist movement, or the old opposition political parties. Jordan's youth, in short, is really the key to Jordan's future, but its more genuinely democratic and less partisan inclinations may be thwarted by one or more of the older social forces noted above. The stakes, to repeat, remain high. They include nothing less than the future of the monarchy, the state, and the nation as the winds of change continue to buffet Jordan and the entire region.

Notes

1. Rex Brynen, "Economic Crisis and Post-Rentier Democratization in the Arab World: The Case of Jordan," *Canadian Journal of Political Science* 25, 1 (1992): 69–97; Malik Mufti, "Elite Bargains and the Onset of Political Liberalization in Jordan," *Comparative Political Studies* 32, 1 (1999): 100–129; Glenn E. Robinson, "Defensive Democratization in Jordan," *International Journal of Middle East Studies* 30, 3 (1998): 387–410.

2. Laurie A. Brand, "The Effects of the Peace Process on Political Liberalization in Jordan," *Journal of Palestine Studies* 28, 2 (1999): 52–67; Jillian Schwedler, "Don't Blink: Jordan's Democratic Opening and Closing," MERIP Press Information Note, July 3, 2002, www.merip.org.

3. For details on the monarchical transition and changes in Jordanian politics, see Curtis R. Ryan, *Jordan in Transition: From Hussein to Abdullah* (Boulder, CO: Lynne Rienner, 2002).

4. Asher Susser, "Jordan: Preserving Domestic Order in a Setting of Regional Turmoil," Middle East Brief No. 27 (Waltham, MA: Crown Center for Middle East Studies, Brandeis University, March 2008), 4–5.

5. Curtis R. Ryan, "'We Are All Jordan' ... but Who Is We?," *Middle East Report Online*, July 13, 2010, www.merip.org/mero/mero071310.

6. Author interview, Amman, Jordan, June 2010.

7. This section draws on Curtis R. Ryan, "Identity and Corruption in Jordanian Politics," Middle East Channel at *Foreign Policy*, February 9, 2012, http://mideast.foreign policy.com/posts/2012/02/09/identity_and_corruption_in_jordanian_politics.

8. Author interview, Amman, Jordan, December 2011.

9. Author interviews with youth activists, Amman, Jordan, May 2012.

10. Author interview with His Majesty King Abdullah II, Basman Palace, Amman, Jordan, May 21, 2012.

11. Curtis R. Ryan, "The King's Speech," Middle East Channel at *Foreign Policy*, June 17, 2011, http://mideast.foreignpolicy.com/posts/2011/06/17/the_kings_speech.

12. Author interview, Amman, Jordan, June 2011.

13. Author interview with Jordanian democracy activist, Amman, Jordan, June 2011.

14. See the account by democracy activist and blogger Naseem Tarawneh, "The Quick Death of Shabab March 24th and What It Means for Jordan," *Black Iris of Jordan* (blog), March 26, 2011, http://www.black-iris.com/2011/03/26/the-quick-death-of-shabab-march-24-and-what-it-means-for-jordan.

15. Author interview with Dr. Fayez Tarawneh, Senate, Amman, Jordan, December 13, 2011.

16. International Crisis Group, "Popular Protest in North Africa and the Middle East (IX): Dallying with Reform in a Divided Jordan," *Middle East Report* No. 118, March 12, 2012, www.crisisgroup.org/en/regions/middle-east-north-africa/iraq-iran-gulf/jordan.aspx.

17. Marwan Muasher, "A Decade of Struggling Reform Efforts in Jordan: The Resilience of the Rentier System" (Washington, DC: Carnegie Endowment for International Peace, 2011).

18. Ryan, "Identity and Corruption."

19. Secular proreform forces make similar arguments. Some activists and analysts even fear that the security services themselves would force a change in monarch if they felt it would help secure the monarchy and their own privileges.

7

Iraq and the Arab Spring:
From Protests to the Rise of ISIS

Ibrahim Al-Marashi

WHILE IRAQ IS GENERALLY not considered an "Arab Spring" state, in the catchall term employed to describe protests and uprisings in the region since 2011, it was affected by international dynamics that occurred afterward. Whenever sustained protests emerged in Iraq from 2011 to 2015, both Iraqis and outside observers labeled those events "Iraq's Arab Spring," attesting to the enduring nature of the metaphor. Thus, symbols and slogans that emerged during the Arab Spring were appropriated by Iraqis to protest their domestic woes and lack of services, giving their grievances greater regional resonance. In terms of Iraq's security situation, the political disruptions after 2011 in the Middle East and in Syria, in particular, led to the resurgence of the Islamic State of Iraq and Syria (ISIS) and a flow of recruits to Iraq from Arab Spring states such as Tunisia and Libya. ISIS essentially represents both a transnational and an Iraqi uprising seeking to transform territory in Syria and Iraq into an Islamic state. Within the field of civil-military relations, Iraq's military provides a study of the relationship between the state and its coercive apparatus after 2011, and of how the armed forces of a Middle Eastern state chose to side with either the people or the regime. Finally, from a regional historical perspective, protests in Iraq allow for the analysis of popular mobilization and the state in the Middle East.

In the conclusion of this volume James Gelvin differentiates between "protest," a tactic to reform or change political elites within a system, and "uprising," which seeks the complete dismantlement of the existing regime.[1] The nuance

Gelvin provides elucidates how the term "Arab Spring" conflates protests with uprisings. The region since 2011 has witnessed both protests and uprisings, or protests that evolved into uprisings and into full-scale civil war and state collapse. Protests and uprisings are not ahistorical phenomena in the Middle East, and the past provides interpretative schemata for those enduring hardships as of January 2011. For example, those living through the Syrian civil war often relate Bashar al-Assad's current use of indiscriminate violence to how his father, Hafiz, crushed the 1982 Muslim Brotherhood uprising in the town of Hama.

In terms of Iraq's historical trajectory and national narrative, the nation was forged by an uprising. In 1920, Iraqis from a variety of ethnosectarian backgrounds from the south to the north protested against British rule after World War I. This event, called the "Great Revolution of 1920," served as a formative event in forging a national identity. Iraq witnessed sustained protests in 1948, known as the Wathba, or the Leap, against the Portsmouth Treaty, a defense agreement signed between the Iraqi monarchy and the United Kingdom, followed by another series of protests in 1952. The events of July 1958, deemed a *thawra*, or revolution, by the new regime, constituted a successful uprising by the military and elements of the public that transformed Iraq from a monarchy into a republic. The first uprising in Iraq that came close to overthrowing the Ba'ath Party occurred in 1991. Known as the *"intifada,"* or "shaking off" (borrowing the Palestinian term that emerged after 1987), it spread among fifteen of Iraq's eighteen provinces. The uprising included defecting soldiers; Iran-based Iraqi Shi'a groups; and both Kurdish parties, the Kurdistan Democratic Party (KDP) and the Patriotic Union of Kurdistan (PUK). The brutal manner in which the Iraqi state repressed the 1991 uprising in the north and south did little to quell Kurdish aspirations for autonomy or independence or Shi'a discontent. Another Shi'a uprising erupted in 1991 in Baghdad and cities in the south after the cleric Ayatollah Muhammad Sadiq al-Sadr, father to Muqtada al-Sadr, was assassinated by the state.[2]

It took a foreign invasion in 2003 to change Iraq's long-entrenched authoritarian government. The US-led Coalition Provisional Authority subsequently dismantled Iraq's one-party regime, including its bureaucracy and armed forces, which created a state vacuum and ensuing insurgency. A network of non-Iraqi insurgents led by the Jordanian Abu Mus'ab al-Zarqawi entered Iraq from Afghanistan and other parts of the region, merged under al-Qaida's banner as al-Qaida of Iraq (AQI), and evolved into the Islamic State of Iraq

(ISI). As ISI, it enforced harsh Islamic living codes in the areas in which it operated, causing resentment among the local population. In coordination with US forces, Iraqi tribal elements coalesced in the Reawakening (Sahwa) and Sons of Iraq forces and expelled ISI from their urban centers. The conflict in Syria provided a space for ISI to recuperate. Once it had established a foothold in Syria, ISI officially broke with al-Qaida's central leadership and added an *S* to become ISIS. Since 2011, sustained protests have emerged within Iraq itself, requesting better governance and opposed to a change of the post-2003 government. Concurrent with these protests, the rise of ISIS in this period constituted an uprising in which Iraqis who sought to uproot the order joined or supported the Islamic State.

THE 2011 PROTESTS

As the Arab Spring began in Tunisia and Egypt in early 2011, Iraqis took to the streets by February. On February 17, protests began in Sulaymaniyya, in the Kurdistan Regional Government (KRG) of Iraq, where followers of the Goran (Change) Movement gathered in solidarity with the protesters in Tunisia and Egypt, calling for the end of the joint PUK-KDP monopoly of power.[3] The fact that Qubad Talabani, the son of Iraqi president Jalal Talabani, took to his blog to write, "Kurdistan is not Tunisia,"[4] demonstrates the fear that a member of the PUK elite had of the symbolic power of these protests.

The protesters in the KRG demanded reliable public services and an end to rampant corruption, nepotism, and unemployment. These calls would resonate a few days later in Tahrir Square in the capital, Baghdad, and in Mosul, Falluja, Tikrit, and Hawija.[5] This "Day of Rage" targeted the central government in Baghdad under Prime Minister Nuri al-Maliki.[6] Issues that motivated these protesters echoed those from the KRG protest, such as government corruption and failure to deliver reliable electricity, drinking water, and jobs. The Day of Rage in Iraq bore some superficial similarities to events in Tunisia and Egypt, including Facebook activism.[7] However, unlike in Tunisia and Egypt, protesters called not for a change in government but for reliability in the delivery of services and an end to corruption.

Nonetheless, the protests were met with a heavy government response. The Iraqi security forces killed twenty-three protesters on February 25, 2011.[8] The Kurdish security services fired on the crowds and then attacked the Goran Party's offices.[9] Apparently, the KRG and central Iraqi state feared a contagion effect from the Arab Spring and used force to suppress the protests despite their calls for reforms and not the overthrow of the state. Political elites failed to address the root causes of the demonstrations, leaving tensions simmering.

The international media that reported on these events situated the protests within a greater Arab Spring narrative, as it provided a convenient catchall term for foreign observers—or simply made the events in Iraq more news-worthy. The moniker would be invoked from this point onward to describe protests in Iraq, called "Iraq's Arab Spring" or, in the case of Arab Sunni pro-tests in the Anbar province, "Iraq's Sunni Spring."[10]

Iraqis remained undeterred from protesting and continued to do so through 2015. What differentiated the outcome of these protests from other disrup-tions throughout the region was that Iraq is a hybrid regime.[11] Such a regime is characterized by a democratic facade but undermined by systemic authori-tarianism and corruption. Hybrid regimes in the region include Iraq and Leb-anon, both of which have political elites that practice sectarian clientage. Iraq and Lebanon allow political pluralism, as both maintain multiple competing parties, elections, and a change in the executive leadership. Thus, protesters sought to change not the system but rather the way career politicians operated within it. The lack of efficient governance and rule of law continues to frustrate the populaces in both states, and since they have relative assurance that they can take to the streets without being killed by security forces, they resort to expressing their grievances in protests, since the ballot box rarely ejects the ruling oligarchs from power. The Arab Spring had endowed Iraq with a set of symbols and language to challenge its hybrid regime.

THE ANBAR CRISIS AND 2013 PROTESTS

Disaffected Arab Sunni Iraqis launched protests in January 2013 in the cities of Falluja and Ramadi in the Anbar province, Mosul in the Ninawa province, and Hawija near Kirkuk. The international media that reported on these protests often invoked the "Arab Spring" metaphor. Reporters even stressed how the Iraqi protests resembled Egypt's Tahrir Square in 2011, with sit-ins and tent cities, which led to headlines such as "Arab Spring–Style Protests Take Hold in Iraq"[12] or "Will Iraq Be Next to Have an Arab Spring?"[13] However, these protests in Iraq did not call for dismantling the system. The protests were in response to the Maliki government's order of the arrest of the bodyguards of an Iraqi Arab Sunni politician, Rafi al-Issawi, the former finance minister, in

December 2012, on the back of a 2011 arrest warrant for Tariq al-Hashimi, the former Iraqi vice president. Maliki had accused both of having links to "terrorist groups," an inflammatory label for the insurgents.

By 2013, Arab Sunnis had reached a breaking point. They were not protesting out of devotion to the Arab Sunni political class. In fact, when Arab Sunni politicians visited the camps, they were pelted by the protesters, who blamed them for failing to represent their interests. The protesters were lodging complaints against a Shi'a-dominated executive and its discrimination against these Arab Sunni politicians, which they perceived as part of a systemic disempowering of their community. The arrests led to increased calls among Arab Sunnis for the reform of a political order that would address their grievances, allowing for their participation in governance and employment opportunities.

Iraq after 2003 witnessed a rearrangement of the patronage system that had existed under Saddam Hussein. The Anbar and Ninawa provinces are home to several tribes that had served as the backbone of the Ba'athist state, and Hussein had cultivated a system of neotribalization after the Gulf War to devolve power to the tribes so as to maintain order after the 1991 Uprising.[14] The collapse of the Ba'athist state in 2003 ended these tribes' privileged status as the elites of the state.

During Saddam's rule, the state had been the largest employer of Iraqis, and membership in the Ba'ath Party had been a prerequisite for a job in the state's behemoth bureaucracy. Security concerns after 2003 ultimately led to the de-Ba'athification process and the dismissal of thousands of experienced bureaucrats and military officers, which deprived Iraq of its pool of midlevel civil servants and soldiers who could maintain order. A large number of them happened to be Arab Sunnis, ultimately leading to a mass of unemployed men among this demographic. The critique of de-Ba'athification among Arab Sunnis did not emerge from an ideological loyalty to the party. For Arab Sunnis, de-Ba'athification was a blanket policy that had dismantled one of the primary vehicles of bestowing patronage under the old order. The new parties in power, the Shi'a Islamist and Kurdish groups, offered bureaucratic posts to members of their communities as a means of patronage.[15] When politicians in post-Ba'athist Iraq were awarded a ministerial post, that ministry was filled with political loyalists rather than talented technocrats. Those loyalists down the hierarchy then rewarded themselves by accepting bribes or creating their own niches of patronage within the ministry. This in turn led to Arab Sunni complaints of systemic discrimination in state hiring practices.[16] They protested against a corrupt system that essentially locked them out of patron-age networks that had benefited their community prior to 2003. Tensions also emerged between the Maliki government and the Sahwa tribal forces, with the latter arguing that the state had failed to support them financially or mil-itarily, or to allow their members to join the armed forces. In their view, the Shi'a-Kurdish parties had excluded the Arab Sunni community from an insti-tutionalized paramilitary and security role in the areas in which they resided. The new Iraqi armed forces had engaged in arbitrary arrests and had extracted payments from citizens at checkpoints. Iraq's Ministry of Interior forces or mi-litia members, who joined Iraq's army and police, employed extralegal violence to pursue the agendas of the Shi'a political factions, which happened to target Arab Sunnis.[17]

In terms of linkages between Iraq and Syria following the Arab Spring, Iraqi Arab Sunni protesters were emboldened by the Arab Sunni uprising against the Alawite Shi'a government in Syria. One protester in Ramadi declared, "We and the Syrians are part of the same struggle. Both our governments are very close to Tehran, and both of us oppose Iranian plans in the region. Iran wants to turn Baghdad and Damascus into its provinces and form a Shiite axis stretching from Tehran to the Mediterranean Sea."[18] This comment also alludes to how Arab Sunni protesters in Iraq expressed grievances over the Ira-nian influence in the Iraqi state,[19] often invoking the pejorative term "Safavid" to describe Maliki's government, a reference to the Turco-Persian dynasty that converted Iran to Shi'ism wholesale in the 1500s and later contested the Otto-man Empire for control over Iraq.[20] Some protesters carried posters of Recep Tayyip Erdogan, leader of Turkey.[21] Erdogan had been an early supporter of the Arab Spring protests in Egypt, Libya, and Syria. He also represented a Sunni leader with hegemonic potential to counter Shi'a Iran in the region and in Iraq. Erdogan emerged as a leader who became embedded within an Iraqi Arab pan-Sunnism, transcending the Arab-Turkish ethnic binary in the face of a perceived Iraqi Arab Shi'a-Persian threat.

This discourse is indicative of a change I noticed inside Iraq and in the di-aspora as the Syrian uprising of 2011 degenerated into a civil war. This conflict reconfigured Iraqi identities, with Iraqi Shi'as, Sunnis, and Kurds empathiz-ing or volunteering to fight with coreligionists or fellow ethnic groups across the border. Disaffected Iraqi Arab Sunnis found common cause with Syria's Arab Sunnis who were revolting against a Ba'athist government. Iraqi Arab Sunnis may have been sympathetic to the Iraqi Ba'ath Party, and the Syrian

Ba'ath government of Bashar al-Assad had given refuge to many of these Iraqi Ba'athists. However, after 2011, the Syrian state was perceived by Iraqi Sunnis as no longer a truly Ba'athist state but instead a reimagined Alawite Shi'a regime, on a par with the Shi'a regime in Iraq. Notwithstanding the doctrinal differences between Syrian Alawism and Twelver Shi'ism (the dominant interpretation practiced in Iraq and Iran), the governments of Bashar al-Assad and Nuri al-Maliki were conflated by Iraqi Sunnis into an axis of repressive Shi'a regimes.

Iraqi Shi'a groups experienced the opposite polarization, identifying with Assad's regime while conveniently forgetting that the Syrian government had enabled most of the sectarian killings from 2004 onward by allowing foreign Sunni jihadists into Iraq. Assad's government and the Alawites of Syria became "Shi'a" by sheer virtue of buying in to the narrative that Damascus was under attack from Salafi depredations[22] and the hegemonic aspirations of Sunni Saudi Arabia.[23] Furthermore, the collapse of the Yemeni state as a result of the events of 2011 allowed for the emergence of the Shi'a Zaidi Houthi movement.[24] Whereas before 2011 Iraqi Twelver Shi'a rarely thought of Syrian Alawis or Yemeni Zaidis as fellow Shi'as, a pan-Shi'ism emerged afterward.[25] However, I noticed this change among some segments of Iraq's Shi'a but by no means all. While a pan-Shi'a identity has taken root among some Iraqi Shi'as, other members of this community are wary of the preponderant Iranian influence over the Iraqi state. Iraqi Shi'a politicians and entire parties formed to protest the control of their Iranian coreligionists over domestic Iraqi affairs, thus sharing a common cause with Arab Sunnis. The Syrian civil war and conflict in Yemen allowed for a reconfiguration of pansectarian identities, but this phenomenon does not apply to all Iraqi Shi'as or Sunnis.

While the protests of 2013 and the ensuing rise of ISIS in Iraq might have the trappings of sectarianism in terms of slogans, discourses, and killings, the mere existence of sectarian cleavages in Iraqi society or doctrinal differences between Shi'a and Sunni is not in and of itself the causal factor sparking intranational tensions. Arab Sunni discontent as of 2013 reflected the conflicts that emerged in a new neopatrimonial system, characterized by patronage and favoritism that mostly benefited a new Iraqi Shi'a and Kurdish elite, but not all Shi'as and Kurds. The emergence of the Goran Party served as a protest movement against the established Kurdish elite, and the Shi'a cleric Muqtada al-Sadr expressed solidarity with the Arab Sunni demonstrators and criticized his fellow Shi'a Nuri al-Maliki.[26] He even appropriated the language of the Arab

Spring, labeling the Anbar protests as "Iraq's Arab Spring."[27] Iraq's politics as of 2013 would be more aptly described in this period as the politics of protest than as sectarian politics, where a deprived Kurdish and Arab Sunni-Shi'a opposition protested against an Arab Shi'a-Sunni political elite that was seen as indifferent to their demands, corrupt, and ineffective in terms of governance.

Sectarian fears are often manipulated by political elites to rally a sectarian core to bolster their power. For example, Maliki blamed the Arab Sunni demonstrations of 2013 on Sunni Turkey and Qatar, which had been the chief backers of Arab Sunni rebellion in Syria.[28] The Maliki government argued that these two states had supported the Islamic State of Iraq and elements of the former Ba'ath Party, which they accused of infiltrating the protests to seek out recruits. In terms of poor decisionmaking during the Arab Spring, both Maliki and Bashar al-Assad deflected blame for internal problems onto Ankara and Doha and then responded with violence to the protesters.

On April 23, 2013, fifty people were killed in clashes between security forces and protesters in Hawija.[29] Further armed clashes followed between the Iraqi security forces and Arab Sunni protesters, occurring during a resurgence of ISIS and its bombing campaign that had reached a level unprecedented since the sectarian conflict from 2006 to 2008. Militants linked to ISIS sought to capitalize on the discontent and built on the momentum of the violence, escalating their attacks against the Iraqi state and military in the hope of earning the sympathy of disgruntled members of the Sunni population.

When Iraq's armed forces fired on the crowd at Hawija, Arab Sunnis no longer considered their military a "people's army." In Tunisia, the military forces not only refused to shoot at the protesters but also forced the president-for-life to step down. The Egyptian military also portrayed itself as a people's army in January 2011 by refusing to shoot at protesters or dislodge the crowds from Tahrir Square. As the literature on civil-military relations explains, military forces choose to rally behind the elite or the people in a moment of crisis, depending on the structure of the armed forces and their composition. Eva Bellin writes, "First, where the coercive apparatus is institutionalized, the security elite have a sense of corporate identity separate from the state. They have a distinct mission and identity and career path. Officers can imagine separation from the state."[30] In the case of Egypt and Tunisia, institutionalized militaries in both states calculated that their power would remain intact even if the leadership were to change. Jason Brownlee, when analyzing the loyalties of militaries and security forces in the region, refers to the 1991 Iraqi Uprising: "Iraq further illustrates how neopatrimonial rule provokes internal crises, but may also enable the regime to repress challenger movements."[31] While Iraq's Shi'a revolted to protest Arab Sunni dominance of the state and military in 1991, it was the Arab Sunni core in the Republican Guard that rallied behind Saddam Hussein in his moment of crisis to maintain their minority rule over Iraq. In 2013, the roles were reversed. An Iraqi Shi'a–dominated military suppressed Arab Sunni calls for greater representation in the Iraqi state, albeit with much less brutality than in 1991.

The role of Republican Guards in Ba'athist Iraq or Syria falls within Mehran Kamrava's rubric of competing military and paramilitary organizations in the Middle East, or "parallel militarism"—a system in which branches of the military are not integrated but are kept separate to create a coup-proof system.[32] While this system is meant to deter the conventional army from launching a coup by creating a counterarmy with primordial connections to the regime, in Iraq in 1991 and Syria in 2011 these elite units were deployed to crush internal uprisings to maintain the minority community's power. Maliki continued Saddam Hussein's practice of fostering elite, smaller units loyal to the leader, alongside the regular Iraqi army. Maliki's "praetorian guardian" consisted of the counterterrorism force known as the Golden Division, derogatorily referred to as Maliki's "private army."[33] The case of Egypt demonstrates the difference in military structures. The armed forces in Egypt in 2011 represented the deep state, an autonomous military institution separate from the executive, which managed to retain its power after Husni Mubarak stepped down.[34] In the case of Iraq, one cannot speak of a deep state but rather a shadow state, with multiple nodes of military and paramilitary forces. The shadow state after 2003 consisted of armed forces where the lines between the official army and paramilitary were blurred, with some militias tied to the Ministry of Interior operating secret prisons without government oversight. The shadow state under Maliki included units such as the Golden Division, which reported directly to the prime minister, outside the chain of command of the regular armed forces.[35] The shadow state, combined with corruption of the ruling elite and their management of the armed forces, left the regular Iraqi army eviscerated, unable to withstand the ISIS offensive. Maliki's parallel militarism gave him a loyal force to crush the Arab Sunni protests in 2013, but such a small force could not have protected the entire Iraqi nation from ISIS in 2014.

While differing from Egypt and Tunisia, the Iraqi deployment of security forces in Hawija and at other Arab Sunni protest sites resonated with how security forces responded in Bahrain and Syria. The coercive apparatus of these two states, drawn primarily from one sectarian minority demographic, defended a sectarian elite against perceived threat from the majority. In Syria, an Alawi elite mobilized fellow Alawis in the armed forces to quell a Sunni rebellion, and in Bahrain, the Sunni elite did the same to the Shi'a majority. However, sectarianism should not be seen as the driving element behind the response of the security forces in all the countries that experienced large-scale protests. In Libya, Muammar al-Gadafi's armed forces, dominated by a coalition of Arab Sunni tribal in-groups around the Tripoli area, sought to crush unrest among fellow Arab Sunnis in the Benghazi area. On the other hand, the armed forces in Egypt and Tunisia were not only institutionalized and independent from the executive but also were not operating in societies divided along tribal or sectarian lines. In the cases of Bahrain, Libya, Syria, and Iraq, the armed forces in a divided society rallied behind the elite in which they shared a tribal or sectarian affiliation, based on the calculation that their in-group status would be lost if the political system fell apart. Only in Libya did the NATO intervention force some in-groups to defect to the rebel side after realizing the Gadafi leadership had a low chance for survival.

The Syrian Civil War and Reemergence of ISIS

The Arab Spring affected Iraq in terms of the loss of vast swaths of territory. The 2013 unrest in the Anbar province as well as the Ninawa province, where Mosul is located, made it difficult for Iraqi forces to police these areas, providing Iraqi Arab Sunnis with a space in which to rearm. With the collapse of Syrian state control in the upper Euphrates area, arms could flow in both directions across the Syria-Iraq border.[36] A former Iraqi insurgent in an International Crisis Group interview said of their armed presence in Iraq, "Iraqi resistance fighters have been scattered across the country, but we are counting on the success of the Syrian revolution to acquire more weapons and mobilise more fighters."[37] Concurrent with the protests of 2013, Iraqi religious centers, security forces headquarters and checkpoints, crowded markets, and politicians were targeted by bombings and assassinations.[38] The proliferation of domestic terror attacks coincided with the failure to address Iraqi Arab Sunni grievances, allowing ISIS and the Naqshabandi Army, a primarily Iraqi group led by the former Ba'athist Ibrahim 'Izzat al-Duri, to recruit among disaffected Iraqis.

More ominously, local Iraqis permitted these groups to operate from within their neighborhoods. During the surge of violence, Maliki accused unspecified tribes of harboring elements of ISIS in Iraq.[39] ISIS, he argued, could never have emerged in Iraq without the tribes' consent. The protests in 2013 created the grievances that paved the way for ISIS to ride the wave of Arab Sunnis' discontent and push into their areas of Iraq. The government's failure to address their demands and subsequent violent response led to disaffected Iraqi tribes acquiescing to, if not enabling, ISIS's renewed presence.

Based on past precedent, AQI, ISIS's predecessor, and its cadre of foreign fighters could not have operated from urban and rural Iraqi settings without the support of local Iraqis. In the beginning of the insurgency in 2003, Iraqis supporting the insurgency and AQI had the same goals: fighting US forces and a predominantly Shi'a-Kurdish government.[40] During the sectarian violence of 2006 to 2008, foreigners in al-Qaida were given local support and refuge in Iraqi neighborhoods by Iraqi Sunni coreligionists. Districts in cities such as Baghdad and Mosul are close-knit communities where a foreigner's presence rarely goes unnoticed. In certain districts in Baghdad, for example, locals knew of the "foreigners," as members of al-Qaida were called, operating from their neighborhoods.[41]

This past acquiescence can explain how ISIS secured de facto control of Falluja by January 2014 without actual fighting to seize the city. The Syrian civil war allowed ISIS a space to operate from and begin infiltrating Falluja and later Mosul with a network of sympathizers. Such networks existed in Mosul before ISIS conducted its military foray into the city in June 2014, which led to the collapse of the Iraqi military forces defending it. By allowing the reemergence of ISIS, disaffected Iraqi factions had communicated to the Maliki government a new bargaining tool vis-à-vis the state[42] without realizing, in the case of Mosul, that ISIS would go on to destroy their cultural fabric and historical heritage.

Iraq became a weak state when the United States attempted to develop institutions after dismantling the personalistic rule of Saddam Hussein. Iraq's government had the potential of becoming a stable, hybrid regime as of 2008, when violence subsided, but by January 2014, with the fall of Falluja, the central government once again faced the problems of governing a weak state where the bureaucracy and military were unable to assert authority over significant tracts of territory.[43] As of 2014, Iraq bore similarities to its neighbor Syria, as well as Yemen and Libya in their post-2011 incarnations. National identities and allegiances began to crumble in all of these weak states, where there had been a legacy of personalistic rulers, such as Gaddafi or Ali Abdullah Saleh of Yemen, creating networks around the leader rather than developing autonomous institutions. Maliki, like these aforementioned leaders, preferred to manipulate internal groups, whether they be tribes, factions within a sect, or elements within the armed forces, against each other, a divide-and-rule strategy typical of personalistic rulers that resulted in a divided populace and security force when ISIS returned in 2014.

Without the events of the Arab Spring erupting in Syria, ISI would not have been able to become ISIS. The uprising in Syria enabled ISIS to launch an uprising in Iraq, establishing a new political system: the Islamic State. Maliki's legitimacy as prime minister since his tenure in 2005 had been based on his record of providing relative stability to Iraq, and the fall of Mosul to ISIS undermined his position. Iraq's top Shi'a cleric, Grand Ayatollah Ali al-Sistani, called for Maliki to step down.[44] The United States and Iran, Arab Sunni protesters, and Sadr also called for Maliki's resignation, blaming his divisive rule for the fall of Mosul. During this crisis, the Golden Division, still loyal to Maliki, mobilized for a few days, sparking rumors that he would launch a coup. He stepped down peacefully, though, and was replaced by another politician within his party, Haider al-Abadi. It was the ISIS attack on Mosul that created the crisis that made Maliki's resignation a possibility, and thus events that began with the Arab Spring, which enabled the resurgence of ISIS, did bring about a change in Iraq's governing elite.

The events that unfolded over the summer of 2014, ending with Maliki's resignation, highlight how the hybrid state nature prevailed, even though it was simultaneously evolving into a weak state. There was no deep state to overthrow Maliki or maintain his power. A change of leadership occurred without violence, maintaining the democratic facade characteristic of a hybrid state, yet the problem of corruption and clientalism persisted, leading to the protests of 2015.

THE POST-ISIS PROTESTS OF 2015

By the end of the summer of 2015, antigovernment protests had erupted in several Iraqi cities, aimed primarily at corruption in the government, which had been blamed for the lack of electricity for air conditioners in Iraq's searing summer of 50-degree Celsius (122-degree Fahrenheit) heat.[45] The protests in Iraq occurred concurrently with those in Lebanon over the failure of the municipal government to collect garbage. Both protests, ostensibly against the state's failure to provide services, evolved into attacking the structure of the two regimes, specifically the sectarian quotas that hindered efficient governance.

Observers continued to situate these protests as Iraq's ongoing Arab Spring, demonstrating the endurance of this metaphor. An Iraqi writer, Ali Mamouri, wrote, "The July 16 killing of Muntazar al-Hilfi by police in al-Madina, north of Basra, during a protest for improved services was redolent of the death of Tunisian Mohamed Bouazizi on Jan. 4, 2011, which sparked the Arab Spring revolutions."[46] International media also situated these 2015 Iraqi and Lebanese protests within the Arab Spring narrative. Anton Issa, writing for the United Arab Emirates–based English-language newspaper the *National*, opened his article with the symbolic immolation that had sparked the Arab Spring: "When Tunisian street vendor Mohamed Bouazizi doused himself with petrol on December 17, 2010, it symbolised the exasperation felt across the Arab world with self-serving elites that had long neglected the public interest."[47] In reporting on protests in Iraq, the Arab Spring and the death of Bouazizi provided a powerful reference point and moniker.

By 2015, Iraq had forged a process of a public seeking to renegotiate the ruling contract with its elites. Iraqis believed they could take to the streets without facing repercussions from the security forces, and the political elite felt the pressure to listen and respond. In contrast to how his predecessor Nuri al-Maliki had responded with violence to the Day of Rage protests in 2011 and the Hawija protest in 2013, Abadi did not resort to breaking up the protests with force. The protests occurred not only in Tahrir Square in Baghdad but also in Basra in the south and the predominantly Shi'a heartland towns of Najaf, Karbala, and Hilla, the constituencies of Iraq's major Shi'a political parties.[48] The 2015 protests against the government's failure to deliver services served as poignant rejoinder to the ingrained notion that Iraq's Shi'a are a monolithic sectarian population, highlighting how a shared Shi'ism between political elites and the Shi'a population did not always determine allegiances in Iraq's politics.

Abadi had the political clout to answer the protesters' demands due to a sermon from Sistani calling upon Iraq's leadership to tackle the corruption at the top that had led to the failure to deliver services. These protests served as a case of "people power" enabled by the *marja'iyya*, the Shi'a clerical establishment, endorsing public discontent—a role reminiscent of that played by Shi'a clerics in endorsing the Iranian tobacco revolt of the early 1890s.

In response to the protests, Abadi initiated a campaign to streamline the executive branch, eliminating several posts, including Iraq's three vice presidencies.[49] The redundant vice presidencies, mere ceremonial roles, were a symptom of Iraq's patronage politics, with government posts being awarded not for a leader's acumen in governance but as part of the bargains struck with the myriad of ethnosectarian parties that form Iraq's post-2003 political landscape.

These protests had also occurred during the military conflict against ISIS. Abadi's response demonstrated that the rally-around-the-flag effect of an ISIS threat was not enough to distract the masses from the lack of state services. The protests also proved embarrassing to Abadi as he battled for the "hearts and minds" of Iraqis under ISIS rule. ISIS had even invested in its own media campaign to demonstrate its ability to deliver services such as reliable electricity in a sprawling metropolis like Mosul.[50] ISIS not only took advantage of Arab Sunni discontent in Iraq but then created a model of governance and reliable services that repudiated the corrupt practices of the Iraqi state.

CONCLUSION

Iraq's protests have been situated within the Arab Spring narrative by Iraqi participants and outside observers. Iraq has also been affected and transformed by the 2011 events that led to the collapse of neighboring Syria and subsequent resurgence of ISIS.

The tradition of political protest has been established in Iraq; such protests most likely demand reform of the state but not its complete dismantlement. In both Iraq and Lebanon, the populations have memories of the anarchy that state collapse entails. Nevertheless, the governments of both states, even though they are elected, are dysfunctional. What remains to be seen is whether Abadi can tackle the insurmountable structural challenges of reforming a political system based on rewarding Iraqi politicians solely due to their ethnic and sectarian backgrounds, managing the war against ISIS, and delivering reliable services—all tasks that his predecessor could not accomplish.

Protests in Iraq will continue, as grievances there, like the grievances that drove the initial Arab Spring protests in Egypt, Tunisia, Yemen, Libya, and Syria, will not dissipate anytime soon. Despite its vast oil wealth, Iraq suffers from poverty, unequal distribution of wealth, and unemployment. Government corruption and violation of basic rights are ongoing problems. Gelvin attributes the Arab Spring discontent to the "decades-long struggle for human dignity."[51] In Iraq, the decades-long struggle continues, whether against the Ba'ath government or the post-2003 "democratic" government that was supposed to symbolize the "new Iraq."

NOTES

1. James L. Gelvin, "Conclusion: The Arab World at the Intersection of the National and Transnational," in *The Arab Spring: The Hope and Reality of the Uprisings*, 2nd ed., ed. Mark L. Haas and David W. Lesch (Boulder, CO: Westview Press, 2017), 300.

2. Alexander Smoltczyk, "The Curse of Saddam City," *Spiegel*, April 28, 2003, www.spiegel.de/international/spiegel/religion-the-curse-of-saddam-city-a-246717.html.

3. Mohammed M. A. Ahmed, *The Iraqi Kurds and Nation-Building* (New York: Palgrave Macmillan, 2012), 30.

4. Qubad Talabani, "Kurdistan Is Not Tunisia," *Qubad's Blog*, January 2011, http://qubadsblog.com/2011/01/kurdistan-is-not-tunisia.

5. Charles McDermid with Karim Lami, "The Missing Ingredient in Iraq's Day of Rage," *Time*, February 25, 2011, http://content.time.com/time/printout/0,8816,2055525,00.html.

6. Ahmed K. Al-Rawi, "The Arab Spring and Online Protests in Iraq," *International Journal of Communication* 8 (2014): 918.

7. Ibid., 918.

8. Stephanie McCrummen, "23 Killed in Iraq's 'Day of Rage' Protests," *Washington Post*, February 25, 2011, www.washingtonpost.com/wp-dyn/content/article/2011/02/25/AR2011022502781_pf.html.

9. Turan Keskin, "The Impact of the Arab Uprisings on the Kurds," in *Authoritarianism in the Middle East: Before and After the Arab Uprisings*, ed. Julide Karakoc (New York: Palgrave MacMillan, 2015), 127–149.

10. Ranj Alaaldin, "Iraq's Sunni Spring," January 8, 2013, http://ranjalaaldin.com/2013/01/08/iraqs-sunni-spring.

11. See Gelvin, "Conclusion," for a definition of "hybrid regimes."

12. Liz Sly, "Arab Spring–Style Protests Take Hold in Iraq," *Washington Post*, February 8, 2013, www.washingtonpost.com/world/middle_east/arab-spring-style-protests-take-hold-in-iraq/2013/02/08/f875ef7e-715f-11e2-b3f3-b263d708ca37_story.html.

13. Colin Freeman, "Will Iraq Be Next to Have an Arab Spring?" *Telegraph*, March 2, 2013, www.telegraph.co.uk/news/worldnews/middleeast/iraq/9904605/Will-Iraq-be-next-to-have-an-Arab-Spring.html.

14. Amazia Baram, "Neo-Tribalism in Iraq: Saddam Husayn's Tribal Policies 1991–1996," *International Journal of Middle Eastern Studies* 29, 1 (February 1997): 1–31.

15. Harith al-Qarawee, "Siyasiu al-manfi fil-'iraq wa iqsa al-dakhil" (Exile politicians in Iraq and the exclusion of home), Al-Monitor, November 3, 2013, www.al-monitor.com/pulse/originals/2013/11/iraq-politician-former-exiles-divide.html#ixzz3lgE48kWJ.

16. Mustafa al-Kadhimi, "Al-Baʿath wal-Baʿathiin . . . wal-jaruh alati tarfadh an tandamal" (The Baʿath and the Baʿthists and the wounds that refuse to heal), Al-Monitor, April 12, 2013, www.al-monitor.com/pulse/ar/originals/2013/04/iraq-politics-baath-party.html#ixzz3lgCos1n9.

17. Robert M. Perito, "The Iraq Federal Police," United States Institute of Peace (October 2011), www.usip.org/publications/the-iraq-federal-police, 5–6.

18. International Crisis Group (ICG), "Syria's Metastasising Conflicts," Middle East Report No. 143, June 27, 2013, www.crisisgroup.org/~/media/Files/Middle%20East%20North%20Africa/Iraq%20Syria%20Lebanon/Syria/143-syrias-metastasising-conflicts.pdf, 12.

19. Ali Abel Sadah, "Ahmed Al-ʿAlwani: Zaʿim radikali lisunna al-Anbar" (Ahmed Al-ʿAlwani: Radical leader of the Sunnis of al-Anbar), Al-Monitor, October 1, 2013, www.al-monitor.com/pulse/originals/2013/10/iraq-sunni-leader-incitement-shiites.html#ixzz3lfzebHmg.

20. Ali Mamouri, "Don Quixote ma zal yuharib tawahin al-hawa . . . fil-ʿIraq" (Don Quixote continues to attack windmills in Iraq), Al-Monitor, January 26, 2014, www.al-monitor.com/pulse/originals/2014/01/iraq-politics-disputes-imagined-ideology.html#ixzz3lg4L6G1P.

21. Alaaldin, "Iraq's Sunni Spring."

22. Ali Mamouri, "Khatar al-tashaddud al-salafi yuwahhid al-shiʿa" (The danger of Salafist militancy unites the Shiʿa), Al-Monitor, October 1, 2014, www.al-monitor.com/pulse/ar/originals/2014/10/shiite-pan-identity-threat-islamic-state-iran.html.

23. Adnan Abu Zeed, "Al-intima al-taifi yuhaddid al-muwaqif al-iraqiyya min ʿsifa al-hazm'" (Sectarian affiliations reveal Iraqi positions on "decisive storm"), Al-Monitor, April 14, 2015, www.al-monitor.com/pulse/ar/originals/2015/04/iraq-sunni-shiite-positions-operation-decisive-storm-yemen.html.

24. F. Gregory Gause III, "Ideologies, Alliances, and Underbalancing in the New Middle East Cold War," *International Relations Theory and a Changing Middle East*, POMEPS Studies 16, September 17, 2015, http://pomeps.org/2015/09/17/international-relations-theory-and-a-new-middle-east/#sthash.mN3r7CmM.dpuf.

25. Omar al-Jaffal, "Al-huthiyyun yahzun bihtimam shiʿa al-ʿiraq" (Yemen's Houthis draw the attention of Shiʿa in Iraq), Al-Monitor, October 16, 2014, www.al-monitor.com/pulse/ar/originals/2014/10/iraq-shiite-support-yemen-houthis.html#ixzz3lfGLmeZE.

26. Ali Abel Sadah, "Muqtada al-Sadr: nida akhir ila maliki baʿad al-silsila tafjirat Baghdad" (Muqtada al-Sadr: Ultimatum to Maliki after a chain of Baghdad explosions), Al-Monitor, May 29, 2013, www.al-monitor.com/pulse/ar/originals/2013/05/sadr-maliki-iraq-warning.html#ixzz3lg5wYkUj.

27. Alaaldin, "Iraq's Sunni Spring."

28. Sly, "Arab Spring–Style Protests Take Hold in Iraq."

29. Mushreq Abbas, "Ahdath al-Hawija takalafa al-intihaziyya al-siyasiyya" (The Hawija incidents and the costs of political opportunism), Al-Monitor, April 25, 2013, www

.al-monitor.com/pulse/ar/originals/2013/04/iraq-hawija-massacre-politics.html# ixzz3lg22X6wl.

30. Eva Bellin, "Coercive Institutions and Coercive Leaders," in *Authoritarianism in the Middle East: Regimes and Resistance,* ed. Marsha Pripstein Posusney and Michele Penner Angrist (Boulder, CO: Lynne Rienner, 2005), 28.

31. Jason Brownlee, ". . . And Yet They Persist: Explaining Survival and Transition in Neopatrimonial Regimes," *Studies in Comparative International Development* 37, 3 (Fall 2002): 44.

32. Mehran Kamrava, "Military Professionalism and Civil-Military Relations in the Middle East," *Political Science Quarterly* 115, 1 (Spring 2000): 67–92.

33. David Witty, "The Iraqi Counter Terrorism Service," Brookings Institute, March 2015, www.brookings.edu/~/media/research/files/papers/2015/03/iraq-counter-service -witty/david-witty-paper_final_web.pdf, 12, 17.

34. See Gelvin, "Conclusion," for an analysis of the "deep state" and "Arab Spring," 295–296.

35. Witty, "The Iraqi Counter Terrorism Service," 23.

36. Omar al-Jaffal, "Suq al-islah al-'iraqiyya yanta'ash bitadhur al-amni wal-sara'a al-suri" (Iraqi weapons market thrives during the deteriorating security situation and Syria battle), Al-Monitor, December 18, 2013, www.al-monitor.com/pulse/ar/originals/2013/12/iraq -weapons-market-surge-syria-conflict.html#ixzz3lfCtSolR.

37. ICG, "Syria's Metastasising Conflicts," 11.

38. Bob Dreyfuss, "The Agony of Iraq—and Its Lesson for Syria," *Nation,* June 19, 2013, www.thenation.com/blog/174881/agony-iraq-and-its-lesson-syria#axzz2YN7hZIQD.

39. Suadad al-Salhy and Patrick Markey, "Al Qaeda, Sunni Insurgents Exploit Iraq's Sectarian Woes," Reuters, June 11, 2013, http://uk.reuters.com/article/2013/06/11/uk -iraq-alqaeda-idUKBRE95A0T120130611.

40. Austin Long, "The Anbar Awakening," *Survival,* 50, 2 (2008): 74.

41. Ami C. Carpenter, "Havens in a Firestorm: Perspectives from Baghdad on Resilience to Sectarian Violence," *Civil Wars* 14, 2 (June 2012): 193.

42. Mushreq Abbas, "Mutamar al-anbar . . . la nataij min dun musaliha dakhiliyya" (Maliki's call for unity conference in Anbar may be too late), Al-Monitor, June 4, 2014, www.al-monitor.com/pulse/originals/2014/06/iraq-maliki-call-unity-conference-anbar -too-late.html#ixzz3lfAQrmfU.

43. For discussion of a "weak state," see Bassel F. Salloukh, "Overlapping Contests and Middle East International Relations: The Return of the Weak Arab State," *International Relations Theory and a Changing Middle East,* POMEPS Studies 16, September 17, 2015, http://pomeps.org/2015/09/17/international-relations-theory-and-a-new-middle -east/#sthash.mN3r7CmM.dpuf.

44. Ali Mamouri, "Kayf najaha al-sistani biizaha al-Maliki" (How did Sistani succeed in ousting Maliki?), Al-Monitor, August 20, 2014, www.al-monitor.com/pulse/originals /2014/08/iraq-sistani-democratic-ways-successors-maliki.html#ixzz3lgLdUFfl.

45. Wassim Bassem, "Muwallidat al-kahriba . . . ramz al-ihbat al-mushari' al-khidmat fil-'iraq" (Electricity power crisis . . . symbol of frustration of the services project in Iraq), Al-Monitor, July 13, 2015, www.al-monitor.com/pulse/originals/2015/07/iraq-electricity -crisis-power-outages-daily-need-economy.html#ixzz3lf6j2CPY.

46. Ali Mamouri, "Jihat mawaliyya al-iran tu'aridh al-ihtijajat al-sha'biyya fil-'iraq" (Groups allied with Iran oppose the needs of the Iraqi people), Al-Monitor, August 25, 2015, www.al-monitor.com/pulse/ar/originals/2015/08/iraq-protests-reforms-iran-najaf -support-oppose.html#ixzz3lf7oBuTL.

47. Antoun Issa, "Why Iraqis and Lebanese Have Reached Breaking Point," National, August 25, 2015, www.thenational.ae/world/middle-east/why-iraqis-and-lebanese-have -reached-breaking-point.

48. Ibrahim Al-Marashi, "Endless Battle: Fighting Systemic Corruption in Iraq," Al-Jazeera, August 11, 2015, www.aljazeera.com/indepth/opinion/2015/08/endless-battle -fighting-systemic-corruption-iraq-150811084000991.html.

49. Mustafa al-Kadhimi, "Islah al-'iraqiyya imam ikhtibarat sa'ba walakinniha mum-kina" (Iraqi reforms in front of difficult test, but possible), Al-Monitor, August 17, 2015, www .al-monitor.com/pulse/ar/originals/2015/08/iraq-abadi-reform-measures-corruption -services-implement.html#ixzz3lf7KJVwp.

50. Saleh Elias, "Risala al-da'ish al-jadida . . . tawfir al-khadimat fi madinat al-mawsil" (Letter from the New Da'ish . . . offering services in the city of Mosul), Al-Monitor, May 13, 2015, www.al-monitor.com/pulse/ar/originals/2015/05/iraq-isis-mosul-services-sector -improvement-internet-roads.html#ixzz3lf5jjMwU.

51. James L. Gelvin, "Conclusion: The Arab World at the Intersection of the National and Transnational," in The Arab Spring: Change and Resistance in the Middle East, 1st ed., ed. Mark L. Haas and David W. Lesch (Boulder, CO: Westview Press, 2013), 241.

PART II

Non-Arab Countries and
the Arab Spring

MARK L. HAAS AND DAVID W. LESCH

T HE PROTESTS THAT OCCURRED throughout much of the Arab world beginning in 2010 affected in critical ways non-Arab countries located both in and out of the Middle East and North Africa. This volume analyzes reactions of five of them: Iran, Turkey, Israel, Russia, and the United States. Leaders in these countries believed that the Arab Spring created significant threats to and opportunities for their core interests. The following chapters discuss why this was the case, as well as the countries' responses to the demonstrations.

The Arab Spring uprisings affected the interests of non-Arab countries primarily by three mechanisms. The first was the anticipated impact of what are known in political science literature as "demonstration effects." This term refers to the tendency for developments in one country, including revolutions, to spur similar outcomes elsewhere.[1]

Demonstration effects were clearly at work during the Arab Spring: protests in one country inspired similar actions in others; hence their spread throughout much of the region. Moreover, the more the protesters succeeded with their objectives—such as the ousting of Presidents Zine El Abidine Ben Ali in Tunisia and Husni Mubarak in Egypt—the more powerful demonstration effects became, thereby making uprisings in other countries even more likely.

Arab leaders, as many authors in the first half of the book document, were acutely aware of the power of these dynamics, which made them fearful that the Arab Spring protests would spread to their own countries. This fear was not, however, restricted to the Arab world. As the chapters by Narges Bajoghli and Arang Keshavarzian and Robert Freedman make clear, both Iranian and Russian elites were concerned that examples of successful uprisings in Arab countries could inspire similar pressures in their own. This concern was particularly high in these countries because both had experienced large-scale popular protests shortly before the Arab Spring began. The protests were against what were perceived to be fraudulent or unfair elections: Iranian president Mahmoud Ahmadinejad's reelection in June 2009 and Russia's December 2012 parliamentary elections coupled with Vladimir Putin's announcement in the same month that he would again run for president (Russian protests continued after Putin's electoral victory in March 2012).

The level of domestic vulnerability, in short, colored how leaders viewed the Arab Spring. The more worried Russian and Iranian leaders were about the stability of their regimes before the Arab Spring demonstrations began, the more likely they were to view these developments negatively because these protests could exacerbate popular challenges to their domestic power. Russian elites in particular were apprehensive from the beginning that the Arab protests could have harmful consequences, both at home and abroad. The Arab Spring challenged Russian leaders' conception of "sovereign democracy," which asserted that the state has the central role in managing movement toward democracy while preserving social stability among contending domestic groups. To the Russians, popular democracy in the Middle East would likely lead to increased conflict and the rise of radical Islamists while also weakening domestic support for their preferred regime type.[2] Although Iranian leaders had more positive views of the Arab Spring than their Russian counterparts, based on a hope that more pro-Iranian regimes might emerge, they, too, frequently viewed the protests warily lest they intensify popular pressures for political change at home.

The view that the Arab Spring augmented the threats to Russian and Iranian leaders' domestic interests increased the incentives for both groups of decisionmakers to support counterrevolutionary policies. Although Russian and Iranian elites did not always act on these incentives (for reasons we discuss later), they did so in key instances, particularly their support for counterrevolution in the Syrian civil war. Roland Dannreuther summarizes the linkage between Russian leaders' concern for their domestic power and their Syrian policies: "As the Russian leadership felt internally threatened by the growing opposition within the country, conflict in the Middle East highlighted the perceived flaws of the imposition of Western liberal democracy and the virtues of Russia's own model of state-managed political order. There was, as such, a significant ideational and ideological dimension to the Russian response to the Arab Spring" and Russia's "uncompromising stance" in support of the Assad regime.[3] Domestic vulnerability and demonstration effects, in sum, resulted in policies toward the Arab world that were dedicated to preserving "order" and protecting state rather than popular sovereignty and humanitarian intervention.

In contrast to the response by Russian and Iranian elites, leaders in other non-Arab countries, especially in Turkey, viewed the Arab Spring combined with the power of demonstration effects as a significant benefit to their interests. As Mark Haas documents in Chapter 9, Turkey, at least until roughly 2014, was a highly popular country among Arab populations, with many viewing its system, which protected political liberties and religious identities while promoting economic dynamism, as a model worthy of emulation. Turkey's leaders agreed that their regime was a model one and hoped that its success would inspire protesters in Arab countries to push for the creation of similar political and economic institutions. Turkish elites, in other words, believed that the success of their regime created demonstration effects that would work for its spread, especially during the politically fluid era of the Arab Spring. The more Arab countries emulated Turkey's system, the more its soft power would increase, which would in turn boost Turkey's regional influence, cooperation, and security.

In addition to the impact created by demonstration effects, a second way in which the Arab Spring has affected the interests of non-Arab powers is due to the widespread belief that states' international-security policies, including choices of allies and enemies, are to a great extent a product of the identities of the dominant decisionmakers (e.g., whether a leader is Sunni or Shia, dictator or democrat, secular or Islamist). In this view, if one group of leaders were to be replaced with another with a different identity, security policies would dramatically alter. This perspective explains a key motive that has pushed outside countries to intervene in others' domestic contests. Iranian leaders, for example, have supported the Assad regime in Syria despite its brutality, not only due to the domestic interest in seeing attempted revolutions fail (see the previous point) but also due to the belief that cooperation with Syria will be greatly reduced if the Alawite (a variety of Shi'ism) regime is overthrown and replaced by a Sunni Islamist one. Similar dynamics help explain Turkish support of Sunni opposition groups in the Syrian conflict as well as Iran's support of Houthi groups (another offshoot of Shi'ism) in the Yemeni civil war.

Once one state dedicated to a particular identity interferes in another's civil conflict, other countries with opposing identities have enhanced incentives to do so as well in order to protect their interests (for more in-depth analysis of this point, see Haas's chapter on Turkey's foreign policies). It is by this process that domestic conflicts frequently result in regional polarization along different lines of identity (ideological, ethnic, and/or religious), thereby transforming civil conflicts into regional ones.[4] The wars in Syria and Yemen can in large part be understood by this logic, specifically as proxy disputes between Saudi Arabia and Iran based on regional sectarian polarization, with the Saudis supporting Sunnis—and usually hard-line Islamists—and the Iranians supporting Shia groups. If states' security policies were primarily a product of factors that transcended the identities of different groups of leaders—such as geography or power distributions—regime changes would have marginal effects on foreign policies. This is clearly not what many elites both in and out of the Middle East and North Africa believe—hence the frequent interference in others' domestic politics.

The incentives pushing leaders to intervene to support identity-based allies in other countries' conflicts have proven in key instances to be more powerful than the fear of revolution spreading and the resulting threats to governments' domestic interests (as discussed earlier in the first point). Iranian elites, for example, have powerful domestic-based reasons to support counterrevolutionary over revolutionary forces, but they have at times aided the latter, including rebels in Yemen and perhaps in Bahrain, where government officials have accused Iran of training militants and supplying them with weapons.[5]

Interestingly, Saudi calculations mirror those of Iranian leaders. The Saudis also have a strong interest in weakening the demonstration effects created by successful uprisings by supporting counterrevolutionary forces throughout the region. They have often acted on these incentives, especially by vigorously aiding follow monarchies. Saudi Arabia sent troops into Bahrain in 2011 (at the request of Bahrain's monarch) to quell domestic unrest. In an effort to tighten and expand cooperation among monarchies as a bulwark against revolution, the Saudis pushed for the Gulf Cooperation Council becoming a more cohesive political and economic federation, while also expanding the group's membership to include Jordan and Morocco. Riyadh has also led a military coalition using force to support the Yemeni government against rebel forces.[6]

Just like the Iranians, however, the Saudis have at times been a force for revolution when opportunities to increase the power of sectarian allies at the expense of enemies, specifically Iran, have arisen.[7] Most notably, Riyadh has been a consistent supporter of the armed resistance in Syria that is dedicated to the overthrow of the Assad regime. In this critical case, efforts to gain an advantage in the regional sectarian struggle with Iran have been more important to Saudi leaders than supporting counterrevolution.

The preceding analysis does not mean that all of the non-Arab countries examined in the following chapters were always heavily ideological in the formation of their foreign policies, either for domestic or international-security reasons. Interestingly, the liberal democratic countries—the United States and Israel—have been in important ways the most pragmatic in the sense that they were the least consistent in aiding their ideological allies in authoritarian states that appeared susceptible to political change. Although US leaders did lead the way in using force to oust Muammar al-Gadafi in Libya, they were noncommittal in the protests that overthrew Ben Ali in Tunisia, acquiesced to the crushing of dissidents in Bahrain, and provided limited support to opposition groups in Syria. These policymakers did push for the removal of Mubarak in response to the Egyptian popular uprisings, but they also offered little protest to the military coup in July 2013 that removed the democratically elected government that had assumed power in the post-Mubarak era.[8] Israel has been even less active in aiding the spread of democratic institutions, for the most part staying out of its neighbors' internal disputes.

These choices by US and Israeli policymakers were due to a significant degree to pragmatic calculations that privileged order and the security of existing allies over the support of democracy. Jeremy Pressman argues in Chapter 12 that this calculation became particularly strong for the Barack Obama administration as the Arab Spring progressed.

American and Israeli hesitancy to support the overthrow of authoritarian leaders in the name of democracy promotion goes beyond pragmatic, nonideological perspectives, however. Leaders in both countries, as both Pressman's analysis and Ilan Peleg's chapter on Israel demonstrate, feared that the removal of dictators from power, even if this was at first followed by the creation of a democracy, might eventually bring to power a more dangerous ideological enemy: radical Islamists.

This type of calculation frequently occurs in systems that contain more than two prominent types of ideological rivals, as is the case in the Middle East and North Africa.[9] In these systems, the overthrow of one ideological enemy might lead not to the ascendance of ideological allies but to the rise of another, more threatening foe. President John Kennedy referred to this danger in a 1961 discussion concerning US policies toward the Dominican Republic: "There are three possibilities in descending order of preference: a decent democratic regime, a continuation of the [dictatorial] Trujillo regime, or a [communist] Castro regime. We ought to aim at the first, but we really can't renounce the second until we are sure that we can avoid the third."[10] As Kennedy's quotation indicates, the existence of multiple ideological enemies limits the incentives to try to topple ideological enemies lest another, more dangerous rival becomes dominant. The same fears, with radical Islamism replacing the fear of the spread of communism, have played an important role in US and Israeli policies toward dictatorial regimes in the Middle East and North Africa both before and during the Arab Spring era.

US and Israeli leaders have not been alone in their fears about the rise of hard-line Islamists. Indeed, all of the non-Arab countries studied in the volume have shared this concern, at least with regard to Sunni-jihadist groups.[11] The fear that disorder caused by the Arab Spring would create openings that extremist groups would exploit (see the analysis of the "tyranny-anarchy loop" in the Part I introduction) is the third principal way in which protests in the Arab world have affected core interests in non-Arab states. This fear was not unreasonable, and the rise to power of the Islamic State of Iraq and Syria (ISIS) made possible by the Syrian civil war confirmed its legitimacy. Leaders in all of the non-Arab countries view this Sunni-jihadist group as an enemy that must be destroyed.

This last statement raises, however, an interesting puzzle that has important implications for the study of international security. If every one of the non-Arab countries studied in this volume—not to mention most Arab and European powers—has an interest in seeing ISIS destroyed, why has no grand alliance formed for this purpose? Part of this failure is due to the incentives for buck-passing policies that exist when multiple states share a common enemy: All want to see the enemy defeated, but all also want others to pay most of the costs to realize this goal (many are likely waiting for the United States in particular to lead the way before committing their resources). Because each state has incentives to free-ride on the balancing efforts of others, the result is that insufficient resources are dedicated to the objective.[12]

A sufficiently powerful anti-ISIS alliance has, however, also failed to form because of the effects created by the region's division into multiple ideological rivalries. The Middle East, in other words, is multipolar in terms of not only power but identity as well. The latter division makes an anti-ISIS alliance difficult to create because it reduces the likelihood that a majority of powers will view ISIS as the greatest danger they confront (the same factor helps explain why an anti-Iranian alliance has not formed).[13] Thus, Turkey wants ISIS destroyed, but not if it means the ascendance of Kurdish nationalism. Iran and Russia want ISIS destroyed, but not if this means the overthrow of the Assad regime. Israel wants ISIS destroyed, but not if it means the empowerment of Iran or a reduction in its isolation. If we bring Arab powers into the analysis, Saudi Arabia wants ISIS destroyed, but not if it means the defeat of all Sunni Islamist groups. As several of the following chapters indicate, alliances in an ideologically multipolar environment like the Middle East are fluid, with an enhanced likelihood of strange bedfellows cooperating (such as US-Russian-Iranian cooperation against ISIS), but also brittle due to the reduced likelihood that states will prioritize threats in the same way. This fact will increase the likelihood of prolonged conflicts by making the defeat of shared enemies less likely.

The impact that the Arab Spring has had on major interests of non-Arab powers means that they will continue to be highly involved in the region. This fact unfortunately creates reasons for pessimism concerning the advancement of rights in Arab states. Past foreign interventions in the Middle East have frequently had destabilizing effects.[14] Many non-Arab countries continue to have significant interests in preventing the spread in the region of rights-based regimes. Even when these outside powers possess common enemies, barriers to stable cooperation are likely to remain substantial.

Despite these major obstacles, there is still hope that at least some non-Arab powers can play a constructive role in advancing the basic rights of Arab peoples and thus many of the ideals that first animated the Arab Spring. At a minimum, a liberal democracy remains the most powerful country in the world. Although many in the Arab world remain hostile to the United States for some of its policies, its democratic institutions possess high levels of appeal.[15] The combination of America's considerable soft and hard power, with effective leadership, could help positively shape the political direction of the region. Moreover, if a Muslim-majority, non-Arab country or region, such as Turkey or the autonomous Kurdish regions of Iraq and Syria, successfully establishes a model that promotes rights while protecting religiosity, the power of demonstration effects will likely once again be at work, creating incentives for emulation and perhaps a renewal of the Arab Spring.

NOTES

1. See Samuel Huntington, *The Third Wave: Democratization in the Late Twentieth Century* (Norman: University of Oklahoma Press, 1991), 100–104.

2. Roland Dannreuther, "Russia and the Arab Spring: Supporting the Counter-Revolution," *Journal of European Integration* 37, 1 (2015): 80, 89–90, 92.

3. Ibid., 77. See also Pavel K. Baev, "Russia's Counter-Revolutionary Stance Toward the Arab Spring," *Insight Turkey* 13, 3 (2011): 11–19. As part of their counterrevolutionary efforts, Russian leaders are trying to promote their own preferred regime type of sovereign democracy. According to Dannreuther, "Russia presents a model, which is conservative in its support of the overriding need of the state to defend its sovereign rights of state and to respond to the societal demands for reform. . . . Compared to the 1990s or even early 2000s, Russia now feels much more confident about promoting this essentially authoritarian Russian model of state power since it is supported by China and by a number of other emerging powers" (Dannreuther, "Russia and the Arab Spring," 93).

4. On this process, see John M. Owen, *The Clash of Ideas in World Politics: Transnational Networks, States, and Regime Change, 1510–2010* (Princeton, NJ: Princeton University Press, 2010).

5. Peter Wonacott, "Bahrain Accuses Iran of Training Militants," *Wall Street Journal*, October 31, 2015.

6. Mehran Kamrava, "The Arab Spring and the Saudi-Led Counterrevolution," *Orbis* 56, 1 (Winter 2012): 96–104; Kareem Fahim and David D. Kirkpatrick, "Saudi Arabia Seeks Union of Monarchies in Region," *New York Times*, May 14, 2012.

7. See F. Gregory Gause III, "Is Saudi Arabia Really Counter-revolutionary?," *Foreign Policy*, August 9, 2011.

8. For other analysis of US and Israeli policies during the Arab Spring era, see Mark L. Haas, "The United States and the Arab Spring: Opportunities and Threats in a Revolutionary Era," in *The Middle East and the United States: History, Politics, and Ideologies*, 5th ed., ed. David W. Lesch and Mark L. Haas (Boulder, CO: Westview Press, 2013), 501–534; Daniela Huber, "A Pragmatic Actor—the U.S. Response to the Arab Uprisings," *Journal of European Integration* 37, 1 (2014): 57–75; Amichai Magen, "Comparative Assessment of

Israel's Foreign Policy Response to the 'Arab Spring,'" *Journal of European Integration* 37, 1 (2014): 113–133.

9. On this tendency, see John M. Owen IV and Michael Poznansky, "When Does America Drop Dictators?," *European Journal of International Relations* 20, 4 (2014): 1072–1099.

10. Quoted in Arthur M. Schlesinger Jr., *A Thousand Days: John F. Kennedy in the White House* (Boston: Houghton Mifflin Co., 1965), 769.

11. Hard-line Islamists dominate the Iranian government, but they are enemies with most Sunni-jihadist groups, who view Shias as heretics.

12. On buck-passing in power multipolarity, see Thomas Christensen and Jack Snyder, "Chain Gangs and Passed Bucks: Predicting Alliance Patterns in Multipolarity," *International Organization* 44, 2 (Spring 1990): 140–147.

13. On this last point, see F. Gregory Gause III, "Why Isn't There an Anti-Iran Alliance?," *Washington Post*, June 3, 2015, www.washingtonpost.com/blogs/monkey-cage/wp/2015/06/03/why-isnt-there-an-anti-iran-alliance. On the concept of ideological multipolarity and how it affects the likelihood of the formation of alliances, see Mark L. Haas, "Ideological Polarity and Balancing in Great Power Politics," *Security Studies* 23, 4 (December 2014): 715–753.

14. See Sean L. Yom, *From Resilience to Revolution: How Foreign Interventions Destabilize the Middle East* (New York: Columbia University Press, 2015).

15. Haas, "The United States and the Arab Spring," 513.

8

Iran and the Arab Uprisings

Narges Bajoghli and Arang Keshavarzian

T HE RISE OF THE Arab Spring movements in 2010 and their subsequent transformations from street protests to militarized conflicts and coun-terrevolutionary coups meant that the Islamic Republic of Iran also changed its view of and relationship to these uprisings and their aftermaths as they unfolded. Three processes, we argue, have been crucial to the Iranian regime's understanding of this conflict, its messages to its domestic audience regarding the uprisings, and its later involvement in certain areas of the Arab Spring. First, the fact that the Arab Spring followed on the heels of the 2009 Green Movement in Iran, which the state violently suppressed, affected the lens through which the state viewed the potential repercussions of the Arab Spring in Iran. Second, the regime reacted to the unfolding events as a result of Iran's larger geopolitical standing in the region, alliances with the regimes in Iraq and Syria, and prolonged rivalry with Saudi Arabia. Finally, the Islamic Republic has lacked a grand regionwide strategy; instead, the regime's approach to the uprisings has been reactive and inconsistent.

In this chapter, we begin by unpacking the relationship between the Green Movement and the Arab Spring; then we contextualize Iran's foreign policy in the region in relation to its own 1979 revolution and US involvement in the region. Next, we discuss Iran's involvement in Syria as Syria's civil war intensified and consider the role of the Islamic State (also known as Islamic State of Iraq and Syria [ISIS], Islamic State of Iraq and the Levant [ISIL], or DAESH) in the wider politics of the region. Finally, we conclude by reflecting on the effects of the Arab Spring on domestic politics in Iran, especially as they relate to domestic opposition to the ruling regime.

THE ARAB SPRING AS AN ALLY TO THE IRANIAN REGIME AND IRAN'S GREEN MOVEMENT

On the eve of the protest movements that began in December 2010 in Tunisia and swept across the Arab world in subsequent months, the Islamic Republic of Iran was facing domestic and international challenges to its authority. Although by the end of 2010, Iran's own popular uprising, the Green Movement—the name adopted by those who protested against the 2009 presidential results[1]— was more a specter than an organized political force, domestic politics remained highly contentious in the aftermath of the elections and the state's crackdown on the ensuing protests. Not only did a significant number of Iranian citizens and voters question the results that ensured Mahmoud Ahmadinejad a second term in office but notable postrevolutionary personalities added their support and social networks to the protest movement that brought millions of Iranians out into the streets in the summer, fall, and winter of 2009.

Mir Hossain Mousavi and Mehdi Karrubi, two of the 2009 presidential candidates and long-standing officials of the regime, questioned the reelection of Ahmadinejad as well as the procedures and organs of the regime that ratified the results and subsequently prohibited dissent. Mohammad Khatami, the popular reformist president (1997–2005), did not shy away from aligning himself with the so-called Greens. Neither did Ali Akbar Hashemi-Rafsanjani, arguably the second-most powerful man in the Islamic Republic. Rafsanjani was a student and confidant of the founder of the regime, Ruhollah Khomeini (1902–1989); was a critical political figure in the parliament in the 1980s; became president immediately after the Iran-Iraq War; and was regarded by many in Iran as the elder statesman second only to the Leader, Ali Khamenei. Thus, when Rafsanjani and his inner circle of associates, including his children, challenged poll results and the handling of the 2009 postelection crisis, the Islamic Republic faced one of the most critical challenges since the overthrow of the shah and the seizure of state power by Khomeini and his allies in 1979.

In response to the rise of the Green Movement and the support of some of the political elite in Iran for it, the regime blended indiscriminate violence against protesters, the use of state-controlled media, and targeted arrests and show trials of activists, journalists, and intellectuals to undermine the Green Movement. Although Khamenei, Ahmadinejad, the judiciary, and the security apparatus managed the conflict by silencing dissent, this response did not address social tensions and grievances, which, with the continued institutional fragmentation of the state,[2] further polarized the polity. Even among supporters of the Leader, conflicts and cleavages became so regular that they belied the Leader's call for unity and the ability of Ahmadinejad to govern during his second term.

If the regime was vulnerable domestically by the time the Arab Spring protests broke out, it was equally under pressure internationally. The Obama administration had succeeded in uniting powerful states against Iran's nuclear program. Cooperation between the United States, the European Union, Russia, and China expanded and deepened multilateral sanctions against Iran's economy. Diplomacy and economic inducements also brought Iran's trading partners, such as India, Korea, and the United Arab Emirates, into line. Restrictions on Iran's ability to trade, attract investment, and use international financial instruments may not have hurt hard-line conservatives in the regime,[3] but it did deepen the economic recession and threaten the livelihood of average Iranians. Meanwhile, the assassination of scientists and sabotage of computer systems in 2010 demonstrated how vulnerable the regime was to foreign efforts to harm its nuclear program.

This international pressure reinforced the Islamic Republic's threat perception that had prevailed since the 1979 revolution. While there had been talk of exporting Iran's revolution to surrounding countries in the 1980s, after the death of Khomeini and the end of the Iran-Iraq War, the Islamic Republic's primary objective was regime survival rather than investing in the overthrow of other regimes with the end of the devastating war.[4] The Hashemi-Rafsanjani presidency (1989–1997) pushed through economic, social, and cultural reforms aimed at creating a social base of professional, technocratic, and educated urban denizens. This constellation of forces constituted the base of the reformist movement that emerged with Khatami's presidency (1997–2005) and continued during the Green Movement in 2009.

Both Presidents Hashemi-Rafsanjani and Khatami sought out strategic openings with European, East Asian, and even Arab states, including Saudi Arabia and Egypt. Yet Iran's primary approach to regional politics in the Middle East followed a distinct pattern, namely, to bypass US-backed regimes that were hostile to Iran and to curry favor at the level of the "Arab street." Iranian leaders have sought to identify counterhegemonic allies and to undermine and embarrass unpopular Arab rulers and political elites for kowtowing to the demands of the United States and for passivity vis-à-vis Israel. This has been Iran's strategy, for instance, in cultivating close relations with Hamas in Palestine as a means to challenge the regional status quo. However, unlike the cases of Hamas in Palestine or Hizbullah in Lebanon, Iran has been unable to identify allies in Tunisia, Egypt, or Bahrain that would willingly and publicly associate themselves with the Iranian government (as is discussed later in the chapter).

Nonetheless, Iranian policymakers continued to believe that the greatest threat facing their regime was the United States' deep regional involvements and security apparatus built on an alliance system in the region including Central Asia. For several decades the United States has been a direct and indirect power within the region. First, the US military has established its own bases and access to ports and logistics centers in the northern Indian Ocean, Persian Gulf, the Caucasus, Central Asia, and the Eastern Mediterranean region. Moreover, the United States has worked closely with the militaries and secret services of Israel, Turkey, Egypt, Saudi Arabia, Pakistan, and other countries. Finally, these security quid pro quos have been augmented by a host of vested economic interests and financial alliances among economic and political elites across the region. During the cold war, investments in security aimed to confront Soviet expansion and ensure the flow of cheap oil to US allies in Europe and Asia. The demise of the cold war saw the emergence of new justifications for these military and financial arrangements. The targets became Saddam Hussein's Iraq, Iran, Somalia, and the Taliban. What was consistent in the eyes of policymakers in Tehran was that US regional hegemony isolated and threatened Iran.

When the George W. Bush administration invaded Iraq in 2003, Iran seized this opportunity not only to support the dislodging of a regime against which it had fought an eight-year war (1980–1988) but also to foster a close alliance with Baghdad as one of the few Arab states sympathetic to Iran. The emergence of a pro-Iranian Shia-dominated government in Iraq did not result in a stable and democratic regime in Baghdad, but it did reverberate through the regional order. Within months of the fall of Saddam Hussein, rulers in Saudi Arabia, Jordan, the United Arab Emirates, Egypt, and other countries warned of a "Shia Crescent" that was presented as a threat to "moderate" Arab states and therefore US regional interests.[5] Advocates of this sectarian view of regional politics claimed that Iran had masterminded a front extending from Tehran to Hizbullah in Lebanon via Iraq and Syria. The complexities of political conditions and the interwoven histories of religious sects in the region were brushed aside in order to convince both Washington insiders and citizens in the region that the primary source of "instability" was not lack of political freedoms, economic opportunities, or social welfare but Iranian "imperial ambitions" dating back millennia and, in more virulent and puritanical Sunni-centric discourse, the rise of heretical forms of Islam—Shia and Alavi Islam.

With the eruption of the Arab Spring nearly eighteen months after the start of the Green Movement in Iran, the hard-line forces and security apparatus of the Islamic Republic remained on alert. Fearful that the wave of protests and initial victories in Arab countries could embolden domestic Green activists, Iranian state television depicted the protests in the Arab world as an "Islamic Awakening" (bidari-e islami) that sought to create Islamic governments throughout the region, and as protests and struggles against regimes that were allies of the United States. This framing of the Arab Spring in religious terms harkened back to Ayatollah Khomeini's initial calls in the early 1980s for the export of Iran's "Islamic Revolution." In particular, the narrative was made to fit the events in Tunisia and Bahrain, where the Islamist al-Nahda party was able to democratically come to power, in the former, and the Shia majority protested against the Saudi-backed Sunni rulers, in the latter.

The Leader, Ali Khamenei, argued that these "revolutions" were akin to the 1978–1979 mass uprising in Iran and were part of an Islamic Awakening.[6] In a Friday prayer sermon on February 4, 2011, while reminding his audience that "the sedition of 88 (2009)" aimed to derail the Islamic Revolution, Khamenei commented, "Today's events in North of Africa, the country of Egypt, the country of Tunisia and certain other countries have another meaning for us people of Iran; they have a special meaning for the Iranian nation. This is the same type of event that is always known as 'Islamic Awakening,' which is the result of the victory of the great revolution of the Iranian nation."[7] He explicitly connected these events to geopolitical concerns, stating, "The Tunisian nation managed to topple a US ally with a treacherous and irreligious ruler." Regarding Egypt, he argued that the uprising was not only because the Egyptian people had risen up against the US-sponsored dictatorship of Husni Mubarak but that the Egyptian regime had not opposed Zionism and had become a companion and servant of Israel against Palestinians, as had been demonstrated in the 2008–2009 war against Gaza. Ahmadinejad, parliamentarians, and hard-line allies of the Leader's office all came out in support of this narrative of the uprisings, even though there were few actual indicators that the Iranian revolution or the ruling regime was a direct inspiration or model for the would-be revolutionaries in Tunisia, Egypt, and beyond.

On the other hand, supporters of the Green Movement also championed the Arab uprisings, claiming that these protests in Tunisia, Egypt, Bahrain, and other locations shared much with their own demands and methods of nonviolent protest against the state. Nonetheless, the official rhetoric throughout the uprisings in Bahrain, in particular on the Islamic Republic of Iran Broadcasting service, showcased scene after bloody scene of Bahraini activists beaten down by police in their attempt at "self-determination." In these events, the Islamic Republic positioned itself as a supporter of the oppressed Muslim masses against Saudi and Western-backed autocrats.

The irony of this was not lost on those who supported the Green Movement in Iran and faced the regime's wrath. Activists called out the Islamic Republic's hypocrisy in its depictions of the Arab Spring on social media sites, especially on Facebook, where users shared news of the Arab Spring from opposition Persian-language websites. The opposition sites depicted the protests as uprisings against oppressive governments and drew connections with Iran's own Green Movement only eighteen months before. In the midst of the eighteen-day Egyptian uprising that culminated in the overthrow of Husni Mubarak, the leader of the Green Movement, Mir Hossain Mousavi, wrote on his Facebook page, "The starting point of what we are now witnessing on the streets of Tunis, Sanaa, Cairo, Alexandria, and Suez can be undoubtedly traced back to the days of the 15th, 18th, and 20th of June 2009, when people took to the streets of Tehran in the millions shouting 'Where is my vote?' and peacefully demanded that they get back their denied rights."[8] A popular chant shared on Facebook and later in protests in Tehran, Isfahan, Shiraz, and Rasht drew parallels between the events in the region and the frustration of some of the Iranian protesters: "Tunisia could do it, but we couldn't" (*Tunis tunist, ma natoonistim*), referring to Tunisia's ability to bring about a revolution following its protests.

In response to the victorious revolutions in Egypt and Tunisia, Green Movement activists echoed the call for a "Day of Rage" protests on February 14, 2011, in solidarity with protesters in Egypt, Bahrain, and Yemen.[9] These actions and claims aimed to revitalize those who were sympathetic toward the Green Movement as well as to expose the Iranian regime's hypocritical stance vis-à-vis protesters. This sort of statement also suggested the possibility of camaraderie between Iranians and Arabs struggling to make popular sovereignty a reality. Yet the Green Movement did not enjoy the political space and resources to realize this objective, nor did activists in the Arab world cultivate/acknowledge/prioritize this potential.

Iran's Day of Rage protests coincided with the annual state-sponsored ten-day celebrations of the victory of the 1979 Iranian revolution, during which state television aired footage of the victorious Egyptian revolution, intercutting scenes from the revolution and the return of Ayatollah Khomeini. The message was clear: The Egyptian masses had been inspired by Iran's revolution and wanted to create a system similar to the Islamic Republic. Despite the depictions and edited footage on national television, the Islamic Republic feared the connections that opposition groups were making between the Arab Spring and Iran's Green Movement. The day before the Day of Rage protests, Mousavi; his wife, Zahra Rahnavard; and Mehdi Karroubi were put under house arrest. Regime loyalists argued that the outspoken statements linking the Green Movement to the Arab uprisings were sufficient evidence to prove that the Green Movement intended to overthrow the regime rather than merely protect civil and political rights. The security apparatus wanted to ensure that a new wave of protests would not emerge and repeatedly claimed that the Green Movement was dead.

Nonetheless, on February 14, 2011, Tehran witnessed the largest protest since the suppression of the Green Movement the year before. In two separate and contested cases, two students, Sane Jaleh and Mohammad Mokhtari (who died the next day from the wounds he suffered), were killed near Azadi Square in Tehran.[10] The families of those killed were barred from talking to media and threatened with retaliation if they spoke to Iranian-diaspora journalists. Jaleh's brother spoke out about the threats in an interview with Iranian journalist Masih Alinejad, who now lives in the United Kingdom. Smaller protests were held in cities in Iran for the anniversary of the deaths of these students, as were gatherings on March 8, the International Day of Women. All of these gatherings were met with the deployment of antiriot forces.[11] None of these gatherings, and their calls of solidarity with the Arab Spring, were reported on Iranian state television, which continued to report only a limited amount of news about the uprisings and continued to refer to them as Islamic Awakenings. By contrast, Iranian-diaspora media sources, whether the more than twenty-four channels broadcast daily on satellite station into Iran or the plethora of news websites online, covered the Arab Spring, and the news further spread on Facebook.

This call to action was one of the final attempts by the Iranian opposition to engage with the Arab Spring as a means to continue its own struggle.

Despite these rhetorical and physical struggles between different wings of the Iranian polity, there was little evidence that Tunisians, Egyptians, Bahrainis, or others took inspiration from events in Iran or imagined fashioning new political orders modeled on Iran's regime. From the officials of the Islamic Republic to their opponents, the Arab uprisings became a reflection of the particular anxieties of the Islamic Republic that did not find a sounding board in the squares being occupied in the rallies of December 2010, January 2011, or February 2011. It seems that Iranian policymakers deep down understood this, and their actions were cautious and reactive rather than strategic or committed. The Arab uprisings simultaneously were a tool in ongoing political struggles inside Iran and, as suggested by the Bahrain case, were becoming a stage in which regional conflicts, especially between Iran and Saudi Arabia, were being enacted. This latter point was most vividly demonstrated after the Syrian protest movement gained a tragic momentum in spring 2011, as discussed in the following section.

Syria: When an Uprising Becomes a Threat

Ironically, just when the regime seemed to have the upper hand vis-à-vis the Greens, the Arab uprisings took a turn that caught Islamic Republic officials off guard and challenged their narrative that those uprisings were an Islamic Awakening against the West and in line with Iranian revolution. As the Arab Spring turned from street protests to sites for larger geopolitical confrontations, the Islamic Republic began to take a more active role in the events. From the legitimate outcry of protesters in Libya against Muammar Gaddafi's rule to NATO intervention and eventual civil war, to Saudi Arabia and the Gulf Cooperation Council's deployment of ground troops to Bahrain, the fast-moving events in the region posed a dilemma for the Islamic Republic. While Iran was buoyed by the thought that a number of regimes allied with the United States and opposed to the Islamic Republic would be overthrown or at least weakened, it was increasingly clear that these political upheavals were both volatile and attracting numerous outside forces and interests. The stakes for Iran were rising just as the outcomes were becoming more unpredictable.

By the summer of 2011, Syria became the focal point of Iran's attention. Unlike Egypt, Tunisia, Libya, Yemen, or Bahrain, Iran has long-standing strategic interests in Syria, and specifically in the Assad family that headed the Baathist party-state. The relationship between Syria's ruling Baath Party and the Islamic Republic stretches back to the early 1980s, when Iraq invaded Iran. As the only Arab country to defend Iran during the bloody eight-year war with Iraq, Syria provided invaluable diplomatic and military support to the Islamic Republic throughout the war. Syria shut down the Iraqi oil pipeline of Kirkuk–Baniyas to deprive the Iraqis of revenue and provided the Iranians with military technology and weaponry. Saddam Hussein's Iraq was Syria's regional foe, and the Syrian state had a vested interest in preventing Iraq from gaining ground in the region.

Due to Syria's support throughout the war, the Islamic Republic has remained loyal to its ally, despite the fact that Syria's Baathist regime is staunchly secular. For the Islamic Republic, in addition to loyalty to Syria for its defense of Iran during the 1980s, Syria is important because it is on the front line of defense against wider Israeli, American, and Saudi influence in the region. Syria has been key to Iran in maintaining Hizbullah in Lebanon and, by extension, providing channels for funding Hamas. Without Syria, the Islamic Republic fears what would happen to Hizbullah; both receive funding and support from the Iranian government. According to Western estimates, Hizbullah receives anywhere from $100 to $200 million in supplies and weaponry per year from Tehran, with much of this transported through Syria.[12]

As the Syrian conflict intensified and more insurgents flowed across Syria's borders to fight, the Iranian government began to see the events in the region as an extension of a proxy war with Saudi Arabia and as an uprising nurtured by the United States and its regional allies. This in effect shed doubt on the sincerity of opposition movements in Syria. Calling attention to the varied groups involved and the money being transferred from Western and Saudi sources to the insurgent groups, the Islamic Republic viewed the Syrian events not as opposition to Assad's rule but as a Saudi and Western intervention against an Alavi ruler allied with Iran. In late June 2011, Supreme Leader Ali Khamenei said, "In Syria, the hand of America and Israel is evident."[13] The Revolutionary Guard has also followed the Leader in believing that the continued civil war in Syria is a foreign intervention against one of the few Arab regimes friendly to Tehran. Initially providing funding for Assad's defense of Syria, as the conflict grew bloodier and more money from Saudi sources reached extremist Sunni armed groups, the Islamic Republic authorized the special forces of the Revolutionary Guard—the Quds Forces, under the leadership of Qassem Soleimani—to provide tactical support to the Syrian military as well as an increasing number of fighters.[14] Beyond this, Iran is also involved in providing billions of dollars in lines of credit to the Syrian government.[15]

For the more hard-line forces in the Islamic Republic and the Revolutionary Guard, the Syrian uprising is similar to Iran's own 2009 Green Movement, which they believe was supported by foreign powers. As such, helping to suppress any opposition movement in Syria also serves as a "lesson" for opposition movements in Iran and its diaspora about the consequences of challenging state rule. Referring to the Mujaheddin-e Khaleq (MKO), the biggest armed Iranian opposition group outside the country, a Revolutionary Guard colonel said in a personal interview, "Look how easily foreign groups duped Syrians and hijacked that movement. If the Islamic Republic hadn't acted the way it did in 2009, I guarantee you the Mujaheddin [based in Iraq and Europe] and [other] outside forces would be wreaking havoc in Iran."[16]

While Khamenei and other spokespersons of the regime downplay the sectarian dimensions of the conflict in Syria, as well as in Iraq and Yemen,[17] the regime has not shied away from legitimating its involvement in Syria and Iraq in religious terms. For instance, the mission and recruitment to defend the Assad regime has been described as a battle to protect "the Two Shrines," a reference to the two holy shrines in Damascus visited by Shia pilgrims—Sayyedeh Roghiyeh and Sayyedeh Zayneb.[18] The emblem of the two Shia shrines is useful for the regime because the Islamic Republic's policy of actively supporting the Baathist regime in Syria poses ideological challenges and contradictions. It is coming to the aid of a political regime that is strongly associated with Arab nationalism and socialism and is headed by Alevis, who have had just as precarious a position in mainstream Twelver Shia theology as they have in Sunni Islam. Hence, the logic of Iranian-Syrian cooperation is grounded in political expediency rather than ideological or sectarian solidarity. As Ari Heinstein notes, "Recognizing that there is limited theological affinity between Alawis and Shia, and that such similarities could be the cause of tension rather than the basis for an alliance, the question of why Iran has so strongly identified with the Alawi Asad regime requires an answer beyond 'sectarianism.' Rather, it is shared strategic aims that have sustained the relationship for 35 years, including mutual interests in seeing Saddam Hussein's Iraq weakened, thwarting American influence in the region, fighting against Sunni radicalism, and strengthening Hizbullah."[19]

During the course of the Syrian uprising, the broader geopolitical context, however, has shifted. Under Hasan Rouhani's administration and with the rise of ISIS in Eastern Syria (discussed further in the next section), Iran and the United States have shared an interest in securing Syria's borders and defeating ISIS militants. Iran not only plays a large role in the civil war but is one of the few countries that has diplomatic relations and leverage with the Assad regime and therefore has strong vested interests in the outcome of this conflict. Despite these factors, up through the suspension of the Geneva talks in February 2016, Western and regional powers have attempted to deal with the spiraling civil war in Syria through the exclusion of Iran. This policy on the part of Western powers and regional states, principally Saudi Arabia, has further hurt attempts to reach a peaceful solution in this civil war, which is fundamentally political rather than religious in nature.[20] The nuclear agreement between Iran and world powers signed in 2015 as well as ceaseless violent conflict dismembering Syria and destabilizing the entire region may provide the conditions for a new strategy to bring about peace in Syria that could include the Iranian government along with a diverse array of Syrians, the Saudi Arabian government, Turkey, the United States, Russia, and other relevant parties.

ISIS as a Threat and Motivation for Engagement

One of the many by-products of the Arab uprisings has been the emergence and development of nonstate actors with "flexible linkages" and alignments with states.[21] This has been most prominent in cases where the weakening or fall of regimes has resulted in the collapse of state structures (e.g., Libya, Syria, and Yemen). In these contexts, armed militias have both filled the vacuum caused by collapsing states and eviscerated state sovereignty and threatened to redraw territorial borders. Iran's response to the mushrooming and empowerment of nonstate actors has been mixed and based on strategic calculations. As the Syrian uprising became increasingly violent due to tactics of the regime and the turn to arms by some segments of the opposition, Iran came to the aide of its ally, the Assad regime, against multiple and sometimes competing militias funded and aided by Saudi Arabia, Qatar, Turkey, the United States, and others. In the case of Yemen, Saudi Arabia and others have claimed that Iran has weighed in on the side of the Houthi rebels against the government in Sanaa that was nominally in power after the fall of Ali Abdullah Saleh.[22] Finally, the fluid and multifaceted conflicts unleashed by the Arab uprisings resulted in the souring of relations between Iran and Hamas. While Iran spent much of the 2000s cultivating relations with Hamas's leadership and outmaneuvering Arab states that had previously patronized Hamas since its founding in the 1980s, 2011 marked the beginning of a rupture. Hamas distanced itself from Iran as it found itself on opposing sides in some conflicts (e.g., Syria) and at least for a short period of time was able to cultivate relations with emerging regimes (e.g., the Muslim Brothers in Egypt, 2012–2013). By 2015, reports suggested that Iran no longer helps finance Hamas.[23]

However, the case of the transnational, and even antinational, Islamic State posed a greater challenge to Iran in 2014.[24] This ultramilitant Sunni militia-cum-caliphate developed in the context of post-2003 Iraq and post-2011 Syria. Its call for jihad took aim at multiple targets in the name of confronting heresy and upholding its interpretation of Islamic law by fashioning a new polity. Within Iraq, ISIS is a synthesis of radical Sunni-oriented local and foreign fighters and former members of the Iraqi military and Baath Party. While ISIS's immediate adversaries were Syrian, Iraqi, and Kurdish troops, in the eyes of Iran, it posed a dual threat. On the one hand, ISIS offered a virulently anti-Shia interpretation of Islam derived from Wahhabism, which made many in Iran suspect that it enjoyed at a minimum the tacit and private financial assistance of Saudi and Qatari citizens. On the other hand, ISIS's military victories in both Syria and Iraq challenged Iran's two closest regional allies—the Baathist regime in Damascus and the Shia- and Kurdish-dominated government in Baghdad. However, it was the situation in Iraq that was more immediately ominous for the Islamic Republic, for ISIS's military victories and territorial gains threatened to lead to either the collapse of the Iraqi central government or the partitioning of Iraq. The prospect of sectarian chaos and an armed and organized extremist Sunni entity on its western border was unacceptable to Tehran. When the city of Mosul, Iraq's second-largest city, fell to ISIS in June 2014, Iran was put on high alert. Mosul is only 541 kilometers (336 miles) west of Sanandaj, the capital of Iranian Kurdistan. The fall of Mosul was an unexpectedly quick one. Although the Iraqi army had nearly 30,000 soldiers stationed in the city, and the attacking force of ISIS was around 1,500, Mosul fell to ISIS control after six days of fighting. Iran quickly responded with arms and military support and sent the highest levels of the Revolutionary Guard's Quds Force as advisers on the ground.

Again, Iran's response appeared to be reactive rather than premeditated. One study concluded that Tehran was initially caught unawares by the rise of

ISIS, particularly its advance into Iraq. It noted that "at first, Tehran minimized the threat from ISIS; then its strategy shifted as the group's progress became more alarming, leading it to become involved 'from behind'. Then, in the light of the progress made by ISIS fighters close to Iranian borders, Tehran changed its approach to the conflict again, further increasing its involvement in Iraq in the effort to pre-empt a potential spillover across its borders."[25] Iran's involvement came through provision of arms and logistical support from the Islamic Revolutionary Guard Corps to the Iraq army, but most notably Shia and Kurdish militias, with which it has long-standing relations and who were more effective on the battlefield.

Meanwhile, the emergence of ISIS in Syria posed a challenge to policymakers in the United States, Turkey, and the Gulf countries, for they found themselves confronting a group successfully battling the Assad regime that they hoped would be toppled. Iran faced no such dilemma, and confronting ISIS was part and parcel of supporting the governments in Syria and Iraq. Yet the conflict with ISIS dramatically illustrated some of Washington's and Tehran's shared objectives. Although the United States and Iran cooperated in Afghanistan after the 2001 fall of the Taliban, and share the goal of maintaining stability in post-Saddam Iraq, in the midst of the tense nuclear negotiations of 2014 and 2015, the old adversaries have found themselves similarly motivated to confront ISIS militarily.

The Legacy of the Arab Uprising
for Iran's Domestic Politics

The Islamic Republic needed to navigate the Arab uprisings in terms of foreign and military policy, but it also posed a challenge and an opportunity in terms of representations and conceptions within Iranian society. As the Arab Spring took a turn for the worse, the media tactics of the Islamic Republic also became more nuanced and sophisticated. The civil war in Syria, the rise of ISIS, and the continued bloodletting and violent conflict in other countries all reinforced the belief among the political elite of the Islamic Republic that they had acted correctly in quickly suppressing the Green Movement. The chaos and violence also left their impression on Iranian citizens and political activists. As a captain in the Revolutionary Guard's navy division explained in a personal interview, "Iran is in the middle of a very volatile region, and we are one of the only countries in the region that is stable now. All of our major cities are safe. We don't have random bombs going off. Do you think there aren't attempts to foment chaos in Iran by outside groups? Of course there are! But we've secured our borders and maintain the country's security."[26]

The narrative of Iran as a "stable country" in a region of violent civil wars and harmful "foreign interventions" spread as clashes in Syria turned into a full-fledged civil war. Mentions in state-controlled Iranian media of the "foreign fighters" in Syria (a category that did not include the proregime Iranian fighters) and of the allegations that Syrian opposition groups who initially preached freedom later made deals with hard-line Islamic forces fit into the Islamic Republic's narrative that opposition groups are not to be trusted and can easily be manipulated. Domestically, the rise of ISIS focused the Iranian public's attention on the volatile consequences of the Arab uprisings. Iranian media and politicians spent much of 2014 depicting ISIS as a dangerous and "un-Islamic" organization.

In an attempt to demonize opposition groups, proregime media makers have received large funds to create films and television series about how the opposition cannot be trusted. In a new distribution strategy, these media were distributed to schoolteachers throughout the country in fall 2014.[27] One such film is *Gorg-ha* (The wolves), a documentary series initially released in 2007 and reissued in 2013. After the fall of Saddam Hussein to American and other Western forces in 2003, Iran gained access to films and archives that revealed the full extent of collaboration between the MKO and the Iraqi government during the 1980–1988 Iran-Iraq War. These archival films show top-level meetings between the MKO's leadership and the security apparatus of Iraq, in which money was exchanged for information and collaboration. Initially, this four-part, eight-hour series aired on national television. With the civil war in Syria, the series was reedited in 2013 to a 90-minute documentary film that attempted to be less "propaganda" and more "just the facts," the producer said in an interview. The film plays a crucial role in the eyes of its filmmakers: It is "proof" that the Islamic Republic is right to distrust any opposition to its rule, just as the opposition in Syria is to be distrusted. The archival footage in the film only confirms the veracity of these claims and makes the betrayal of the MKO as "light as day," as one Basiji filmmaker stated in a personal interview.[28] Films such as this, as well as *The Unfinished Story of My Daughter, Somayeh* (2014), another film about the deceit of the MKO, are now taught in schools and some universities and shown repeatedly on national television. The films have even traveled in special "festivals" in which proregime cultural centers have set up temporary movie theaters to show these films in towns that do not have their own theaters.

Although the MKO has occupied the position of a bogeyman for the Islamic Republic from its inception, new depictions of opposition groups as untrustworthy gained considerable traction with the rise of the Green Movement. The director of *The Unfinished Story of My Daughter, Somayeh,* Morteza Payeshenas, who has made a handful of films about the fierceness of the MKO, said of his reasoning to make these films, "You have all these people on the streets [in Iran] protesting and unhappy. At least inform them who not to believe in and whose arms not to go into in all of this."[29]

In a September 2014 interview with US media, President Rouhani commented about ISIS, "They want to kill humanity. And from the viewpoint of the Islamic tenets and culture, killing an innocent people equals the killing of the whole humanity. And therefore, the killing and beheading of innocent people in fact is a matter of shame for them and it's the matter of concern and sorrow for all the humans and all the mankind."[30] While the regime clearly opposed ISIS and sought to rally support for its opposition, even Iranian citizens ambivalent toward the regime and the military viewed ISIS as a threat. One Iranian was quoted as saying, "Personally I don't like the Revolutionary Guard. But when our territorial integrity is at stake, what choice do we have?"[31] She continued, "DAESH is really frightening, and I'm scared. I feel like they could pose a serious threat to us." Meanwhile, clerics have weighed calling for holy war (jihad) "in defense of the integrity of Iraq and especially its sacred [Shia] shrines." As the Iran correspondent for the *New York Times* noted, "And as the reality of war [against ISIS] is brought home, the attitude of many here toward the Revolutionary Guards Corps is changing. In 2009, when millions took to the streets to protest the re-election of President Mahmoud Ahmadinejad, it was the Guards . . . who attacked many of those on the streets. But the well-documented mass killings by ISIS . . . have caused ordinary Iranians to rethink their views. On websites such as the reformist Entekhab news site, where in the past anonymous commentators rarely missed an opportunity to criticize the Guards, the group is now regularly lauded."[32]

These anxieties were expressed even by those who have been sympathetic to the reform movement in Iran. "Look, I know Mousavi personally, and my daughters and wife voted for him and protested in the Green Movement," one Air Force Commander of the Revolutionary Guard said in a personal interview. "But after some time, we've realized that the Mujaheddin played a large roll in fomenting unrest in the country following the protests. We have to stand strong, or we'll turn into Syria."[33] Although the Mujaheddin figured prominently in the post–Green Movement rhetoric used by the regime and regime supporters, there is no evidence of the exiled Islamist-leftist organization playing any role in the Green Movement or attracting more followers after the uprising. The MKO has become a scapegoat for any and all opposition to the Islamic Republic. Saeed Laylaz, a prominent reformist economic journalist in Iran who was jailed during the 2009 Green Movement, explained it this way: "We realize that if we want to emphasize our own points of view over those of our competitors within this system, the result will be another Syria. This is a great Islamic revolution and we have to sit round the table and try to solve problems step by step. Iran and Turkey are the only stable and quiet countries in the region." He added, "I prefer to have a strong and powerful Revolutionary Guard Corps rather than a weak one, even though they have done bad things to me."[34]

This concern with stability and order may also be a factor in shaping public opinion; a poll conducted in 2015 suggested that 40 percent of Iranians believed that protesters "had no right" to demonstrate after the contested 2009 elections, and 40 percent believed that police response to protestors was "justified."[35] It is these sorts of misgivings toward "street politics" that helped encourage Iranians to return to institutionalized politics and participate in the 2013 presidential elections. Voter turnout reached 72 percent despite the electoral crisis of 2009. And once the ballots were counted, it was clear that the plurality of Iranians had voted for Rouhani, a candidate who took on a more reformist position in response to demands of reformist activists.[36] Notably, he has called his presidency a "government of moderation and hope," two assets running out of supply in the region since the authoritarian backlash against the Arab uprisings.[37]

CONCLUSION

By unpacking the relationship between Iran and the Arab Spring, this chapter has attempted to demonstrate the ways in which Iran's response to the ever-changing Arab Spring was an evolving process related to regional vicissitudes as well as real and imagined internal and external threats. The Islamic Republic of Iran changed its posture toward the Arab uprisings as the movements transformed from street protests to militarized conflicts and counterrevolutionary coups. While the Islamic Republic has not been able to dictate politics during the Arab Spring, its reactions have had consequences for the protest movements in the region, regional geopolitics, US-Iranian relations, and domestic politics in Iran.

Not only did the Arab uprisings not lead to the collapse of the Iranian regime, as some had championed and predicted,[38] but in many respects the regime's position vis-à-vis domestic critics and regional powers has been strengthened. As states and conflicts in the Middle East became more unstable and protracted following the uprisings and counterrevolutionary dynamics, Iran's position in the region slowly strengthened. Iranian citizens and activists recalibrated their politics as international sanctions, post–Green Movement repression, and regional violence "strengthen[ed] . . . a pragmatist and activist model of oppositional politics in Iran."[39] With the signing of the Joint Comprehensive Plan of Action in 2015, or the Iran Deal, the Islamic Republic stands to slowly see sanctions against the country removed, relations with Western powers potentially normalize in the future, and further cooperation with the United States and Western powers to delimit the reach of ISIS in the region. As Waleed Hazbun observes, "Iran's nuclear program has helped project its self-image as a major regional power, but it has been used more to gain leverage vis-à-vis the US than to expand its power regionally. Iran gains regional influence through political, financial, and military support of its allies in Iraq, Syria, Lebanon, and Palestine—places with similar insecurity concerns due to the erosion of state authority."[40] What is less clear is whether Iran's own state authority can be channeled for the betterment of the people of the region and Iran. This is, after all, the central demand that inspired many in Tehran in 2009 and Tunis in 2011 to confront their rulers.

Notes

1. Negar Mottahedeh, #iranelection: Hashtag Solidarity and the Transformation of Online Life (Stanford, CA: Stanford University Press, 2015); Arash Reisinezhad, "The Iranian Green Movement: Fragmented Collective Action and Fragile Collective Identity," Iranian Studies 48, 2 (2015): 193–222; and Nader Hashemi and Panny Postel, eds., The People Reloaded: The Green Movement and the Struggle for Iran's Future (Brooklyn, NY: Melville House, 2010).

2. Arang Keshavarzian, "Contestation Without Democracy: Elite Fragmentation in Iran," in Authoritarianism in the Middle East: Regimes and Resistance, ed. Marsha Pripstein Posusney and Michelle Penner Angrist (Boulder, CO: Lynne Rienner, 2005), 63–88.

3. Bijan Khajehpour, Reza Marashi, and Trita Parsi, "'Never Give In and Never Give Up': The Impact of Sanctions on Tehran's Nuclear Calculations" (Washington, DC: National Iranian American Council, March 2013); Ali Fathollah-Nejad, "Why Sanctions Against Iran Are Counterproductive: Conflict Resolution and State-Society Relations," *International Journal* 69, 1 (2014): 48–65.

4. On the importance of regime security, rather than neorealist approaches to international relations that stress external threats and system-structural factors, see Gregory Gause III, "Balancing What? Threat Perceptions and Alliance Choice in the Gulf," *Security Studies* 13, 2 (2003/2004): 273–305; and Curtis Ryan, "Regime Stability and Shifting Alliances in the Middle East," POMEPS, August 20, 2015; http://pomeps .org/2015/08/20/regime-security-and-shifting-alliances-in-the-middle-east.

5. Morten Velbjorn and Andre Bank, "Signs of a New Arab Cold War," *Middle East Report* 242 (Spring 2007): 6–11.

6. Interestingly, Khamenei began to discuss his notion of an "Islamic Awakening" in 2010, before the Arab uprisings, as a means to confront the anti-Iran posture of the United States, Israel, and regional regimes allied to the West as well as the spread of Islamophobia. Payam Mohseni, "The Islamic Awakening: Iran's Grand Narrative of the Arab Uprising," *Middle East Brief* No. 71, Brandeis University: Crown Center for Middle East Studies, April 2013.

7. Ali Khameinei, "Friday Prayer Speech," February 4, 2011 (11,15, 1379), www.leader.ir /fa/speech/7772.

8. Quoted in Mohseni, "The Islamic Awakening," 5.

9. Ladane Nassiri, "Iran Cheers Revolts as Ahmadinejad Foes See Parallel," February 4, 2011, Bloomberg, www.bloomberg.com/news/articles/2011-02-14/iran-cheers-egypt -tunisia-revolts-as-ahmadinejad-stifles-domestic-dissent.

10. Farnaz Fasihi, "In Tehran, Funerals Bring New Clashes," *Wall Street Journal*, February 27, 2011, www.wsj.com/articles/SB10001424052748703961104576148070942697648.

11. Hamid Farokhnia, "25 Bahman and the Green Revival," February 15, 2011, *Frontline*, www.pbs.org/wgbh/pages/frontline/tehranbureau/2011/02/25-bahman-and-the-green -revival.html.

12. See Scott Wilson, "Lebanese Wary of a Rising Hezbollah," *Washington Post*, December 20, 2004, www.washingtonpost.com/wp-dyn/articles/A12336-2004Dec19 .html; and Matthew Levitt, "Hezbollah Finances: Funding the Party of God," Washington Institute, February 2005, www.washingtoninstitute.org/policy-analysis/view/Hizbullah -finances-funding-the-party-of-god.

13. Geneive Abdo, "How Iran Keeps Assad in Power in Syria," *Foreign Affairs*, August 25, 2011, https://www.foreignaffairs.com/articles/iran/2011-08-25/how-iran-keeps-assad -power-syria.

14. Simon Tisdall, "Iran Helping Syria Crack Down on Protestors, Say Diplomats," *Guardian*, May 9, 2011, www.theguardian.com/world/2011/may/08/iran-helping-syrian -regime-protesters.

15. See Scott Lucas, "Syria Analysis: Iran's Economic Stakes in the Assad Regime," EA Worldview, June 7, 2015, http://eaworldview.com/2015/06/syria-analysis-irans-economic-stakes-in-the-assad-regime.

16. Interview with coauthor Narges Bajoghli, Tehran, 2013.

17. "Ejazeye nufuz va huzur-e amrikai-ha dar iran ra nemidim," *Fars News Agency*, Mordad 26, 1394, www.farsnews.com/newstext.php?nn=13940517000702.

18. "Farmandeh peyshin sepah pasdaran va az 'modafan-e haram' dar suriyeh koshteh shod," Radio Zamaneh, Khordad 7, 1393, www.radiozamaneh.com/148582. See also Toby Matthiesen, "Syria: Inventing a Religious War," *New York Review of Books*, June 12, 2013, www.nybooks.com/blogs/nyrblog/2013/jun/12/syria-inventing-religious-war. It should be noted that neither shrine has actually been under attack or near the conflict zone.

19. Ari Heinstein, "Iran's Support for Syria Pragmatic, Not Religious (or, Who Are the Alawites?)," Informed Comment, August 19, 2015, www.juancole.com/2015/08/secular-alawites-crescent.html.

20. Kayhan Barzegar, "To Defeat ISIS, Get Iran on Board," *Foreign Affairs*, February 8, 2015, https://www.foreignaffairs.com/articles/iran/2015-02-08/defeat-isis-get-iran-board.

21. Bülent Aras and Richard Falk, "Authoritarian 'Geopolitics' of Survival in the Arab Spring," *Third World Quarterly* 36, 2 (2015): 322–336.

22. This allegation has been challenged by many experts, including US intelligence officers. Ali Watkins, Ryan Grim, and Akbar Shahid Ahmed, "Iran Warned Houthis Against Yemen Takeover," *Huffington Post*, April 20, 2015, www.huffingtonpost.com/2015/04/20/iran-houthis-yemen_n_7101456.html?utm_hp_ref=tw; Juan Cole, "The Iranians Are Coming!," Middle East Online, May 14, 2015, www.middle-east-online.com/english/?id=71308; and Graham E. Fuller, "How to Decipher Yemen, Where the Enemy of Your Enemy Is Also Your Enemy," *Huffington Post*, March 30, 2015, www.huffingtonpost.com/graham-e-fuller/decipher-yemen_b_6965564.html.

23. Aras and Falk, "Authoritarian 'Geopolitics' of Survival in the Arab Spring," 325–326; and Jack Moore, "Iran Ceases Financial Aid to Hamas in Gaza, Official Claims," *Newsweek*, July 28, 2015, http://europe.newsweek.com/iran-ceases-financial-aid-hamas-gaza-official-claims-330889.

24. For a thoughtful and detailed discussion of Iran's policy toward ISIS, see Dina Esfandiary and Ariane Tabatabei, "Iran's ISIS Policy," *International Affairs* 91, 1 (2015): 1–15.

25. Ibid., 2.

26. Interview with coauthor Narges Bajoghli, Tehran, 2014.

27. Narges Bajoghli, "Paramilitary Media: Revolution, War, and the Making of the Islamic Republic of Iran," PhD diss., 2016.

28. Interview with coauthor Narges Bajoghli, Tehran, 2013.

29. Ibid.

30. *NBC Nightly News* interview with Ann Curry, September 17, 2014.

31. "Many Iranians Want Military to Intervene Against ISIS," *Guardian*, June 27, 2014, www.theguardian.com/world/iran-blog/2014/jun/27/iran-isis-military-intervention.

32. Thomas Erdbrink, "With War at Doorstep, Iran Sees Its Revolutionary Guards in a Kinder Light," *New York Times*, June 17, 2014, www.nytimes.com/2014/06/18/world/middleeast/with-war-at-doorstep-iran-sees-its-revolutionary-guards-in-a-kinder-light.html.

33. Interview with coauthor Narges Bajoghli, Tehran, 2014.

34. Jonathan Steele, "In a Middle East Racked by Turmoil Iranians Have Fallen in Love with Stability," May 19, 2015, Middle East Eye, www.middleeasteye.net/news/middle-east-racked-turmoil-iranians-have-fallen-love-stability-685330821#sthash.8gofWNTY.dpuf.

35. IranWire, "View from Iran: The Green Movement," June 23, 2015, http://en.iranwire.com/features/6576. It should be noted that responses to these sorts of sensitive political questions via telephone polling are questionable at best.

36. Mohammad Ali Kadivar and Ali Honari, "Iran's Grass-roots Politics and the Nuclear Deal," *Washington Post*, April 6, 2014, www.washingtonpost.com/blogs/monkey-cage/wp/2015/04/06/irans-grass-roots-politics-and-the-nuclear-deal.

37. Farideh Farhi, "The Iranian Evolution: A Shift in Tehran and the National Mood," Muftah, April 22, 2014, http://muftah.org/iranian-evolution.

38. Geneive Abdo, Arash Aramesh, and Shayan Ghajar, "New Round of Clashes Leaves Iran Reeling," *Huffington Post*, March 3, 2011, www.huffingtonpost.com/geneive-abdo/new-round-of-clashes-leav_b_829853.html.

39. Mohammad Ali Kadivar, "A New Oppositional Politics: The Campaign Participants in Iran's 2013 Presidential Elections," *Jadaliyya*, June 22, 2013, www.jadaliyya.com/pages/index/12383/a-new-oppositional-politics_the-campaign-participa.

40. The Iran Project, *Iran and the Arab World after the Nuclear Deal Rivalry and Engagement in a New Era*, Waleed Hazbun, 50, http://belfercenter.ksg.harvard.edu/files/Impact%20on%20Arab%20World%20-%20Web.pdf?utm_source=SilverpopMailing&utm_medium=email&utm_campaign=Payam_IranDealImpactonArabWorld%20%281%29&utm_content=.

9

Turkey and the Arab Spring:
The Rise and Fall of Democracy
Promotion in a Revolutionary Era

MARK L. HAAS

ALTHOUGH TURKEY DURING the Arab Spring did not experience the domestic upheaval that many of its Middle Eastern neighbors did, the revolutionary developments of 2011 and 2012 did result in major changes in Turkey's international relations.[1] Most notably, Turkish leaders' Middle Eastern policies during the first years of the Arab Spring became increasingly ideological as the Arab Spring progressed, with a growing focus on democracy promotion in the region as a central strategy for promoting Turkey's interests. This objective, among other important outcomes, led to major frictions with Syria and Iran and to a tightening of relations with key allies, especially the United States. After 2013, however, Turkey largely retreated from democracy promotion and instead began to support, at least tacitly, some highly illiberal Islamist parties, including al-Qaeda affiliates and the Islamic State of Iraq and Syria (ISIS).

The primary objective of this chapter is to explain these developments. My analysis will proceed in three main steps. First, I will provide a theoretical argument that accounts for why leaders often believe that the spread of their ideological principles to other countries is likely to benefit their interests. Second, I will detail how Turkey's policies in response to the Arab Spring largely support this analysis, thereby demonstrating the frequent centrality of ideologies to states' most important international decisions. In the third section, I argue that Turkey's increasing authoritarianism at home after 2012 helps explain the shift away from democracy promotion. I conclude with a summary of major findings.

IDEOLOGICAL EXPORTATION AND STATES' SECURITY

Turkish leaders' policies during the first few months of the Arab Spring were inconsistent. After large-scale popular protests began in Egypt in January 2011, Prime Minister Recep Tayyip Erdoğan was one of the first foreign leaders to call for Husni Mubarak's resignation and for the initiation of major political reforms. President Abdullah Gül was also the first head of state to meet with the Egyptian Supreme Council of the Armed Forces, which governed the country after Mubarak's ouster, and other Turkish leaders after the revolution promised close strategic ties with the new Egyptian government. Foreign Minister Ahmet Davutoğlu, for example, asserted that Turkey wanted to create an "axis of democracy" with Egypt as it transitioned from an authoritarian to a democratic regime.[2] Turkey established a "High-Level Strategic Cooperation Council" with Egypt in September 2011, the purpose of which was to boost economic and political ties between the two countries. Ankara also actively encouraged increased trade with and investment in Egypt. In September 2012, Turkey announced a $2 billion loan, and the following May, it provided $250 million to Egypt as part of a joint military defense project.[3]

Turkish leaders' reactions to the Libyan uprisings that began in February 2011 were, however, much different. The Turkish government did not cooperate with UN-mandated efforts to freeze Muammar al-Gadafi's assets, and in February and March, Turkish leaders openly opposed the creation by NATO forces of a no-fly zone designed to protect Libyan civilians from their government. Turkey, as Prime Minister Erdoğan put it, rejected "the foreign intervention in friend and brother Libya."[4] Even after NATO air strikes began in March, Ankara continued to argue against the use of force and instead pushed for a cease-fire so that Gadafi could implement political reforms. By May 2011, however, Erdoğan advocated that Gadafi surrender power and leave Libya.[5] Turkey participated in the military operations to oust Gadafi with six aircraft and five ships.[6] Ankara at this time also recognized the authority of the National Transitional Council (NTC) and committed $300 million in financial support. After Gadafi's death, Turkey aided the NTC by committing to train 3,000 Libyan soldiers and to a major increase in trade.[7]

Turkey's leaders demonstrated a similar reluctance to support the uprisings in Syria, at least during their first few months. These policymakers originally opposed international intervention in Syria on behalf of the protesters and instead recommended that any reforms be initiated and controlled by the Bashar al-Assad regime. The Turkish government even put its prestige on the line by sending senior officials to Damascus to meet with Assad. These officials subsequently vouched for the Syrian dictator's reformist intentions and credentials.[8] Turkey's politicians, in sum, sometimes were in the vanguard of advocating regime change during the Arab Spring and other times were openly opposed to revolutionary forces, especially during the early stages of protests.

By August 2011, however, Turkey's leaders had become much more consistently and forcefully supportive of democracy promotion in Syria. This change contradicted a number of contemporaneous predictions. Prominent analysts in the summer of 2011 forecasted that Turkey would not pursue ideology-based policies in cases, like Syria, that would jeopardize its major material interests.[9] Outcomes, though, turned out to be very different from these predictions. As scholar of Turkish politics Tarik Oğuzlu explained, "As the crisis deteriorated in Syria [over the summer of 2011], Turkish leaders made it clear that Turkey desires to see a more democratic, representative and plural order taking root." Importantly, this preference was part of a regional strategy that placed renewed emphasis on the spread of democracy as a key precondition for positive relations with Turkey: "The discourse adopted by Turkish statesmen suggests that Turkey's neighbors need to transform in a way to respond to the society's demands and, most importantly, search for good governance if they want to earn Turkey's friendship and cooperation."[10] Şaban Kardaş expressed a similar analysis in the fall of 2011: "A conspicuous aspect of Turkey's response [to the Arab Spring] has been the increasing salience of democratic principles in the making of Turkey's regional policy. . . . Turkey over time abandoned its resistance to regime change and embraced and even openly advocated a democracy promotion agenda."[11]

Why would Turkey's leaders pursue increasingly ideology-based foreign policies when the costs of these actions were likely to be quite high (as I detail later in this chapter)? What, in other words, were the likely benefits for Turkey of democracy promotion? In order to answer these questions, we must first understand how political ideologies systematically shape states' security interests. I will then demonstrate how Turkey's foreign policies—at least for the first two years of the Arab Spring—were consistent with these fundamental patterns.

I define ideologies as leaders' preferences for ordering the political world. Ideologies, in other words, reflect the core institutional, economic, and social goals that politicians try to realize or preserve in their states.[12] Do politicians, for example, advocate for their country the creation or continuation of representative or authoritarian political institutions? Capitalist or socialist economies? Theocratic or secular values? Full rights of citizenship for some or full rights for all groups in their state? Prominent ideologies include communism, fascism, liberalism, monarchism, and religious fundamentalism.

Leaders' ideological beliefs have major implications not only for domestic politics but also for foreign policies. The literature on ideologies and international relations indicates that significant ideological differences dividing states' leaders can affect their international decisions by shaping their understandings of the threats that they pose to one another's interests.[13] Ideological differences shape leaders' threat perceptions and consequent foreign policies by two main pathways. First, ideological differences play a key role in affecting *how leaders assess one another's international intentions.* The greater the ideological differences dividing decisionmakers, the more likely they are to assume the worst about one another's objectives. Ideological enemies tend to believe that conflict between them is in the long run inevitable. Even if ideological rivals in the present exhibit no hostility toward one another—or are even currently cooperating with one another—leaders will often assume that such amicability is temporary and is bound to be replaced eventually with overt animosity.

Second, large ideological differences are likely to shape leaders' threat perceptions by *affecting their understandings of the dangers to their most important domestic interests*—namely, the preservation of their political power and the regime type they support. The greater the ideological differences dividing decisionmakers in different states, the greater their fears of domestic subversion are likely to be. Leaders will tend to worry that the success of ideological enemies abroad will be contagious, ultimately boosting the political fortunes of like-minded individuals at home, even to the point of revolution. The tendency for developments in one country to spur or inspire similar outcomes elsewhere is known as "demonstration effects." This tendency helps explain why revolutions often cluster in time, including those in Europe in 1848 and the "color" revolutions in Eastern Europe in the 2000s as well as the Arab Spring protests and uprisings.

The opposite threat relationships often hold for states' leaders who are dedicated to similar ideological beliefs. Policymakers who share core ideological principles are likely both to interpret one another's international intentions in a mostly favorable light and to believe their domestic interests to be interconnected. On this last point, leaders will often view the success of ideological allies abroad as a boost to their domestic interests; success of particular ideological beliefs in other countries will likely increase their legitimacy and popularity at home. Conversely, when co-ideologues are weakened abroad, this development increases the likelihood of similar outcomes domestically. Trust in others' international intentions and beliefs in the interconnectedness of domestic interests have often resulted in significant cooperation among proponents of multiple ideological groups, including liberals, monarchists, fascists, religious fundamentalists, and even communists.[14]

The aforementioned effects of ideologies on leaders' threat perceptions shape their foreign policies in key ways. Among the most important of these is an enhanced, security-based interest in ideological exportation. Because leaders tend to believe that hostilities with ideological enemies are in the long run unavoidable and cooperation with ideological allies likely, they will view the conversion of ideological rivals to their own legitimating principles as a way of reducing the number of enemies in the system and increasing the number of allies. Fears of subversion to the principles of international ideological enemies add domestic incentives to work for the spread of one's principles abroad. Taken together, these beliefs explain why politicians of virtually all ideological beliefs—monarchical, liberal, fascist, communist, and religious—have attempted to export, including by force, their defining ideological principles and institutions.[15]

The incentives for regime promotion abroad are likely to be particularly powerful during periods that John M. Owen labels ones of high "ideological polarization," which he defines as the "progressive segregation of a population into two or more [ideological] sets, each of which cooperates internally and excludes externally."[16] Ideological polarization is most likely to occur when elites in various countries are dedicated to different ideological beliefs (i.e., there is not large agreement across states that one particular set of ideological principles is clearly superior to others) and when states (either one's own or others) are vulnerable to regime change or war occurs that makes such domestic change more likely.

The vulnerability of regimes during periods of high ideological polarization is the key factor that magnifies the incentives for states to try to export their ideological principles. If state X that is dedicated to ideology A is susceptible to revolution from ideology B, then adherents to A and B in other countries will have a strong security interest in seeing their co-ideologues emerge victorious in X. Proponents of ideology A in other states will fear that a takeover of ideology B in state X will result in a reduction of their international influence (including the loss of a likely ally) as well as a probable gain in influence (including the creation of a likely ally) for proponents of ideology B in other countries. The same calculations will create incentives for supporters of ideology B abroad to aid revolutionary forces in state X. The fluidity of internal politics in domestically vulnerable states, in sum, will tend to push leaders in other countries to view outcomes as a security gain or a loss for either themselves or their ideological rivals. Spain's revolutionary domestic situation from 1936 to 1938, for example, pushed both fascist Germany and Italy and communist Russia to spend considerable resources on ideological exportation in these years. Both sets of powers believed that the ideological outcome of the Spanish Civil War would have major international effects, most notably on Spain's choices of allies and enemies.

To put the preceding analysis another way, when states are vulnerable to revolution, representatives of rival ideological beliefs in other countries are caught in an "ideological security dilemma."[17] Successful regime change from ideology A to ideology B in state X will tend to make proponents of B in other countries more secure. The more ideology B's principles spread, the fewer ideological enemies they have. B's increase in security, though, will make proponents of ideology A less secure. The greater the number of governments that are dedicated to ideology B, the more proponents of A will feel surrounded by ideological enemies. Given these anticipated outcomes resulting from the ideological contest in state X, proponents of ideology A will confront powerful incentives to interfere in X to maintain the ideological—and thus security—status quo, while B will be inclined to interfere to take advantage of a newly created opportunity to increase international influence and security at A's expense.

It is worth highlighting that the preceding incentives that push states to try to promote their principles in ideologically contested regimes will exist even if the former are not themselves particularly vulnerable to regime change. Others' ideological vulnerability increases the likelihood of states gaining or losing an ally or enemy depending on the ideological outcomes in each of these domestic contests. The incentives for ideological exportation, though, will become even more powerful if the exporting state is plagued by internal ideological divisions. When governments are themselves vulnerable to regime change, they will fear that revolution abroad will increase the likelihood of revolution at home. These states, as a result, will confront powerful domestic-based incentives (in addition to the security-based ones discussed above) to try to boost the power of co-ideologues in other countries.

TURKEY'S INTEREST IN DEMOCRACY PROMOTION IN THE EARLY YEARS OF THE ARAB SPRING

Although a primary focus of this chapter's analysis is Turkish leaders' interest in regime exportation during the early years of the Arab Spring, it is worth noting that Turkey's policymakers pushed for the spread of democracy in neighboring countries based on the Turkish "model" well before the revolutionary developments of 2011 and 2012. President Turgut Özal of the Motherland Party, for example, asserted in 1991 that Turkey's regime type was "a good example for the rest of the Islamic world.... Our experience with economic reform in the past 10 to 11 years ... and also our experience in the past 45 of democracy" would allow Turkey to become an ideological inspiration for others.[18] A year later Prime Minister Süleyman Demirel of the True Path Party declared that "Turkey is committed to being a model [for former Soviet Republics] of democracy, rule of law, tolerance, respect for human rights and economic liberties." In 1993, Demirel stated that "in Central Asia we are the emissaries of Europe. We are the Europeans who are taking European values to Central Asia."[19]

Tansu Çiller (also of the True Path Party) made similar statements after she became prime minister in 1993.[20] Çiller often told US and other Western politicians that there were "essentially two models in the Islamic world: Turkey and Iran," and that it was a major interest for Western states to support Turkey in this ideological struggle.[21] The policies of ideological exportation in reaction to the Arab Spring were thus not new; they were a continuation of long-standing preferences, spanning numerous Turkish political parties that had been in existence since at least the end of the cold war. This fact is important because it demonstrates the systematic effects that ideologies tend to have on states' security policies. Analyzing Turkish leaders' reactions to the Arab Spring both confirms and helps us understand these enduring tendencies of international politics.

During the Arab Spring, Turkey was governed by the Justice and Development Party (JDP), which first came to power in 2002. JDP leaders—at least until roughly 2013 (see later discussion)—were some of the most forceful advocates of political liberalization in Turkey's history. JDP policymakers, for example, adopted the UN Charter of Human Rights and the European Charter for the Protection of Human Rights and Basic Liberties as core ideological references for the party.[22] These politicians also passed major liberalizing reforms in a number of areas, including freedoms of expression, association, assembly, and religion; the prevention of torture; minority rights; and civil-military relations.[23] Much of this legislation was designed to alter Turkish domestic politics in order to meet the criteria necessary for Turkey to join the European Union (EU).

Like their predecessors, JDP leaders in the 2000s also called for liberalization in neighboring regions, especially the Middle East, as a key means of improving Turkey's security. Indeed, from virtually the time of their ascension to power in 2002, JDP politicians, as Philip Robins summarizes, committed themselves to be "proselytizers of democratization among the membership of the [Organization of the Islamic Conference]."[24] These policymakers, according to scholar Aysegul Sever, believed that "an improvement in democracy, economy, and human rights in the Middle East [would result in] . . . improvements in the regional security situation. The [JDP] government agreed that a democratic Middle East with a well-functioning socio-economic system would serve Turkish security interests."[25]

Although JDP leaders before the Arab Spring repeatedly declared an interest in the spread of democracy as a means of advancing Turkey's interests and dedicated important resources to the realization of this objective, there were significant limits to these policies.[26] Two factors were particularly important in reducing these politicians' push for liberalization in the Middle East. The first resulted from a combination of relatively high levels of trust and a norm against threatening fellow Muslim-majority countries, even if these countries were illiberal in terms of their domestic politics.

The JDP was established largely by reformers who were members of Islamist parties (Welfare and Virtue) that had been banned from political activity by Turkey's Constitutional Court in 1998 and 2001, respectively. JDP leaders were much more liberal politically than their Islamist predecessors, but the advancement of Islamic identity and interests remained more central to these individuals' worldview than to that of almost all other governing parties in Turkey's history. As scholar M. Hakan Yavuz explains, "Most ministers, advisors and parliamentarians of the AKP [JDP] stress Islam as their core identity and define national interests within an Islamic framework. . . . The leadership of the AKP believes that Turkey in general and the AKP in particular represent Islamic civilization."[27] Consistent with these views, JDP leaders claimed that Islam should be a key unifying social force in Turkey, regardless of other cultural or ethnic differences.[28] The same beliefs created an interest in the protection of Islamic rights in other countries as well as feelings of solidarity with and trust in other Muslim-majority countries. As an expression of these feelings, JDP leaders often referred to their counterparts in fellow Muslim-majority countries as "siblings," "brothers," or part of a collective "we."[29]

JDP leaders' commitment to Islamic solidarity affected both the incentives to export liberalism to other countries and the policies that were deemed acceptable to achieve this end. Because feelings of trust toward other Muslim-majority countries applied even to states, such as Iran and Syria, that were dedicated to highly illiberal ideological principles, the perceived need to try to spread liberal ideological principles abroad as a means of alleviating threats to Turkey's security was lowered.[30] If, in other words, illiberal Muslim-majority states were not viewed as particularly high threats due to JDP leaders' beliefs in Islamic solidarity, the security-based imperative to convert ideological rivals was reduced. Reinforcing this trend was the fact that JDP politicians' commitment to Islamic solidarity created a normative stigma against threatening fellow Muslim-majority countries. This position limited the means available to Turkey in efforts to promote liberalism abroad.

A second factor that reduced JDP leaders' interest in liberalism promotion was a belief in the accuracy of the core predictions of economic liberal theory, namely, that increasing trade among states is a powerful force for peaceful relations.[31] Because the positive relationship between trade and peace exists largely independently of regime type, cooperative relations and thus improvements in security can obtain independently of political liberalization in other countries.

The importance to JDP leaders of Islamic solidarity and the rise of the "trading state" mentality formed the foundation of what became known as the "zero problems" doctrine of Turkish foreign policies. The doctrine referred to Turkey's commitment to maintain peaceful, nonthreatening relations with all neighboring countries (especially Muslim-majority ones), as long as these states do the same toward Turkey.

The objective of zero problems was in fundamental tension with the goal of promoting liberalism in illiberal countries. Because pushing for liberalization would have invariably created significant "problems" with illiberal regimes (assuming the latter had little interest in reform), the pursuit of one of these objectives necessarily meant downplaying the other. Zero problems was thus in key ways a status quo doctrine that worked for cooperative relations with existing (even authoritarian) governments in Middle Eastern countries, but not necessarily their peoples.

Understanding the incentives, in play since the end of the cold war, pushing Turkey to support liberalization in the Middle East and the barriers to the adoption of such policies on the part of JDP politicians is critical to explaining Turkey's inconsistent reactions to the early major developments of the Arab Spring described earlier. The doctrine of zero problems was not very salient to Turkey's relations with Egypt. Turkey had little financial investment in this country (thus the economic liberal foundations of zero problems were not in play), and relations between Mubarak and Erdoğan were cool, if not competitive.[32] Supporting the Egyptian uprisings thus did not necessitate the sacrifice of a "problem-free," cooperative relationship. Existing frictions and little economic interaction with Egypt, in other words, meant that there was not a major conflict between Turkish leaders' zero problems doctrine and their commitment to support the spread of democracy. This reality made the latter choice much easier to make in the Egyptian case.

Similar dynamics did not, however, exist for Turkey in relation to Libya and Syria. Turkey at the beginning of the Arab Spring had $15 billion worth of investments in Libya and 25,000 citizens living and working there.[33] Personal relations between Gadafi and Erdoğan were also good. In December 2010, for example, the Turkish prime minister had received the Gadafi International Prize for Human Rights. Turkish leaders' early refusal to offer support for the Libyan rebels against Gadafi's dictatorship is an example of economic interests and dedication to problem-free relations trumping goals of liberalism promotion.

Similar calculations that dominated in the Libyan case were on display during the early months of the uprisings in Syria. Turkey's relations with Syria were the crowning jewel of the zero problems strategy. Syria was a highly illiberal state with which Turkey had had very hostile relations in the recent past. The two states had even come close to war in the late 1990s due to Syria's continued support of the militant Kurdistan Workers Party (PKK), a terrorist organization dedicated to Kurdish independence.[34]

Under JDP leadership, however, relations with Syria steadily improved. In 2010, the two countries formally agreed to significantly enhance their cooperation against Kurdish terrorists. By 2011, Turkey was Syria's largest trading partner, and Syrians and Turks no longer required visas to visit each other's country.[35] These economic and strategic considerations no doubt played a central role in Turkey's initially tepid response to the Syrian uprisings highlighted at the beginning of this chapter. Turkey's early reaction to the demonstrations in Syria seemed to be another example of commitment to zero problems superseding dedication to democracy promotion and material interests trumping ideological ones.

By the fall of 2011, however, Turkey had become a forceful supporter of the overthrow of the Assad regime. Prime Minister Erdoğan even likened Assad to "Hitler, Mussolini, and Ceausescu of Romania."[36] The JDP government moved to the forefront of supporting the protesters in Syria, including forcefully condemning the Syrian regime's brutality, cutting off dialogue with it, supporting punishing international sanctions (including helping to freeze the Syrian government's financial assets, stopping financial transactions with Syrian banks, imposing a travel ban on senior Syrian leaders, and working to stop weapons sales to Syria), and hosting an armed opposition group dedicated to the overthrow of the Assad government. (This group, the Free Syrian Army, was not an Islamist one, which contrasts with much of Turkey's policies in the later years of the Syrian conflict, as discussed below). There are also claims that Turkey helped provide tanks to the rebels and even allowed them to initiate attacks across the border in Syria from inside a camp that was guarded by the Turkish military.[37] The Turks also pushed the United States to open by force "humanitarian corridors" into Syria that would allow aid to be sent to besieged cities in Syria's interior.[38]

Turkey's policies that worked for regime change in Syria had major costs, both immediate and potential, which made these actions all the more noteworthy. In terms of doctrinal and normative costs, Turkey's Syria policies after the summer of 2011 both violated the taboo against threatening fellow Muslims and demonstrated the failure of the zero problems strategy. Turkey's leaders by the fall of 2011 concluded that it was not possible to have problem-free relations with some illiberal regimes.

Likely more important to Turkish policymakers were the potential material costs created by pushing for regime change in Syria. This policy meant enmity not only with Syria but also with Iran.[39] Syria and Iran are longtime allies, and Tehran has remained committed to helping the Assad regime stay in power despite the popular uprisings and their brutal suppression. Iranian officials warned Turkey of "adverse consequences" if it continued to work for Assad's downfall and advised that Turkey "draw lessons from the bitter historical experiences of other countries" that opposed Iran.[40] The risks of escalation between Turkey and either Syria or Iran were significant. Syrian forces in April 2012, for example, shelled Syrian refugee camps located inside Turkey, and Syrian leaders have stated that Turkey's level of support for the demonstrators was "considered to be declaring war" on Syria.[41]

Relations between the two countries became particularly tense in June 2012 after Syria shot down a Turkish military jet that had briefly flown into Syrian airspace.[42] In November 2012, Turkey requested that NATO place Patriot missiles on the border with Syria. This was done the following January.[43] A more likely scenario than war, however, is that both Iran and Syria could retaliate for Turkey's interference in Syrian politics by once again empowering Kurdish rebels in Turkey, thereby fueling Turkey's most threatening domestic problem.[44] These security dangers stand in addition to significant potential economic costs, since the trade levels between Turkey and Syria and Iran were substantial.[45] Spurring the rebellion will also most likely result in massive refugee flows into Turkey. By the end of 2015, Turkey hosted over 2 million Syrian refugees.

Turkey's leaders moved to the forefront of the push for regime change in Syria despite the major risks associated with this policy because the costs were more than offset by the anticipated benefits associated with this pursuit. The key reason that the benefits of democracy promotion were believed to be so high was due to the ideological polarization of the Middle East and North Africa that resulted from the Arab Spring uprisings and the subsequent domestic vulnerability revealed in numerous countries. As the Arab Spring and the consequent ideological polarization of the Middle East and North Africa progressed, the security benefits created by regime promotion intensified to the point where they became more powerful for Turkish leaders than countervailing incentives (e.g., adherence to the zero problems doctrine).

There is little doubt that Turkey's key decisionmakers, at least by the summer of 2011, viewed the Middle East and North Africa as an ideologically polarized system in which Turkey's interests were intertwined with the ideological outcomes in other countries. Prime Minister Erdoğan referred to this interconnectedness of interests in his parliamentary victory speech in June 2011, the first of such speeches by Erdoğan that focused on foreign policies: "I greet with affection the peoples of Baghdad, Damascus, Beirut, Amman,

Cairo, Tunis, Sarajevo, Skopje, Baku, Nicosia and all other friends and brother peoples who are following the news out of Turkey with great excitement. . . . Today, the Middle East, the Caucasus and the Balkans have won as much as Turkey."[46] Erdoğan was clearly referring to the power of demonstration effects, namely, that the success in Turkey of a party dedicated to democracy, human rights, and Islamic identity would inspire similar ideological groups throughout the Islamic world. Foreign Minister Davutoğlu made a similar reference in May 2011 when he asserted that "the Arab Spring is also a Turkish Spring," meaning that Arab countries' liberation from authoritarian rule replicated Turkey's political development.[47]

Turkey's support of kindred ideological parties would not be merely inspirational, however. Instead, Erdoğan promised in his June 2011 parliamentary victory speech that Turkey would "become much more active in regional and global affairs. . . . We will take on a more effective role. We will call, as we have, for rights in our region, for justice, for the rule of law, for freedom and democracy."[48] This speech marked the beginning of the reassertion of democracy promotion at the expense of the zero problems doctrine.

Kardaş summarizes Turkey's policies pushing for democracy promotion as follows (writing in October 2011):

> Over time, Turkey moved to claim ownership of the democratic wave and tried to lead the regional transformation, which basically took two forms. In the countries undergoing regime change in a relatively peaceful fashion, Turkey accelerated contacts with the groups that stood to gain in the new political structures. In the countries where the regimes have resorted to violence, Turkey increasingly supported the popular opposition, as well as calling on the regimes to heed people's demands for political reforms. . . . Turkish leaders, officials, academics, or representatives from NGOs [nongovernmental organizations] or think tanks have [also] been frequently touring [these] countries, and at the same time, many delegations have been visiting Turkey. President Abdullah Gül's visit soon after Mubarak's fall and Erdoğan's Arab Spring tour [i.e., state visits to Egypt, Tunisia, and Libya], on one hand, and Turkey's hosting of the leaders of the Egyptian youth movement, on the other, are illustrative examples of this multi-level interaction.[49]

Turkey's leaders became increasingly interested in democracy promotion during the first years of the Arab Spring because the vulnerability of regimes throughout the Middle East and North Africa created an opportunity for Turkey to increase its influence in these regions. Numerous public opinion polls and related data in 2011 and 2012 documented that Turkey—especially in states such as Tunisia, Egypt, and Libya that were trying to create new political systems after ousting authoritarian governments—was the most popular country in the Islamic world. One 2012 poll found that 80 percent of respondents had a favorable view of Turkey, and 60 percent considered Turkey's political system under the JDP a model for their country.[50] Leading political parties in Tunisia and Egypt explicitly modeled themselves on the JDP in Turkey.[51] The sources of this popularity and emulation were clearly ideologically based. The success of the JDP in creating a dynamic economy and advancing political rights while also protecting religious identities was a source of tremendous appeal throughout the Islamic world. To put this analysis another way, Turkey under the JDP's leadership—due to this party's ideological principles—possessed large amounts of "soft power" (which is the ability to influence other countries through persuasion and attraction of beliefs) in relation to Muslim-majority countries.

Turkey's leaders, however, could maximize their soft-power influence only if groups dedicated to similar ideological principles governed. The domestic vulnerability created by the Arab Spring uprisings significantly increased the likelihood of such developments coming to pass. As this probability increased, so, too, did Turkey's incentives to support democracy promotion. As one senior Turkish official stated in the fall of 2011, "What's happening in the Middle East is a big opportunity, a golden opportunity" for Turkey. Suat Kiniklioğlu, the JDP's deputy chairman of external affairs, similarly asserted that his government's reactions to the Arab Spring were designed "to make the most of the influence we have in a region that is embracing our leadership."[52] Foreign Minister Davutoğlu even suggested that Turkey could provide a force for liberalization and cooperation in the Middle East analogous to that played by the EU in Europe.[53]

If Turkish policymakers refused to support co-ideologues in other countries (i.e., if Turkey's leaders maintained their commitment to zero problems with authoritarian regimes), Turkey was likely to squander its potential influence based on ideological affinity. This apparently was already starting to happen in the early months of the Arab Spring. According to one analyst writing in April 2011, "Erdoğan's reticence in addressing the violent crackdowns on civilians in Libya and Syria has also sparked criticism that he has double-standards when he picks fights," which was leading to Turkey's increasing isolation.[54] Another observer wrote in November 2011, "After initially adopting a neutral stance [toward the Arab Spring demonstrations], Turkey soon recognized that its indecisiveness was damaging its image" in the Islamic world.[55] For example, after Turkey's government originally refused to support a NATO-enforced no-fly zone in Libya, anti-Turkish demonstrators in a number of Libyan cities burned Turkey's flag and attempted to overrun Turkey's consulate.[56] There were thus important costs to Turkey created by *not* adopting ideology-based policies in an ideologically polarized era. Turkey's leaders, as a consequence, confronted increasingly powerful incentives to support democracy promotion in neighboring regions as a key means of enhancing its reputation and influence.

It is worth noting that prominent countries recognized the opportunity that Turkey had to advance its interests if it engaged in regime promotion in an ideologically polarized era. Iranian leaders, for example, derided Prime Minister Erdoğan's calls for Egypt and Tunisia to adopt secularism in their new constitutions. The Iranians no doubt hoped to see these countries adopt more hard-line Islamist governments. Ayatollah Mahmoud Hashemi Shahroudi, the former chief of Iran's judiciary, scornfully dismissed Turkey's efforts to spread democracy in the Middle East as an example of "liberal Islam" that was designed to try to counter Iran's regional influence.[57] Ali Akbar Velayati, senior adviser to Supreme Leader Ali Khamenei, made similar statements, as did Yahya Safavi, the former commander of the Revolutionary Guard Corps.[58] These assertions indicate that the Iranians believed that they were caught with Turkey in an ideological security dilemma, as I discussed earlier. The more Turkey was able to spread its ideological principles in those states made vulnerable by the Arab Spring, the more Iran's regional influence would be curtailed. Ali Nader, an Iranian analyst at the RAND Corporation, summarizes the relationship between Turkey's support of regime promotion and threats to Iran's interests as follows: "Iranian conservatives . . . worry that Turkey is presenting an alternate model to the Islamic Republic in the region. . . . The Iranian government claimed that the Arab Spring has been inspired by the Iranian Revolution of 1979. . . . Turkey [is] basically offering itself as [an alternative] model for the Arab population in the region. This contradicts with Iranian interests."[59]

American policymakers recognized similar dynamics. US leaders in the wake of the Arab Spring pushed for Turkey to assert itself as an ideological model throughout the Islamic world.[60] The Americans clearly believed that the spread of Turkey's "liberal Islamic" system was an effective way of protecting US interests. If Turkey, allied with the United States in NATO, did not provide the ideological inspiration in domestically vulnerable regimes, more radical, and more anti-American, Islamist groups might. The result of these ideology-based calculations and policies was an increased closeness in US-Turkish relations.

INCREASING AUTHORITARIANISM AND THE RETREAT FROM DEMOCRACY PROMOTION

Despite Turkish leaders' significant interest in promoting democratization in authoritarian regimes during the first two years of the Arab Spring protests, beginning at the end of 2013, this interest, as well as the opportunity to realize it, waned. Both outcomes were due in large part to a common source: increasing authoritarianism in Turkey. In August 2011, President Gül had explained his country's interest in replacing Assad's regime with a democratic one because "today in the world there is no place for authoritarian administrations, one-party rule, closed regimes."[61] Within a few years of this statement, however, Turkey was increasingly resembling the type of regime Gül asserted was obsolete. This shift toward authoritarianism reduced the appeal of the Turkish model to democratic movements in the Arab world, as well as Turkish leaders' interest in supporting these groups.

The year 2013 proved to be an important turning point in the evolution of Turkish domestic politics. In June, Turkish police suppressed large-scale protests (centered in Gezi Park in Istanbul) of governmental policies. Nearly a dozen protesters were killed and thousands wounded. In December, a massive governmental scandal came to light. Erdoğan and members of his immediate family, as well as senior ministers in the party and close business associates, were accused of bribery and corruption that had resulted in the illegal accumulation of millions of dollars. Erdoğan responded to this crisis by concentrating his power while greatly weakening the checks and balances among branches of government. He did so by firing thousands of prosecutors, judges, and police officers who were involved with the investigation into the scandal.[62]

The trends of repressing core civil liberties and stifling popular dissent and criticism continued into 2014. Freedom House in this year downgraded Turkey's press from "partly free" to "not free" after the government engaged in repeated attacks on the media, including raiding newspaper and television headquarters, arresting journalists, banning over 50,000 websites, and blocking access to YouTube and Twitter in the lead-up to the March 2014 local elections. (According to Reporters Without Borders, by 2015, Turkey ranked 149th in the world in press freedoms.)[63] In 2015, the government passed a bill that broadens police power and increased penalties for protesters.[64]

As a result of these developments, Turkey's democracy since 2012 has been in steady decline, as assessments by a number of prominent organizations, including Freedom House, Amnesty International, and Human Rights Watch, have noted. The country is perilously close to becoming an "illiberal democracy," that is, a country in which leaders are democratically elected but lack safeguards—such as separation of powers and checks and balances—that protect basic liberties and minority rights. Scholars have documented that illiberal democracies are frequently aggressive internationally, often because leaders in such regimes tend to appeal to hyper- and exclusionary nationalistic rhetoric and policies to secure votes.[65]

Compounding the effects of the preceding domestic developments is that Erdoğan after 2012 more frequently appealed to exclusivist, polarizing rhetoric and actions, particularly with regard to religion and nationality.[66] These appeals are designed to increase the size and dominance of the JDP—which would, among other things, allow the party to change the constitution to significantly increase the power of the presidency, which Erdoğan has held since August 2014. A greater emphasis on political Islam serves to rally the JDP's base, while enhanced stress on Turkish nationalism is likely to draw votes from Turkey's right-wing nationalist party, the Nationalist Action Party. With regard to Islamist-based policies, the government in December 2014 recommended the most sweeping school-curriculum change in decades, including increased Islamic religious education and Ottoman-language lessons.[67] Women's rights in Turkey, according to numerous analysts, are also on the decline, as Erdoğan has asserted conservative views on gender that appeal to his base. Erdoğan stated in 2014, for example, that the two sexes are not equal and that men are custodians of women. Violence against women has significantly increased.[68] In May 2013, the government passed new laws that curb alcohol sales and consumption, which also reflect a conservative Islamist agenda.

Erdoğan has also adopted more hard-line nationalist policies, including in 2015 renewing the war against Kurdish separatists. This shift occurred despite the major progress that had been made in resolving this conflict in previous years after the JDP allowed for some cultural pluralism, such as approving a public television channel broadcasting in Kurdish and the study of the Kurdish language at private universities. There had been a cease-fire in the conflict between the government and Kurdish parties since 2013.

The more illiberal and polarized Turkey becomes, the less appeal it has as a model to democratic parties in the Arab World. For example, Rashid al-Ghannouchi, who was the cofounder and leader of Tunisia's moderate Islamist party, Ennahda, frequently pointed to Turkey during the first two years of the Arab Spring as a model for democratization. Beginning in 2013, however, he not only excluded Turkey from his list of sources of emulation but openly criticized Erdoğan's increasingly majoritarian understanding of democracy instead of one that cultivated pluralism and protected minority rights.[69] Ghannouchi's position reflects a wider shift, as both survey data and media reports in multiple Arab states have become increasingly critical of Turkey. The country's domestic scandals and increasing repression are frequently cited as central reasons for the growing belief that Turkey is no longer a prominent model worthy of copying.[70]

At the same time that individuals and parties in Arab countries became less receptive to viewing Turkey as a model for democratization, Erdoğan's foreign policies were shifting. Turkey's leaders still claimed an important interest in the domestic developments in Arab countries—including continued support for regime change in Syria and Egypt—but the content of that objective changed. Instead of a general support for democratization, Turkey by 2014 tended to support only Islamist parties, and sometimes highly illiberal ones.[71] Turkey's relations with Libya, for example, deteriorated in 2014 after Erdoğan sent a special envoy to meet with representatives of a Muslim Brotherhood–led rival government that is trying to supplant the democratically elected and internationally recognized Libyan regime based in Tobruk.[72] In February 2015, Libya's prime minister, Abdullah al-Thinni, threatened to take action against Turkey (presumably including weakening relatively robust economic relations) if "Turkish interference" in Libya's domestic politics that "negatively affect the country's security and stability" continued.[73]

Most alarming, Turkey has provided, at a minimum, tacit support of radical Islamist groups in Syria—including Jabhat al-Nusra (Syria's al-Qaeda affiliate) and ISIS.[74] The objectives of this support are to overthrow the Assad regime while simultaneously preventing the empowerment of Syria's Kurdish parties, which al-Nusra and ISIS also target. The Erdoğan government even reportedly allowed al-Nusra the use of Turkish territory to attack Kurdish (and Armenian) strongholds in Syria.[75] Turkey has also been lax in stopping ISIS fighters from migrating from Turkey into Syria, leading many to conclude that JDP leaders are more interested in seeing Kurdish groups than ISIS defeated.[76] Turkey in 2015 joined with ISIS—in a concurrent but not in a coordinated way—in attacking Syrian Kurds (Turkey by air, ISIS on the ground). These policies have made Turkey's relations with the United States much more complicated and sometimes tense. US leaders have repeatedly pressured Ankara to tighten border security to stop the flow of supplies and foreign fighters into Syria. Tensions have also been created by the fact that the Syrian Kurdish groups that Turkey does not want empowered and has sometimes harmed have been the most reliable US ally in fighting ISIS.

Erdoğan's support of hard-line Islamists has resulted in further disillusionment about Turkey by democratic parties in the Arab world. Tunisia's foreign minister Taieb Baccouche in 2015 accused Turkey of indirectly aiding terrorism in Libya—which, in turn, threatened Tunisia—by allowing foreign fighters to cross into Syria through Turkey. Baccouche told reporters in April that "we have asked our ambassador in Turkey to draw the attention of the Turkish authorities to the fact that we do not want a Muslim nation such as Turkey to help directly or indirectly terrorism in Libya by facilitating the movement of terrorists."[77]

These foreign policies are not surprising when they are analyzed in the light of Erdoğan's growing authoritarianism and his increased emphasis on the centrality of Islam and Turkish national identity to the evolution of Turkey's domestic politics. It is natural that increasing authoritarianism at home will reduce the incentives pushing Turkey's leaders to support democracy abroad. Moreover, the more Erdoğan has emphasized the importance of Turkish national and Islamist identities, the greater the interest in seeing the weakening abroad of rival ethnic groups, especially the Kurds, even if this means at times tacitly supporting (at the minimum) the ascendance of highly illiberal Islamist groups such as ISIS by turning a blind eye to the movement of weapons and fighters across Turkey's border. The lines of polarization are the key determinate of a country's interest in domestic developments in other states. When the axis of polarization in Turkey was democratic versus nondemocratic groups (as it was when Turkey's elected leaders feared a military coup), the primary ideology-based international incentive was to promote democracy.[78] When, however, Turkey is polarized along religious and nationalist lines—as it has been since 2013—democracy promotion becomes ancillary to supporting core-ligionists and conationalists while trying to harm rivals of these groups.[79]

CONCLUSION

This chapter has had two primary objectives. The first was to document Turkish leaders' dominant reactions to the Arab Spring uprisings and protests. The second was to demonstrate how a key dimension of these policies—an increasing interest in ideological promotion during the first two years of the Arab Spring—was part of an important pattern in international relations. Because ideological relationships often have major effects on leaders' threat perceptions, policymakers frequently confront powerful incentives to try to export their ideological principles as a means of increasing the number of allies in the system and reducing the number of enemies. These incentives tend to be especially strong during periods of ideological polarization. Ideologically polarized eras are created when states—as was the case during the Arab Spring—are vulnerable domestically to revolution. At these times, ideological rivals will be particularly sensitive to ideology-based opportunities and threats based on the domestic outcomes in other countries.

Turkish leaders' behavior during the first two years of the Arab Spring supports this pattern. JDP politicians were originally highly inconsistent in advocating democracy promotion when the Arab Spring began. They supported demonstrators in countries with which Turkey had little shared economic interest and strategic cooperation (e.g., Egypt) and stood by regimes with which Turkey shared important material interests (Libya, Syria). Over time, however, the Turkish government became much more assertive for regime change, even in countries that shared major interests with Turkey. The key reason for this shift was the realization that nonideological foreign policies were hurting Turkey's interests by squandering its large reserve of soft power throughout the Islamic world. Turkey was extremely popular because of its commitment to democracy and Islamic identity. Not supporting popular protests for basic rights during the Arab Spring would have dealt a major blow to this popularity by demonstrating Turkey's hypocrisy and selfishness. Supporting democracy movements, in contrast, offered the opportunity of helping groups in other countries come to power that were highly sympathetic to Turkey while simultaneously tightening Turkey's ties with established liberal allies led by the

United States. Helping to spread democracy based on the Turkish model also inhibited proponents of rival ideological beliefs—such as Iran—from increasing their regional influence. Democracy promotion, in short, offered Turkey major opportunities to increase its security.

Turkey's increasing authoritarianism and domestic polarization along ethnic and religious lines after 2012, however, pushed Erdoğan to change foreign policies once again. The more his government championed religious and national identities while weakening the foundations of liberal democracy, the less important democracy promotion became in relation to supporting abroad conationalists and coreligionists. Although the nature of the policies changed, Turkey's domestic politics, especially involving core identity issues, continued to have major international effects in the Arab Spring era.

NOTES

1. I want to thank the Earhart Foundation and the Richard Paluse Mission-Related Research Award from Duquesne University for providing generous financial support of the research that contributed to this chapter.

2. Quoted in Anthony Shadid, "Turkey Predicts Alliance with Egypt as Regional Anchors," *New York Times*, September 18, 2011. See also Nathalie Tocci, Ömer Taşpınar, and Henri J. Barkey, *Turkey and the Arab Spring: Implications for Turkish Foreign Policy from a Transatlantic Perspective* (Washington, DC: German Marshall Fund, 2011), 3.

3. Bilgin Ayata, "Turkish Foreign Policy in a Changing Arab World: Rise and Fall of a Regional Actor?," *Journal of European Integration* 37, 1 (2015): 105.

4. Quoted in Steven A. Cook, "Arab Spring, Turkish Fall," *Foreign Policy*, May 5, 2011, http://foreignpolicy.com/2011/05/05/arab-spring-turkish-fall-2.

5. Ibid.

6. Yaşar Yakış, "Turkey After the Arab Spring: Policy Dilemmas," *Middle East Policy* 21, 1 (Spring 2014): 98.

7. Ayata, "Turkish Foreign Policy in a Changing Arab World," 101–102.

8. Şaban Kardaş, "Turkey's Syria Policy: The Challenge of Coalition Building," *On Turkey* (German Marshall Fund of the United States), February 17, 2012, 1; Tarik Oğuzlu, "The 'Arab Spring' and the Rise of the 2.0 Version of Turkey's 'Zero Problems with Neighbors' Policy," Center for Strategic Research Papers (Ankara, Turkey: Center for Strategic Research, February 2012), 6.

9. Cook, "Arab Spring, Turkish Fall"; Tocci, Taşpınar, and Barkey, *Turkey and the Arab Spring*, 3.

10. Both quotations are from Oğuzlu, "The 'Arab Spring,'" 7, 10.

11. Şaban Kardaş, "Turkey and the Arab Spring: Coming to Terms with Democracy Promotion?," Policy Brief (Washington, DC: German Marshall Fund of the United States, October 2011), 1. See also Ayata, who describes Turkey "as an actor eager to spearhead the transitions from autocratic regimes to popular democracies." Ayata, "Turkish Foreign Policy in a Changing Arab World," 96.

12. For others who define ideology in this way, see John M. Owen, *The Clash of Ideas in World Politics: Transnational Networks, States, and Regime Change, 1510–2010* (Princeton, NJ: Princeton University Press, 2010); Stephen M. Walt, *Revolution and War* (Ithaca, NY: Cornell University Press, 1996); Mark L. Haas, *The Ideological Origins of Great Power Politics, 1789–1989* (Ithaca, NY: Cornell University Press, 2005); Mark L. Haas, *The Clash of Ideologies: Middle Eastern Politics and American Security* (New York: Oxford University Press, 2012); and Mark L. Haas, "Missed Ideological Opportunities and George W. Bush's Middle Eastern Policies," *Security Studies* 21, 3 (July-September 2012): 416–454. Parts of this chapter's argument and evidence are derived from these last three sources.

13. See Haas, *Ideological Origins*, 5–18; Haas, *Clash of Ideologies*, 7–15; Owen, *Clash of Ideas*, 32–52; and Walt, *Revolution and War*, 32–45.

14. For case-study analyses demonstrating how ideological convergence, or increasing ideological similarities among states, is often an important source of international conflict resolution, see Owen, *Clash of Ideas*, 54–55, 68–70, 77, 115–119, 154–157, 196–199, 267–269; and Benjamin Miller, *When Opponents Cooperate: Great Power Conflict and Collaboration in World Politics* (Ann Arbor: University of Michigan Press, 1995), 39–42, 53–55, 241.

15. For extensive analysis of regime promotion by multiple ideological groups over the past five hundred years, see Owen, *Clash of Ideas*. Owen finds that since 1510, states have used force on more than two hundred separate occasions to alter or preserve the ideological principles and institutions of another country.

16. Ibid., 40.

17. The traditional security dilemma is a realist international relations concept that asserts that it is very difficult for one state to make itself feel safe without making a neighboring country feel less safe. When one state increases its military spending to enhance its security, others will feel more endangered.

18. Quoted in David Aikman, "Hoping Saddam Hussein Would Just Go Away," *Time*, May 13, 1991.

19. Both Demirel quotations are from Idris Bal, *Turkey's Relations with the West and the Turkic Republics: The Rise and Fall of the "Turkish Model"* (Aldershot, UK: Ashgate, 2000), 81, 52.

20. Ibid., 59.

21. Quoted in Yalim Eralp, "An Insider's View of Turkey's Foreign Policy and Its American Connection," in *The United States and Turkey: Allies in Need*, ed. Morton Abramowitz (New York: Century Foundation Press, 2003), 116. Turkish leaders' interest in regime

promotion in the 1990s was more than just talk. For details on the significant resources dedicated to these policies, see Haas, *Clash of Ideologies*, 212–213.

22. Metin Heper and Şule Toktaş, "Islam, Modernity, and Democracy in Contemporary Turkey: The Case of Recep Tayyip Erdoğan," *Muslim World* 93, 2 (April 2003): 176.

23. For details, see William Hale and Ergun Özbudun, *Islamism, Democracy, and Liberalism in Turkey: The Case of the AKP* (London: Routledge, 2010), 57–62.

24. Philip Robins, "Turkish Foreign Policy Since 2002: Between a 'Post-Islamist' Government and a Kemalist State," *International Affairs* 83, 1 (2007): 302.

25. Aysegul Sever, "Turkey's Constraining Position on Western Reform Initiatives in the Middle East," *Mediterranean Quarterly* 18, 4 (Fall 2007): 133.

26. For details on the resources dedicated to democracy promotion, see Haas, *Clash of Ideologies*, 221–222.

27. M. Hakan Yavuz, *Secularism and Muslim Democracy in Turkey* (Cambridge: Cambridge University Press, 2009), 209.

28. Ibid., 264–265.

29. For details on these points, see Haas, *Clash of Ideologies*, 192.

30. Probably the best example of JDP leaders' trusting relations toward other Muslim-majority countries was relations with Iran for most of the 2000s. Although Iranian capabilities were growing substantially in this decade, JDP politicians' threat perceptions toward Iran were much lower compared to those possessed by preceding Turkish leaders. For details, see Haas, *Clash of Ideologies*, 187–192.

31. Oğuzlu, "The 'Arab Spring,'" 4; Greg Sheridan, "World's a Stage for Turkey," *Weekend Australian*, January 21, 2012.

32. Tocci, Taşpınar, and Barkey, *Turkey and the Arab Spring*, 3.

33. Ibid.

34. For details, see Robert Olson, *Turkey's Relations with Iran, Syria, Israel, and Russia, 1991–2000: The Kurdish and Islamist Questions* (Costa Mesa, CA: Mazda, 2001).

35. Cook, "Arab Spring, Turkish Fall"; Richard Weitz, "Global Insights: Turkey Turns on Syria's Asad," *World Policy Review*, December 6, 2011.

36. Quoted in Sebnem Arsu, "Turkish Premier Urges Asad to Quit in Syria," *New York Times*, November 22, 2011.

37. Liam Stack, "In Slap at Syria, Turkey Shelters Anti-Asad Fighters," *New York Times*, October 27, 2011; Judy Dempsey, "The Hazards in Turkey's New Strategy," *New York Times*, October 24, 2011; Yakış, "Turkey After the Arab Spring," 99.

38. "Turkey Expected to Pressure US on Syria, Iran," *BBC Monitoring Europe*, February 13, 2012.

39. Tensions between Turkey and China and Russia also increased after the latter two powers vetoed in February 2012 a UN resolution that would have backed an Arab plan that urged Assad to give up power and start a transition to democracy. Turkish foreign minister Davutoğlu expressed his frustration with the two great powers: "Unfortunately,

yesterday in the UN, the Cold War logic continues. Russia and China did not vote based on the existing realities but more a reflexive attitude against the West." Quoted in Joseph Logan and Patrick Worsnip, "Russia, China Veto of Syria UN Resolution Sparks Outrage," Reuters, February 5, 2012.

40. Quoted in "Paper Looks into Regional Competition Between Turkey, Iran," BBC Monitoring Europe, October 18, 2011.

41. Quoted in Harvey Morris, "Time to Dial the Turkey-Syria Hotline," *New York Times*, April 10, 2012. See also Neil MacFarquhar, Sebnem Arsu, and Alan Cowell, "Tensions Mount as Syria Truce Seems Elusive," *New York Times*, April 10, 2012.

42. Eric Schmitt and Sebnem Arsu, "Backed by NATO, Turkey Steps Up Warning to Syria," *New York Times*, June 26, 2012.

43. Ayata, "Turkish Foreign Policy in a Changing Arab World," 104.

44. Syria did pursue this tactic. For details, see ibid., 103.

45. For details, see United Nations Commodity Trade Statistics Database, http://comtrade.un.org/db.

46. Quoted in Susanne Güsten, "Mandate for a New Turkish Era; Erdoğan Boldly Changes Tack with Broad Outreach to a Region in Turmoil," *International Herald Tribune*, June 16, 2011.

47. Quoted in Ayata, "Turkish Foreign Policy in a Changing Arab World," 99.

48. Quoted in ibid.

49. Kardaş, "Turkey and the Arab Spring," 2, 3.

50. "Some See Turkey as a Useful Model for New Arab Regimes," Agence France-Presse, February 5, 2012. For similar polling data, see "Erdoğan Most Popular Leader by Far Among Arabs," Inter Press Service, November 21, 2011; and Ayata, "Turkish Foreign Policy in a Changing Arab World," 96, 110 (fn. 1).

51. "Emerging Arab Islamists Look to 'Turkish Model,'" *Daily News Egypt*, December 4, 2011; Asef Bayat, "Arab Revolts: Islamists Aren't Coming!," *Insight Turkey* 13, 2 (2011): 12–13.

52. Both quotations are from Anthony Shadid, "In Riddle of Mideast Upheaval, Turkey Offers Itself as an Answer," *New York Times*, September 26, 2011.

53. Ibid.

54. Pelin Turgut, "How Syria and Libya Got to Be Turkey's Headaches," *Time*, April 30, 2011.

55. Sinan Ulgen, "Turkey's 'No Problems' Policy Is Problematic," *Daily Star* (Lebanon), November 28, 2011.

56. Sarah Akram, "Turkey and the Arab Spring," *Strategic Studies* 31, 3 (September 2011): 23–31.

57. Quoted in Mustafa Akyol, "The Problem with 'Zero Problems,'" *New York Times*, November 15, 2011; and in Gonul Tol, "Ankara Is Trying to Have It Both Ways," *New York Times*, November 15, 2011.

58. "Senior Adviser to Iran's Supreme Leader Says Turkey's Secularism Not Suitable for Arab States," Al Arabiya News, December 13, 2011, https://english.alarabiya.net/articles /2011/12/14/182516.html; "Paper Looks into Regional Competition."

59. Ali Nader et al., "Arab Spring and Its Effect on Turkey's Regional Policy," SETA Policy Debate, October 2011, 7. See also Robert F. Worth, "Effort to Rebrand Arab Spring Backfires in Iran," New York Times, February 2, 2012.

60. Mark Landler, "New Challenges for Obama and Turkey's Premier," New York Times, September 19, 2011.

61. Quoted in Morris, "Time to Dial the Turkey-Syria Hotline."

62. John Hannah, "Erdogan's Deadly Ambitions," Foreign Policy, September 21, 2015, http ://foreignpolicy.com/2015/09/21/erdogans-deadly-ambitions-turkey-elections-president.

63. Reporters Without Borders, "2015 World Press Freedom Index," available at https:// index.rsf.org/#!/, accessed November 28, 2015. Turkey's repression reached a comitragic low point in December 2015 when the government imprisoned a Turkish physician for comparing Erdoğan to Gollum, the repulsive creature from J. R. R. Tolkien's Lord of the Rings books, in his personal Facebook account. Berivan Orucoğlu, "It Is, by Far, the Worst Time to Be a Turkish Journalist: A Doctor on Trial for Comparing President Erdoğan to Gollum Is Only the Most Visible Example of Ankara's Growing Crackdown on Freedom of Expression," Foreign Policy, December 18, 2015, http://foreignpolicy.com/2015/12/18/ it-is-by-far-the-worst-time-to-be-a-turkish-journalist.

64. See "Erdoğan's Formula for Consolidating Clout in Turkey," New York Times, November 2, 2015; Andrew Finkel, "Brave New Turkey," New York Times, December 21, 2014.

65. A prominent recent example of this phenomenon is Serbia in the 1990s, after Slobodan Milošević was elected president in 1989. On illiberal democracy and aggression, see Edward D. Mansfield and Jack Snyder, Electing to Fight: Why Emerging Democracies Go to War (Cambridge: MIT Press, 2005).

66. Lisel Hintz, "The Heinous Consequences of Turkey's Polarization," Washington Post, October 15, 2015; Mustafa Akyol, "Paranoia and Polarization in Turkey," New York Times, April 16, 2015.

67. Peter Emre, "Turkish President Erdoğan Seeks to Reshape Secular Education; Education Council Recommends Religion Classes, Ottoman Language Lessons," Wall Street Journal, December 5, 2014.

68. "Is Life Getting Worse for Women in Erdoğan's Turkey?," BBC News, March 4, 2015.

69. Kemal Kirişci, "The Rise and Fall of Turkey as a Model for the Arab World," Brookings Institute, August 15, 2013, www.brookings.edu/research/opinions/2013/08 /15-rise-and-fall-turkey-model-middle-east.

70. Sotiris S. Livas, "Turkey's Image in the Middle East via the Arab Media," Turkish Review, January 1, 2015; Sevgi Akarçeşme, "Turkey's Imperial Ambitions Have Led to Disillusionment Among Middle Eastern Elites," Today's Zaman, July 11, 2015; Ayata, "Turkish Foreign Policy in a Changing Arab World," 96.

71. This was not the case in the early years of the Arab Spring. In 2011, Erdoğan drew the ire of the Egyptian Muslim Brotherhood when he stated on Egyptian television that Egyptians should "not be wary of secularism. I hope there will be a secular state in Egypt." Quoted in Marc Champion and Matt Bradley, "Islamists Criticize Turkish Premier's 'Secular' Remarks," *Wall Street Journal*, September 15, 2011. Moreover, unlike after 2013, the JDP's foreign policies for its first decade in power were built on a multicultural foundation that did not focus on ethnicity. See Ömer Taşpınar, "Turkey's Strategic Vision and Syria," *Washington Quarterly* 35, 3 (Summer 2012): 127–140.

72. Quoted in Salim Avci, "Turkey's Relations with North African States on Shaky Ground Due to Differing Regional Policies," *Today's Zaman*, April 11, 2015.

73. Turkey's support for Islamist parties is not always in tension with democracy promotion. The Erdoğan government remains a staunch supporter of Egypt's Muslim Brotherhood in the wake of the military coup that ousted it from power in 2013. This support has resulted in very tense relations between the two countries, including Egypt's expulsion of Turkey's ambassador in 2013.

74. This support has further tarnished Turkey's image among Arab populations. See Jean-Loup Samaan, "The Rise and Fall of the 'Turkish Model' in the Arab World," *Turkish Policy* 12, 3 (2013): 66–67.

75. Aaron Stein, "Turkey's Evolving Syria Strategy," *Foreign Affairs*, February 9, 2015, https ://www.foreignaffairs.com/articles/turkey/2015-02-09turkeys-evolving-syria-strategy.

76. Anne Barnard and Michael R. Gordon, "Goals Diverge and Perils Remain as U.S. and Turkey Take on ISIS," *New York Times*, July 27, 2015.

77. Quoted in Avci, "Turkey's Relations with North African States on Shaky Ground Due to Differing Regional Policies."

78. The JDP by 2013 had greatly reduced the military's ability to play a major role in political affairs, including by arresting large numbers of officers who were accused of disloyalty to the government and replacing them with loyalists. See "Erdoğan and His Generals: The Once All-Powerful Turkish Armed Forces Are Cowed, If Not Quite Impotent," *Economist*, February 2, 2013.

79. A key factor that led Turkey in November 2015 to shoot down a Russian military plane flying near the Turkish-Syrian border—which not surprisingly resulted in a crisis between the two countries—was Russia's bombing of ethnic kin of Turks, Turkmen, in Syria. See Keith Bradsher, "Range of Frustrations Reached Boil as Turkey Shot Down Russian Jet," *New York Times*, November 25, 2015.

10

Israel's Response to the Arab Spring: A Perfect Storm or an Opportunity for Change?

Ilan Peleg

WHAT IS KNOWN TODAY as the Arab Spring has been interpreted by most Israeli politicians and public commentators in extremely negative, sometimes even apocalyptic terms.[1] Pessimism in regard to this series of uprisings, demonstrations, and violent conflicts has also dominated the historical analogies invoked by many Israeli analysts. Most Israelis have tended to view this political earthquake as inviting long-term regional instability, facilitating the rise of radical sociopolitical forces in their already "rough neighborhood," and producing increased hostility toward Israel and its allies. Even though one commentator interpreted the Israeli reaction to the Arab Spring as merely "a frosty response," in reality the reaction of most Israelis has been much more negative.[2]

While many of those reactions are understandable and even justified, the outbreak of the Arab Spring for the most part had nothing to do with Israel or its long-term hostile relationships with the Arab world.[3] The uprisings started in Tunisia, a country relatively detached from the Israeli-Palestinian conflict, and their central gravitational point has been the call of the Arab masses for democratization and economic equality—demands aimed at the traditional authoritarian Arab regimes and protesting their corruption. The absence of an "Israeli agenda" for the Arab protesters, especially in the beginning of the uprising, has been noted by many commentators. And yet, with the passage of time, Israelis and others have tended to look at the Arab Spring as dramatically impacting Israel's position in a highly negative way.[4] This chapter, in contrast, will offer a more balanced approach to the Arab Spring and its impact on Israel.

First, this chapter will describe the Israeli reaction to the Arab Spring by focusing on the "majority opinion" among Israelis as well as on some alternative voices among politicians, commentators, and the general Israeli public. Second, the chapter will explain why most Israelis have reacted the way they have, attempting to contextualize the Israeli reaction by examining historical, ideological, and political factors. Third, the chapter will highlight some of the actual policies adopted by Israel in regard to the Palestinians, the Arabs, and the world at large under the impact of these dramatic regional events. Fourth, the chapter will dwell on the sensitive and overwhelmingly important relations between Israel and the United States in the wake of the Arab Spring, emphasizing both similarities and differences in the American and Israeli responses to these Middle Eastern events. And finally, the chapter will try to assess the longer-term impact of the Arab Spring on Israeli politics and on Israel's relationships with other nations in the region and beyond.

DESCRIBING THE ISRAELI REACTION

The reactions of many Israelis to the Arab Spring contain elements of collective, large-scale groupthink. Although Irving Janis introduced the term "groupthink" into the lexicon of political analysis to describe small-group propensities for irrational response to foreign policy challenges,[5] some of the Israeli collective reactions to the Arab Spring fit his concept rather well. Politicians, commentators, and analysts have tended to reinforce each other in an almost endless chorus, ushering in a competition of negative superlatives rarely seen in responses to other events.

Government spokespersons sometimes encouraged the Israeli public in its strong threat perception of the Arab Spring.[6] The most authoritative among those voices was Benjamin Netanyahu's. In a major November 2011 Knesset address, the prime minister said he believed the Arab Spring had taken the Arabs "not forward, but backward." In his view, Israel was now surrounded by a potentially hostile sea of "illiberal, anti-Western, anti-Israeli and anti-democratic" fundamentalism.[7] While his pessimistic reading of the regional map was understandable, it further promoted the apocalyptic national mood already established by other commentators.

The Israeli reaction to the Arab Spring has had several prominent elements, emphasizing in particular a few specific threats:

1. Domestic political instability in the Arab countries, especially those neighboring Israel. Analysts have noticed, correctly, that the quietest Israeli borders over the past several decades have been with nondemocracies such as Egypt, Jordan, and Syria, while the borders with more democratic political entities, such as Lebanon, the Palestinian Authority on the West Bank, or Hamas-ruled Gaza, have been significantly less stable.

2. Regional instability leading eventually to the possible renewal of Arab-Israeli wars in which all or most Arab states would align against Israel under some kind of renewed Nasserite ideology, pan-Arabism, or even, more frighteningly, pan-Islam. Several Israelis raised specifically the possibility of a two-front war. An even more nightmarish scenario would be an important country such as Egypt getting closer to Iran, Israel's archenemy in the Middle East.[8]

3. The danger that moderate countries, particularly Egypt and Jordan, would break diplomatic relations with Israel as a result of internal pressures and that this would further isolate Israel in the region and in the world. Many in Israel have expressed fears that the 1979 peace treaty with Egypt might be abrogated or vacated from its content. At the same time, in a November 2011 public opinion poll, 50.6 percent of Israeli Jews thought that the treaty would not be officially canceled but that relations with Egypt would be harmed.[9]

4. The rise of Islamists of all stripes, but especially radical Islamic movements in the Arab countries. Barry Rubin, editor of the *Middle East Review of International Affairs*, wrote an article under the title "Egypt Gets Its Khomeini: Qaradawi Returns in Triumph," comparing the leader of Egyptian Muslims to the Iranian Muslim revolutionary.[10] The fear of many Israelis has been that Islamists will come to power either through democratic elections or through violent means during the revolutionary period. The argument has been that once they get power, the Islamists will either abrogate the peace treaty their country has signed with Israel altogether (e.g., in the case of Egypt) or will adopt a more hostile position toward the Jewish state than did their predecessors (e.g., in the case of Syria).[11] More specifically, Israelis have often expressed the fear that

certain Islamists, particularly Egypt's Muslim Brotherhood, will have a negative influence over Hamas in Gaza, thus complicating Israel's relations with the Palestinians.[12]

5. The possibility or even likelihood of a rise in Palestinian radicalism. Many Israelis read the marches of Palestinians toward the Syrian-Israeli cease-fire line on the Golan Heights in May and June 2011 as a danger sign for the future, linking the Arab Spring and the Palestinian issue. The Israeli public was split on the likely radicalization of the Palestinians in the territories: 57.6 percent of Jews thought that the likelihood of radicalization was low, and only 37.8 percent thought it was high (the Israeli Arab public was even less worried about the chances for such radicalization). As for the impact of the Arab Spring on Israeli Arab citizens, almost 66 percent of the Jews and more than 75 percent of the Arabs thought that the likelihood of an Arab revolt in Israel was low. Regarding the overall impact of the Arab Spring on Israeli-Palestinian peace, Israeli Jews were split almost equally (with a slight majority viewing it as negative); Israeli Arabs were more positive.[13] One consequence of the Arab Spring was a Hamas-PLO agreement to unite, but the Netanyahu government quickly dismissed it as a negative move.

6. An increase in anti-Israeli terrorism if neighboring Arab regimes lose control over areas adjacent to Israel or if those regimes actively support and even passively cooperate with terrorist groups. Many Israelis have been particularly worried about the lack of effective Egyptian control over the Sinai.[14] While this concern was pertinent, terrorism in the Sinai actually intensified Egyptian-Israeli cooperation, including Israeli agreement to increased deployment of Egyptian forces in the Sinai.

7. A lack of strong or decisive reactions to the events and long-term consequences of the Arab Spring by outside powers, especially the United States. Many Israeli commentators accused the United States of not truly understanding the Middle East and not reacting forcefully enough to the events; the US reaction to the Egyptian demonstrations was particularly criticized. As early as February 2011, most Israeli Jews (unlike most Israeli Arabs) thought that the United States was wrong "when it supported anti-Mubarak demonstrators in Egypt."[15]

8. Increased political pressure on Israel from outside powers, especially the United States, in order to preempt or restrain political radicalization in the Arab world, counter Iran, and achieve other allegedly American

goals.[16] Many commentators thought that Israel would eventually have to pay a political price for the Arab Spring.

9. The possibility that "popular regimes [in the Arab world] may prove less tolerant of a Jewish state in their midst than the Washington-dependent dictatorships they displaced."[17] The fundamental idea here has been that the Arab populace is inherently and inalterably anti-Israel and that therefore popular regimes would be more inclined toward anti-Israel policies than elite-based regimes.

10. The possibility of a revolt in Israel. Only a relatively small minority of Israeli Jews (7.3 percent) thought there was such a possibility, although more Arabs in Israel (21.1 percent) thought it was possible. In rejecting the possibility of an internal uprising, most Israelis reasoned that their country was a democracy and that the public could change the government through elections.

Combining all or most of those factors into a seemingly coherent whole, most Israelis have adopted a rather pessimistic view of the events in the Middle East since December 2010. A few specific assaults have been connected to this overall sense of vulnerability, including repeated attacks on the Sinai gas pipeline from Egypt, an assault on the Israeli Embassy in Cairo, an August 2011 terrorist attack near Eilat, launching of rockets from Gaza, and so forth.

Analytically speaking, the overwhelmingly negative reactions of many Israelis to the Arab Spring were based on problematic reasoning. First, they reflected a tendency to overgeneralize rather than recognition that situations vary among different countries and societies. Second, negative events (such as the fall of Husni Mubarak) generated a huge echo chamber of endless negativity rather than a balanced analysis. Third, and most importantly, the thinking process of many Israelis has been dominated by false dichotomies, such as the one between democracy and Islam. For example, Israelis often assume that any strengthening of the Islamic factor in Arab countries will come necessarily at the expense of democracy (even though Islamists were the target of authoritarian secular Arab regimes and fought, in fact, for more democracy) and that any Islamist participation in governance will be disastrous for Israel, the United States, and the West in general.

These types of interpretations failed to look at the Arab Spring in broader terms, ignoring popular desires for democratic institutions, broad-based political freedoms, effective and corruption-free governance, and so forth. The dichotomy of democracy versus Islam, superimposed on the Arab Spring, has been clouding assessment of the event, not clarifying it. Interpreting the Arab Spring "Islamically" has encouraged some Israelis to become overly defensive.

The developments in the Arab world have shaken the self-confidence of Israelis. Writing in the *Washington Post* during the outset of the Egyptian demonstrations, Aaron David Miller, who had served as an adviser to several American presidents, observed, "It is impossible to overstate the angst, even hysteria, that Israelis are feeling about their neighborhood as they watch what is unfolding in the streets of Cairo."[18]

Side by side with the negative views held by most Israelis, an alternative, more optimistic (although significantly less popular) perspective emerged.[19] This antihegemonic view had a few elements:

1. An argument that more-democratic regimes in the neighboring countries might create more stability in those countries.[20] Yossi Beilin, a former Israeli minister of justice, described the Arab Spring positively as the "empowerment of the Arab society."[21] He speculated that this empowerment would mean more involvement in efforts to bring peace to the region. Moreover, in a Brookings Institution poll conducted between November 10 and November 20, 2011, 46 percent of Israelis expressed sympathy toward the Arab Spring, agreeing that it was about "ordinary people seeking dignity, freedom and a better life"; 44 percent thought that if the Arab Spring led to more democracy in the Arab world, that would be better for Israel.[22]

2. A possibility of an emerging regional pro-Western camp in the Middle East committed to democracy. While most politicians on the right of the political spectrum in Israel, headed by Prime Minister Netanyahu, sounded the alarm about the Arab Spring, former Defense Minister Moshe Arens stated that the Arab Spring could benefit democracy in the region as a whole.[23] Others have seen the Arab Spring as weakening the radical axis and opening the gate for new (if secret) alliances, including increased cooperation directed at Iran, one of Israel's primary enemies.

3. An argument that Israel's peace treaties with Egypt and Jordan were highly stable, reflective not merely of Israel's interests but also of the long-term interests of those countries, and that therefore those treaties were not seriously endangered by the Arab Spring. Analysts adopting

this position argued that a new political elite in Egypt would quickly realize the enormous benefits from the peace treaty with Israel and would
act to maintain it.

4. An assertion that not all Islamists were radicals and that, in fact, some
   of them (including the Muslim Brotherhood in Egypt and other countries) were moderate and democratically inclined (having been the main
   victim of totalitarianism in their own countries). Some commentators
   emphasized the possibility of Israeli-Sunni cooperation against the Shia-
   led Iranians.

5. Attention to the fact that the Palestinian territories remained calm
   throughout the Arab Spring and that the West Bank was being led by
   moderates. Some commentators thought that the Muslim Brotherhood–
   led government in Egypt that succeeded Mubarak (though it was ousted
   by a military coup in July 2013) could have fulfilled an important role
   of mediating between Israelis and Palestinians and that such mediation
   could have eventually produced a peace settlement between the parties.
   Moreover, Hamas has emerged in opposition to the Syrian regime, which
   has helped to divide some of Israel's enemies.

6. Recognition by some analysts that whatever the public sentiment in the
   Arab countries resulting from the Arab Spring, some of them will not
   be able to dramatically change their foreign policy, including that toward
   Israel. For example, any post-Mubarak regime in Egypt will have huge
   internal challenges and will need international and especially American
   assistance, which will prevent it from severing relations with Israel.

It is worth noting that the analysis offered by Israeli commentators has
been dominated by what might be called "the prophets of doom," whereas the
general public seems to be somewhat more balanced in its opinions. Thus, in
March 2011, Israeli Jews and Arabs were asked separately to assess whether the
antiregime struggles in the various Arab states were positive or negative from
an Israeli perspective. Among Jews, a full 46.7 percent saw the events as positive and 29.7 percent considered them as negative; among Arabs, the numbers
were 55.5 percent and 34.4 percent, respectively.[24] When asked to assess the
demonstrations from the perspective of the Arab people, 53.1 percent of the
Jews thought they were positive and merely 29.3 percent thought they were
negative; 65.5 percent and 28.9 percent of Arabs held the corresponding opinions. So at least at the beginning of the uprising, the Israeli Jewish public was

not sold on the idea that these developments were negative. Opinions seem to have shifted in a negative direction with the passage of time.

In May 2011, the Peace Index reported that in assessing the impact of the Arab Spring on Israel, 38.9 percent of Israeli Jews thought that Israel's situation had worsened, while less than 11 percent thought it had improved.[25] This change might have reflected the impact of the numerous negative interpretations of experts, public commentators, and politicians. Even more negative results were reported in November 2011: This time the assessment of the situation as "worsening" had reached 68.5 percent of the Israeli Jewish public.[26]

EXPLAINING THE ISRAELI RESPONSE

In order to explain comprehensively the overwhelmingly negative Israeli response to the Arab Spring, we need to adopt three different, albeit related, forms of analysis: historical, ideological, and political. Historically, this reaction ought to be understood as part of the long-term hostility between Arabs and Israelis—hostility that has created and sustained an understandable nervousness and a proclivity for negative reactions on both sides of the generally hostile border between Israel and its Arab neighbors. So it is no wonder that the regionwide instability associated with the Arab Spring has generated deep anxiety among most Israelis. Furthermore, many Israelis have looked at the events of the Arab Spring against the background of the last two decades or so, appreciating the fact that recent Arab-Israeli relations have been more positive than in the past, especially in terms of Israel's relations with Egypt and Jordan as well as less-formal relations with other moderate, pro-Western Arab countries. From an Israeli perspective, the Arab Spring has put in jeopardy the development of better Arab-Israeli relations in years to come.

But beyond this historical perspective, Israel's negative reaction to the Arab Spring has an ideological dimension. Many Israelis have tended to view the Arab world as fundamentally hostile to their national goals and even their independent national existence as a sovereign Jewish state in the Middle East. This has been particularly the case for those who belong to the nationalist right, including the current government and its leader, Prime Minister Netanyahu. Viewing the Arab world as hostile has been at the center of the right's belief system.[27]

Netanyahu's ideology has been fundamentally nationalist, promoting maximal territorial expansion and viewing the Arab world, including the Palestinians, as inalterably hostile to Israel.[28] Within this ideological framework, any change in the Arab world—including increased democratization—that might have negative implications for Israel's security, including events that are part of the Arab Spring, is likely to be magnified. This is precisely what has happened in reaction to the Arab Spring. Netanyahu himself became the leader of the "negativist" camp, interpreting the events in the most apocalyptic terms possible.

Israeli reaction to the Arab Spring had a clear political component. The political reality in Jerusalem since 2009 has been that of a right-wing government with a commitment to prevent the repartition of Palestine despite enormous worldwide expectations that a two-state solution must be implemented. In that light, the reaction of the Netanyahu government, and of the Israeli public led by it, could have been expected. It is a government with no trust whatsoever in the Arab "street" and minimal trust in Arab elites, with the exception of Western-sustained autocrats such as Mubarak or traditional monarchies such as the one in Jordan.

The Israeli reaction to the Arab Spring became part and parcel of an overall, ongoing debate in Israel on the nature of the Middle East and Israel's relations with it. The "hawks," under the active leadership of the government, tended to adopt a completely negative attitude toward the Arab Spring, while the "doves," more liberal circles in the opposition to the current government, allowed for a more cautious and sometimes moderately positive attitude. Thus, for example, some commentators on the right found that the Arab Spring "proves once again that the Arab-Israeli conflict is not the central problem in this region [the Middle East]" and therefore that "this is not the time for Israel to be taking territorial or other risks."[29] Other hawks argued that there was no reason to believe that democracy would result from any of the Arab revolutions, as if Arabs were constitutionally unable to democratize. More "dovish" elements saw the potential for democracy in the demonstrations of the Arab masses.

HIGHLIGHTING OLD-NEW ISRAELI POLICIES

Although it has been commonly argued—even assumed—that the Arab Spring "changed everything" in terms of Israel's position in the Middle East, it could be conversely argued that Israel's position in the region has not changed a great deal.[30] Israel continues to be a regional power, easily the strongest military power in the area, although it is unpopular with the vast majority of the countries in the region and even less popular with the Arab masses. The pessimists' stance has been that as the influence of the masses in the region grows,

Israel's position will markedly deteriorate; equally, to the extent to which new political elites adopt the policies of old political elites, continuity in terms of Israel's position will prevail. To date, we have seen little evidence that the new elites have adopted new policy positions, particularly in foreign policy.

One of the most interesting questions is whether, and in what ways, the Arab Spring has led to actual, observable changes in Israeli policy. While the fundamental approach, attitudes, and goals of Israel's foreign policy seem to have remained fairly constant, in some tactical areas changes have been introduced:

1. The Arab Spring has strengthened the reluctance of the current Israeli government to move forward toward a negotiated agreement of the Israeli-Palestinian conflict and take action to facilitate such an agreement (e.g., by stopping settlement activity on the West Bank). The overall, sometimes unverbalized argument has been that in a time of regional instability, Israel could not and should not transfer territories to the Arabs, including the Palestinians. While Netanyahu did not have a reputation for aggressively pushing the peace process before the beginning of the Arab Spring in late 2010, the onset of regional instability made it significantly easier for him to promote his hawkish line even further, especially within Israel. Thus, the Arab Spring, a series of events that were initially unlinked to Arab-Israeli relations, became the last nail in the "peace process coffin."

2. The Arab Spring has had some impact on budgetary allocation in Israel. Pressures to cut the large defense budget, particularly as a result of social protest in Israel during the summer of 2011 (itself a phenomenon impacted by the Arab Spring), have been resisted with the argument that Israel may soon have to face the Arab armies again, possibly in an all-out war. In general, the powerful defense lobby has been successful in maintaining the large defense budget.

3. The Arab Spring has caused some changes in the relationships between Israel and the neighboring Arab states, although it is too early to fully assess those changes. The relationship between Israel and Egypt, cold but stable under Mubarak, became even more distant during the Morsi era, although even then the Egyptian government responded positively to Israeli needs (e.g., rescuing Israeli personnel from the besieged Israeli Embassy). Relations have subsequently improved since the military coup led by General Abdel Fattah al-Sisi, and the equally crucial relations with Jordan have also been maintained. Thus, for example, Foreign Minister

Avigdor Lieberman gave a speech in which he openly endorsed the territorial integrity of the Hashemite Kingdom, a very important posture in view of possible Palestinian pressures to the contrary.[31] Even in the case of Syria, a declared enemy, the Israeli government remained rather detached from international efforts to unseat Bashar al-Assad. Interestingly, despite the hostility of many Israelis toward Syria and the Assad regime, the Israeli public has been split over the benefit of a possible collapse of that regime, and an overwhelming number of Israeli Jews (84.1 percent) supported the idea that "Israel should sit quietly on the sidelines" while the Syrian conflict goes on.[32] The Israeli Jewish public was more sympathetic (49.8 percent) to the idea of Western countries providing aid to the opposition forces.[33] The Israeli government remained uninvolved, strengthening the perception that it preferred the Middle East status quo to the evolution of a more participatory new order.

4. As a result of the Arab Spring, Israel seems to be pursuing more energetically new relationships with a number of countries in the Eastern Mediterranean, Africa, and parts of the Arab world. There has been somewhat of a return to David Ben-Gurion's so-called periphery strategy, in which Israel tried to compensate for the hostility of its immediate Arab neighbors by developing strong geostrategic relations with countries such as Iran and Turkey, Christian elements in Lebanon, the Kurds, and so forth. Among Israel's recent "diplomatic targets" have been several European countries, including Greece, Italy, Bulgaria, and Romania, but also Cyprus in the Eastern Mediterranean.[34]

5. One real, although somewhat indirect, consequence of the Arab Spring was the agreement reached between the PLO and Hamas to create a united Palestinian front. It is interesting to note, however, that most Israelis, and most particularly the Netanyahu government, dismissed this agreement as unpromising and negative. The prime minister found in this agreement yet another reason for Israel's inability to negotiate with the Palestinians.

All in all, the Arab Spring has strengthened the "wait-and-see" policy of the Netanyahu government.[35] The political division in the Israeli public has enabled Netanyahu to stay on the sideline on most issues. Given its ideology and structure, there is little reason to think that the Netanyahu government would have moved toward a final resolution of the question of Palestine had the Arab

Spring never sprung. The Arab Spring gave Netanyahu and the Israeli right new arguments against the establishment of a Palestinian state, but it did not create those arguments. Netanyahu's traditionally grim view of the region was fortified by the recent developments but did not fundamentally change as a result of them.

In asking the Israeli public (in March 2011) what ought to be done in view of the Arab Spring, the Peace Index reported that the vast majority of Israeli Jews—70.2 percent—agreed with the claim that Israel should remain passive "at this stage," while only 40 percent of Israeli Arabs agreed with this position.[36] It is hard to know whether the Israeli Jewish public simply accepted the position of the Netanyahu government or dictated it. What is clear, however, is that there was no concentrated effort by the government to convince the public to see any positive element in the Arab Spring.

In the competition between the pessimists and the optimists in regard to the interpretation of the Arab Spring, the former have clearly prevailed. Their position has become even more dominant than before. A more diverse picture of the Arab Spring emphasizing the fall of Arab autocrats and the possibility of democracy was ignored in favor of an exclusive emphasis on the dangers of instability and Islamism. This position justified and legitimized Netanyahu's do-nothing approach, particularly on the Palestinian front. Rather than pushing for a Palestinian settlement as a way to promote stability, the government adopted a passive position, using the Arab Spring as a pretext for paralysis.

No other country has been more important for the pessimist/optimist battle than Egypt. The debate has been focused on the nature of Egypt's Islamist movements, especially the Muslim Brotherhood. While the pessimists interpreted it as a radical movement, the optimists have emphasized its pragmatic and even moderate character. They thought that with the Brotherhood's influence over Hamas in Gaza, Egypt could fulfill an important role in negotiating a deal between Israelis and Palestinians. With the rise to power of General Sisi, however, this debate became less urgent.

DWELLING ON THE AMERICAN FACTOR AND THE EMERGING DIVERGENCE

The Arab Spring caught both Israel and the United States by surprise. Intelligence services officers, foreign ministries bureaucrats, academics, and politicians were completely unprepared for these events. As close allies and essentially two pro-status-quo states, the United States and Israel could have been expected to have similar reactions. Yet they didn't, and this divergence of opinions may very well increase in years to come. In many ways, the Arab Spring complicated US-Israeli relations, already characterized by different views on a variety of issues.

From an Israeli perspective, the deepening rift between Israel and the United States occasioned by the Arab Spring has been worrisome. When the Arab Spring began, Israelis hoped and expected that America would automatically express its strong, unwavering support for its friends in the Middle East, mostly also Israel's friends, whatever their domestic stance with their publics or chance of survival in the face of popular uprising. The United States took a different position. While the Israeli position toward the unrest was extremely negative (especially in the case of Egypt), supportive of the existing regimes (e.g., in the case of Jordan), or ambivalent (e.g., in the case of Syria), the American position was verbally sympathetic to what Washington perceived as a democratic wave against authoritarian tradition. At the same time, Washington was careful not to get directly involved in yet another "shooting war" in the Middle East.[37] While the Israeli policy looked decisive, the American position looked like waffling, and while Israel emerged as clearly supporting the old regimes, the US position was much more nuanced. Moreover, Washington showed sympathy to the rebels in the different Arab countries.

Israeli strategic thinkers noted the dramatic change. Efraim Inbar, a prominent Israeli analyst, wrote about the United States that "its friendship with Israel is no longer self-evident,"[38] a position incompatible with the statements of practically all American political figures, including President Barack Obama. Inbar speculated that "Israeli use of force as a preventive or preemptive move could exacerbate the strained Jerusalem-Washington relationship,"[39] a far-reaching conclusion in view of the centrality of such a move on Israel's part.

The most important "test case" in terms of Israeli-American divergence was Egypt. When the US administration decided not to support President Husni Mubarak against the Cairo demonstrators, Israelis of all stripes saw that as a sign of US unreliability and even untrustworthiness. The American argument that Mubarak had lost the confidence of the Egyptian people after more than three decades of authoritarian and abusive rule, manifested clearly in his attempt to pass on the presidency to his son, failed to convince most Israeli commentators, let alone government officials. The Egyptian uprising, and the

American reaction to it, heightened the tension between Washington and Jerusalem, tensions that have dominated their relations since Obama's inauguration and Netanyahu's resumption of the Israeli premiership (2009).

Interestingly, many Israelis saw a direct link between the situation in Egypt and the issue of whether a resolution on the Palestinian issue was even possible. This was reflective of the tendency among Israelis to look at everything systemically, as if all parts of the complicated Middle East were connected and as if all were aligned against them. As a result of the unrest in Egypt, many Israelis concluded that "the only border Israel can fully control today is the one with the West Bank,"[40] thus leading them away from a two-state agreement with the Palestinian Authority. This Israeli position further antagonized Washington. Obama put the resolution of the Israeli-Palestinian issue at the top of his Middle East agenda upon assuming office in January 2009, clearly in opposition to Netanyahu's stance.

Dov Waxman has argued persuasively that "at the root of today's tensions [between Israel and the United States] are increasingly differing strategic perspectives."[41] Haim Malka has expressed this idea somewhat differently, stating that "increasingly U.S. and Israeli responses to their common challenges and threats differ significantly."[42] While Waxman talks about "strategic perspectives" and Malka about "responses to common challenges," both emphasize divergence of opinion and policies as well as a negative trajectory in US-Israeli relations in years to come. I agree with this reading of the situation but wish to emphasize its multiple roots—a disagreement about the resolution of the Israeli-Palestinian conflict, the use of force in the Middle East, the appropriate response to the Iranian challenge, and, indeed, the overall response to the Arab Spring.

In looking into US and Israeli responses to the Arab Spring, we must note the negativity on both sides. Israelis have tended to look at the Obama administration's reaction to the Arab Spring as naive, timid, shortsighted, and unsophisticated, guaranteeing the emergence of foes to Western power. Americans saw Israel, particularly the one led by Netanyahu, as "stuck somewhere between denial and defiance."[43] But this divergence of views was not merely about name-calling or gaining points in an endless debate between a superpower and its regional ally. It was also about supporting different "teams." While many Israelis stood on the side of the autocrats (notably Egypt's Mubarak and Jordan's King Abdullah II) or, at most, showed "neutrality" (e.g., toward Syria's Assad), the US administration expressed support for the democratic forces challenging those autocrats. While Israel feared the ascendance of democracy in the Arab world, assuming that it would reflect the hostility of Arab public opinion toward Israel, the United States seemed to have concluded that the uprising could not and should not be stopped. While the public debate was ostensibly about being on the "right side of history," it was actually about being politically on the victorious side.

The Israeli-American "debate" has been particularly sharp in terms of the appropriate response to the Islamists in the new constellation of political power in the Middle East. In the Israeli belief system, Islamists are not to be trusted under any and all circumstances. They are implacable enemies of the Jewish state. For the United States, the picture is more complicated and more nuanced. There are some radical Muslims and some moderate Muslims, and the United States needs to find a way to talk to the latter, especially if and when they come to power. Israelis tend to argue that Islamists should not be allowed to come to power; Americans do not believe that they can be prevented from doing so—and certainly not through the use of force.

In general, American-Israeli disagreement about the Arab Spring has to be understood structurally; it reflects the difference between the narrower view of a local power and the broader perspective of a superpower. Most Israelis expect the United States to show unshakable commitment to Israel, its overall interests, and, especially, its security. Americans look at their commitment to Israel as only one component of their multifaceted regional and even global policy. Other components include US relations with Arab states as well as America's "desire to advance democratization in the region and gain the goodwill of the new Arab leaders."[44] For the United States, strong ties with Arab countries are vital. Moreover, for the United States, the resolution of the Palestinian problem through a two-state solution is a key component for establishing a stable Middle East. For many Israelis, including major elements within the current government, this American design is highly problematical. For many Americans, the Palestinian issue is a source of instability and therefore a source of the Arab Spring, a position that many Israelis do not accept.

In many ways, Israeli commentators are caught on the horns of a dilemma. On the one hand, they view Israel as continuing to be dependent on American support. On the other, they see the American position in the Middle East and in the world in general as declining. Their interpretation of the US regional standing is that it is on the retreat. Inbar, in a comprehensive analysis of the overall post–Arab Spring, titles his section on the United States "The Decline of American Clout."[45] Rather harshly, he views the US response to recent Middle East events as "confused, contradictory, and inconsistent."

Conclusion: Assessing the Long-Term Impact and Exploring the Unpredictable

While we cannot know what will be the final results of the momentous events known as the Arab Spring, some trends are identifiable. In general, there has been a tendency by most analysts to exaggerate the negative impact of the Arab Spring on Israel's position in the Middle East. A more balanced view, as well as "a calmer and more nuanced portrait of the Middle East's complex reality," is called for.[46] Such an approach would quickly reveal that Israel's military supremacy in the region has increased, especially given the decline of Iraqi and Syrian capabilities.[47]

The Arab Spring, along with other developments in the area, has further intensified Israel's isolated position in the region and possibly beyond. Given that post-Spring Israel is even more reluctant than pre-Spring Israel to reach a territorial settlement with the Palestinians, it seems that post–Arab Spring Israel will continue to be highly isolated, a position marked by a continuing divergence of interests, perceptions, and policies with the country's "natural friends," the United States and Western European countries.

In realpolitik terms, the single most important geostrategic result of the Arab Spring was the fall of the Mubarak regime. Nevertheless, pessimistic and almost apocalyptic predictions in regard to Egyptian-Israeli relations have not come to pass. Speculation about the abrogation of the Egyptian-Israeli peace treaty (1979) and the return of Egypt to pan-Arab policies à la Nasser have not materialized, even when Egypt was led by a Muslim Brotherhood government.

Much of the negativity in analyzing Egyptian-Israeli relations has focused on the Sinai. On August 18, 2011, there was a terrorist attack from the Egyptian-held Sinai across the border into Israel. Several civilians were killed, and several Israeli politicians blamed Egypt. Four Egyptian border-police officers were killed in the incident as well, leading to an attack on the Israeli Embassy in Cairo, the recalling of the Egyptian ambassador from Tel Aviv, and mutual accusations between the two countries. Nevertheless, despite this serious public crisis and cross-border violence, both countries worked toward a peaceful settlement of the dispute, assisted actively by the United States. While the Arab street exploded, the generals acted to calm passions.

The issue of the Sinai, like other Israeli-Arab issues, has deeper roots than cross-border tensions. But despite the pessimism of the Israeli press, there are mutual interests in solving such issues by peaceful means. When it comes to the Sinai, an area characterized by lawlessness for decades, Israel and Egypt share deep concern about the chaotic nature of the situation. Therefore, there is reason to believe that they can find a way to deal with future incidents.

This sense of realism ought to be applied to other areas as well. The Israelis are naturally worried about the "isolating processes" that they believe have come to dominate the Middle East as a result of the Arab Spring. But just as the Sinai was unstable long before the Arab Spring, Israel's isolation in the area, indeed in the world, was evident long before the Arab Spring erupted. While many Israeli commentators note the aggressive attitude of Iran and the unfriendly attitude of Turkey toward Israel, those are not really new phenomena.

All in all, when we look at the actual policies of most Arab governments, they seem to be rather stable. In Egypt, for example, the Supreme Council of the Armed Forces, then the Morsi government, and now the Sisi regime have been committed to the regional status quo, honoring Egypt's international obligations. The peace treaty between Israel and Egypt is among the most important obligations that Egypt has taken upon itself over the past thirty-five years. It is linked to a whole gamut of Egyptian relations with the outside world, including, most importantly, Egypt's relations with the United States.

Beyond the specific issues related to the Arab Spring, the danger is that the overall interpretation of it might continue to be radically negative and completely controlled by the traditional Israeli narrative. Thus, there has been a strong tendency in Israel to link any change in the Arab world with "Islamism" and to correlate Islamism with nondemocratic, anti-Israeli, and anti-Western attitudes. The asserted dichotomy between Islamism and democracy is simplistic and often wrong. A more balanced and therefore more positive perspective ought to be considered, giving a chance for improvement in regional relations.

Columnist Rami Khouri has described the Arab Spring as "the birth of Arab politics."[48] If Khouri is right, even partially, Israel must find a way of reaching out to the new forces active in this new politics, a way of combining a realist foreign policy with a progressive bent.

Some Israeli commentators have conflated the Arab Spring with the overall decline of the Arab Middle East, a conclusion that emphasizes the instability generated by the upheavals and the rise of non-Arab powers.[49] It is, however, somewhat premature to reach such a conclusion because the Arab Spring may energize the Arab world, especially if new forces emerge. Moreover, the weakening of the Arab world is not necessarily a benefit to Israel. Some of the non-Arab forces that have allegedly emerged at the expense of the Arab states—notably Iran and Turkey—are increasingly anti-Israeli. Arab states that suffer from internal instability, such as Egypt, Syria, Lebanon, and Jordan, may become a source of constant regional volatility and therefore of threats on Israel's borders. A rapprochement between some of the weakened Arab states and a non-Arab foe of Israel—for example, an Egyptian-Iranian alliance—could be truly threatening for Israel.

Another potentially long-term development resulting from the Arab Spring is the rise of Saudi Arabia to a leadership position in the region, possibly heading a broad anti-Iranian coalition. In fact, despite the overwhelming Israeli pessimism in regard to the Arab Spring, such a long-term result could work in Israel's favor, particularly regarding Iran. The active role of Saudi Arabia not merely in its close neighborhood (Bahrain, Yemen) but also in other parts of the Middle East (Syria) indicates that such a scenario is, in fact, emerging as part of the Middle East geostrategic landscape.

Above all, the Arab Spring has made peace in the Middle East between Israelis and Arabs more remote than ever before. While some of this assessment is based on cold, realistic calculation—how can Israel conclude peace with anyone in such an unstable region?—much of it is about a psychological state of mind. It is about the triumph of anxiety. The Arab Spring strengthened the fear factor in Israel, and especially the political forces associated with that fear factor, the traditional right. Although some commentators have argued that the Arab Spring might result in tougher Israeli security demands if and when Israeli-Palestinian negotiations start (e.g., presence on the Jordan River, demilitarization of the Palestinian state), the deeper meaning of the Arab Spring is that negotiations are simply unlikely to start at all.

The assumption of many Israeli analysts has been that the Arab world is unwaveringly hostile to Israel and that no matter what Israel does, this hostility will remain constant. Moreover, they have further assumed that the new forces in the region, especially the Islamists, are even more hostile to Israel than traditional nationalist circles and that Israel cannot change that hostility through its actions. It seems to me that such fatalistic assumptions could lead inevitably to one and only one result—no change in Israeli policy. Such a result would be tragic, a classic case of self-fulfilling prophecy. It is reflected in the 2015 reelection of Benjamin Netanyahu.[50]

NOTES

1. See, for example, the recent commentary in Benny Morris, "Israel and the 'Arab Spring,'" Byline, July 8, 2015, www.byline.com/column/17/article/146, and the Peace Index of the Israel Democracy Institute (IDI), which has collected large amounts of information on the attitudes of Israelis. In assessing the response of the Israeli public to the Arab Spring, I will rely heavily on the Peace Index; whenever possible, I will use other sources as well. In this essay, I will use "Arab Spring" as shorthand for the Middle East demonstrations, protest, and violent acts (including the wars in Libya and Syria) since December 2010. Concepts such as "awakening," "uprising," or even "revolution" will be used interchangeably.

2. Daniel L. Byman, "Israel: A Frosty Response to the Arab Spring," in *The Arab Awakening: America and the Transformation of the Middle East*, ed. Kenneth M. Pollack (Washington, DC: Brookings Institution Press, 2011), 250–257.

3. Even many people who took a pessimistic view of the Arab Spring have admitted this fact.

4. Maybe the most comprehensive early assessment of the impact of the Arab Spring on Israel's overall situation has been offered by Efraim Inbar, "The 2011 Arab Uprisings and Israel's National Security," *Mideast Security and Policy Studies* No. 95 (Ramat-Gan, Israel: The Begin-Sadat Center for Strategic Studies, Bar-Ilan University, February 2011); and Efraim Inbar, "Israel's National Security Amidst Unrest in the Arab World," *Washington Quarterly* 59, 3 (Summer 2012): 59–73.

5. Irving L. Janis, *Victims of Groupthink: A Psychological Study of Foreign-Policy Decisions and Fiascoes* (Boston: Houghton Mifflin, 1972).

6. Byman, "Israel," calls this perception, alternatively, the "fear factors," 250. Among the most prominent official spokespeople promoting the negative view were Prime Minister Netanyahu and several ministers in his government (e.g., Avigdor Lieberman, Yuval Steinitz, and Moshe Ya'alon).

7. Quoted in Leslie Susser, "Seize the Spring," *Jerusalem Report*, February 27, 2012, 20.

8. When Egypt allowed two Iranian ships to go through the Suez Canal, Israelis took notice. Yet to date, an Egyptian-Iranian alliance has not materialized. There is plenty of evidence that the major Sunni Arab countries, such as Egypt and Saudi Arabia, fear the growing Iranian influence in the region as much as Israel does.

9. IDI, Peace Index, November 2011, available at www.peaceindex.org.

10. Quoted in Eric Rozenman, "The 'Arab Spring': Democratic Promise or Threat?," *Midstream* (Spring 2011): 9.

11. Much of the "analysis" of what the Islamists may or may not do in regard to Israel tends to be rather speculative, often not based on any hard evidence.

12. Hamas has its origins in the Egyptian Muslim Brotherhood. Yet if the Brotherhood comes to power in Egypt, it may decide to try moderating Hamas in Gaza.

13. IDI, Peace Index, March 2011, available at www.peaceindex.org.

14. Inbar calls it the "Somalization" of the Sinai. See Inbar, "The 2011 Arab Uprisings," 15.

15. IDI, Peace Index, February 2011, available at www.peaceindex.org.

16. For speculation about such a scenario, see Aaron David Miller, "2011: The Year of the (Bad) Initiative," *New York Times*, March 11, 2011.

17. Rozenman, "The 'Arab Spring,'" 8–11.

18. Aaron David Miller, "Why Israel Fears a Free Egypt," *Washington Post*, February 4, 2011.

19. See, for example, Nimrod Goren and Jenia Yodkevich, eds., *Israel and the Arab Spring: Opportunities in Change* (Ramat Gan, Israel: Mitvim, 2013), a collection of twelve essays on different aspects of the Arab Spring; and Ehud Eiran, "The Arab Spring: Opportunities," *Palestine-Israel Journal* 18, 1 (2012): 66–70.

20. Interestingly, this position was initially promoted by Benjamin Netanyahu in his book *A Place Among the Nations* (New York: Bantam, 1993); see esp. 248–249. Yet he came out strongly against the Arab Spring, describing it as a danger for Israel.

21. Yossi Beilin, "The Empowerment of Arab Society," bitterlemons.org, June 13, 2011, www.bitterlemons.org/inside.php?id=96.

22. Shibley Telhami, "Jewish Citizens of Israel," in *2011 Public Opinion Polls of Jewish and Arab Citizens of Israel*, Brookings Institution, 3–5, www.brookings.edu/~/media/research/files/reports/2011/12/01%20israel%20poll%20telhami/1201_israel_poll_telhami_presentation. On the other hand, the majority of Israelis thought that the impact of the Arab Spring on Israel was "mostly for the worse" (51 percent) rather than "mostly for the better." Those contradictions reflect the fact that the Israeli public has been torn in regard to the Arab Spring.

23. Moshe Arens, "Growing Mideast Democracy Could Benefit Israel," *Haaretz*, April 5, 2011. While Arens mentioned the concern about Islamist takeover, his tone was less alarmist than that of many other right-leaning commentators.

24. IDI, Peace Index, March 2011.

25. IDI, Peace Index, May 2011, available at www.peaceindex.org.

26. IDI, Peace Index, November 2011.

27. It should be noted that while the right adopted the public view that the Arab Spring was a threat to Israel, some right-wingers quietly adopted the opposite view. See, for example, Zvika Krieger, "The Right-Wing Israeli Case That the Arab Spring Is Good for Israel," *Atlantic*, May 20, 2012.

28. See, for example, Ilan Peleg, "The Israeli Right," in *Contemporary Israel: Domestic Politics, Foreign Policy, and Security Challenges*, ed. Robert O. Freedman (Boulder, CO: Westview Press, 2009), 21–44.

29. Comments by General Uzi Dayan, reported by the Begin-Sadat Center for Strategic Studies, "What Arab Spring?," Bulletin No. 28 (Spring 2012).

30. I share in this respect the opinion expressed by Brent E. Sasley, "Israel and the Arab Spring: But the Season Doesn't Matter," *Huffington Post*, December 28, 2011, www .huffingtonpost.com/brent-sasley/israel-arab-spring_b_1171821.html.

31. For a pessimistic view on Jordan, see Herb Keinon, "Anti-normalization Forces Gaining Strength in Jordan," *Jerusalem Post*, August 10, 2011; and Eli Lake, "Muslim Brotherhood Seeks End to Israel Treaty," *Washington Times*, February 3, 2011.

32. IDI, Peace Index, February 2012, available at www.peaceindex.org.

33. Ibid.

34. Inbar, "The 2011 Arab Uprisings," 25.

35. Yossi Klein Halevi, "Israel's Neighborhood Watch: Egypt's Upheaval Means That Palestine Must Wait," *Foreign Affairs*, February 1, 2011.

36. IDI, Peace Index, March 2011.

37. For example, the United States reacted very differently to the Syrian revolt than to the Libyan revolt.

38. Inbar, "The 2011 Arab Uprisings," 10.

39. Ibid.

40. Halevi, "Israel's Neighborhood Watch."

41. Dov Waxman, "The Real Problem in U.S.-Israeli Relations," *Washington Quarterly* 35, 2 (Spring 2012): 71–87.

42. Haim Malka, *Crossroads: The Future of the U.S.-Israel Strategic Partnership* (Washington, DC: Center for International and Strategic Studies, 2011), 56.

43. Waxman, "The Real Problem," 75.

44. Byman, "Israel," 256.

45. Inbar, "The 2011 Arab Uprisings," 5–7.

46. Such a position is reflected in Hilo Glazer, "Israelis Telling the Middle East Like It Is," *Haaretz*, June 28, 2015; a more nuanced position could be seen also in Benedetta Berti, "Weathering the 'Spring': Israel's Evolving Assessments and Policies in the Changing Middle East," Analysis No. 277, Italian Institute for International Political Studies, November 2014.

47. Efraim Inbar, "The Middle East Turmoil and Israel's Security," Middle East Forum, April 13, 2015, www.meforum.org/5174/israel-middle-east-security.

48. Quoted in Salman Shaikh, "A Failure to Communicate," *Foreign Policy*, February 9, 2012, http://foreignpolicy.com/2012/02/09/a-failure-to-communicate-2.

49. See, for example, Inbar, "The 2011 Arab Uprisings," 4.

50. Morris, "Israel and the 'Arab Spring.'"

11

Russia and the Arab Spring

Robert O. Freedman

I think that these processes [of the Arab Spring] have no direct impact on us. Although one should recognize that there are certain financial costs as we had to stop our involvement in some economic projects and military and technical cooperation in some cases. I am sure that the ongoing events cannot break the huge, mutually fruitful potential of cooperation that has been stockpiling for years. . . . [However,] if the region's countries turn out to be under weak control of the central authorities, this would be fertile soil for international terrorism's efforts, illicit drug trafficking, trans-border crime, and illegal migration.

—Russian deputy foreign minister Mikhail Bogdanov,
Interfax, July 5, 2011

Introduction

THE ARAB SPRING caught Russia, as it did the United States and indeed the rulers of the countries affected, unawares.[1] In a dynamic somewhat reminiscent of the events in Eastern Europe in 1989, the revolutions quickly spread from Tunisia to Egypt and then to Yemen, Libya, Bahrain, Syria, and Jordan.[2]

As far as the Russian leadership was concerned, there appeared to be some initial concern that the revolutions in the Arab world could spread to Russia as well. Russia itself was marked by an autocratic government, widespread corruption—something Prime Minister Dmitry Medvedev, when he was Russia's president, had openly complained about—and rising prices, with inflation reaching nearly 10 percent in 2010.[3] Indeed, Russia's prodemocracy opposition cheered the events in Tunisia and Egypt, with comments such as "The [revolutionary] train stopped at the station in Cairo. Next stop: Moscow" and "Start packing your bags, Vladimir."[4] Medvedev took a tough line on such attitudes, and in an almost cold war–era response asserted that the revolts in the Arab world were instigated by "outside forces" that were also trying to topple the Russian government. In Medvedev's words, "Let's face the truth. They have been preparing such a scenario for us, and now they will try even harder to implement it."[5]

However, Medvedev's concern initially appeared very much exaggerated. First, Russia had gone through a chaotic period only a decade before under Boris Yeltsin, and with the exception of a relatively small group of reformers, Russians at first showed little inclination to oust the ruling duo of Medvedev and Vladimir Putin by street protests. Second, unlike the case in Egypt, the Russian religious authorities in the Orthodox Church had closely aligned themselves with the regime (a situation somewhat reminiscent of Czarist Russia). As far as Western instigation of the Arab Spring was concerned, Russia's leading Middle East expert (and former prime minister and foreign minister) Yevgeny Primakov, no friend of the United States, publicly ruled out the idea that the United States had orchestrated the revolts, asserting that he was convinced, after visiting the United States, that the developments in Egypt had "provided a true shock for the Americans."[6]

Nonetheless, following the announcement in the fall of 2011 that Putin would again run for president—an action that would allow him to stay in power until 2024—coupled with the fraudulent Duma (parliamentary) elections of December 4, 2011, it suddenly appeared that the Arab Spring had indeed come to Russia as tens of thousands of Russians took to the streets to protest. As will be shown later in this chapter, the mass protests were to affect Russian policy toward the Arab Spring in general and toward the situation in Syria in particular.

In weighing the rapidly changing situation in the Middle East caused by the Arab Spring, Moscow could note some short-term gains to its Middle East position as well as the possibility of some long-term losses. By early March 2011, the price of Brent oil had risen 24 percent since the beginning of January, reaching more than $110 per barrel. This enabled Russia to meet its projected budget deficit from the increased oil revenues and even rebuild its sovereign wealth fund, which had been depleted by the 2008 world economic crisis, even though Russia remained plagued by capital flight.[7] In addition, with the possibility of natural gas supplies to Europe being cut off due to the turmoil in the Middle East and North Africa—the Europeans had been trying to diversify their sources of natural gas by buying LNG (liquefied natural gas) from the Middle East so as to lessen their dependence on Moscow—Russia saw the possibility of increasing its natural gas sales to Europe. Indeed, in a visit to Brussels in late February, Putin took pride in pointing to Russia as a reliable natural gas supplier.[8]

On the downside, however, Moscow had to worry about its own oil and gas investments in the Middle East, which were at risk if the turmoil got worse, as well as the possible loss of arms and industrial deals it had signed with countries such as Libya and Syria. Another problem for Moscow lay in the possibility that conservative Islamist forces, both of the Salafi and Muslim Brotherhood type, could be the big winners of the Arab Spring, particularly if free and fair elections were held in countries such as Tunisia, Egypt, and Syria. Given that Russia's North Caucasus continued to simmer with Islamic unrest, with continuing Islamist attacks in Dagestan, Chechnya, northern Ossetia, and Ingushetia and an Islamist terror attack on Moscow's Domodedovo airport in January 2011, Moscow had cause for concern. Islamist victories in Egypt, Tunisia, and Syria, and possibly in Libya as well, could give added impetus to the Islamic uprising in the North Caucasus—something Putin had tried to prevent by having Russia admitted to the Organization of the Islamic Conference as an observer and by courting Saudi Arabia.[9] Indeed, in Brussels Putin had stated, rather prophetically, "Regardless of the calming theories that radical groups coming to power in North Africa is unlikely, if it happens it cannot but spread to other areas of the world, including the Northern Caucasus."[10]

On the other hand, in countries such as Tunisia and Egypt, the ouster of leaders closely linked to the United States and the West held some potential benefits for Moscow. Especially in Egypt, the close link between the Mubarak regime and Washington made the United States highly unpopular, despite US president Barack Obama's speech in Cairo in June 2009 in which he promised greater outreach to the Muslim world based on respect and protection of rights. Whether or not Moscow could benefit from the situation was, however, an open question. Egypt's Supreme Council of the Armed Forces, which was essentially running the country into June 2012 and appeared to be doing so even after the Egyptian presidential elections, had close ties with the US military, and there was a good bit of suspicion that the Egyptian army would be highly influential in the new government. (The Egyptian military was to stage a coup d'état in July 2013.) In addition, because of a serious drought in Russia in 2010, Putin had declared a ban on wheat exports in August 2010, thereby considerably complicating Egypt's efforts to import the grain because Russia had accounted for more than half of Egypt's wheat imports before the embargo. The end result was that when Russia again began to export wheat in 2011, the Egyptians excluded Russia from a June 2011 tender, with the vice chairman of Egypt's State Wheat Purchasing Agency stating, "Last year the Russians failed to ship some quantities that were agreed upon, even before the ban came into effect, and that is why I am wary of the Russian side. When we are sure that the Russian side is stable, we will re-include it."[11] While Egypt subsequently did buy Russian wheat, it was at a sizable discount.

RUSSIA AND LIBYA

If Russia hoped to make gains in Tunisia and Egypt, it sought to avoid losses in Libya and Syria, whose regimes were seriously challenged by the Arab Spring. Indeed, the Russian leadership may have remembered the "Death to Russia" signs carried by antiregime demonstrators in Iran in 2009. In the case of Libya, Russia appeared to be following what might be termed a zigzag policy, first opposing sanctions on Libya and then agreeing to them; first opposing a no-fly zone over Libya and then agreeing to it; and then, while criticizing NATO for using excessive force in Libya, agreeing to serve as a mediator between the Libyan rebels and the Gadafi regime, even as it urged Muammar al-Gadafi himself to step down.

What explains these apparent contradictions in Russian policy? In part, they were caused by disagreements between Medvedev and Putin that broke out into the open over the no-fly zone. In part, they were caused by Moscow's disinclination to oppose the Arab consensus, which supported both sanctions and the no-fly zone. By offering to mediate the conflict, Russia was able to demonstrate its importance in the Middle East. And by maintaining ties with both the Gadafi regime and the rebels, who with NATO support had been able to consolidate their position in the city of Benghazi by May 2011, Moscow evidently hoped to preserve both its investments and its markets in Libya no matter which side eventually won the civil war.

Unlike the situation in Tunisia and Egypt, Russia had major economic interests in Libya. According to a Russian arms supply specialist, Russia had signed $2 billion in arms contracts with Libya and had another $1.8 billion in contracts under negotiation.[12] Thus, Russia could lose almost $4 billion in arms sales should Gadafi fall. In addition, during his 2008 trip to Libya, Putin had signed a number of major industrial agreements, which were now also in jeopardy. Consequently, when the United States and its NATO allies began to call for sanctions against the Gadafi regime because of its brutal crackdown on dissidents, the Russian Foreign Ministry claimed that the proposed sanctions would not be effective and rejected them, although Russian foreign minister Sergei Lavrov, in a joint statement with foreign policy chief Catherine Ashton of the European Union (EU), did say, "We condemn and consider unacceptable the use of military force to break up peaceful demonstrations."[13]

Several days later, however, Medvedev reversed the Foreign Ministry's position and agreed to the sanctions, which included an arms embargo, joining in a unanimous Security Council Resolution (No. 1970) that also called for Gadafi's actions to be referred to the International Criminal Court. As Medvedev stated, "We strongly call on the current Libyan authorities to show restraint and not allow a worsening of the situation and the killing of civilians. If they do not, such actions will qualify as crimes, carrying all the consequences of international law."[14]

Gadafi, however, rejected Medvedev's threat, and as Libyan government forces bore down on Benghazi, there were increasing calls for a no-fly zone to protect the inhabitants of that city. These calls came not only from the United States and the European Union but also from the Arab League, an organization that Moscow, as it was seeking to increase its influence in the Middle East, was loathe to oppose. Although Lavrov initially denounced the proposed military intervention as "unacceptable,"[15] Medvedev overruled him, and the end result was that Russia chose to abstain on the UN Security Council Resolution (No. 1973) authorizing the no-fly zone, thus allowing it to be adopted. Russia's abstention, however, brought to the surface a major dispute in the Russian leadership over Libya policy. Medvedev had already fired the Russian ambassador to Libya for opposing the sanctions,[16] but Putin, speaking at a missile factory in Votkinsk, publicly denounced the resolution, calling it "defective and flawed" and asserting, "It allows everything. It resembles 'Medieval calls for Crusades.'"[17] Medvedev, in turn, publicly contradicted Putin several hours later, stating, "In no way is it acceptable to use expressions that ensure the clash of civilizations, such as crusades and so forth. This is unacceptable. Otherwise everything may wind up far worse."[18] The Putin-controlled Duma, perhaps trying to prevent the dispute from escalating, adopted a compromise position, voting 350–32 to call on NATO to stop all military action against Libya but also stating that the Russian abstention on Resolution No. 1973 was "appropriate."[19]

Over the next several months, as NATO air strikes increased in intensity, Russian criticism of NATO military action grew, but Moscow proved unable to stop the NATO attacks. By the latter part of May, therefore, Moscow adopted a new policy, one of mediation between the rebels and the Gadafi regime. It invited representatives of both sides to Moscow, and at the G-8 Summit in late May, Medvedev, after meeting with President Obama, offered to try to persuade Gadafi to step down from power. As might be expected, Gadafi was less than enthusiastic about the Russian mediation offer, and Libyan deputy foreign minister Khalid Kaim stated at a news conference that Libya had expected solidarity from Russia after forty years of close commercial and political links, not a deal made in France that aligned Moscow with the West in an attempt to oust Gadafi. Kaim also stated that Libya would not accept any mediation efforts from Moscow unless Russia worked through the African Union—long an ally of Gadafi's.[20]

It appears that Moscow got Gadafi's message because after appointing Mikhail Margelov, chair of the Russian Federation Council's International Affairs Committee, as special envoy to Libya, Medvedev sent him to meet the Libyan rebels in Benghazi. And then Margelov was dispatched to the African Union summit in Equatorial Guinea in late June, where, after meeting with a number of African leaders, he stated that Russia would step up its contacts with the African Union in seeking a settlement on Libya.[21] Moscow appeared now to back the African Union's road map for settling the Libyan conflict, which, in calling for "broad dialogue" between the sides, was unacceptable both to the Libyan rebels and to NATO. However, the African Union's offer to mediate the talks seemed to eclipse the monthlong Russian effort. Medvedev, who personally met with President Jacob Zuma of South Africa when he was on a visit to Moscow in early July, nevertheless sought to highlight Russia's close cooperation with the African Union in its peacemaking efforts.[22]

Unfortunately for Moscow, however, by September, the Gadafi regime had fallen to a Western-backed National Transitional Council, and Russia turned out to be the major loser diplomatically, economically, and militarily. The lesson Moscow took from this development was not to allow another UN Security Council resolution to be passed that could, as in the case of Libya, lead to regime change. This concern was to dominate Russian policy toward Syria after the fall of Gadafi, and Moscow was also to blame the post-Gadafi chaos in Libya on the NATO intervention.

RUSSIA AND SYRIA

Unlike the situation in Libya, Russian policy toward the Syrian uprising has been much more consistent. Although the crackdown by the Bashar al-Assad regime on its citizens was every bit as brutal as that by Gadafi, not only has Moscow opposed Libya-type military intervention in Syria, it has also opposed sanctions against the Assad regime. This has been the case because Syria has long been a major ally of Moscow in the Middle East, and, unlike the mercurial regime of Muammar al-Gadafi, the Assad regime had real, if diminishing, influence in the Arab world. The regime has ties to Hizbullah, which since February 2011 has been the dominant power in Lebanon, and, to a lesser degree, to Hamas, which controls Gaza and had its headquarters in Damascus until the intensification of the Assad regime's crackdown on protesters in 2011. In addition, Syria has close ties to Iran, and Moscow, whose relations with Iran had deteriorated after the Security Council sanctions resolution against Iran in 2010, appears to have little interest in further alienating Tehran with pressure on the Islamic Republic's primary Arab ally, Syria. Syria also was a major market for Russian arms, most recently the Bastion antiship missile, the Pantsir air defense system, and the Yakhont cruise missile system,[23] and unlike the case in Libya, Moscow had been given the use of naval facilities in Tartus by the Syrian government. Finally, unlike the case in Libya, there was no Arab consensus on dealing with Syria.

Consequently, when the uprising in Syria began, Moscow steadfastly opposed foreign intervention, especially intervention legitimized, as it had been in Libya, by a UN Security Council resolution.[24] When Assad did make some halfhearted reforms, they were praised by Moscow, with Lavrov urging the Syrian protesters to engage in a dialogue with the Syrian regime.[25]

As in the case of Libya, however, Moscow sought to keep ties not only with the Syrian government but also with the Syrian opposition. Thus, the Russian Afro-Asian Solidarity and Cooperation Society invited a delegation of the opposition to visit Moscow. This was a low-level invitation reminiscent of

the Soviet Afro-Asian People's Solidarity Association making similar invita-
tions during the Soviet era to maintain contact with opposition groups.[26] As
far as both Syria and Libya were concerned, Moscow was trying to salvage its
position no matter who came out on top in the struggle for power. However,
as the Syrian regime intensified its crackdown on antiregime protesters, the
Syrian opposition and much of the Sunni Arab world, led by Saudi Arabia,
became highly critical of Russia, thereby threatening Russia's position in the
Arab world, which Putin had tried so hard to build.

The fall of Gadafi seemed to inspire the Syrian opposition, and demonstrations against the Assad regime intensified. But Moscow continued to support
Assad, as evidenced by its opposition to any anti-Syrian vote in the UN Human Rights Council. Antiregime demonstrators burned Russian flags in protest. Then, at a news conference in Moscow on September 9, Syrian opposition
leader Ammar al-Qurabi pointedly noted, "Russia was late in recognizing the
new authorities in Libya. This is the second mistake. The first mistake was
made in Iraq [with Saddam Hussein]. We wish that Moscow would not repeat
a mistake of this kind for the third time—in respect to what is happening in
Syria."[27]

But Moscow did not heed Qurabi's warning. On October 4, 2011, as civilian
casualties mounted in Syria, Russia vetoed a proposed anti–Syrian Security
Council resolution that, while containing no sanctions, did warn that sanctions would be forthcoming if the Syrian government continued oppressing
its citizens. The resolution also condemned the Syrian regime for "systematic
human rights violations and the use of force against civilians."[28] However, in
an apparent attempt to salvage its reputation in the Sunni Arab world following the veto, Russia announced visits of Syrian opposition delegations at the
Foreign Ministry level, a major step above the level of the Russian Afro-Asian
Solidarity and Cooperation Organization, the previous venue of such visits. In
addition, Medvedev issued the strongest criticism of Assad to date in a statement asserting, "If the Syrian leadership is incapable of conducting reforms, it
will have to go." Medvedev, however, then qualified his statement by adding,
"This decision should be taken not by NATO or certain European countries;
it should be taken by the Syrian people and the Syrian leadership."[29] Meanwhile, the then Syrian National Council president, Burhan Ghalioun, who
represented what was then the leading opposition group to Assad, bemoaned
the Russian (and Chinese) veto, stating, "Supporting Bashar al-Assad in his
militarist and fascist project will not encourage the Syrian people to stick to

peaceful revolution."[30] Ghalioun's remarks were prophetic because, following the Russian veto, as Assad felt emboldened to step up his military crackdown on the demonstrators, they fought back, which ultimately led to the emergence of a Free Syrian Army rebel force.

As the fighting escalated, the Arab League, meeting in Cairo, called for a "national dialogue" between Syria's government and the opposition to help end the violence and avoid "foreign intervention in Syria." This call also warned Syria that it faced expulsion from the Arab League if it did not comply.[31] From Moscow's point of view, the Arab League's resolution, which the Syrian representative at the League repudiated as a "conspiracy,"[32] had a number of positive elements. First, it called for a dialogue between the Syrian regime and its opponents—just what Moscow was trying to achieve by inviting opposition delegations to Moscow. Second, its desire to avoid "foreign intervention" coincided with Moscow's goal, as the Russian leadership clearly wished to avoid a repetition of the Libyan experience. Given this situation, Russia decided to back the Arab League plan. Unfortunately for Moscow, rather than toning down his repression of the domestic opposition, Assad increased it, leading Moscow to deplore the regime's actions in the Syrian city of Homs as "inevitably alarming." However, in an attempt to be "evenhanded," Moscow also blamed "armed extremists who were provoking retaliation from the authorities to derail the League of Arab States initiative."[33] But Moscow soon found that it could not play the evenhanded game in Syria and soon shifted back to fully supporting Assad. Thus, when the Arab League, witnessing Assad's accelerated crackdown, suspended Syria's membership, Lavrov called the suspension "incorrect" and blamed the United States and NATO for it.[34]

The end result of the failed negotiations was a more decisive Russian shift to the side of the Syrian government. In January 2012, a Russian naval flotilla visited the Russian base in Syria at Tartus—an action hailed by the governor of Tartus as evidence of the "honorable position adopted by Russia which stood by the Syrian people."[35] Russian ships also came to Syria to resupply the Assad regime with weapons and ammunition.

In adopting this position, the Russian leadership was clearly taking a major gamble. By backing Syria, it was alienating most of the Sunni Arab world, especially the Gulf Cooperation Council (GCC), led by Saudi Arabia. In looking for reasons for this policy, besides Russia's major investments in Syria and its desire to prevent the loss of another ally to the West, we need also to consider Russian domestic politics. While Putin was confronted by Moscow's deteriorating diplomatic position in the Middle East because of Russia's support for the Assad regime, in December 2011, he was confronted by a version of the Arab Spring at home. Some of the same issues that had motivated Arabs to take to the streets were also at work in Russia: rising prices, leaders who had been in power for too long, and rampant corruption. Two events appear to have precipitated the protests in Russia: Putin's decision to switch places with Medvedev (Putin had been Russia's president from 2001 to 2008 and then became prime minister while Medvedev became president) and run again for president in March 2012 and the Duma election of December 4, 2011, which was widely seen as fraudulent. Fifty thousand people took to the streets of Moscow on December 10 to protest the election results and to call for new elections. As TV cameras rolled, there were shouts from the crowd of "Russia without Putin." Further demonstrations followed, on December 24 of 100,000 people and on February 4, 2012, of 160,000 people despite the bitter cold. Unlike in the case of Egypt, however, the demonstrators succeeded neither in bringing down the Putin regime nor in preventing Putin's reelection on March 4, 2012, although demonstrations continued after the election.

Putin's Attempts to Salvage the Russian Position in the Middle East

Throughout February, as Putin concentrated on the Russian presidential election, the Russian position in the Middle East deteriorated as Moscow found itself isolated in no fewer than three UN votes concerning Syria. It faced increasingly sharp criticism not only from the United States and such EU states as France and Britain but also from GCC Arab states. As a result, in March, Russia made a few gestures to the Sunni Arab world by offering some measured criticism of the Assad regime, and in the latter part of March, Russia joined a watered-down UN Security Council presidential letter calling for a cease-fire in Syria. Nonetheless, despite the criticism, Moscow remained a strong backer of Assad and worked hard to prevent any UN sanctions against his regime.

Moscow's Middle East position had suffered a major blow when, on February 4, 2012, it vetoed a weak UN Security Council resolution that, while criticizing Syria, did not call for an arms embargo or for Assad's resignation, as a recent Arab League peace plan had done. The Soviet veto took place even though Assad was escalating his crackdown on Syrian protesters. Despite a visit by Lavrov to Damascus after the veto, the crackdown continued un-abated, which made matters worse for Moscow. Opposition leader Ghalioun strongly criticized the veto, stating that Russian credibility had been lost amid the continuous shelling of the Syrian people. Ghalioun called Lavrov's visit to Damascus "an interference in Syrian affairs" that was "targeted against the Syrian people."[36] Saudi Arabia also criticized Moscow, saying it should have coordinated with the Arab League before the veto.[37] Prominent Sunni Islamic scholar Yusuf al-Qaradawi carried the criticism further, calling on Muslims to boycott the products of Russia and China (which also vetoed the resolution) because the money that Muslims spend on their products "turns into a weapon that kills Syrians."[38] Arab League secretary-general Nabil al-Arabi remarked that Russia and China had lost diplomatic credibility in the Arab world after the veto.[39]

Following the veto, the opponents of the Assad regime introduced a reso-lution in the UN General Assembly strongly condemning the Syrian crack-down and calling on Assad to relinquish power to his vice president (this had been part of the Arab League plan, which also called for the formation of a national unity government and free elections in Syria). The resolution also called on UN secretary-general Ban Ki Moon to appoint a special envoy for Syria. The resolution, which Moscow could not veto, passed overwhelmingly, with 137 in favor, 12 (Russia was one of the 12) opposed, and 17 abstaining.[40] The negative Russian vote led Saudi foreign minister Saud al-Faisal to step up Saudi criticism of Moscow: "The stand of those countries that thwarted the UNSC Resolution and voted against the Resolution in the General Assembly on Syria, gave the Syrian regime a license to extend its brutal practices against the Syrian people."[41]

By early March 2012, it must have appeared to Russian leaders that they had to back off from their close embrace of the Assad regime—at least orally—if Moscow were to salvage even a part of its position in the Middle East. Foreign Ministry spokesman Alexander Lukashevich stated on March 2 that Moscow was not treaty-bound to help Syria if it were invaded,[42] and Lavrov, later in the month, asserted, "We believe the Syrian leadership reacted wrongly to the first appearance of peaceful protests and . . . is making very many mistakes." Lavrov added that "the question of who will lead Syria in a transition period can only be decided in a dialogue between the government and its opponents." Lavrov maintained, however, that demanding Assad resign as a condition for such a dialogue—as the Syrian opposition was doing—was "unrealistic."[43]

In addition to somewhat distancing itself from the Assad regime—if only in words—Moscow sought to rebuild its relationship with the Arab League throughout March. This was no easy task, however, as both Qatar and Saudi Arabia clashed with Lavrov at the March 2012 meeting in Cairo. Saudi Arabia had been incensed by a statement issued by the Russian Foreign Ministry on March 4 that Saudi Arabia was supporting terrorism by aiding the Syrian opposition. The Saudis called the statement "dangerous and irresponsible."[44] For its part, Qatar remained incensed at a comment made by Vitaly Churkin, Russia's ambassador to the United Nations, who reportedly had threatened to "wipe Qatar off the map" at a UN meeting in February.[45] By mid-March, Moscow's strategy was to build on one element of a February 17 UN General Assembly resolution—a call for a special UN envoy to Syria—and to shape it to protect the Assad regime from serious pressure. The end result on March 22 was the watered-down, nonbinding UN presidential letter calling for a cease-fire by both sides to be monitored by UN officials, a withdrawal of the Syrian army from populated areas, freedom of movement for journalists, and facilitation of a Syrian-led political transition to a democratic, plural political system. The letter also, very vaguely, warned of "further steps as appropriate."[46] The whole process was to be under the supervision of UN special envoy Kofi Annan, a former UN secretary-general. Whether or not the Annan mission would work, however, was a very open question, given the opposition's unwillingness to negotiate with Assad, whom they considered a murderer, and Assad's hesitancy throughout the month of April 2012 to remove the Syrian army from populated areas, end his crackdown on protesters, or allow foreign journalists—as well as UN monitors—free passage throughout Syria. Indeed, Annan was later to resign in frustration, as did his successor, Lakhdar Brahimi, whose efforts to achieve a peace settlement at Geneva ended in failure.

PUTIN EXPLOITS OBAMA'S RISK-AVERSE MIDDLE EAST STRATEGY

Despite all the problems for Russia's position in the Arab world caused by its ongoing military and diplomatic support for the Assad regime in Syria, Moscow benefited not only from the continuing disunity in the ranks of the Syrian opposition but also from the unwillingness of President Obama to provide serious military support for the opposition. While Obama strongly protested

Moscow's veto of the anti-Syrian UN resolutions, he was unwilling to go beyond verbal criticism of the Assad regime.

In the midst of his 2012 reelection campaign, the Obama mantra was "I
got us out of Iraq [all US troops had left by the end of 2011], I'm getting us
out of Afghanistan [US troops were then set to leave in 2014], and I'm not
getting us into Syria." Consequently, Obama did almost nothing as the Assad
regime murdered increasing numbers of Syrians, some by starvation and others by barrel bombs. The only thing Obama did in 2012 was to threaten action
against the Syrian government if it used poison gas against the Syrian opposition. Even in this case, Obama's critics complained that the US president had
given Assad carte blanche to use all kinds of force up to poison gas against his
opponents, something certain to cause more Syrian deaths.[47]

Once the election was over, Obama's advisers in the State Department,
Defense Department, and CIA urged him to provide weapons to the Syrian
opposition, which at the time (November–December 2012) was not yet dominated by Islamic forces. The president refused, however, apparently hoping—
in vain, as it turned out—that diplomacy, through an international conference
at Geneva that Russia would help to arrange, would solve the problem.[48]

A real challenge to the Obama administration, however, came in August
2013 when the available evidence indicated that the Assad regime had used
poison gas against the Syrian opposition—thus crossing the "red line" that the
president himself had set. While both US secretary of state John Kerry and
Obama himself gave strong speeches denouncing the use of poison gas, in the
end Obama accepted a Russian plan that would prevent a US attack on Syria
by getting the Assad regime to hand over its stocks of poison gas to an international body for destruction and also to destroy its facilities for making the
gas. The Obama decision was criticized on a number of grounds. First, could
the United States be sure that Assad would, in fact, give up all his poison
gas?[49] Second, by agreeing to the deal, Obama ensured that Assad would stay
in power long enough to implement it. Perhaps the most important criticism
of all, however, was that Obama had allowed one of his red lines to be crossed
without taking military action, which set a very bad precedent. A number of
Middle Eastern countries, especially US allies Israel and Saudi Arabia, worried that Obama would now allow another of his red lines to be crossed: preventing Iran from acquiring a nuclear weapon.[50] These fears were reinforced
in November 2013 when the United States, together with other members of

the UN Security Council and Germany, entered into formal negotiations with Iran to limit, but not eliminate, the Iranian nuclear program.

From the Russian point of view, both the poison gas agreement with Syria and the start of negotiations with Iran were highly advantageous. The agreement with Syria accomplished a number of objectives. First, it helped ensure that Bashar al-Assad, an ally of Russia, would remain in power. Second, Putin prevented a US attack on Syria, which would have presented Russia with a difficult choice as to how to respond. Third, the agreement, mediated by Putin, enabled Russia to reinsert itself into the heart of Middle East diplomacy, and Putin was widely praised for averting a war between the United States and Syria. Although it is not yet known whether there was a direct connection, the risk aversion demonstrated by Obama during the Syrian crisis may have been a factor in Putin's thinking when he annexed the Crimea six months later.

As far as the Iran negotiations were concerned, Moscow foresaw a number of benefits if an agreement were reached. First, Russia could be expected to assist Iran in the negotiations, which would help Moscow rebuild its ties to Tehran following the cancellation of the promised SAM-300 surface-to-air missile system agreement, much as Russian aid to Iran's ally, Syria, had helped rebuild ties to that country. Second, were an agreement to be concluded, there would be increased business for Russian firms, including the possibility of constructing another nuclear reactor (Russia had built Iran's first nuclear reactor at Bushehr), as well as lucrative arms deals including, most probably, the replenishment of the Iranian air force and navy. Also, with oil prices still high at the time (Brent oil was almost $108 per barrel in November 2013),[51] Russia was probably not too concerned about competition from Iran's oil fields. A final benefit to Moscow came from the growing perception in the Middle East following the Syrian poison gas agreement and the start of negotiations with Iran that the United States had begun to disengage from the region and was now concentrating more and more on Asia.

Moscow benefited once again—at the expense of the United States—when the Islamist government of Egypt, led by President Mohamed Morsi, leader of the Muslim Brotherhood, was overthrown by a popularly supported military coup d'état led by General Abdel Fatah el-Sisi in July 2013. The United States seemed unsure how to respond to the coup d'état and in October 2013 temporarily froze military aid to Egypt (F-16 fighter jets, Apache helicopters, and harpoon missiles)—this at a time when Egypt was battling an Islamist uprising in its Sinai Peninsula—and Russia saw this as an opportunity to exploit.

Obama's policy seemed to alienate both the Muslim Brotherhood supporters of Morsi and the new military regime in Egypt. Thus, a month after the US freezing of military aid, Russian foreign minister Sergei Lavrov and Russian defense minister Sergei Shoigu traveled to Egypt (the first visit of a Russian defense minister to Egypt in forty years), where they had discussions with the new Egyptian leadership about both economic and military cooperation, including the possibility of Russia building a nuclear reactor for Egypt.[52] The visit served the interests of both countries. From the Egyptian side, it was a demonstration that Egypt would not be taken for granted by the United States, and for Russia, it was another opportunity to demonstrate that it was a major player in the Middle East—despite its support of Syria—because Egypt was one of the most important countries in the Arab world. One year later, the two countries signed a $3.5 billion preliminary agreement on Russian arms sales to Egypt, which reportedly included air defense systems and fighter jets, although whether the deal was ever fully consummated remains unclear. In 2014, Sisi made two visits to Moscow, the latter as Egypt's president, and in 2015, Putin made a state visit to Egypt when an agreement was signed for Russia to build a nuclear reactor there.[53]

There was also some speculation that Putin and Sisi had agreed to funnel arms to the anti-Islamic forces in Libya, as Egypt appeared to be increasingly concerned about the security threat emanating from Libya, which was degenerating into chaos.[54]

Besides providing a mechanism for reinforcing Russian-Egyptian relations, the rise of the Islamic State of Iraq and Syria (ISIS), which had captured large swaths of Syrian and Iraqi territory in 2014, provided additional benefits to Moscow, although it also held some serious potential dangers. First, the rise of ISIS reinforced the political position of Bashar al-Assad, who could now claim that he was fighting Islamic extremism (ISIS and the Al-Qaeda-linked Al-Nusra Front). Second the halfhearted and less-than-competent response of the United States to the rise of ISIS in both Iraq and Syria raised further questions about US policy in the Middle East as the US-trained Iraqi army lost the city of Mosul (along with large amounts of US-supplied weaponry). The US response of providing 3,500 military trainers plus limited anti-ISIS air strikes also appeared to be too little and too late, although the United States was able to forge an anti-ISIS alignment of the Gulf Arab states and Jordan. However, the belated US decision to start the training of anti-Syrian rebels with the goal of fighting ISIS and not Assad led not only to great difficulty in recruiting Syrian rebels—the vast majority of whom wanted to fight Assad, not ISIS—but also to the collapse of the first rebel unit trained by the United States, with the capture of its commander and a number of its soldiers by the Al-Nusra Front.[55]

The issue of ISIS also played a role in Russia's relations with Turkey, as it was an irritant in the ties between the two countries. Turkey's prime minister (and later president) Recip Erdogan was a supporter of both ISIS and the Al-Nusra Front, in part because of his own increasingly Islamist position and also because he wanted to use the two Islamist organizations (as well as the Islamist Ahrar al-Sham organization) as tools to overthrow Assad. Thus, Erdogan supplied arms and other support to the Islamist organizations and turned a blind eye when ISIS recruits used Turkey as a transit point to go to Syria. Nonetheless, Erdogan worked hard to maintain a positive relationship with Russia (at least until November 2015, when Turkey shot down a Russian jet, which resulted in a major crisis in Turkish-Russian relations, as discussed later). In part, this was due to Turkey's energy dependence on Russia, which supplied more than 55 percent of Turkey's natural gas. Moscow also promised to build a new series of natural gas pipelines to Turkey, the so-called Turkish Stream project, which would make Turkey an energy hub.[56] Erdogan's policy toward Russia was also a result of Turkey's isolation due to conflicts with Syria; Israel; and, after the ouster of Mohamed Morsi, Egypt. In addition, relations with the United States had cooled considerably after Obama's earlier hope that Turkey would provide a "model" of Islamic democracy to the Arab world. Erdogan's increasing authoritarianism, his crackdown on the Gezi Park protesters in 2013, and his arrest of Turkish journalists, let alone his support for ISIS and the Al-Nusra Front, considerably soured relations with the United States. This left Turkey bereft of allies and more dependent on Russia.

However, on July 20, 2015, when an ISIS terrorist attack on the Turkish border city of Suruc killed thirty-three Turks, Erdogan apparently decided to change his policy toward ISIS. His actions included tightening control over the porous Turkish-Syrian border and offering to the United States the use of Turkey's Incirlic air base to attack ISIS forces. This greatly eased American logistical problems in bombing ISIS, given the relatively short distance from Incirlic to ISIS positions in Syria.

From Moscow's perspective, Erdogan's changed position held both advantages and disadvantages. On the one hand, if Erdogan's crackdown on ISIS was genuine—and there were some both in Turkey and in the United States who doubted his sincerity in combating this group—Moscow would be pleased to have another ally against it. On the other hand, given Erdogan's desire to oust Assad, Moscow had to be concerned that Turkey might use the opportunity to hit Syrian forces as well as the Kurdistan Workers Party (PKK) and other Kurdish groups within Syria.

Perhaps the most important threat ISIS posed to Russia was not to its position in the Middle East but to Russia domestically, with the threat that Russian citizens trained by ISIS would return to Russia to carry out acts of terrorism. Indeed, Foreign Minister Lavrov, on July 9, 2015, stated that 2,000 Russian citizens were fighting for ISIS.[57] Lavrov, who on April 22, 2015, had said he considered ISIS "our main enemy right now," had cause for concern.[58] ISIS had been recruiting Russian Muslims from the restive North Caucasus region for several years, and on June 22, 2015, the Islamic State proclaimed a new governorate in the North Caucasus region.[59] Moscow also faced the problem of ISIS recruiting disaffected migrant workers from Central Asia, who were often mistreated in Moscow, and adherents of a revived Islamic Movement of Uzbekistan (IMU). The IMU is an organization that had threatened Central Asia—which Russia considers its "soft underbelly"—in the 1999–2001 period prior to the US invasion of Afghanistan after 9/11, which badly damaged the IMU. After taking refuge in Pakistan, the IMU rebuilt itself and, having declared its adherence to ISIS, posed a renewed threat to Central Asia.

By the end of 2014, facing a rising threat from ISIS and a weakening of the military position of Syria's Assad regime, despite all the aid given to it by Russia, Iran, and Hizbullah, Moscow again sought to work out a political settlement of the Syrian war. This involved stepped-up contacts with supporters of Syrian rebels who were invited to Moscow; an attempt to win over Saudi Arabia to a compromise agreement that would leave Assad, or at least Syrian leaders favorable to Moscow, in power; and an overture to the United States.

In the case of Saudi Arabia, much as in the case of Egypt, Moscow sought to exploit the Saudi unhappiness with US policies in the Middle East. Russia was helped by the change of government in Saudi Arabia when, in January 2015, King Abdullah died and was replaced by King Salman bin Abdul Aziz, who appointed his son, Mohamed bin Salman, as deputy crown prince and minister of defense. Like Egypt, Saudi Arabia had become disenchanted with the United States because of what it perceived as a pro-Iranian tilt in US policy as well as a perceived desire by the United States to withdraw from the Middle East, which would have left Saudi Arabia vulnerable to the more populous and powerful Iran. Mohamed bin Salman, just as General Sisi had done, used his visit to Moscow to demonstrate to the United States that Saudi Arabia had other options, although it was unlikely that Saudi Arabia (or Egypt) would give up its military ties to the United States, which was its defender of last resort. During the meeting, Saudi Arabia and Russia signed a memorandum of understanding to cooperate on nuclear energy development and to jointly invest up to $10 billion, although details of the two agreements were not made public.[60] There was also a discussion of the sharp drop in world oil prices (Brent oil hovered around $50), which negatively affected both economies, although the Russian economy was more seriously affected given the heavy sanctions placed on it because of its annexation of Crimea and aid to rebels in eastern Ukraine. For its part, Moscow needed Saudi aid in convincing the Syrian rebels to agree to a Syrian settlement that would protect Russian interests. The two sides, however, could not reach an agreement, as the Saudi foreign minister insisted that Assad had to be ousted in order to reach agreement on Syria, a demand also made by the Syrian rebel groups that Moscow was cultivating.[61]

If Moscow had little success with Saudi Arabia, at least on the subject of Syria, it appeared to fare little better with the United States. Perhaps hoping that the US-Russian cooperation in evidence during the P5+1 nuclear negotiations with Iran would continue (these negotiations were aimed at preventing Iran from acquiring a nuclear weapon), and that Obama's desire not to get too heavily involved in Syria would make it easier to reach an agreement on Syria, Lavrov held a series of meetings with Secretary of State Kerry in 2015 on the best ways to both fight ISIS and achieve a Syrian agreement. Nonetheless, following several meetings with Kerry in August 2015, Lavrov stated that the two countries were as yet unable to reach an agreement: "We all agree that the Islamic State is the common threat, common evil. We agree that we need to join efforts to fight this phenomenon as soon and as effectively as possible. For now we don't have a joint approach on how specifically we can do it, given the standoff between various players on the ground, including armed units of the Syrian opposition."[62]

THE RUSSIAN MILITARY INTERVENTION IN SYRIA

Given Russia's failure to mobilize US and Saudi support for its diplomatic efforts, and with the military position of the Assad regime continuing to deteriorate, Putin decided to bolster Assad with a major Russian military effort.

Overflying Iraq and Iran to reach Syria, Russian transport aircraft and fighter jets established a major military base on the Assad airfield near Latakia, complete with advanced Russian tanks, armored personnel carriers, artillery, air defense missiles, fighter-bomber aircraft, and 2,000 ground troops (later to expand to 4,000).[63] After extending the runway on the airfield, at the end of September 2015, Russia began a major bombing campaign, primarily against Assad's opponents in the Aleppo and Idlib regions of Syria. Though Russia claimed that its military actions were aimed at the Jihadist groups ISIS and Jabat Al-Nusra, well over 90 percent of its targets were non-Jihadist opponents of the Assad regime such as elements of the Free Syrian Army supported by the United States, as Russian officials initially argued that any armed opponent of the Assad regime was, by definition, a "terrorist."[64] In choosing his targets this way, Putin downplayed the threat to Russia from ISIS, despite the protestations of Russian officials to the contrary as the effort to preserve the Assad regime clearly took precedence over what Moscow had claimed was the battle against terrorism.

In the early stages of its intervention, Moscow appeared to have a free hand in Syria, as President Obama stated in a news conference that the United States would not engage in a proxy war with Russia in Syria.[65] Meanwhile, Iran stepped up its military aid to Syria by providing increased numbers of Iranian troops and, together with Hizbullah forces and what remained of the Syrian army, formed a coalition against the non-ISIS elements of the Syrian opposition. The Russian military concept of operation appeared to be that a combination of Russian air strikes and advances by Assad's coalition forces would enable the Syrian leader to regain the land he had lost earlier in 2015. In addition to attacking the non-ISIS elements of the Syrian opposition so as to bolster the Assad regime—thereby demonstrating that Russia stood by its allies—Putin also exploited the Russian military effort in Syria to demonstrate Russia's new military prowess. Thus, along with air strikes by Russian fighter-bombers, Moscow fired twenty-four cruise missiles into Syria from its gunboats on the Caspian Sea (although four missiles reportedly fell into Iran, well short of their targets),[66] used Russian heavy bombers flying from Russian territory to attack Assad's enemies, and even fired missiles from a Russian submarine.[67] Since one of Putin's goals was to demonstrate that Russia was again a great power and that Russian interests had to be taken into consideration when decisions of importance were made by other global powers, the intervention into Syria gave him the opportunity to make these points.

After more than three weeks of bombing, Russia's military success appeared to be mixed, with Assad's coalition gaining some ground in the north of Syria but losing ground in the south.[68] At this point, Putin moved on the political front. After inviting Assad to Moscow—where the Syrian leader either agreed to a political settlement of the Syrian conflict or was pressured into agreeing—Putin called for an international conference to set up a political framework whereby the Assad regime and "moderate" elements of the Syrian opposition would (1) agree to a cease-fire, (2) establish a transitional government, (3) write a new constitution, and (4) prepare for new parliamentary and presidential elections.[69] Moscow's agenda was accepted by the United States; the Obama administration may have believed that such a conference, if it made progress, would lessen the growing pressure on the United States to take more decisive action in Syria, especially after the fiasco of its failed rebel training program was revealed. The international conference took place in Vienna at the end of October. Unlike similar diplomatic meetings in the past in Geneva, this time Iran was included in the deliberations, symbolizing its return, following the signing of the P5+1 nuclear agreement in July, to a central position in Middle East diplomacy. Having Iran, a major Russian ally in the battle for Syria, in the talks must be considered a political victory for Moscow. Perhaps to reinforce its ties with Tehran, Russia and Iran completed their negotiations on the SAM-300 deal, and by December 2015, some components of the missiles were reportedly already on their way to Iran.[70]

Despite a veneer of agreement at the Vienna conference, two major issues had to be resolved if the war in Syria, which by October 2015 had already claimed more than 250,000 lives and created millions of refugees, was to come to an end. The first concerned the role, if any, for Bashar al-Assad in the transitional process, and whether or not he would be allowed to run in the proposed presidential election. The second issue involved the selection of "moderate" opposition groups to participate in the talks to set up the transitional government, although both ISIS and Jabat Al-Nusra were excluded from the proposed talks.[71] As far as Assad's role in the transition talks was concerned, it was not completely clear whether Russia and Iran held the same position. The Iranian leadership is committed to Assad, its fellow Shia (secular though he may be), because he is its main link to Hizbullah in Lebanon, but the Russians may not be as firmly wedded to the Syrian leader. Assuming the transitional government comes into being—a very big assumption—and that it would permit Moscow to keep its new air base near Latakia[72] and its naval facility in Tartus (another big assumption), it is certainly conceivable that Putin might agree to Assad's departure from power. This development would not only facilitate the end of the Syrian civil war but also enhance Moscow's position among Sunni Arabs, as Russia would no longer be so closely identified with the Shia alignment of Assad, Hizbullah, and Iran.[73]

The diplomatic situation dramatically changed for Moscow a few days after the Vienna meeting when a bomb exploded on a Russian charter airliner flying back to Russia from the Egyptian Red Sea resort of Sharm el-Sheikh, a bombing for which ISIS claimed responsibility. Moscow waited seventeen days before acknowledging that the plane had been downed by a terrorist bombing. The delay was probably due to the fact that the terrorist act would appear to be a major backlash against Russia's intervention in Syria. Indeed, when asked by a reporter in early November at the beginning of the investigation into the causes of the crash whether Russia's involvement in Syria might have served as a motive for the attack on the plane, Putin's spokesman Dmitry Pskov asserted that "these hypothetical theories are completely inappropriate."[74] To avert such speculation, Putin waited to acknowledge that terrorism was responsible for the downing of the charter airliner until after the massive terrorist attack in Paris on November 13, 2015. The Paris attack enabled Putin to call for an international coalition against ISIS and to seek a joint anti-ISIS effort with France. Russian foreign minister Lavrov also exploited the Paris attack to demonstrate that Assad was not the problem, but ISIS was.[75] Belatedly, Moscow began to step up its bombings of ISIS targets, especially the ISIS capital of Rakkah, Syria, although the majority of the Russian sorties were still targeted at Assad's non-Jihadist opponents.

In addition to losing the airliner to ISIS terrorists, Russia suffered another blow on November 24 when a Russian fighter-bomber that had penetrated Turkish airspace over the southwestern Turkish province of Hatay was shot down by the Turkish air force. Russian-Turkish relations had already been damaged by previous Russian incursions into Turkish airspace, and the Turks had given Russia yet another warning only a few days before the Russian jet was shot down. Indeed, following the earlier Russian incursions, Turkish president Erdogan had warned Moscow that Turkey could go elsewhere for its natural gas supplies.[76] Nonetheless, the shooting down of the Russian plane led to a major deterioration of Russian-Turkish relations. Putin called the Turkish action "a stab in the back by accomplices of terrorists"[77] and imposed a series of economic sanctions on Turkey, including a halt to selected agricultural imports, the termination of chartered Russian tourist flights to Turkey,[78] and putting the planned Russian-Turkish natural gas pipeline project on hold.[79] For his part, Erdogan was incensed at the Russian reaction, again noting that Turkey could get its natural gas from other suppliers.[80] The two countries also traded charges about buying oil from ISIS.[81] Meanwhile, following the shooting down of its fighter-bomber, Russia further strengthened its military position in Syria by installing SAM-400 missiles at its air base near Latakia and deploying the missile cruiser *Moskva*, with antiaircraft capability, near the coast of Syria.[82] Moscow also intensified its bombing of the Turkish-supported Turkmen rebels who were located in northwest Syria, near where the Russian plane had been shot down, while at the same time moving to aid the Kurdish rebels in Syria who Erdogan claimed were part of the PKK.[83]

The shooting down of the Russian fighter-bomber as well as a helicopter sent to rescue the pilot, along with the bombing of the Russian charter airliner over the Sinai and the shelling of the Russian Embassy compound in Damascus, all served to demonstrate to Putin that Russian intervention would not be a cost-free operation. Nonetheless, Putin soon moved to demonstrate that these setbacks would not deter Russia from acting in Syria, and Moscow stepped up its military aid to the Assad regime. As the fighting intensified in December, with Assad's forces now on the offensive, helped by Russian air strikes that hit civilian as well as military targets, the Obama administration continued to be unwilling to make a serious move of its own to help the embattled pro-Western opposition forces, as Obama appeared convinced that Russia would be bogged down in the Syrian quagmire.[84] This left both the diplomatic and the military initiative in Moscow's hands. Thus, the UN Security Council Resolution of December 22, 2015, on Syria (number 2254) made no mention of the departure of Bashar al-Assad, a diplomatic requirement long called for by the United States and the US-backed Syrian opposition.[85] On the military front, the position of the US-backed forces continued to deteriorate under the onslaught both of Russian air strikes and of Syrian government coalition forces. Secretary of State Kerry appeared to be increasingly desperate to stop the fighting, which was causing tens of thousands of additional refugees to flee, while other Syrians faced the increasing danger of death by starvation.[86] What emerged from US-Russian negotiations to stop the fighting was not a cease-fire but an agreement on a vaguer "cessation of hostilities."[87] While the agreement, which became operative in the latter part of February 2016, slowed down the tempo of the fighting and allowed some food convoys to reach starving Syrians, the agreement also allowed the Assad regime to consolidate its gains and strengthened Assad's bargaining position as the Geneva peace talks resumed. However, from the Russian perspective, it may have strengthened the Syrian government position a bit too much, as the Assad regime not only now refused to discuss Assad's ouster from power during the negotiations but also began to talk about reconquering all of Syria.[88]

This, apparently, was too much for Moscow, as Putin announced a partial withdrawal of Russian forces from Syria on March 14. In Putin's words, "I think that the task that was assigned to the Ministry of Defense and the armed forces as a whole has achieved its goal, and so I order the defense minister to start tomorrow withdrawing the main part of our military forces from the Syrian Arab Republic."[89] Having helped to keep the Assad regime in power, Putin evidently did not want to invest further resources in the operation that would be needed for the Assad regime to recapture all of Syria, particularly at a time of growing strains on the Russian economy. As senior Russian analyst Fyodor Lukyanov noted, "This is a way to show Assad his own weakness. This is a signal to him that we will not abandon you, but if you think you can use us for your own success, that's not our job."[90] Nonetheless, Putin continued to maintain significant amounts of military power in Syria, and it was with Russian assistance that, two weeks after Putin's withdrawal statement, Syrian forces recaptured the city of Palmyra from ISIS.[91]

CONCLUSION

The Arab Spring caught the Russians, like everyone else, by surprise. After exhibiting an initial concern that the popular uprisings in the Arab world would spread to Moscow—something that would happen in the late fall of 2011—the Russian leadership sought to formulate a policy to deal with the new situation. While Moscow hoped to take advantage of the ouster of pro-Western leaders in Tunisia and Egypt, it also was genuinely worried that Islamist regimes might come to power in these countries, with a negative impact on Russia's restive North Caucasus region. In addition, while it certainly profited from the temporary rise in oil prices caused by the Arab Spring (they were to drop sharply in 2015), Moscow had to be concerned about the possible toppling of regimes in Libya and Syria—regimes with which it had major economic, political, and military ties.

Putin's stubborn support for the Assad regime, while advancing some of Russia's interests as Putin defines them (e.g., preserving an ally, preventing the toppling of a fellow authoritarian regime, trying to prevent the empowerment of radical Islamist groups), has also had major costs. Russian policies during the Syrian civil war have alienated key Sunni Arab states, such as Saudi Arabia and Qatar, countries Putin had been trying to win over since 2007. Indeed, in many ways, as a result of his backing of Syria, by 2012, Putin was back to his Middle East position of 2005–2006, when Russia's primary support in the Middle East came from the rogue regimes of Syria and Iran as well as from Hizbullah and Hamas (although Hamas's move away from Syria has weakened this "rogue coalition"). Second, backing the Shia Assad regime increased Russia's negative image throughout the Sunni Arab world. Moreover, with the rise of ISIS and the weakening of the military position of the Assad government in Syria in 2014—despite all the military aid given to it by Russia, Iran, and Hizbullah—Moscow faced serious problems internally and externally because of the threat of returning ISIS fighters carrying out terrorist attacks in Russia and because of the threat ISIS posed to Syria. In response, Moscow in 2015 engaged in both major new military and diplomatic interventions to try to end the Syrian conflict. While Moscow's diplomatic efforts in 2015 failed, its military actions proved far more successful. Interestingly enough, when Russia began its air strikes in Syria at the end of September 2015, its main targets were the pro-Western Syrian opposition groups, not ISIS and the al-Qaeda-linked al-Nusra Front, which may have indicated that Putin did not judge the ISIS threat to be very serious, despite his rhetoric to the contrary. The end result of the Russian bombing campaign was that the pro-Western forces were weakened. Indeed, by March 2016, the Assad regime and its allies were on the offensive, and pro-Western Syrian opposition forces were very much on the defensive. Russian military power had accomplished a number of objectives for Putin. First, it bolstered the Assad regime, an ally of Moscow, and enabled it to go on the offensive. Second, Moscow acquired a very important air base in Syria that enabled it not only to control the airspace throughout Syria but also to fly sorties over the Mediterranean. In some ways, this was reminiscent of the Soviet position in Egypt in the late 1960s, when a desperate Nasser sought Soviet air support against Israel. Third, the Russian military intervention demonstrated Russia's importance in world affairs—a big plus for Putin domestically—as the United States needed Russian aid to reach a cease-fire in Syria, shaky as it may prove to be. Fourth, it helped bring Russia out of the diplomatic isolation it had suffered after its annexation of Crimea. Fifth, it demonstrated the capabilities of the Russian military, and Moscow may hope that this demonstration will generate additional arms sales. Finally, the Russian intervention helped improve Russian-Iranian relations, which had been suffering from Moscow's cancellation of the SAM-300 deal in 2010. However, it should also be noted that much of Putin's success in Syria in 2015–2016 was due to the failure of the Obama administration to challenge his policies there. Should a more activist US president be elected in November 2016, Putin might well find himself in a more difficult position in Syria.

Nonetheless, by March 2016, the most important question for Russian strategy in Syria was the fate of Syrian leader Bashar al-Assad. Were Moscow to insist that Assad play a major role during the proposed transition government and even run again for president of Syria, Putin could once again demonstrate that Russia stands by its allies. Such a stance would further reinforce Russia's ties with Assad's main ally, Iran. However, if Russia takes such a position, not only would the proposed transitional process most probably collapse but Putin would alienate almost all of the Sunni Arab world—with the possible exception of Egypt, which Putin has been carefully cultivating. Even that relationship may be in question, however, given Egypt's heavy economic dependence on Saudi Arabia. On the other hand, if Putin agrees to the timely exit of Assad from power, not only would the Russian leader receive regional and world credit for facilitating the process to end the Syrian civil war, he would also enable Russia to begin to rebuild ties to the Sunni Arab world. Putin's decision to partially withdraw Russian forces from Syria in mid-March 2016 may have been a hint as to which way the Russian leader was leaning on this question. In any case, it will be interesting to see which choice Putin makes or whether he decides to let Syria continue to fester, thereby assuring Russia a continuing role in the diplomacy surrounding the ongoing conflict there.

In sum, the Arab Spring, which also paid a visit to Russia, has posed serious problems for Moscow. In its response to the first five years of the Arab Spring, Russian policy, while highly visible, has also been highly reactive and, in the case of Libya, not well coordinated. Even though the Arab Spring has proven to be diplomatically costly for the United States, especially in Egypt, the Arab Spring may, in the long run, also prove costly to Putin's regime—despite its massive military intervention in Syria beginning in the fall of 2015—if it continues to support the Assad regime in Syria.

Notes

1. I want to thank my student Alex Shtarkman for his research help on this chapter.

2. For a perceptive analysis of the early Russian reaction to the Arab Spring, see Stephen Blank and Carol Saivetz, "Russia Watches the Arab Spring," Radio Free Europe/Radio Liberty, June 24, 2011. For a Russian view, see Sergei Filatov, "The Middle East: A Perfect Storm," *International Affairs* (Moscow) 57, 3 (2011): 55–74.

3. Charles Clover, "Inflation Severs Russians' Fragile Grip on Material Comforts," *Financial Times*, July 5, 2011.

4. Viktor Davidoff, "Egypt's Lessons for Moscow," *Moscow Times*, February 14, 2011.

5. Quoted in Nabi Abdullaev, "Kremlin Sees Peril in Arab Unrest," *Moscow Times*, February 24, 2011.

6. Ibid.

7. See Andrew E. Kramer "Russia Cashes In on Anxiety over Supply of Middle East Oil," *New York Times*, March 7, 2011.

8. See Stephen Castle, "Putin Questions Europe's Foreign and Energy Policies," *New York Times*, February 24, 2011. Of course, Ukrainians, who twice had their gas cut off by Moscow, might question Russia's reliability.

9. See Robert O. Freedman, "Russia Returns to the Middle East: 2005–2011," *Maghreb Review* 36, 2 (2011): 127–161.

10. Quoted in Reuters, "Russia Tells West Not to Meddle in North Africa," *Moscow Times*, February 25, 2011.

11. Quoted in Bloomberg, "Egypt Rejects Russian Wheat," *Moscow Times*, June 22, 2011. See also Bloomberg, "Russia Targets Asia with the Largest Discount on Wheat," *Moscow Times*, August 3, 2011.

12. "UN Sanctions on Libya May Cost Russia $4 Billion," *Moscow Times*, February 28, 2011.

13. Quoted in Nikolaus Von Twickel, "Moscow Opposes Sanctions for Libya," *Moscow Times*, February 25, 2011.

14. See "UN Sanctions on Libya."

15. Reuters, "Russia—Outside Meddling in Libya 'Unacceptable,'" *New York Times*, March 10, 2011.

16. Ellen Barry, "Leaders' Spat Tests Skills of Survival in the Kremlin," *New York Times*, March 25, 2011.

17. Reuters, "Putin Rips 'Medieval Crusade' in Libya," *Moscow Times*, March 22, 2011.

18. Ibid.

19. "Russian Duma Calls on West to Stop All Military Operations in Libya," Interfax, March 23, 2012 (World News Connection [hereafter WNC], March 23, 2011).

20. Ellen Barry, "In Diplomatic Reversal Russia Offers to Try to Persuade Qaddafi to Leave Power," *New York Times*, May 28, 2011.

21. "Margelov Discusses Libya with African Leaders," Interfax, June 29, 2011 (WNC, June 29, 2011).

22. Göskel Bozkurt, "Medvedev—Pressure NATO on Libya," *Turkish Daily News*, July 4, 2011.

23. Konstantin Pakhalyuk, "Between Asad and the Opposition," politikom.ru, July 5, 2011 (WNC, July 6, 2011).

24. Neil MacFarquhar, "Push in UN for Criticism of Syria Is Rejected," *New York Times*, April 27, 2011.

25. "US Denies Support for Syrian Road Map," *Turkish Daily News*, July 1, 2011.

26. See Robert O. Freedman, *Moscow and the Middle East: Soviet Policy Since the Invasion of Afghanistan* (New York: Cambridge University Press, 1991).

27. Quoted in "Syrian Opposition Warns Russia That Its Unclear Stance May Damage Its Image," Interfax, September 9, 2011 (WNC, September 9, 2011).

28. Quoted in Colum Lynch, "Russia and China Block Syria Resolution at UN," *Washington Post*, October 5, 2011.

29. Quoted in "Russia's Medvedev Tells Asad to Reform or Else," NOW (Lebanon), October 7, 2011 (WNC, October 7, 2011).

30. Quoted in "Russia, China Vetoes Slammed," *Turkish Daily News*, October 5, 2011.

31. "Syria Slams Arab League for Acting as Tool of the West," *Turkish Daily News*, October 20, 2011.

32. Ibid.

33. "Russia Backs Arab League Initiative for Syria," Rossiya TV, November 10, 2011 (WNC, November 10, 2011).

34. Agence France Press (AFP), "Russia Condemns Syria's Suspension from the Arab League," *Turkish Daily News*, November 15, 2011.

35. AFP, "Russian Naval Flotilla to Leave Syrian Waters," *Turkish Daily News*, January 8, 2012.

36. "Ghalioun: Credibility of Russian Foreign Policy 'Gone,'" NOW (Lebanon), February 8, 2012 (WNC, February 8, 2012).

37. "Saudi Arabia Urges Russia to 'Advise' Syria to End Bloodshed," *Jordan Times*, March 5, 2012.

38. "Sunni Scholar Sheikh Yousuf Al-Qaradawi Calls to Boycott Russian and Chinese Products, States They Are the Enemies of the Arab Nation," Al Jazeera, February 5, 2012 (cited in Middle East Media Research Institute Report, February 6, 2012).

39. Reuters, "Russia, China Lose Credit in Arab World—Arab League Chief," *Jordan Times*, February 7, 2012.

40. Rick Gladstone, "General Assembly Votes to Condemn Syrian Leader," *New York Times*, February 17, 2012.

41. Quoted in "Arabs, Russians Discuss Syria amid Splits," NOW (Lebanon), March 10, 2012 (WNC, March 10, 2012).

42. "Russia Not Bound to Aid Syria in Case of Invasion—Spokesperson," RIA Novosti, March 2, 2012 (WNC, March 2, 2012).

43. Quoted in Reuters, "Russia: Syria's Asad Regime Has Made Many Mistakes," *Haaretz*, March 21, 2012.

44. "Saudi Daily: Riyadh Hits Out at Russia's Falsehoods," *Arab News Online*, March 8, 2012 (WNC, March 8, 2012).

45. "The Moscow-Riyadh War of Words: A Conversation with Dr. Theodore Karasik," Saudi-U.S. Relations Information Service Report, April 9, 2012, 6, http://susris.com/2012/04/09/the-moscow-riyadh-war-of-words-a-conversation-with-dr-theodore-karasik.

46. Rick Gladstone, "UN Council Unites over Plan for Syria," *International Herald Tribune*, March 23, 2012. See also Geoff Dyer and Charles Clover, "UN Backs Annan Peace Plan," *Financial Times*, March 23, 2012.

47. For an overall critique of Obama's Middle East policy, see Robert O. Freedman, "US Policy in the Middle East: Breakthrough or Breakdown?," *Contemporary Review of the Middle East* 1, 3 (September 2014): 243–252.

48. On this point, see former US secretary of state Hillary Rodham Clinton, *Hard Choices* (New York: Simon and Shuster, 2014), 459–464.

49. In fact, Assad did hide some of his chemical weapons. See Adam Entous and Naftali Bendavid, "Mission to Purge Syria of Chemical Weapons Comes Up Short," *Wall Street Journal*, July 23, 2015. See also the testimony of former US ambassador to Syria Robert Ford, "The Use of Chemical Weapons in Syria," before the US House of Representatives Foreign Affairs Committee, June 17, 2015.

50. On this point, see former US CIA director and secretary of defense Leon Panetta, *Worthy Fights: A Memoir of Leadership in War and Peace* (New York: Penguin, 2014), 450.

51. See the report of the US Energy Information Agency, August 5, 2015.

52. "Special Forces with the Embassy: Interview with Russian Foreign Minister Sergei Lavrov," *Rossiskaya Gazata*, November 23, 2013 (translated in the *Current Digest of the Russian Press* [hereafter CDRP] 65, 47 [2013]: 18).

53. Yury Paniyev, "Big Political Visit," *Nezavisimaya Gazeta*, February 11, 2015 (CDRP 67, 7 [2015]: 16).

54. For more on this speculation, see Ayah Aman, "Egypt Acts as Middleman for Russia-Libya Arms Deal," Al-Monitor, February 19, 2015.

55. See Missy Ryan, "After Setbacks, US Military Looks for Ways to Recalibrate New Syrian Force," *Washington Post*, August 12, 2015. Moscow, meanwhile, had taken a dim view of the US air strikes, saying they were illegal unless agreed to by the Syrian government

or legitimized by a UN Security Council resolution. See "Russia Slams U.S. Air Strikes Against Islamic State in Syria," *Moscow Times*, September 23, 2014.

56. For a good analysis of Russian-Turkish relations in early 2015, see Semih Idiz, "Huffing and Puffing at the Russian Bear," *Hurriyet Turkish Daily News*, May 6, 2015.

57. "Foreign Minister Lavrov Says 2,000 Russians Have Joined Islamic State," *Moscow Times*, July 9, 2015.

58. Joanna Paraszczuk, "Lavrov: Islamic State Is Russia's Main Enemy," *Under the Black Flag*, Radio Free Europe/Radio Liberty, April 22, 2015, www.rferl.org/content/lavrov-islamic-state-russias-main-enemy/26972850.html.

59. See "Islamic State Declares Foothold in North Caucasus," *Moscow Times*, June 24, 2015.

60. See Reuters, "Russia, Saudi Arabia Sign Nuclear Cooperation Deal," *Moscow Times*, June 19, 2015, and Reuters, "Russia and Saudi Arabia to Invest $10 Billion in Joint Fund," *Moscow Times*, June 21, 2015.

61. See Reuters, "Russia, Saudis Fail in Talks to Agree on Fate of Syria's Asad," *Moscow Times*, August 12, 2015.

62. Quoted in Reuters, "Russia Says No Common Approach in Fighting Islamic State," *Moscow Times*, August 5, 2015.

63. See Dion Nissenbaum and Philip Shishkin, "Russian Build-Up in Syria Worries U.S.," *Wall Street Journal*, September 15, 2015.

64. Foreign Minister Lavrov stated in early October as the Russian air strikes got under way, "Nobody's really heard about the moderate opposition." Cited in Andrew E. Kramer, "Russian Soldiers Join Syria Fight," *New York Times*, October 6, 2015. See also the comments by General Andrei Kartapolev, commander of Russian forces in Syria, who told *Komsomolska Pravda*, "In the West they talk about a 'moderate opposition,' but we so far haven't seen any in Syria. Any person who takes up arms and fights the legal government, how 'moderate' can he be?" Cited in Ilya Arkhipov, Stepan Kravchenko, and Henry Meyer, "Putin Officials Said to Admit Real Syrian Goal Is Far Broader," Bloomberg, October 19, 2015, www.bloomberg.com/news/articles/2015-10-19/putin-officials-said-to-admit-real-syrian-goals-are-far-broader.

65. Gregory Korte, "Obama Says He Won't be Drawn into 'Proxy War' with Russia over Syria," *USA Today*, October 2, 2015.

66. Neil MacFarquhar, "Russia Allies with France Against ISIS," *New York Times*, November 18, 2015.

67. See David Axe, "Russia Pounds ISIS with Biggest Bomber Raid in Decades," *Daily Beast*, November 17, 2015, www.thedailybeast.com/articles/2015/11/17/russia-pounds-isis-with-biggest-bomber-raid-in-decades.html.

68. See Sam Jones, "Hopes of Syria Deal Rise as Russia Starts to Shift Stance," *Financial Times*, November 22, 2015. See also Eric Cunningham, "Russia's Syria Intervention Makes Scarce Progress on the Ground," *Washington Post*, November 14, 2015.

69. See Carol Morello, "Diplomats Call for Ceasefire in Syria," *Washington Post*, October 31, 2015.

70. Vladimir Kozhin, Putin's aide for military-industrial trade with foreign nations, said the contract was "under way." Quoted in *Moscow Times*, December 4, 2015.

71. Somini Sengupta, "World Powers Set High Goals for Syria Ceasefire, but Pitfalls Await," *New York Times*, November 20, 2015.

72. General Kartapolev said Russia was planning to create a single unified military base in Syria that would include sea, air, and ground components. Cited in Mathew Bodner and Daria Litvinova, "Russia to Build Unified Military Base in Syria, Says General," *Moscow Times*, October 16, 2015.

73. For an analysis arguing that it was possible to split Russia from Iran, see Jay Solomon, "US, Allies Seek to Erode Russia-Iran Partnership," *Wall Street Journal*, November 19, 2015.

74. Quoted in Andrew Roth, "Shards of Inconclusive Clues Emerge on Jet Crash," *Washington Post*, November 4, 2015.

75. Lavrov had stated, "I cannot agree therefore with the logic that Asad is the cause for everything. The Paris attack has shown, alongside with ISIS claiming responsibility for it, that it doesn't matter if you are for Asad or against him. ISIS is your enemy, so it is not about Asad." Cited in Julie Hirshfeld Davis, "Talks on Syria Truce and Transition Take on New Urgency After Attacks," *New York Times*, November 15, 2015.

76. Erdogan had stated after the first three Russian air penetrations of Turkish airspace, "We can't accept the current situation. Russia's explanation on the airspace violations are not convincing. . . . We are Russia's number one natural gas consumer. Losing Turkey would be a serious loss for Russia. If necessary, Turkey can get its natural gas from many different sources. . . . If the Russians don't build Akkuyu [the nuclear plant] another will come to build it." Quoted in Reuters, "Angered by Air Strikes, Turkey's Erdogan Warns Russia on Energy Ties," *Turkish Daily News*, October 8, 2015.

77. Quoted in Serkan Demitras, "Syria Turns into Turkish-Russian Battlefield," *Turkish Daily News*, November 24, 2015.

78. See "Russia Approves Sanctions Against Turkey over Downed Plane," *Turkish Daily News*, December 2, 2015.

79. Katherine Hille, "Putin Says Turkey Will Regret 'Murdering' Servicemen," *Financial Times*, December 9, 2015. For his part, Erdogan claimed that Turkey had stopped the negotiations on the Turkish Stream pipeline because Turkey's demands were not met. "Turkey Has Shelved Turkish Stream Pipeline Project, Says President Erdogan," *Turkish Daily News*, December 5, 2015.

80. "Ankara Shuns Moscow's Potential Gas Threat with Qatari Accord," *Turkish Daily News*, December 2, 2015.

81. "Erdogan: Ankara Has Proof of Russian Involvement in I.S. Oil Trade," *Radio Free Europe/Radio Liberty*, December 3, 2015.

82. See Judah Ari Gross, "Russia Deploys S-400 Missile Battery in Syria, State Media Says," *Times of Israel*, November 26, 2015; and "Russia Deploys Missile Cruiser Off Syria Coast, Ordered to Destroy Any Possible Target," RT.com, November 25, 2015.

83. Turkish foreign minister Ahmet Davutoglu denounced the attacks on the Turkmen in Syria, stating, "No one can legitimize attacks on Turkmen in Syria, using the pretext of fighting the Islamic State." Quoted in Keith Bradsher, "Range of Frustrations Reached Boil as Turkey Shot Down Russian Jet," *New York Times*, November 25, 2015.

84. For a detailed discussion of the Obama administration's policy toward Syria, see Jeffrey Goldberg, "The Obama Doctrine: The US President Talks Through His Hardest Decisions About America's Role in the World," *Atlantic*, April 2016, www.theatlantic.com/magazine/archive/2016/04/the-obama-doctrine/471525.

85. The text of UN Security Council Resolution 2254 can be found on the UN website, www.un.org/press/en/2015/sc12171.doc.htm.

86. See David Ignatius, "John Kerry's Desperate Push on Syria," *Washington Post*, February 9, 2016; and "Putin's Syria Victory: John Kerry's Ceasefire Lets Assad Consolidate His Strategic Gains," editorial, *Wall Street Journal*, February 13, 2016.

87. See David Sanger, "US and Russia Agree on Plan for a Cease-Fire," *New York Times*, February 12, 2016.

88. See Sammy Katz, "Assad Vows to Reclaim Whole of Syria, Warns Could Take 'Long Time,'" *Times of Israel*, February 12, 2016; and Agence France-Presse, "Syria: Anger over Assad Ahead of Peace Talks," *Australian*, March 14, 2016. Syrian foreign minister Walid Muallem had said in Damascus prior to the resumption of the Geneva talks, "We will not talk with anyone who wants to discuss the (Syrian) presidency. . . . Bashar al-Assad is a red line. The opposition is operating under delusions that they will take power in Geneva that they failed to take in battle." Quoted in Hugh Naylor and Karen DeYoung, "Syria's Warring Parties Return to Geneva to Talk Peace, but Hopes Are Low," *Washington Post*, March 13, 2016.

89. Quoted in Michael Pearson, "Russia to Withdraw Forces from Syria," CNN, March 15, 2016, www.cnn.com/2016/03/14/world/russia-syria-withdrawal.

90. Quoted in Sam Dagher, "Syria Defies Russia in Bid to Keep Assad," *Wall Street Journal*, April 11, 2016.

91. See Raja Abdulrahim, "Syria Retakes Palmyra from Islamic State," *Wall Street Journal*, March 28, 2016.

12

US Policy After the Uprisings: Alliances, Democracy, and Force

Jeremy Pressman

IN RESPONSE TO the Arab Spring and subsequent events, US alliances in the Middle East have remained largely static. After some initial rhetorical flourishes, President Barack Obama's administration has chosen continuity over change on most questions where US security interests seem to conflict with pressures for democracy or reform. The same is true of the US commitment to a market-based or neoliberal order. As Schwedler, Stacher, and Yadav so eloquently put it, "The alarm clock has sounded, but Washington has elected to hit the snooze."[1]

On the question of military force, however, the Obama administration has broken with its predecessor, the administration of President George W. Bush, with many of the contested cases occurring in the Middle East. Despite vociferous criticism and pressure from elements of the US elite, Obama has frequently avoided or minimized using military force and expressed a preference for multilateral diplomacy. Obama did initially ramp up troop levels in Afghanistan; intervene in Libya; order the killing of Osama bin Laden in Pakistan; approve an intensive drone war in Yemen, Pakistan, and elsewhere; and begin bombing the Islamic State of Iraq and Syria (ISIS). But he also limited US intervention in Syria relative to what his critics demanded; attempted withdrawals of most US forces in Iraq and then Afghanistan; did not bomb Iran's nuclear facilities; and did not dramatically expand US military help for Ukraine despite Russia's meddling in Eastern Ukraine.

As of mid-2016, the Obama administration had not launched a ground invasion of any other country. The administration negotiated the removal of chemical weapons from Syria; opened diplomatic relations with Cuba; and, along with other powers, signed a nuclear agreement with Iran. Is this avoidance of military intervention a sign of US weakness and appeasement or US caution and prudence? Obama's political opponents in Washington, as well as many in the region, including leaders of major US allies such as Egypt, Israel, and Saudi Arabia, often suggest the former. To Obama's critics, the United States' "hegemonic status is diminishing."[2] As the president has continued to outline the need to pursue diplomacy and remained wary of war, the dividing line among both US policymakers and pundits on the US role in the Middle East and the world has come into sharp relief.[3] For Fabbrini and Yossef, this very split explains the seeming incoherence of US policy in the region: "the difficulties the national political elites had in agreeing on the US role in the region, on identifying US friends and foes, and on elaborating a shared interpretation of the changes taking place in Arab world."[4] The Obama administration's reaction to the Arab Spring tends to emphasize that while the United States has a large role to play, it cannot solve many of the Middle East's most pressing problems of civil war, refugees, and weak states.

When the Arab Spring started, the United States also faced the question of engaging with Islamists in places such as Egypt and Tunisia. But given the domestic pushback against Islamist political forces, the Obama administration never really ended up having a deep, policy-changing engagement with Egypt's Muslim Brotherhood or other newly empowered Islamist forces.[5]

Before looking at three individual countries in depth—Egypt, Bahrain, and Syria—it is worth noting that the Arab Spring as a whole has been a short-term failure if the metric is progress toward democratic systems. In other words, bear in mind that the environment in which the United States is setting policy has been unstable, violent, and not moving in a democratic direction.[6] The state of the region is not wholly independent of US contemporary or historical US policy, but I contend it is much more driven by events on the ground in the specific countries than by US decisions. Protests arose independent of US help.[7]

In Bahrain, the ruling Khalifa monarchy has brutally suppressed the mass protest movement. In Egypt, the military deposed the Muslim Brotherhood president. In 2016, as in 2010, Egypt's president is a former military leader

elected in a questionable election. The Abdel Fattah el-Sisi government targeted Muslim Brotherhood members, journalists, and many liberal activists.
Libya, Syria, and Yemen are all in a state of civil war, with extensive meddling
by foreign states both inside and outside the region. The Syrian humanitarian
crisis is massive. Yemen is experiencing large-scale domestic conflict, fueled in
part by military intervention by foreign powers (especially Saudi Arabia, the
United States, and Iran). Only in Tunisia has the constitutional and democratic process moved in a positive direction, and even there terrorist attacks
have taken a toll.

US SECURITY INTERESTS VERSUS GROWTH OF DEMOCRATIC REGIMES

In this unstable environment, a central tension in US policy has been between
US security interests and the growth of democratic regimes. Tamara Cofman
Wittes has highlighted the "conflicts-of-interests problem" whereby US officials see short-term security needs as more pressing than the prospect of democratization and democracy.[8] Initially in 2011, Huber argues, Obama had the
United States play a dual role with the advent of the Arab Spring: "Remain an
anchor of regional security but at the same time boost its role of being *a modest
advocate of democratic change*."[9] But by 2013, Huber continues, several events
influenced the Obama administration to downplay democratic change and focus on security, including the Benghazi attack that resulted in the death of US
ambassador to Libya J. Christopher Stevens and others on September 11, 2012;
Syria's Assad government's use of chemical weapons in the Syrian civil war;
and the violent ouster of Mohamed Morsi and the Muslim Brotherhood in
July 2013 in Egypt. One can see the renewed emphasis in a speech the president
gave at West Point in May 2014: "In countries like Egypt, we acknowledge that
our relationship is anchored in security interests—from peace treaties with
Israel, to shared efforts against violent extremism."[10] He did mention pressing
for reform, but it appeared to have secondary status. The anchor? Security.

In making the distinction between security and democratization, one also
needs to distinguish between US statements and US policy and action. Since
2011, one can point to US rhetoric that seems supportive of democratization
and reform. On May 19, 2011, President Obama stated a change in US policy
was in order: "We have the chance to show that America values the dignity

of the street vendor in Tunisia more than the raw power of the dictator." He named traditional US interests in the Middle East but then questioned the viability of "a strategy based solely upon the narrow pursuit of these interests." US support for universal rights and political and economic reform "is not a secondary interest." And he pledged to act: "Today I want to make it clear that it is a top priority that must be translated into concrete actions, and supported by all of the diplomatic, economic and strategic tools at our disposal."[11]

But my point is that one did not see US policy change to make that rhetoric and the lofty principles the guiding light of US aid and action. Most of the time, at decisionmaking moments when US regional security interests, as they are usually understood, conflict with democratization or human rights, the former still win out (as was usually the case before the Arab Spring, going all the way back to World War II).[12] In sum, US policy on the democracy-security nexus since 2011 does not look all that different from US policy prior to the Arab Spring. Security trumps democratization.

ECONOMIC ISSUES AND US POLICY

Though it is not the central focus of this chapter, another useful way to look at the Arab uprisings and overall US policy is in terms of economic issues. Economic corruption, mismanagement, and crony capitalism fueled public rage in, for example, Egypt and Tunisia.[13] When Acharya weighed the two impulses, economic and political reform, he concluded, "The Arab uprisings were more of a protest against corrupt and repressive regimes than a call for the establishment of Western style liberal democratic institutions."[14]

In the context of the economic issues, the United States was off the mark, according to Heydemann; Washington focused upon corruption and crony capitalism but missed the fact that market failure and inequality—a basic questioning of capitalism itself—were at the heart of much of the mass Arab protests.[15] Labor movements were crucial catalysts in Egypt's protests. "Obama's policy," Schwedler, Stacher, and Yadav argued, "constitutes a doubling-down on the failed neoliberal economic policies."[16] Hinnebusch further contended that the counterrevolution, led by US allies including Sisi's Egypt, Israel, and Saudi Arabia, sought to protect the neoliberal capitalist order.[17]

Now we turn to considering how US policy has played out in Egypt, Bahrain, and Syria.

EGYPT

In Egypt since 2011, the main characteristic of US policy has been continuity. For decades, the United States has been a partner with Egypt's military dictatorship. In Jason Brownlee's view, the United States provided Egypt's military regime with protection from foreign threats, subsidies for its armed forces, and help to the security services in exchange for benefits such as intelligence sharing, overflight rights, access to the Suez Canal, joint military exercises, and a market for arms sales, all linked to preserving the peace treaty with Israel and protecting the Persian Gulf along the lines of the Carter Doctrine.[18] On the whole, and despite some verbal sparring between officials, that has changed little under President Obama.

There have been some important, partial breaks in US policy toward Egypt, but each is far short of what the United States could have done had it wanted to cut ties with the Egyptian military, push hard for democratization, or both. Egypt's armed forces quickly came to see that breaking with then Egyptian president Husni Mubarak was in their own interest. Obama broke with Mubarak after a few days of mass protests in 2011, and the United States also used military-to-military contacts to encourage the armed forces not to fire on the protesters and to reinforce the message about Mubarak.[19] But the United States never turned full bore on the Egyptian military and its centrality as a pillar of the regime.

With Mubarak gone and the Supreme Council of the Armed Forces (SCAF) in charge in Cairo, the United States encouraged Egypt to hold elections and move toward civilian rule, and Egypt did so.[20] The SCAF did not seem interested in governing indefinitely, and the dialogue between the two sides did not turn acrimonious.

One example of a moment when the Obama administration could have sided more with Egypt's reformists against the military regime was when protests erupted and violence flared in December 2011. In the aftermath of a widely seen video of an Egyptian woman being beaten and dragged in the street, Secretary of State Hillary Rodham Clinton strongly criticized what had happened in Egypt but did not attach a specific consequence: "This systematic degradation of Egyptian women dishonors the revolution, disgraces the state and its uniform, and is not worthy of a great people."[21] Clinton did not call for specific changes to the political structure. She criticized what had happened without criticizing the military generally or the SCAF. A month later, the White House released a very positive-sounding summary of a call between Obama and Field Marshal Hussein Tantawi, head of the SCAF. There were few hints of Egyptian-US differences.[22]

The Muslim Brotherhood dominated the parliamentary elections, and Mohamed Morsi, its candidate, won the presidential election in June 2012, seemingly diminishing the military's power. Obama officials "adopted a businesslike approach"[23] and worked with President Morsi and other Brotherhood leaders as Egypt's elected officials. Maybe a different US administration would have been more hostile toward the Muslim Brotherhood. Even so, it was not as if the Obama administration worked to get the Brotherhood elected or warmly embraced the Brotherhood and President Morsi.

And when, in July 2013, the military removed President Morsi in a coup, the United States declined to call it a coup even though just before it occurred, US officials had urged the Egyptian military not to forcibly depose Morsi. Had the Obama administration called Morsi's removal a coup, it would have been legally required to suspend US military and financial assistance to Egypt until a democratic government took power. When, especially in August 2013 during the Rabba massacre, the armed forces brutally suppressed Muslim Brotherhood supporters through arrests, torture, and killing over eight hundred civilians, the United States chose not to fundamentally reorient its policies against the military. Sisi was elected president in June 2014 with 97 percent of the vote. Perhaps US measures in October 2013, such as withholding some fighter aircraft or canceling military exercises, were more than a slap on the wrist, but they were not much more.[24] Washington refrained from using most of the military leverage it had over Egypt.

In December 2014, the administration delivered delayed Apache helicopters. In spring 2015, the US administration fully relented, releasing the Harpoon missiles, F-16 aircraft, and M1A1 Abrams tank kits whose delivery it had held up. The Obama administration has not stated any plans to cut Egypt's annual military aid allocation of $1.3 billion.[25]

Wittes has suggested that the Obama administration made one important change by ending the US practice of cash-flow financing. Such financing often led to arms contracts that obligated the United States to provide military aid to Egypt years into the future.[26] But in the whole picture of US military aid to Egypt, that is a meaningful but limited correction.

Obama's 2015 climbdown came despite the fact that the Sisi administration, and really the Egyptian military since 2011, has been aggressively suppressing civil society and blocking both Egyptian reformers and their international NGO allies. Regionally, the democratization movement is in trouble, targeted by Egypt and other dictatorships. Scholars have called into question the efficacy of foreign support for such efforts throughout the region.[27] Do these foreign-funded programs even help promote democracy? Though the United States was, through the US Agency for International Development, the International Republican Institute, and the National Democratic Institute, supporting democratization efforts in a way that one might see as a minor counterweight to tight relations with the repressive Egyptian armed forces, those efforts have become even less weighty as the Arab Spring has continued. To Heydemann, the United States has much less space for supporting civil society in today's Egypt or Bahrain. Moreover, new US initiatives in that vein, like the proposed Middle East and North Africa Incentive Fund, never got off the ground.[28] In 2015, aid for Tunisia was in flux.[29]

In sum, Washington had several moments when it could have chosen political reform over maintaining ties with the Egyptian military, which has ruled Egypt for most if not all of the Arab Spring,[30] and each time, the US government took no or limited steps rather than advancing wholesale change in the formulation of US policy. The Obama administration passed up opportunities such as the trials of prodemocracy NGO workers (including a number of Americans), the toppling and trial of Morsi, and the continued repression of regime opponents.

BAHRAIN

In 2011, after protests swept Bahrain, the United States called generally for restraint and for working out differences in political, not violent, fashion, but Washington did not strongly object to the Saudi-led military repression of the Bahraini opposition movement. The Obama administration passed up the opportunity to castigate or sanction either of two of its close allies, Bahrain and Saudi Arabia, when the reform movement was forcibly suppressed on March 14, 2011, and in the years thereafter. The United Arab Emirates, another US ally, also provided Bahrain with support for the crackdown.

The US president suggested that the way forward was a government-opposition dialogue, exactly the concept the United States rejected and Russia advanced in the Syrian case.[31] The United States did limit security assistance in October 2011, but high-level Bahraini-US meetings have continued. The

United States was not totally silent. For example, in September 2013, it was one of forty-seven countries that joined the UN Office of the High Commissioner for Human Rights (OHCHR) to express "serious concern" about the human rights situation.[32] The government of Bahrain has regularly expressed its displeasure with US criticism and with US officials meeting with Bahraini opposition figures.[33]

While it would be easy to point to Bahrain's hosting a base for the US Navy (the Fifth Fleet) in order to explain the overall gentle US reaction, a stronger reason for the US position was the Saudi-US alliance and Saudi outrage when the Obama administration publicly turned against Egypt's Mubarak just weeks prior to the uprising in Bahrain.[34] Furthermore, the United States wants ties with Bahrain, and Saudi Arabia, to help push back both Iran and ISIS.[35] In 2015, the United States praised Bahrain for "working closely with us on the counter-ISIL campaign."[36] Bahrain has long claimed that its domestic "unrest is an Iran-inspired effort to overthrow the monarchy."[37]

In May 2012 and June 2015, the US government allowed arms or security assistance to the Bahrain Defense Force and National Guard (but not the Ministry of Interior) that had been partially cut off in 2011.[38] In the 2015 case, the US Department of State contended that Bahrain "has made some meaningful progress on human rights reforms and reconciliation."[39] Human rights watchers disagreed, claiming the policy change took place "in the absence of any real or meaningful political reform."[40] In early August 2015, the US government approved a possible sale of $150 million of equipment for Bahrain to maintain its F-16 fighter aircraft.[41] In the Bahrain case, continued military ties have been coupled with only light US concerns about reform and human rights.

Syria

The Syrian civil war is a massive humanitarian crisis with many casualties, over 7 million internally displaced Syrians, and over 5 million refugees as of mid-2016. In 2011, the Assad regime decided to respond to domestic political protests and demands for reform, the Syrian outbreak of the Arab Spring, with brutal, violent repression. The government violence overcame the popular protest movement, and today the Syrian army and many militias fight in Syria (and some fight into Iraq as well). Syrian government forces, Lebanon's Hezbollah, the Islamic State, al-Nusra, the People's Protection Units (or YPG), and many others each control parts of a deeply fragmented Syria.

The United States has been a leader in funding humanitarian aid for displaced Syrians, with $4.1 billion in aid for 2012–2015.[42] At the same time, the United States has resettled very few Syrian refugees.

But the central debate about US policy toward Syria has been whether the United States should have intervened militarily in the civil war and what impact that intervention might have had. In 2014, the United States began to bomb ISIS targets in Syria and Iraq, and it has also trained a very small number of opposition fighters. But US training of rebels has proceeded slowly, perhaps with the exception of CIA efforts.[43] Proponents of intervention have called for military strikes on the Assad regime, establishing a safe zone inside Syria to protect civilians, and much more rapid and significant support of the Syrian opposition. The Obama administration has not pursued these options.

Critics view US policy as ineffective and responsible for the humanitarian crisis and ongoing war. US military intervention, critics claim, could have stopped civilian suffering, defeated the Assad regime, prevented the rise of ISIS, and shortened the civil war. In 2013, Michael Hudson wrote, "Washington is baffled, almost paralysed by the ongoing tragedy in Syria."[44] In 2015, Shadi Hamid tweeted about the US training program for Syrian fighters, "The US has basically lost an entire year in building up/supporting rebel forces that can fight ISIS & Assad. Tragic, missed opportunity."[45] Writing in the *Guardian*, Natalie Nougayrède was highly critical of the Obama administration: "Syria is going down as the US president's most serious, tragic, far-reaching and long-lasting foreign policy failure." It was a profound moral failure, as the United States "largely failed to uphold a convincing moral stand in the face of one of the worst humanitarian catastrophes since the second world war." The civilian suffering, Nougayrède alleged, opened the door to the growth of ISIS.[46]

President Obama and others have been reluctant to intervene more deeply and have highlighted several concerns.[47] In 2012, Obama noted that "the opposition is hugely splintered." The fragmentation makes the choice of allies and enemies more challenging. Militant Salafist groups such as ISIS and al-Nusra are capable of some military success versus Assad, but they are not a good fit with US preferences. The Free Syrian Army, a possible US partner, never emerged as a major player on the military battlefield. Meanwhile, the policies of other states matter as well; unlike in Libya, Obama said, Russia frequently has blocked UN Security Council action on Syria.[48] Other arguments included the idea that US "military adventurism" could have worsened US "credibility" in the region.[49] Bahgat and Sharp suggested that "less foreign intervention by the United States and other powers is likely to help Arab countries to determine their future without blaming foreign countries."[50] Furthermore, the past US intervention in Iraq spawned many of today's problems in Syria.[51]

Some broader research bolsters the position of those wary of military intervention in the Syrian civil war. Jacob D. Kathman and Reed M. Wood have found that international military intervention in a situation like Syria might worsen the violence in the short term, even if such impartial intervention would help end mass killing in the long run.[52] And what some pundits in the United States have called for is not *impartial* US military intervention but rather action that sides with some part of the opposition. Patrick M. Regan and Aysegul Aydin's research on external interventions suggests that diplomatic intervention—mediation—is most effective at ending violence and saving human lives.[53]

One issue that has been particularly controversial is the US response to Syria's use of chemical weapons. In August 2012, President Obama warned Syria:

> I have, at this point, not ordered military engagement in the situation. . . .
> We have been very clear to the Assad regime, but also to other players on the ground, that a red line for us is we start seeing a whole bunch of chemical weapons moving around or being utilized. That would change my calculus. That would change my equation. . . . We have communicated in no uncertain terms with every player in the region that that's a red line for us and that there would be enormous consequences if we start seeing movement on the chemical weapons front or the use of chemical weapons. That would change my calculations significantly.[54]

The Syrian government continued using chemical weapons on multiple occasions. Almost exactly a year later, in August 2013, the Syrian government used a banned chemical weapon, sarin, to attack an opposition area, Ghouta, in the suburbs of Damascus. Hundreds or thousands were killed. The Obama administration considered a military response, but the British Parliament expressed its opposition, and congressional support was mixed.

Instead of a direct US attack, the United States and Russia, a close Assad ally, negotiated the removal of Syria's chemical-weapons stockpile, an approach ultimately backed by the UN Security Council. The Organisation for the Prohibition of Chemical Weapons (OPCW) then supervised the removal of Syria's cache of chemical weapons and their precursors and rendered inoperable Syrian production facilities.[55] From one perspective, this was a major breakthrough: "Ridding the Assad regime of these deadly [chemical] weapons without a military offensive campaign should be seen as an important achievement."[56] Critics focused on Obama's August 2012 "red line" and charged that his failure to use military force signaled US weakness and damaged US credibility.

Whereas the situations in Egypt and Bahrain have reached a period of short-term stability, the war and humanitarian crisis in Syria, as in Libya and Yemen, remains in flux.

CONCLUSION: THE OVERALL ROLE OF THE UNITED STATES

Analysts are divided about the US role in the failure of the Arab Spring protest movements to spur deeper political reform. Some cite domestic or regional factors beyond US control. The survival of monarchic regimes in the Middle East is due to the loyalty and support of the monarchs' extended families (and the resultant unity) and, in many of these states, oil rents. External strategic factors, such as arms sales, are secondary.[57] Places such as Libya, Syria, and Yemen are different from countries that democratized in the third wave of democratization. They have more violence, have more external support (e.g., from China or Russia) for antidemocrats, and experience extensive meddling by Arab Gulf countries.[58]

That said, other scholars have characterized the US impact in a range of ways. For example, some, such as Barak Mendelsohn, also highlight regional dynamics when assessing US options: "The magnitude and complexity of the changes in the region would have made the wish to shape developments in alignment with U.S. interests unrealistic even during the heyday of the American imperium."[59] To Bahgat and Sharp, "US efforts to influence or shape the [Arab reform] process have largely proven unproductive."[60]

Why has the United States not had influence and control over the Arab Spring? Maybe it was simply beyond US control. The problems are too large and internally rooted. Perhaps the Obama administration made the wrong policy choices; it was hesitant, ad hoc, and incoherent when it needed to be visionary and decisive. Maybe it is a structural issue, and US power is in decline. Or perhaps this is the wrong question, using too short-term a lens. In the bigger picture, at the strategic level, not much has changed in terms of US national interests: oil and gas flow from the region at a reasonable price; Israel still exists; and the United States continues to battle a Salafist foe.

Notes

1. Jillian Schwedler, Joshua Stacher, and Stacey Philbrick Yadav, "Three Powerfully Wrong—and Wrongfully Powerful—American Narratives About the Arab Spring," in *The Dawn of the Arab Uprisings: End of an Old Order?*, ed. Bassam Haddad, Rosie Bsheer, and Ziad Abu-Rish (London: Pluto Press, 2012), 40.

2. Barak Mendelsohn, "U.S. Strategy in a Transitioning Middle East: Reviving 'State Responsibility,'" *Orbis* 58, 2 (2014): 198–211.

3. Michael A. Cohen, "Party Divide on Use of Force Resurfaces in Iran Deal Debate," *World Politics Review*, August 12, 2015, www.worldpoliticsreview.com/articles/16446/party -divide-on-use-of-force-resurfaces-in-iran-deal-debate. One could also throw one's hands up given that different policies all produced negative outcomes, heavy suffering, and instability in Iraq (major US ground invasion), Libya (aerial, US-led intervention), and Syria (no or limited US military intervention).

4. Sergio Fabbrini and Amr Yossef, "Obama's Wavering: US Foreign Policy on the Egyptian Crisis, 2011–13," *Contemporary Arab Affairs* 8, 1 (2015): 65–80.

5. See Jeremy Pressman, "Same Old Story? Obama and the Arab Uprisings," in *The Arab Spring: Change and Resistance in the Middle East*, ed. Mark L. Haas and David W. Lesch (Boulder, CO: Westview Press, 2013), 219–237.

6. For example, see Daniela Huber, "A Pragmatic Actor—the US Response to the Arab Uprisings," *Journal of European Integration* 37, 1 (2015): 57–75; and Nikolaos Zahariadis, "Penelope Unraveling: The Obama Administration's Policy in the Eastern Mediterranean," in *The Eastern Mediterranean in Transition: Multipolarity, Politics and Power*, ed. Spyridon N. Litsas and Aristotle Tziampiris (Burlington, VT: Ashgate Publishing, 2015), 88.

7. Ashley Barnes, "Creating Democrats? Testing the Arab Spring," *Middle East Policy* 20, 2 (Summer 2013): 55–72. On theorizing the diffusion of the crisis across Arab countries, see many useful citations in Marc Lynch, Deen Freelon, and Sean Aday, "Syria in the Arab Spring: The Integration of Syria's Conflict with the Arab Uprisings, 2011–2013," *Research & Politics* 1, 3 (October 2014): 1–7.

8. Tamara Cofman Wittes, *Freedom's Unsteady March: America's Role in Building Arab Democracy* (Washington, DC: Brookings Institution Press, 2008), 17–18.

9. Huber, "A Pragmatic Actor."

10. "Remarks by the President at the United States Military Academy Commencement Ceremony," West Point, New York, May 28, 2014, www.whitehouse.gov/the-press -office/2014/05/28/remarks-president-united-states-military-academy-commence ment-ceremony.

11. "Remarks by the President on the Middle East and North Africa," May 19, 2011, www .whitehouse.gov/the-press-office/2011/05/19/remarks-president-middle-east-and-north -africa.

12. Or, including the economic angle, political reform and accountability lose out to "vital" military (pro-US) and economic (neoliberal) interests. See Schwedler, Stacher, and Yadav, "Three Powerfully Wrong—and Wrongfully Powerful—American Narratives About the Arab Spring," 44.

13. Imad Salamey, "Post–Arab Spring: Changes and Challenges," *Third World Quarterly* 36, 1 (2015): 111–129.

14. Amitav Acharya, "How the Two Big Ideas of the Post–Cold War Era Failed," *Washington Post*, June 24, 2015, www.washingtonpost.com/blogs/monkey-cage/wp/2015/06/ 24/how-the-two-big-ideas-of-the-post-cold-war-era-failed.

15. Steven Heydemann, "America's Response to the Arab Uprisings: US Foreign Assistance in an Era of Ambivalence," *Mediterranean Politics* 19, 3 (2014): 299–317. Some of the elite-level displeasure was with the way crony capitalism, centered around Gamal Mubarak and the building of ties to foreign players, threatened national capitalists, including the armed forces. See Paul Amar, "Why Mubarak Is Out," in *The Dawn of the Arab Uprisings: End of an Old Order?*, ed. Bassam Haddad, Rosie Bsheer, and Ziad Abu-Rish (London: Pluto Press, 2012), 83–90.

16. Schwedler, Stacher, and Yadav, "Three Powerfully Wrong—and Wrongfully Powerful—American Narratives About the Arab Spring," 38.

17. Raymond Hinnebusch, "Globalization, Democratization, and the Arab Uprising: The International Factor in MENA's Failed Democratization," *Democratization* 22, 2 (2015): 335–357. See also Victoria E. Collins and Dawn L. Rothe, "United States Support for Global Social Justice? Foreign Intervention and Realpolitik in Egypt's Arab Spring," *Social Justice* 39, 4 (2014): 1–30.

18. Jason Brownlee, *Democracy Prevention: The Politics of the U.S.-Egyptian Alliance* (Cambridge: Cambridge University Press, 2012). For a different and broader argument about how US policy blocked Arab democratization, see Amaney A. Jamal, *Of Empires and Citizens: Pro-American Democracy or No Democracy at All?* (Princeton, NJ: Princeton University Press, 2012).

19. Marc Lynch, *The Arab Uprising: The Unfinished Revolution of the New Middle East* (New York: PublicAffairs, 2012), 92, 94–95.

20. I am not claiming that Egypt held elections and moved toward civilian rule solely because of US policy.

21. "Secretary Clinton's Remarks on Women, Peace, and Security," December 19, 2011, Washington, DC, www.state.gov/secretary/20092013clinton/rm/2011/12/179173.htm. See also Agence France-Presse, "Clinton: Egypt's Treatment of Women a 'Disgrace,'" *Egypt Independent*, December 20, 2011, www.egyptindependent.com/node/559071. Shatz agreed that the United States was relatively soft on the SCAF. See Adam Shatz, "Whose Egypt?," *London Review of Books*, January 5, 2012, www.lrb.co.uk/2011/12/20/adam-shatz/whose-egypt.

22. "Readout of the President's Call with Egyptian Field Marshal Tantawi," January 20, 2012, www.whitehouse.gov/the-press-office/2012/01/20/readout-president-s-call-egyptian-field-marshal-tantawi.

23. Gawdat Bahgat and Robert Sharp, "Prospects for a New US Strategic Orientation in the Middle East," *Mediterranean Quarterly* 25, 3 (2014): 27–39.

24. See also Heydemann, "America's Response to the Arab Uprisings," 303. For a different view, see Fabbrini and Yossef, "Obama's Wavering."

25. For the view that the Obama administration let the Sisi government off the hook, see Editorial Board, "With Washington's Complicity, Egypt Cracks Down on Critics," *New York Times*, July 16, 2015, www.nytimes.com/2015/07/16/opinion/with-washingtons-complicity-egypt-cracks-down-on-critics.html. The editorial is in the same vein as Brownlee's work (see Brownlee, *Democracy Prevention*).

26. Tamara Cofman Wittes, "The Politics of Restoring Egypt's Military Aid," *Washington Post*, April 2, 2015, www.washingtonpost.com/blogs/monkey-cage/wp/2015/04/02/the-politics-of-restoring-egypts-military-aid.

27. Matthew Baum and Philip B. K. Potter, "No One Talks About Democratization Any More. Is There a Better Policy?" *Washington Post*, July 5, 2015, www.washingtonpost.com/blogs/monkey-cage/wp/2015/07/05/no-one-talks-about-democratization-any-more-is-there-a-better-policy. For a rebuttal, see Erica Chenoweth, "How Can States and Non-State Actors Respond to Authoritarian Resurgence?," Political Violence @ a Glance, July 7, 2015, http://politicalviolenceataglance.org/2015/07/07/how-can-states-and-non-state-actors-respond-to-authoritarian-resurgence. For an earlier critique, see Thomas Carothers, "The Continuing Backlash Against Democracy Promotion," in *New Challenges to Democratization*, ed. Peter Burnell and Richard Youngs (New York: Routledge, 2010), 66. See also Jeff Bridoux and Malcolm Russell, "Liberal Democracy Promotion in Iraq: A Model for the Middle East and North Africa?," *Foreign Policy Analysis* 9, 3 (July 2013): 327–346.

28. Heydemann, "America's Response to the Arab Uprisings," 310, 312–313.

29. Julian Pecquet, "Senate Hits the Brakes on Tunisia Aid Boost," Al-Monitor, July 15, 2005, www.al-monitor.com/pulse/originals/2015/07/tunisia-aid-senate-block-terror-us-congress.html.

30. The only question is whether one should say that the armed forces ruled Egypt during Morsi's year as president. The military still constituted the backbone of Egypt's deep state during that time, so I think that is a defensible position. Had Morsi held on and deepened his hold on power, perhaps we might look back differently on the question of who ruled Egypt in 2012–2013.

31. "Remarks by the President on the Middle East and North Africa." See also Charles W. Moore, "Bahrain, a Vital U.S. Ally," *Washington Times*, December 1, 2011. Moore was commander of the US Navy's Fifth Fleet from 1998 to 2002.

32. The forty-seven countries did not include any Arab countries. "Joint Statement on the OHCHR and the Human Rights Situation in Bahrain," September 9, 2013, http://

freeassembly.net/wp-content/uploads/2013/10/Switzerland_Cross_Regional_GD_01
.pdf.

33. Michael C. Hudson, "Geopolitical Shifts: Asia Rising, American Declining in the Middle East?," *Contemporary Arab Affairs* 6, 3 (2013): 458–466.

34. Shatz, "Whose Egypt?" See also Lynch, *The Arab Uprising*, 140, 228; and Andrew F. Cooper, Bessma Momani, and Asif B. Farooq, "The United States and Bahrain: Interpreting the Differentiated U.S. Responses to the Arab Spring," *Digest of Middle East Studies* 23, 2 (Fall 2014): 360–384.

35. Sayed Alwadaei, "Losing Leverage on Bahrain" (op-ed), *New York Times*, July 7, 2015, www.nytimes.com/2015/07/08/opinion/losing-leverage-on-bahrain.html.

36. John Kirby, "Lifting Holds on Security Assistance to the Government of Bahrain," US Department of State, June 29, 2015, www.state.gov/r/pa/prs/ps/2015/06/244478.htm.

37. Hudson, "Geopolitical Shifts."

38. For more details, see Kenneth Katzman, "Bahrain: Reform, Security, and U.S. Policy," Congressional Research Service report, May 8, 2015, www.fas.org/sgp/crs/mideast/95-1013.pdf, 26–27.

39. Kirby, "Lifting Holds on Security Assistance to the Government of Bahrain."

40. Andy Valvur, "US Resumes Aid to Bahrain Military," *Deutsche Welle*, June 30, 2015, http://dw.com/p/1FpsS.

41. Andrea Shalal, "U.S. Approves $150 Million Deal for Bahrain F-16 Support," Reuters, August 7, 2015, www.reuters.com/article/2015/08/07/usa-bahrain-aircraft-idUSL1N10I2J220150807.

42. The figure was current as of August 4, 2015. "Humanitarian Funding to Syria Humanitarian Response FY 2012–2015," www.usaid.gov/crisis/syria.

43. Roy Gutman, "First Contingent of U.S.-Trained Fighters Enter Syria," July 16, 2015, www.mcclatchydc.com/news/nation-world/world/article27446395.html; Missy Ryan, "After Setback, U.S. Military Looks for Ways to Recalibrate New Syrian Force," *Washington Post*, August 12, 2015, www.washingtonpost.com/world/national-security/after-setbacks-us-military-looks-for-ways-to-recalibrate-new-syrian-force/2015/08/12/e6c5664e-4103-11e5-8e7d-9c033e6745d8_story.html; and Greg Miller and Karen DeYoung, "Secret CIA Effort in Syria Faces Large Funding Cut," *Washington Post*, June 12, 2015, www.washingtonpost.com/world/national-security/lawmakers-move-to-curb-1-billion-cia-program-to-train-syrian-rebels/2015/06/12/b0f45a9e-1114-11e5-adec-e82f8395c032_story.html. For a very different perspective, see Joel Veldkamp, "How to Understand Those 60 Trainees," August 14, 2015, www.joshualandis.com/blog/how-to-understand-those-60-trainees.

44. Hudson, "Geopolitical Shifts."

45. Shadi Hamid, @shadihamid, https://twitter.com/shadihamid/status/618773738163687424. See also Matt Schiavenza, "Why the U.S. Can't Build an Opposition Army in Syria," *Atlantic*, August 2, 2015, http://theatln.tc/1SQxHii.

46. Natalie Nougayrède, "If Barack Obama Ever Had a Strategy for Syria, It's Been Turned on Its Head," *Guardian*, August 10, 2015, www.theguardian.com/commentisfree

/2015/aug/10/barack-obama-strategy-syria-procrastination-civilians-protecting-rebels. See also Anne-Marie Slaughter, "How the World Could—and Maybe Should—Intervene in Syria," *Atlantic*, January 23, 2012, http://tinyurl.com/7smzyua.

47. For example, see Steven Simon, "Staying Out of Syria," *Foreign Affairs*, October 26, 2014, https://www.foreignaffairs.org/articles/iraq/2014-10-26/staying-out-syria.

48. Jeffrey Goldberg, "Obama to Iran and Israel: 'As President of the United States, I Don't Bluff,'" *Atlantic*, March 2, 2012, www.theatlantic.com/international/archive/2012/03/obama-to-iran-and-israel-as-president-of-the-united-states-i-dont-bluff/253875. See also Marc Lynch, "The 'Arm the FSA' Bandwagon," *Foreign Policy*, February 9, 2012, http://foreignpolicy.com/2012/02/09/the-arm-the-fsa-bandwagon.

49. Robert Mason, "The Obama Administration and the Arab Spring: Waiting for a Doctrine," in *The International Politics of the Arab Spring: Popular Unrest and Foreign Policy*, ed. Robert Mason (New York: Palgrave, 2014), 42.

50. Bahgat and Sharp, "Prospects for a New US Strategic Orientation in the Middle East."

51. C. J. Polychroniou, "Chomsky: U.S. Spawned a Fundamentalist Frankenstein in the Mideast," Alternet, October 6, 2014, www.alternet.org/books/chomsky-us-spawned-fundamentalist-frankenstein-mideast.

52. I appreciate Erica Chenoweth pointing out this research. Jacob D. Kathman and Reed M. Wood, "Managing Threat, Cost, and Incentive to Kill: The Short- and Long-Term Effects of Intervention in Mass Killings," *Journal of Conflict Resolution* 55, 5 (October 2011): 735–760.

53. Patrick M. Regan and Aysegul Aydin, "Diplomacy and Other Forms of Intervention in Civil Wars," *Journal of Conflict Resolution* 50, 5 (October 2006): 736–756.

54. "Remarks by the President to the White House Press Corps," www.whitehouse.gov/the-press-office/2012/08/20/remarks-president-white-house-press-corps, August 20, 2012.

55. For a history of Syria's chemical program, including the OPCW phase, see www.nti.org/country-profiles/syria/chemical, last updated March 2016.

56. Bahgat and Sharp, "Prospects for a New US Strategic Orientation in the Middle East."

57. André Bank, Thomas Richter, and Anna Sunik, "Long-Term Monarchical Survival in the Middle East: A Configurational Comparison, 1945–2012," *Democratization* 22, 1 (2015): 179–200.

58. Heydemann, "America's Response to the Arab Uprisings," 312–313.

59. Mendelsohn, "U.S. Strategy in a Transitioning Middle East," 198. See also F. Gregory Gause III, "Don't Just Do Something, Stand There!" *Foreign Policy*, December 21, 2011, http://foreignpolicy.com/2011/12/21/dont-just-do-something-stand-there.

60. Bahgat and Sharp, "Prospects for a New US Strategic Orientation in the Middle East."

13

Conclusion: The Arab World at the Intersection of the National and Transnational

JAMES L. GELVIN

O N DECEMBER 17, 2010, Muhammad Bouazizi set himself on fire in front of the local government building in the Tunisian town of Sidi Bou Zid. The self-immolation touched off protests that swept the country, reaching Tunisia's capital ten days later. Less than a month after Bouazizi's desperate act, military and political leaders saw the writing on the wall, and after the army surrounded the presidential palace, President Zine El Abidine Ben Ali stepped down and fled to Saudi Arabia. For the first time in history, popular protest brought down an Arab head of state.

About a week and a half after Ben Ali fled, protesters began their occupation of Tahrir Square in Cairo. After security forces and goons for hire failed to dislodge them, and after the military declared its neutrality, the protest movement gained momentum. Over the course of the next two weeks, strikes and protests spread throughout Egypt. On February 11, 2011, the army took matters into its own hands: It deposed President Husni Mubarak and established a new government under the Supreme Council of the Armed Forces. This phase of the Egyptian uprising was over in a mere eighteen days.

The uprisings in Tunisia and Egypt created the template—a false template, as it were[1]—through which the media and the general public have viewed the success or failure of other uprisings in the region. There are three aspects of this template. First, in the public imagination at least, both uprisings were largely peaceful, with tech-savvy youths playing the lead role in the drama (an exaggeration on both counts). Second, both uprisings brought down autocrats when the "people's army" refused to shoot at protesters. Third, both got rid of autocrats in a matter of weeks.

No matter what inspiration other uprisings that broke out in the Arab world in subsequent weeks derived from the Tunisian and Egyptian models, however, it would be wrong to look at them through the lens of the first two. It is true, for example, that after Egypt, a similar-style protest movement emerged in Yemen that upstaged an ongoing protest led by political "outs" seeking "in." Nevertheless, it had very un-Tunisian, un-Egyptian results, and Yemen soon descended into the first of two postuprising civil wars. After protests modeled on those of Egypt broke out in Bahrain, the government struck back violently and, using the excuse that Iranian subversion was behind the protests, invited in troops and police from neighboring Saudi Arabia and the United Arab Emirates to help "restore order." In Saudi Arabia and Morocco, kings who had presented themselves as "reformers" faced their own protest movements, which demanded expanded representation, an end to corruption, and constitutional checks on monarchic power—but, significantly, not the end of the regime, as the protests in Tunisia and Egypt had demanded. The governments were able to placate their populations—in the former kingdom with promises of a $300 billion benefits package to its citizens, in the latter with superficial reforms.

Uprisings in both Libya and Syria were longer, more brutal affairs. In Libya, a "Day of Rage" was held after the arrest of a prominent human rights lawyer. Violent protests subsequently spread, and, with the help of a fierce NATO air campaign, *thuwwar* (revolutionaries) managed to overthrow the government of Muammar al-Gadafi. Unfortunately, they proved incapable of putting in place a government agreeable to all, and violence continued. And after months of predictions that "it couldn't happen in Syria," it did, when a local incident in Daraa sparked wider protests. Unlike their Libyan counterparts, however, opposition forces in Syria were not able to overthrow the regime they opposed or even to act in unison, and so Syria, too, descended into civil war with no end in sight.

These were the main sites of protest. There were others, less publicized. So how are we to understand what is going on?

Metaphorically Speaking

There are two metaphors commonly used to describe what has happened in the Arab world since December 2010. The first and most commonly used metaphor is "Arab Spring." Despite its popularity, it falls short for two reasons. First, it is misleading: The optimism the phrase connotes has long since been shattered, and the metaphor discounts the often-sizable contributions made to the uprisings by non-Arab communities, such as the Berber community in North Africa. Second, events in the Arab world during 2010–2011 cannot be viewed as a discrete phenomenon that might be isolated within the span of a single "season." Not only did uprisings continue to erupt in the region long after the arrival of the 2011 summer solstice but the so-called Arab Spring was but one phase of a three-decades-long struggle for human and democratic rights and social and economic justice in the region—a struggle that brought hundreds of thousands, from Morocco to Bahrain, out into the streets.[2]

The second metaphor commonly used to describe what has been happening in the Arab world since Bouazizi's death is "wave." There are pluses and minuses to this metaphor as well. On the plus side, there is no denying that later Arab uprisings borrowed techniques of mobilization and symbols from earlier ones. Town squares that became the sites of protest throughout the Arab world were renamed "Tahrir" after the main site of protest in Cairo, and many uprisings began with a scheduled Day of Rage, also borrowed from the Egyptian model. Then there is the highly touted use of social networking sites for the purpose of mobilization, not to mention the common demands for human and democratic rights and social justice.

There are, however, two main objections to the wave metaphor. Most significantly, the metaphor makes it seem that the spread of the uprisings and protests from state to state was inevitable, like a wave washing over a beach. Its use thus obscures the fact that the uprisings and protests spread as a result of tens of thousands of individual decisions made by participants who chose on a daily basis to face the full repressive power of the state. The wave metaphor also obscures the fact that the goals and styles of the uprisings and protests have varied widely from country to country. The goal of some has been the complete overthrow of the regime, while the goal of others has been the reform of the regime. In some places, initial protests came about after meticulous preparation; in others, the spark was spontaneous. And there have been times when uprisings have been predominantly peaceful and other times when they took a violent turn.

Despite its problems, the wave metaphor might be salvaged if we remain aware that what has been taking place in the Arab world has both transnational and national elements. The transnational elements are found mainly in terms of inputs: Over the course of the past half century, all Arab states came to share similar characteristics, and over the course of the past two decades, all Arab states have faced similar conditions and shocks that made them vulnerable to popular anger. The national elements are found in terms of the trajectories taken by the uprisings: Variations in local history, state structure, and state capability opened up possibilities and foreclosed options for each. This made it impossible for Libyans and Syrians, for example, to replicate the relative peacefulness and quick resolution that marked the initial phases of the Tunisian and Egyptian uprisings. Foreign intervention (or lack thereof) has also played a role in determining the trajectories of protests, as might be seen most pointedly in the cases of Libya, Syria, and Bahrain.

TRANSNATIONAL INPUTS

Overall, there are five transnational factors that made all states in the Arab world vulnerable to popular anger. First, beginning in the late 1970s, and accelerating over the course of the past decade and a half, the United States and international banking institutions persuaded or coerced regimes throughout the region to adopt social and economic policies associated with neoliberalism. These policies shredded the post–World War II ruling bargain that had connected Arab governments with their populations.

Before the 1980s, states throughout the Arab world had played an uncontested role in their national economies in an effort to force-march economic development. They also provided a wide array of social benefits for their populations, including employment guarantees, health care, and education. In addition, consumer goods such as food and petroleum products were subsidized by the state. In some states—Nasser's Egypt, postindependence Algeria, Gadafi's Libya, post-1958 Iraq, Syria at various times, and others—regimes justified their policies using a populist discourse that extolled anticolonialism and the virtues of the revolutionary masses. In others—Jordan and Saudi Arabia, for example—rulers appealed to tradition or efficiency. Whether "revolutionary" or "reactionary," however, governments came to the same destination, although via different routes. In return for their generosity, Arab states expected obedience. Overall, then, the ruling bargain connecting states with their populations might be summed up in three words: benefits for compliance.[3]

During the last quarter of the twentieth century, as development stalled and economies stagnated, neoliberalism came to replace dirigisme as the dominant economic paradigm globally. Neoliberalism got its tentative start in the Arab world in December 1976, when Egypt negotiated a $450 million credit line with the International Monetary Fund (IMF). In return, the Egyptian government pledged to cut commodity supports and direct subsidies. Over the course of the next three decades, the IMF negotiated ever more expansive agreements with cash-strapped governments in the region. These agreements were fairly consistent across the board: Governments agreed to cut and target subsidies, remove price controls, privatize government-owned assets, balance their budgets, liberalize trade, deregulate business, and the like. Neoliberalism thus violated the norms of the ruling bargain.

Populations throughout the Arab world confronted the new dispensation by engaging in acts of resistance that ranged from revolt (so-called IMF riots) to labor activism. Those populations found two aspects of neoliberalism particularly repellent. The first is the fraying of the social safety net and threats to middle-class welfare, particularly threats to across-the-board subsidies for food and fuel. At the recommendation of the IMF, those subsidies were replaced by subsidies targeted to those who live in "absolute poverty." The second aspect of neoliberalism populations found repellent was the sell-off of publicly owned enterprises. For many, privatization threatened state-employment guarantees. Furthermore, privatization did not lead, as promised, to free-market capitalism but rather to crony capitalism, as regime loyalists took advantage of their access to the corridors of power. Privatization also widened the gulf between rich and poor. The worst of the crony capitalists—Ahmad Ezz in Egypt, Rami Makhlouf in Syria, anyone named Trabelsi in Tunisia—thus came to symbolize systemic corruption in the buildup to the uprisings.

Accompanying the neoliberal revolution was the so-called Human Rights Revolution, which began in the mid-1970s—the second factor that made states in the region vulnerable to uprisings. Between 1948, when the UN General Assembly adopted the Universal Declaration of Human Rights, and the late 1970s, "human rights" referred to a bundle of rights, including collective rights (such as the right of national self-determination), economic rights, and individual rights. In the wake of the Human Rights Revolution, whenever the subject of human rights was broached in international conferences and legal proceedings, the point of reference was inevitably individual political, civil, and personal rights.

As I have argued elsewhere,[4] neoliberalism and this restrictive definition of human rights were cut from the same cloth. Both counterposed a system that gave autonomous, decisionmaking, rights-bearing citizens pride of place against one in which autonomy, decisionmaking, and rights-bearing were attributes of the state. Both pitted the individualism of the West against the collectivism of the Soviet and the increasingly assertive Third World blocs. Indeed, both were used by the United States to undercut the foundations and very raison d'être of states within the two blocs. This was particularly important in the mid- to late 1970s, when Third World states threatened the global economic order by asserting such collective rights as the right to economic development and the right to own and set the price for the raw materials they exported themselves.

The Arab world was not impervious to the new dispensation. A wide variety of individuals, from leftists and liberals to members of the loyal opposition and even Islamists, found human rights to be an effective tool in the struggle against their autocratic governments. Hence the proliferation of nongovernmental organizations tasked to monitor their government's compliance with the new norm. And hence the protests and uprisings for human and democratic rights and against autocratic regimes alluded to earlier. It was no accident, then, that the uprisings of 2010–2011 initially spoke in the language of human and democratic rights, no matter how they evolved over time.[5]

The third factor that made regimes vulnerable was their brittleness. The years between the onset of the economic crisis of 2008 and the first uprising were not good ones for governments throughout the world. Governments found themselves caught between bankers and economists recommending austerity, on the one hand, and populations fearing the end of the welfare state they had come to know, on the other. While uprisings were spreading in the Arab world, governments fell in the United Kingdom, Greece, Ireland, Portugal, Spain, Iceland, Italy, and elsewhere and were challenged in France and the United States. Throughout it all, not one government was overthrown, nor were political institutions uprooted. Blame fell on politicians and parties and the policies they pushed.

In the Arab world, popular representatives could not be turned out of office because there were no popular representatives. This is why populations throughout the region took to the streets as their first option. This also explains why the most common slogan during this period was "Down with the *nizam* [regime]," not "Down with the government [*hukuma*]."

In addition to these three deep-seated factors were two contingent ones that made regimes in the Arab world vulnerable. The first of these was demography. In 2011, approximately 60 percent of the population of the Arab world was under the age of thirty. Even more telling is the percentage of youth between the ages of fifteen and twenty-nine, the period during which most enter the job market and compete on the marriage market. In 2010, youths between the ages of fifteen and twenty-nine made up 29 percent of the population of Tunisia, 30 percent of the population of Egypt, and 34 percent of the population of Libya. They also made up the bulk of the unemployed (for example, in Egypt they made up 90 percent of the unemployed).[6]

Demography is not, of course, destiny, and frustrations about job or life prospects do not necessarily translate into rebellion. And youth was hardly the only segment of the Arab population that mobilized during the uprisings: In Tunisia and Egypt, labor played a major role; in Libya and Syria, parents protesting the way the state had dealt with their children sparked them. Nevertheless, by 2010, there was a cohort of youths throughout the Arab world with a significant set of grievances. Under the proper circumstances, this cohort was available to be mobilized for oppositional politics.

The final factor that made regimes in the Arab world vulnerable was a global rise in food prices. Between mid-2010 and January 2011, the world price of wheat more than doubled. Economists attribute this price rise to a number of factors, from speculation to drought to more acreage in the United States and Europe devoted to growing corn for biofuel.[7]

The Arab Middle East is more dependent on aggregate food imports than any other region in the world. At the time of its uprising, Egypt was the world's largest wheat importer. In addition to its dependence on food imports, however, there are two other reasons that skyrocketing food prices are a particular burden in the Arab world. First, the portion of household spending that went to pay for food in the Arab world ranged as high as 63 percent in Morocco. Compare that to the average percentage of household spending that goes to pay for food in the United States: 7 percent—a figure that includes eating as entertainment (that is, dining outside the home).[8] The second reason the damage caused by skyrocketing food prices in the Arab world is particularly punishing is neoliberalism: Pressure from the United States and the IMF has constrained governments from intervening in markets to fix prices and has forced governments to abandon across-the-board subsidies for food.

These five factors, then, made all regimes throughout the Arab world vulnerable to popular anger. They should not be seen as causing the uprisings, however. To attribute causation to these or any other factors overlooks a key variable—the human element—that determines whether an uprising will or will not occur. That being said, the remarkable fact remains that starting in December 2010, uprisings or protests of one sort or another broke out in all but possibly four of the twenty-two member states of the Arab League,[9] demonstrating that the term "Arab world" connotes more than a geographic expanse.

NATIONAL OUTCOMES

Once uprisings began to break out in the region, they took a number of forms. In the main, the uprisings that have broken out thus far might be placed into five clusters.

The first cluster consists of Tunisia and Egypt, where militaries stepped in to depose long-ruling autocrats who faced widespread disaffection. The militaries thus cut the revolutionary process short. This prevented a thorough housecleaning in both states. Tunisia and Egypt are unique in the Arab world: Beginning in the nineteenth century, both experienced two centuries of continuous state-building. As a result, in both there were long-lived, functioning institutions autonomous from the executive branch of the government. The military is one of those institutions, but there are others as well, including the judiciary and security services. Together, these institutions make up what political scientists call the "deep state."[10] When faced with an unprecedented crisis, the institutions of the deep state closed ranks to protect the old order.

The struggle between the deep state and the forces promoting change in both places defined the course of the two uprisings. When moderate Islamist organizations—Ennahda in Tunisia, the Muslim Brotherhood in Egypt— won popular mandates to form governments, the deep state joined forces with remnants of the old regime and more secular-oriented groups within the population in defiance. In Egypt, the Brotherhood saw itself locked in a battle to the death with its adversaries, who felt likewise. It therefore refused to share power with them and even pushed through a constitution it drafted when it appeared that the judiciary was about to dissolve the constitutional assembly on procedural grounds. As the crisis escalated—and as the Egyptian economy went into a free fall—hundreds of thousands of Egyptians took to the streets. Once again, the military stepped in, dissolved the Brotherhood government, had a constitution drafted that enhanced the power of the deep state, and established a regime far more repressive than Mubarak's (according to the Egyptian Centre for Economic and Social Rights, between July 2013, when the military retook power, and November–December 2013, the military killed 2,665 of its fellow citizens, wounded 16,000, and arrested 13,145).[11]

Things in Tunisia did not end up as badly. Unlike the Egyptian Muslim Brotherhood, Ennahda did not overplay its hand. As a matter of fact, from the beginning, Ennahda reached out to opposition parties and brought them into the government. And when faced with the same crises and oppositional forces faced by the Egyptian Muslim Brotherhood, Ennahda, as well as its opponents, stepped away from the precipice. Ennahda not only dissolved the government it dominated and called for new elections, it signed on to the most liberal constitution in the Arab world. Although the economic and political stability of Tunisia continues to be threatened by jihadi violence, if any of the uprisings is to have a happy ending, the Tunisian uprising is the most likely candidate.

The second cluster of states undergoing uprisings consists of Yemen and Libya, where regimes fragmented, pitting the officers and soldiers, cabinet ministers, politicians, and diplomats who stood with the regime against those who joined the opposition.

The fragmentation of regimes in the two states is not surprising: In contrast to Tunisia and Egypt, both Yemen and Libya are poster children for what political scientists call "weak states." In weak states, governments and the bureaucracies upon which they depend are unable to assert their authority over the entirety of the territory they rule. Nor are they able to extend their reach beneath the surface of society. It is partly for this reason that populations in weak states lack strong national identities and allegiances. Such is the situation in both Yemen and Libya.

To a certain extent, the weakness of the Yemeni and Libyan states came about as a result of geography. Neither country has terrain that makes it easy to govern—Yemen because of the roughness, Libya because of the expansiveness of their respective terrains. To a certain extent, the weakness is a result of their history (or lack thereof). Both states are relatively recent creations, artificially constructed from disparate elements. Yemen had been divided between an independent North Yemen and South Yemen until 1990. Contrasting social structures found in each Yemen reflect the legacies of formal imperialism in the south and the absence of formal imperialism in the north. The United Nations created an independent federated Libya in 1952 from the remnants of three former Italian colonies that had been kept separate until 1934. Even then, regional differences remained. Finally, the weakness of the Yemeni and Libyan states was a product of the ruling styles of their leaders: Both President Ali Abdullah Saleh of Yemen and Muammar al-Gadafi of Libya purposely avoided establishing strong institutions in favor of a personalistic style of rule that gave them more leeway in playing off tribes and other internal groupings against each other.

Because regimes in both states fragmented, there was no unified military to step in to end the uprisings, as had happened in Tunisia and Egypt. As a result, uprisings in both states were violent and invited foreign meddling. In the case of Yemen, the Gulf Cooperation Council, the United States, and the United Nations intervened to foster a "national dialogue," which, since the outside world was more interested in stability than democratic transition, mainly included the preuprising political elites interested only in claiming their share of the pie. In the end, foreign powers got neither democratic transition nor stability. Not only did a southern secessionist movement reassert itself, but the northern Houthi movement, which represents Yemen's Zaidi minority, joined forces with Ali Abdullah Saleh to take control of the capital and depose the government that the Gulf Cooperation Council, the United States, and the United Nations had installed. Once again, an international coalition led by Saudi Arabia intervened to restore the preuprising system—only this time it was with a Libya-style air campaign. Four years after the initial uprising, Yemen became a humanitarian nightmare facing continued civil war and breakup.

As for Libya, locally based militias—some Islamist, some not—vied for control over resources, territory, and political power in the immediate aftermath of the uprising. Over time, Islamist militias, on the one hand, and non-Islamist militias and regime holdovers, on the other, coalesced into two opposing camps represented by two different governments. As in the cases of Tunisia and Egypt, then, the main fault line in Libyan politics in the aftermath of the February 2011 uprising became one separating Islamists from their anti-Islamist opponents. Unlike the case of Tunisia, however, outside powers have fueled the Libyan flames, with Qatar initially supplying the Islamists with weaponry and Egypt and the United Arab Emirates spearheading military intervention on behalf of their secular opponents.

A third cluster of states includes Syria and Bahrain, where regimes maintained their cohesion against the uprisings. One might even say that in Syria and Bahrain, regimes had no choice but to maintain their cohesion against uprisings. Thus, once uprisings broke out in these states, there was little likelihood that one part of the ruling institution would turn on another, as happened in Tunisia or Egypt, or that the ruling institution would splinter, as happened in Libya and Yemen.

In Syria and Bahrain, rulers effectively "coup-proofed"[12] their regimes by, among other things, exploiting ties of sect and kinship to build a close-knit, interdependent ruling group. In Syria, this group consisted of Bashar al-Assad, his extended family, and members of the minority Alawite community. Thus, at the time of the outbreak of the uprising, President Assad's cousin was the head of the presidential guard, his brother was commander of the Republican Guard and Fourth Armored Division, and his now deceased brother-in-law was deputy chief of staff. None of them could have turned on the regime; if the regime went, they would go, too. As a matter of fact, few persons of note have defected from the regime, and of those who have—one brigadier general, a prime minister (which in Syria is a post of little importance), and an ambassador to Iraq—not one was Alawite.

The core of the regime in Bahrain consists of members of the ruling Khalifa family who hold critical cabinet portfolios, from the office of prime minister and deputy prime minister to ministers of defense, foreign affairs, finance, and national security. The commander of the army and commander of the royal guard are also family. As in Syria, members of a minority community—Sunni Muslims, who make up an estimated 30–40 percent of the population—form the main pillar and primary constituency of the regime. The regime has counted on the Sunni community to circle its wagons in the regime's defense, although the uprising started out as nonsectarian in nature, as had Syria's. But as happened in Syria, repression by a regime identified with a minority community, along with the regime's deliberate provocation of intersectarian violence to ensure that communities upon which the regime depends for support would stick with it until the bitter end, sectarianized the uprisings and intensified the level of violence.

Foreign intervention has played a critical role in determining the course of the uprisings in both Bahrain and Syria. The one thousand Saudi and Emirati soldiers and policemen who crossed the causeway connecting the island nation of Bahrain with the mainland took up positions throughout the capital, Manama. This freed up the Bahraini military and security services (led by members of the ruling family and made up of Sunnis from Pakistan, Jordan, and elsewhere) to crush the opposition. The regime then embarked on a campaign of repression that was harsh even by Gulf standards. Regime opponents have faced mass arrests and torture in prison, all demonstrations have been banned, insulting the king can result in a prison sentence of up to seven years, and security forces armed with riot gear have cordoned off rebellious Shi'i villages, terrorizing residents with nighttime raids. It is also illegal to possess a Guy Fawkes mask, the accessory of choice of anarchists and members of Occupy movements the world over.[13] All the while, the regime has hidden behind the facade of a series of national dialogues whose outcomes the regime fixed.

While foreign intervention helped curtail the Bahraini uprising, it had the opposite effect in Syria. Both supporters of the regime—Iran, Russia, and Hizbullah—and supporters of the opposition—the West, Saudi Arabia, Qatar, Turkey, and others—have funneled arms and money to their proxies, while Hizbullah fighters and, perhaps, Iranian soldiers, joined the fray. This has not only served to escalate the violence but also created the environment in which the Islamic State of Iraq and Syria—later just the "Islamic State"—might incubate before it set out to create its caliphate from portions of the two states. To date, the foreign backers of the government have been more effective in their efforts than the foreign backers of the opposition for two reasons. First, the latter group supports a number of groups acting at cross-purposes—ranging from the inept "moderate" forces supported by the West to salafis supported by the Qataris and Saudis. Second, they themselves act at cross-purposes: The West, fearing a sectarian bloodbath and the strength of Islamist groups within the opposition, has been ambivalent, at best, about facilitating a clear-cut opposition victory. On the other hand, the Saudis and Qataris have supported groups that seek to rule postuprising Syria according to a strict interpretation of Islamic law.

All told, by 2014, Syria hosted approximately 120,000 opposition fighters who have joined upward of 1,000 opposition groups, many of which have taken control over villages and towns and the surrounding countryside. The fact that the Syrian uprising turned into a proxy war that outside powers on both sides are willing to escalate when the need arises means that a negotiated settlement is unlikely—that is, unless the West and Iran reach a rapprochement. As the United Nations and Arab League special envoy to Syria Lakhdar Brahimi put it, in the end the uprising will quite possibly lead to the "Somalization" of Syria. That is, like Somalia, Syria will remain a state on paper only, while real power will be divided among the government and rival gangs that control their own fiefdoms.

The fourth cluster of states consists of four of the seven remaining monarchies—Morocco, Saudi Arabia, Kuwait, and Oman—in which uprisings occurred. Here the word "uprising" is a misnomer: With the exception of the uprising in Bahrain (and Jordan), *protests* in the Arab monarchies share two important characteristics that set them apart from *uprisings* in the Arab republics: They have, for the most part, been more limited in scope, and they have demanded reform of the *nizam*, not its overthrow.

It is not altogether clear why this discrepancy has been the case—or, for that matter, whether it will continue to be so. Some political scientists have maintained that the reason why the demand in monarchies has been for reform and not revolution is that monarchs have an ability that presidents—even presidents for life—do not have: They can retain executive power while ceding legislative power to an elected assembly and prime minister. As a result, the assembly and prime minister, not the monarch, become the focal point of popular anger when things go wrong.[14] Unfortunately, this explanation rings hollow. While it might hold true for Kuwait, which has a parliament that can be, at times, quite raucous, Saudi Arabia does not even have a parliament, and the king *is* the prime minister. Others argue that oil wealth enables monarchs to buy off their opposition or prevent an opposition from arising in the first place. This might explain the Gulf monarchies, but Morocco (which had an uprising that the king enfeebled with a few cosmetic reforms) does not have oil, while Bahrain—which has had a long history of rebellion and had a full-fledged uprising in 2011—is hydrocarbon-rich.

It is entirely possible that in the future it might be necessary to reassess whether a monarchic category even exists. Bahrain was not the only monarchy in which opposition leaders called for the removal of the king. The same occurred in Jordan during demonstrations in November 2012, and although those demonstrations soon ran out of steam, there is no way to determine how deep the sentiment runs or whether it might reemerge in the future. And while the world was focused on the anemic demonstrations of social-networking youths in Saudi Arabia's capital, violent protests, which met with violent suppression, broke out in the predominantly Shi'i Eastern Province of the country. Taking these latter protests into account challenges the notion that protests in the monarchies were limited in scope. Ultimately, the small number of monarchies included in this category (four out of eight in the region) makes any conclusions about a monarchic exception problematic.

The fifth and final cluster includes the only three states in the Arab world that, at the end of 2010, the *Economist* Intelligence Unit listed as governed by "hybrid regimes": Iraq, Lebanon, and Palestine. According to the *Economist*, hybrid regimes maintain a democratic facade: There are, for example, elections, but those elections have substantial irregularities and are hardly free and fair. Rampant corruption and clientage further erode the rule of law and frustrate the popular will.[15]

The uprisings in the three states share characteristics that reflect regime structure: Populations had relative freedom to mass on the streets (often alongside disgruntled members of the ruling elite), demanding accountability from dysfunctional elected governments. Protests unfolded over time, and as governments proved unable or unwilling to break the political gridlock and answer even the most rudimentary needs of their populations, those populations expanded their demands to include an overhaul of the entire political system. Hence, demonstrations that began throughout Iraq on February 25, 2011, protesting the lack of potable water, electrical shortages, and high unemployment, along with those that began in Beirut in August 2015 protesting the government's inability to secure the removal of garbage (hence the campaign's evocative name, "You Stink") and other services, morphed into demonstrations demanding the removal of oligarchs and an end to the sectarian systems in which they were bred.[16] Although the outcomes of both sets of protests cannot be predicted, it is unlikely that ruling elites in either Iraq or Lebanon will consent to changes that would result in their disempowerment. Instead, a more likely scenario is that they will unite to crush the movement, or that one or another faction within their ranks will attempt to co-opt it.

It should also be mentioned that in Iraq, a separate protest movement began in the winter of 2014 in the Sunni areas of the country. Protesters demanded the end of discriminatory policies against their community perpetrated by the Shi'i government of Prime Minister Nuri al-Maliki. The government met those protests with extreme violence (as it did the initial protests), encouraging many Sunnis to sit on their hands or openly support the Islamic State when it began its conquests.[17]

Since Palestinians live under exceptional conditions, the uprising in Palestine naturally followed a slightly different path. In January 2011, a group calling itself Gaza Youth Breaks Out issued its first manifesto, which stated, "There is a revolution growing inside of us, an immense dissatisfaction and frustration that will destroy us unless we find a way of canalizing this energy into something that can challenge the status quo and give us some kind of hope."[18] That energy was "canalized" through the March 15 Youth Movement, a loose association of social media–savvy young people similar to Egypt's April 6 Youth Movement, which had sparked the uprising there. Like the April 6 Youth Movement, the March 15 Youth Movement began its protests with a Day of Rage in which tens of thousands of Palestinians took part. Rather than demanding the ouster of the regime, as their Egyptian compatriots had done, however, movement leaders demanded reconciliation between Fatah and Hamas, which had gone their separate ways in 2007, dividing the Palestinian national movement. The final stage (so far) in the Palestinian uprising took place in the West Bank in September 2012 after the government raised prices on food and fuel. Spurred on by the same sort of labor activism that had proved decisive in the Egyptian uprising, protesters soon escalated their demands from the economic to the political: They called for the dismissal of the prime minister of the Palestinian Authority (and, in some cases, the resignation of its president, Mahmoud Abbas); the dismantling of the Authority; renunciation of the Oslo Accord and its associated economic protocols; and the establishment of a Palestinian state within the 1967 borders, with East Jerusalem as its capital.[19] The protest deeply shook the Palestinian leadership. It not only led to the firing of the Palestinian Authority prime minister but also encouraged Abbas to seize the initiative and assuage public opinion by taking the case for Palestinian statehood to the General Assembly of the United Nations.

Overall, the scorecard for the uprisings that began in 2010–2011 is depressing. In Egypt and all the monarchies, the forces of reaction snuffed out the demands for change. Although the state system as a whole is not threatened—thanks in large measure to the support of both great and regional powers for the status quo—Libya and Yemen do face fragmentation, mainly because of their marginal importance to the regional and international order. Syria's bloodbath shows no sign of abating, and Iraqis now face more serious challenges than shortages of potable water and electricity. Regionally, there has been a rise in sectarianism, fueled by a combination of the Syrian civil war; the *takfiri* policies of the Islamic State, according to which the group differentiates between "true" Muslims who are to be left in peace and "apostate" Muslims who are to be killed; and the Iranian-Saudi rivalry. And with all due respect to the aspirations of protesters in Iraq and Lebanon, once societies or politics within states become sectarianized—once people segregate themselves among "their own kind" or representation or employment opportunities are allocated according to religious affiliation—sectarianism is unlikely to disappear. Only the uprising in Tunisia shows signs of success—that is, if one puts aside the elephant in the room that might have ultimately doomed the uprisings in all non-oil-producing states anyway: the wretched shape of the Arab economies. No one predicts that that problem will be resolved anytime soon.

But even if the initial optimism ignited by the uprisings has dimmed, their legacy cannot be entirely discounted. Just as no revolution during the 1848 "Springtime of Nations" ousted any autocrat, its outbreak signaled in retrospect that the field of political contestation in Europe had opened up to include liberal and nationalist alternatives to the old order. While historical analogies are inevitably deficient, a corresponding lesson might be drawn from the recent spate of uprisings. Only this time, uprisings have signaled that global norms of human and democratic rights remain on the table in the Arab world.

NOTES

1. On the false lessons of the Egyptian uprising, see James L. Gelvin, "Everything You Think You Know About the Egyptian Revolution Is False," History News Network, February 11, 2014, http://historynewsnetwork.org/article/154685.

2. See James L. Gelvin, *The Modern Middle East: A History*, 4th ed. (New York: Oxford University Press, 2015), 329–333.

3. See James L. Gelvin, "American Global Economic Policy and the Civic Order in the Middle East," in *Is There a Middle East? The Evolution of a Geopolitical Concept*, ed. Michael Bonine, Abbas Amanat, and Michael Gasper (Stanford, CA: Stanford University Press, 2011), 191–206; and Steven Heydemann, "Social Pacts and the Persistence of Authoritarianism in the Middle East," in *Debating Arab Authoritarianism: Dynamics and Durability in Nondemocratic Regimes*, ed. Oliver Schlumberger (Stanford, CA: Stanford University Press, 2008), 21–38.

4. Gelvin, *The Modern Middle East*, 267–268.

5. See James L. Gelvin, "Reassessing the Recent History of Political Islam in Light of the Arab Uprisings," in *The Arab Uprisings: Catalysts, Dynamics, and Trajectories*, ed. Fahed al-Sumait, Nele Lenze, and Michael C. Hudson (Lanham, MD: Rowman and Littlefield, 2014), 115–134.

6. See Farzaneh Roudi, "Youth Population and Employment in the Middle East and North Africa: Opportunity or Challenge" (New York: United Nations Secretariat, 2011), www.un.org/esa/population/meetings/egm-adolescents/p06_roudi.pdf; and "Egypt Human Development Report 2010: Youth in Egypt: Building Our Future" (Cairo: Egyptian Institute of National Planning/United Nations Development Programme, 2010).

7. Elena Ianchovichina, Josef Loening, and Christina Wood, "How Vulnerable Are Arab Countries to Global Food Price Shocks?" (Washington, DC: World Bank, 2012), www-wds.worldbank.org/servlet/WDSContentServer/WDSP/IB/2012/03/29/000158 349_20120329154735/Rendered/PDF/WPS6018.pdf.

8. "Eight Reasons Food Prices Are Rising Globally," Rediff Business, October, 17, 2011, www.rediff.com/business/slide-show/slide-show-1-8-reasons-why-food-prices-are-rising -globally/20111017.htm; Business Insider, "The Twenty-Five Countries That Will Be Screwed by a World Food Crisis," Wall Street Cheat Sheet, October 12, 2010, www.cheatsheet.com/ breaking-news/the-25-countries-that-will-be-screwed-by-a-world-food-crisis.html.

9. Depending on the definition of protests or uprisings being used, the four in which it might reasonably be said that uprisings have not occurred are the Comoros, Somalia, Qatar, and the United Arab Emirates.

10. For a nuanced exploration of the deep-state phenomenon in Egypt, see Nathan J. Brown, "Egypt's Wide State Reassembles Itself," *Foreign Policy*, July 17, 2013, http://foreign policy.com/2013/07/17/egypts-wide-state-reassembles-itself.

11. "Statistics Reveal Casualties Since Military Coup in Egypt," Middle East Monitor, January 2, 2014, www.middleeastmonitor.com/news/africa/9021-statistics-reveal -casualties-since-military-coup-in-egypt.

12. See James T. Quinlivan, "Coup-Proofing: Its Practice and Consequences in the Middle East," *International Security* 24 (Autumn 1999): 131–165.

13. Samuel Muston, "Anti-protest: Bahrain Bans Import of Plastic Guy Fawkes Masks," *Independent*, February 25, 2015, www.independent.co.uk/news/world/middle-east/anti protest-bahrain-bans-import-of-plastic-guy-fawkes-masks-8510615.html.

14. See, for example, Jack A. Goldstone, "Understanding the Revolutions of 2011: Weakness and Resilience in Middle Eastern Autocracies," *Foreign Affairs*, May-June 2011, www .foreignaffairs.com/articles/north-africa/2011-04-14/understanding-revolutions-2011.

15. See "Democracy Index 2010: Democracy in Retreat," *Economist* Intelligence Unit, www.eiu.com/public/thankyou_download.aspx?activity=download&campaignid =demo2010, accessed August 5, 2015.

16. Anne Barnard, "Lebanese Protesters Aim for Rare Unity Against Gridlocked Government," *New York Times*, August 29, 2015, www.nytimes.com/2015/08/30/world/

middleeast/lebanon-protests-garbage-government-corruption.html; Tim Arango, "Protests in Iraq Bring Fast Promises, but Slower Changes," *New York Times*, August 31, 2015, www.nytimes.com/2015/09/01/world/middleeast/protests-in-iraq-bring-fast-promises -but-slower-changes.html.

17. Dexter Filkens, "What We Left Behind," *New Yorker*, April 28, 2014, www.newyorker .com/magazine/2014/04/28/what-we-left-behind.

18. "GYBO Manifesto 2.0," Gaza Youth Breaks Out, https://gazaybo.wordpress.com/ about, accessed August 5, 2015.

19. "The Palestinian Protests of September 2012: The Birth of a Social Movement," (Doha: Arab Centre for Research and Policy Studies, September 17, 2012), http://english .dohainstitute.org/release/94454f0f-ed0b-40cl-b9b3-58cb6f0b525.

About the Contributors

Narges Bajoghli is a postdoctoral Fellow at the Watson Institute for International and Public Affairs at Brown University. She holds a PhD in sociocultural anthropology from New York University. Her research examines the role of proregime cultural producers in Iran, focusing on media producers in the paramilitary Basij and Ansar-e Hezbollah organizations as well as the Islamic Revolutionary Guard Corps.

Laurentina Cizza holds a master of arts degree in international relations and Middle Eastern studies from Johns Hopkins University School of Advanced International Studies (SAIS), where she concentrated on North Africa and Libya. She has coauthored peer-reviewed book chapters with Karim Mezran in both Italian and English dealing with the fallout of the Arab Spring in Libya. She is also the program manager of Libya-Analysis.com, founded by Libya researcher Jason Pack. In addition to Libya and North Africa, her research interests include Mediterranean security, migration, and national identity studies. She has a background in risk management analysis and program management in the field of international development.

Julia Clancy-Smith is Regents Professor of Modern North African, Middle Eastern, and Mediterranean History at the University of Arizona, Tucson. She is the author of *Mediterraneans: North Africa and Europe in an Age of Migration, c. 1800–1900* (University of California Press, 2011), which won three book awards, and *Rebel and Saint: Muslim Notables, Populist Protest, Colonial Encounters (Algeria and Tunisia, 1800–1904)* (University of California Press, 1997), which received three awards. She also coedited *Walls of Algiers: Narratives of the City Through Text and Image* (University of Washington Press, 2009).

Robert O. Freedman is the Peggy Meyerhoff Pearlstone Professor of Political Science Emeritus at Baltimore Hebrew University and is currently Visiting Professor of Political Science at Johns Hopkins University, where he teaches courses on Russian foreign policy and on the Arab-Israeli conflict. Among his recent publications are *Russia, Iran, and the Nuclear Question: The Putin Record* (Strategic Studies Institute of the US Army War College, 2006) and *Israel and the United States: Six Decades of US-Israeli Relations* (Westview Press, 2012). He is currently completing a book on Putin and the Middle East.

James L. Gelvin is Professor of History at the University of California, Los Angeles. A specialist in the social/cultural history of the modern Middle East, he is the author/editor of five books, including *The Arab Uprisings: What Everyone Needs to Know*, 2nd ed. (Oxford University Press, 2015) and *The Modern Middle East: A History*, 4th ed. (Oxford University Press, 2015), along with numerous articles and chapters in edited volumes.

Mark L. Haas is professor in the Political Science Department at Duquesne University in Pittsburgh. He is the author of *The Clash of Ideologies: Middle Eastern Politics and American Security* (Oxford University Press, 2012) and *The Ideological Origins of Great Power Politics, 1789–1989* (Cornell University Press, 2005) and coeditor with David Lesch of *The Middle East and the United States*, 5th ed. (Westview Press, 2013). His scholarly articles have appeared in such leading journals as *International Security, International Organization, International Studies Quarterly, Security Studies*, and *Review of Politics*.

Arang Keshavarzian is Associate Professor of Middle Eastern and Islamic Studies at New York University. He is the author of *Bazaar and State in Iran: The Politics of the Tehran Marketplace* (Cambridge University Press, 2007). His essays have appeared in a number of edited volumes and journals, including *Politics and Society, International Journal of Middle East Politics, Geopolitics, Middle East Report,* and *Economy and Society*. He is currently on the editorial committee of *Middle East Report* (www.merip.org). His research examines the ways in which forms of accumulation and control produced multiple and competing geographic spaces and scales in the Persian Gulf during the twentieth century.

David W. Lesch is the Ewing Halsell Distinguished Professor of History at Trinity University in San Antonio, Texas. He is the author or editor of fourteen books, including *Syria: The Fall of the House of Assad* (Yale University Press, 2013) and *The Arab-Israeli Conflict: A History* (Oxford University Press, 2009), and is coeditor with Mark Haas of *The Middle East and the United States*, 5th ed. (Westview Press, 2013).

Ibrahim Al-Marashi is Associate Professor in the History Department at California State University–San Marcos. He is the coauthor of *Iraq's Armed Forces:*

An Analytical History (Routledge, 2008) and *The Modern History of Iraq*, 4th ed. (Westview Press, 2016), with Phebe Marr.

Karim Mezran is the Senior Resident Fellow for North Africa at the Atlantic Council's Rafik Hariri Center for the Middle East. In addition, he is an adjunct professor of Middle East studies at the Johns Hopkins School of Advanced International Studies (SAIS), where he teaches courses on the history and politics of North Africa. Previously he was director of the Center for American Studies in Rome. He holds a PhD in international relations from SAIS Johns Hopkins University. His recent publications include "Libya: Negotiations for Transition" in *Arab Spring: Negotiating in the Shadow of the Intifadat,* "Libya" in *Political and Constitutional Transitions in North Africa: Actors and Factors,* and "Libya in Transition: From Jamahiriya to Jumhuriyyah?" in *The New Middle East: Protest and Revolution in the Arab World.*

Ilan Peleg is the Charles A. Dana Professor of Government and Law at Lafayette College and an Adjunct Scholar at the Middle East Institute in Washington, DC. He is the author, most recently, of *Israel's Palestinians: The Conflict Within,* coauthored with Dov Waxman (Cambridge University Press, 2011); *The Foreign Policy of George W. Bush* (Westview Press, 2009); and *Democratizing the Hegemonic State: Political Transformation in the Age of Identity* (Cambridge University Press, 2007). His previous publications include a political biography of Menachem Begin (1987), an edited book on the emergence of a binational Israel (1989), a book on human rights in the West Bank and Gaza (1995), and many articles on the Israeli right.

Jeremy Pressman is Associate Professor in the Department of Political Science and Director of Middle East Studies at the University of Connecticut. His publications include *Warring Friends: Alliance Restraint in International Politics* (Cornell University Press, 2008) and "American Engagement and the Pathways to Arab-Israeli Peace," *Cooperation & Conflict* 49, 4 (December 2014). He is on Twitter @djpressman.

Bruce K. Rutherford is Associate Professor of Political Science at Colgate University. His publications include *Egypt After Mubarak: Liberalism, Islam, and Democracy in the Arab World* (Princeton University Press, 2008 and 2012); "What Do Egypt's Islamists Want? Moderate Islam and the Rise of Islamic Constitutionalism," *Middle East Journal* 60, 4 (Autumn 2006); "Egypt: The Origins and Consequences of the January 25 Uprising," in *The Arab Spring: Change and Resistance in the Middle East,* ed. Mark Haas and David Lesch (Westview Press, 2013); and "Surviving Under 'Rule by Law': Explaining Ideological Change in Egypt's

Muslim Brotherhood," in *Constitutionalism, the Rule of Law, and the Politics of Administration in Egypt and Iran*, ed. Said Arjomand and Nathan Brown (State University of New York Press, 2013).

Curtis R. Ryan is Professor of Political Science at Appalachian State University in North Carolina. He holds a PhD from the University of North Carolina, Chapel Hill. He served as a Fulbright Scholar at the Center for Strategic Studies in Jordan (1992–1993) and was twice named a Peace Scholar by the US Institute of Peace. He is the author of *Inter-Arab Alliances: Regime Security and Jordanian Foreign Policy* and *Jordan in Transition: From Hussein to Abdullah* as well as articles in *Middle East Journal, Middle East Insight, Arab Studies Quarterly, Israel Affairs, Southeastern Political Review, Journal of Third World Studies, Middle East Policy,* and *Middle East Report.*

Jeannie L. Sowers is Associate Professor of Political Science and the International Affairs Program Chair at the University of New Hampshire. Her research focuses on the political economy of environment and natural resource issues in the Middle East and North Africa. She is the author of *Environmental Politics in Egypt: Activists, Experts, and the State* (Routledge, 2013) and coeditor of *The Journey to Tahrir: Revolution, Protest, and Social Change in Egypt* (Verso, 2012). She holds a PhD from Princeton University and a BA from Harvard University. She has published articles in *Climatic Change, Development and Change, Journal of Environment and Development,* and *Middle East Report* and serves on the editorial boards of *Global Environmental Politics* and *Middle East Report.*

Steve A. Yetiv is the Louis I. Jaffe Professor of International Relations at Old Dominion University. He is the author, most recently, of *Myths of the Oil Boom: American National Security in a Global Energy Market* (Oxford University Press, 2015); *Explaining Foreign Policy: U.S. Decision-Making in the Gulf Wars,* 2nd ed. (Johns Hopkins University Press, 2011); and *The Petroleum Triangle: Oil, Globalization, and Terror* (Cornell University Press, 2011).

Index

CPSIA information can be obtained
at www.ICGtesting.com
Printed in the USA
LVOW01s0252090716
495459LV00001B/1/P